The Basics of Economics

Recent titles in
Basics of the Social Sciences

The Basics of Western Philosophy
Eugene Kelly

THE BASICS OF ECONOMICS

David E. O'Connor

Basics of the Social Sciences

GREENWOOD PRESS
Westport, Connecticut • London

Library of Congress Cataloging-in-Publication Data

O'Connor, David E. (David Edward)
The basics of economics / David E. O'Connor.
p. cm. — (Basics of the social sciences)
Includes index.
ISBN 0–313–32520–0 (alk. paper)
1. Economics. 2. Economics—History. I. Title. II. Series.
HB71.027 2004
330—dc22 2004008304

British Library Cataloguing in Publication Data is available.

Library of Congress Catalog Card Number: 2004008304
ISBN: 0–313–32520–0

First published in 2004

Greenwood Press, 88 Post Road West, Westport, CT 06881
An imprint of Greenwood Publishing Group, Inc.
www.greenwood.com

Printed in the United States of America

The paper used in this book complies with the Permanent Paper Standard issued by the National Information Standards Organization (Z39.48–1984).

10 9 8 7 6 5 4 3 2 1

Contents

List of Figures and Tables

FIGURES

TABLES

Acknowledgments

The author recognizes the following individuals for their contributions to this publication: Desmond McCaffrey, Instructional Developer at the Institute for Teaching and Learning, University of Connecticut, for the production of the book's charts, graphs, and diagrams; Linda Mathes, Jane White, Jan Nuhn, and Peter Salesses of the Edwin O. Smith High School Library Media Center for technical assistance; the Government Publications research staff at the Homer Babbidge Library, University of Connecticut, for its research support; Anne Thompson, Senior Development Editor, and Marie Ellen Larcada, Senior Acquisitions Editor, of the Greenwood Publishing Group, for their encouragement, advice, and guidance; and Liz Kincaid, Photo Researcher, for her assistance in locating and obtaining photo permissions.

The author recognizes the following organizations and agencies for their work on behalf of economic education in the United States. Two of the unsung heroes are the National Council on Economic Education (NCEE) and the Foundation for Teaching Economics (FTE). Over the years their innovative programs for teachers and students and their instructional materials have advanced the cause of economic literacy at the elementary, middle, and high school levels. Deep appreciation is also extended to the National Council for the Social Studies (NCSS) for its continued support of economic education in the nation's schools. Finally, kudos are offered to the many U.S. government agencies and multilateral organizations that collect and disseminate important economic information to citizens.

The author recognizes the inspirational work of civil society organizations, which, collectively, work to improve the human condition. Civil society organizations, including nongovernmental organizations, private foundations, independent think tanks, charitable groups, and others give a voice to the marginalized and distressed and raise awareness among all peoples. Royalties earned from this publication will support Feed the Children, one such group with ties to the local and the global.

Preface

It seems that change is the only constant in people's economic lives. Throughout history, changes in the human condition have stimulated discussion about how to best answer society's basic economic questions of what, how, and for whom to produce. Over the past two and a half centuries, the economic debates matured. Professional economists developed and tested theories in the laboratory of everyday life. Some theories reinforced the status quo, while other fomented revolution. All attempted to explain and influence the economic behaviors of people.

Today the study of economics is highly scientific. Yet even with centuries of study and the use of sophisticated computer modeling techniques, economists are unable to untangle some of our most vexing economic mysteries. For instance, during the 1990s, the U.S. economy reveled in its conquest of inflation and unemployment. Optimism reigned as the confident nation experienced a decade of economic growth, rising productivity, a raging bull market, and soaring federal budget surpluses. By the early 2000s, however, the economy soured. People's confidence dipped as grim reports of recession, joblessness, bearish investment, massive federal deficits, and crippling corporate scandals dominated the headlines.

A recurring, if irregular, cycle of economic boom and bust is one of many dilemmas that economists have grappled with over time. It has been said that "the owl of Minerva [the ancient Roman goddess of wisdom] takes flight when darkness has fallen." Dark economic conditions have traditionally jostled people's worldview and have served as a springboard to new economic thinking, the rise of reform movements, even revolution. The global depression of the 1930s, for example, brought nations and empires to their knees and prompted momentous changes in the concept of limited government in much of the industrialized world. Depression-era economists such as Frances Perkins and John

Maynard Keynes led the charge to dump the time-honored laissez-faire doctrine and to radically expand the role of government in promoting economic growth, stability, and security. Robert Heilbroner often referred to economists as the "worldly philosophers" to highlight the direct impact of economic thinking on people's quality of life. It would be difficult to overstate the role that these worldly philosophers played in shaping the world's economic landscape.

Educators, businesspeople, government officials, and others often voice support for economic literacy as a prerequisite for informed decision making in today's fast-paced, complex, and dynamic economy. In recent years, public concern about economic illiteracy stiffened state and federal resolve to raise academic standards in economics and other core subjects. In 1994 President Bill Clinton signed into law the historic Goals 2000: Educate America Act (Public Law 103–227), which identified economics as a core subject in the nation's schools. In 2002 President George W. Bush signed the No Child Left Behind Act (Public Law 107–110), which echoed the Goals 2000 call for mastery of essential subjects. Under this 2002 legislation, 4 of the 10 core subjects—history, geography, civics and government, and economics—were nestled beneath the academic umbrella of historians and social scientists.

The Basics of Economics explores the fundamentals of economic literacy. In language that is clear and precise, this reference guide introduces and applies the basic economic concepts, analyzes economic choices and decisions, examines competing theories, traces historical trends and movements, explains the operation of the U.S. economy, and probes the impact of globalization on the world economy. Timely, relevant tables, charts, graphs, diagrams, and photographs reinforce the narrative. In short, this user-friendly reference book provides a wealth of information to students, teachers, and the public about the theory and practice of economics.

The book's front matter consists of three features, each of which facilitates quick access to important information. A "List of Tables and Figures" enables users to quickly locate more than 60 tables, charts and graphs, diagrams, and formulas that accompany the running narrative of the book's 13 chapters. These graphics provide timely, authoritative statistical data in a format that invites readers to make economic comparisons and discern economic trends. The graphics also illustrate economic processes such as economic growth, product and factor market flows, and price determination. A list of "Common Abbreviations in Economics" identifies key economic organizations, agreements, institutions, technologies, and vocabulary from *automated clearinghouse* (ACH) to *World Wide Web* (WWW). A "Timeline of Key Economic Events of the Modern Era: 1750 to 2005" traces the impact of reform movements, economic theories, revolutionary actions, government policies, and other events that contributed to the maturing of economics into a social science. The logical starting point for the timeline is the life and times of Adam Smith, the founder of modern economics.

The Basics of Economics is organized into 13 focused chapters. Chapters 1–4 provide a foundation for the study of economics. Chapter 1, "Economics as a Social Science," defines economics, introduces basic economic vocabulary, outlines an economic way of thinking, and cautions readers about common fallacies in reasoning. Chapter 2, "A Survey of Economic History and Economic Thought," traces the uneven progression of civilizations through four stages of economic history: primitive food gathering and hunting, agriculture and animal domestication, manufacturing and the factory system, and the information age. It also delves into the rise and fall of several leading schools of economic thought, including the mercantilists, physiocrats, classical economists, marginalists, Marxists, and Keynesians. Later chapters explore other schools, including the neoclassical economists, supply-siders, and monetarists. Chapter 3, "The Rise of Modern Capitalism: The Power of the Market," and chapter 4, "The Other Isms: Socialism, Communism, and Fascism," examine the historical circumstances that gave rise to revolutionary economic theories and to radical changes in nations' economies. These chapters also examine a variety of twentieth-century economies and the general demise of all isms except capitalism by the 1990s.

Chapters 5–8 examine in detail some of the major decision makers in the microeconomy—businesses, consumers, workers, and financial institutions. Chapter 5, "Business Firms: The Basic Production Unit," introduces readers to the supply side of the market by examining business firms, mainly sole proprietorships, partnerships, and corporations. The chapter also delves into business decision making, the conduct of business operations within different market structures, and the role of government in protecting competition. Chapter 6, "Consumers Organize: Consumer Behavior and Consumer Power," is concerned with the demand side of the market. The chapter investigates the factors that influence consumer behavior, including advertising; the growth of consumer power, including the consumer movement; and market prices, including the interaction of supply and demand. Chapter 7, "Workers Organize: The Labor Force and Labor Power," features the role of workers and entrepreneurs in the production process. It deals with factors that influence worker behaviors, wage determination, and the growth of worker power through trade unionism. Chapter 8, "Financial Markets: The Arteries of Economic Activity," explores the world of money and the financial institutions that facilitate saving and investing. The chapter examines the role of banks, stock exchanges, and other financial institutions in channeling trillions of dollars into productive investments. It also features the expanding role of the Federal Reserve System, the nation's central bank, in maintaining the integrity and stability of the American financial system.

Chapters 9–10 analyze the performance of the overall economy, or macroeconomy. Chapter 9, "Perspectives on Economic Growth," explains measurements of economic growth, such as gross domestic product (GDP), and examines the main economic and political determinants of economic growth in America and abroad. The chapter also analyzes the costs and benefits of economic growth, especially those related to quality of life issues. Chapter 10, "In Search of Economic Stability," investigates the types and causes of inflation, unemployment, and recession. The chapter explains how government stabilization policies, mainly monetary policy and fiscal policy, address disruptive fluctuations in price levels, employment, and national output. It also probes related issues such as taxation and tax policy, federal deficits and the national debt, and income distribution and poverty.

Chapters 11–12 deal with globalization, economic interdependence, and the chasm between the world's rich and poor nations. Chapter 11, "Globalization: Creating a Global Marketplace," examines the three pillars of globalization—international trade, foreign direct investment, and cross-border financial flows. The chapter explores the forces that support the globalization juggernaut, such as the World Bank, International Monetary Fund, and World Trade Organization. It also examines dents in globalization's armor, which include uneven economic development, vocal discontent of civil society organizations, creeping protectionism, and the specter of financial contagion. Chapter 12, "The Challenge of Sustainable Economic Development," describes the common characteristics of developing countries, the poorer nations of the global south. The chapter examines the process of economic development and prospects for transforming the vicious cycle of poverty into the virtuous cycle of development.

Chapter 13, "Careers in Economics," describes current employment opportunities for the three types of economists: business economists, academic economists, and government economists. Economists are professional social scientists who command a wage that is double the average wage for workers in the American labor force. Many economists earn advanced academic degrees, which, in the highly competitive job market for economists, is crucial to securing rewarding positions in the private or public sectors. Holders of degrees in economics are also attractive candidates for jobs in related occupations such as market research, advertising, securities dealing, and banking.

Each of the 13 chapters concludes with (1) four or more brief biographies of people who have been key to the economic issues discussed in that chapter, with some 55 individuals profiled in total, and (2) a list of useful sources to consult.

The book's back matter consists of five handy reference tools. A comprehensive "Glossary of Selected Terms" serves as an economics dictionary, providing readers with quick access to definitions. All terms with definitions in this glossary are **boldfaced** within the text. The "Key Economic Web Sites" is a useful tool for researchers who wish to investigate topics in greater detail or update statistical data. These Web sites connect students, teachers, and other readers with multilateral organizations, such as the United Nations, World Bank, and International Monetary Fund; U.S. government departments and agencies, such as the Bureau of Labor Statistics, Bureau of Economic Analysis, and International Trade Administration; and private research groups, such as the Population Reference Bureau, Freedom House, and World Resources Institute. A "Selected Videotapes" list provides an overview of classroom-tested audiovisual teaching aids. An "Index to Biographies" provides an alphabetized list of the 55 individual biographies that appear in the book. These biographies examine the lives and major contributions of economists and economic thinkers, past and present. The biographies are clustered by topic within the book's 13 chapters. For instance, biographies in chapter 12, "The Challenge of Sustainable Economic Development," offer perspectives on the subject by leading international scholars, including British economist Sir Arthur Lewis, Peruvian economist Hernando de Soto, Indian economist Amartya Sen, and Swedish economist Gunnar Myrdal. The book concludes with a detailed "General Index," which enables readers to locate a specific subject, including multiple references to a subject. Related topics are cross-referenced to facilitate further research.

The study of economics is part art, part science. The basic principles of economics are derived from ongoing experimentation using computer models and simulations and other research. Yet the study of economics is grounded in the real world, a world that refuses to stand still! Changing conditions make the study of economics a dynamic one that offers fertile ground for new research, new theories, and new ideas. Not surprisingly, economists' views often differ, adding fodder to vigorous public policy debates. The welfare of people, both local and global, hangs in the balance.

Since the dawn of civilization, people have groped for answers to the basic economic questions of what, how, and for whom to produce. How people chose to answer these universal questions shaped the course of history, just as today's choices will inevitably affect the quality of life for future generations. Over time, the ideas of economists have been used to justify the toppling of nations and empires. They have also helped strengthen existing political and economic systems and humanize society's treatment of the poor and other economically distressed groups. Sometimes shouted from the barricades, sometimes whispered in the halls of academia, economic ideas have played a central role framing the institutions, practices, and attitudes of the modern world. *The Basics of Economics* attempts to capture the spirit of economics, its fundamental concepts, its guiding principles, its leading personalities, and its inexorable journey toward becoming a purer science.

Common Abbreviations in Economics

ACH	automated clearinghouse
ADB	Asian Development Bank
ADB Group	African Development Bank Group
AEA	American Economic Association
AFL	American Federation of Labor
AFL-CIO	American Federation of Labor-Congress of Industrial Organizations
ASEAN	Association of Southeast Asian Nations
ATM	automated teller machine
ATS	alternative trading system
B2B	business-to-business (transactions)
B2C	business-to-consumer (transactions)
BBB	Better Business Bureau
BBSS	Broker Booth Support System
BEA	Bureau of Economic Analysis
BIF	Bank Insurance Fund
BIS	Bank for International Settlements
BIT	bilateral investment treaty
BLS	Bureau of Labor Statistics
B/P	balance of payments
CBO	Congressional Budget Office
CBOT	Chicago Board of Trade
CCC	Civilian Conservation Corps
CCI	Consumer Confidence Index
CCP	Chinese Communist Party

CD	certificate of deposit
CEA	Council of Economic Advisors
CEO	chief executive officer
CFA	Consumer Federation of America
CFCs	chlorofluorocarbons
CFO	chief financial officer
CI	Consumers International
CIA	Central Intelligence Agency
CIO	Congress of Industrial Organizations
CIS	Commonwealth of Independent States
CME	Chicago Mercantile Exchange
CPI	consumer price index
CPSC	Consumer Product Safety Commission
CR	Consumers' Research
CR	continuing resolution
CSO	civil society organization
CU	Consumer's Union
CWA	Civil Works Administration
DAC	Development Assistance Committee
DJIA	Dow Jones Industrial Average
Dow	Dow Jones Industrial Average
EBRD	European Bank for Reconstruction and Development
ECN	electronic communications network
ECOWAS	Economic Community of West African States
EEOC	Equal Employment Opportunity Commission
EIA	Energy Information Administration
EMU	European Monetary Union
EPA	Environmental Protection Agency
ETS	Educational Testing Service
EU	European Union
FC	fixed costs
FDA	Food and Drug Administration
FDI	foreign direct investment
FDIC	Federal Deposit Insurance Corporation
FFIEC	Federal Financial Institutions Examinations Council
FICA	Federal Insurance Contributions Act
FLSA	Fair Labor Standards Act
FOMC	Federal Open Market Committee
FTAA	Free Trade Area of the Americas

FTC	Federal Trade Commission
FTZ	free trade zone
FX	foreign exchange
FY	fiscal year
GATT	General Agreement on Tariffs and Trade
GDP	gross domestic product
GEM	*Global Entrepreneurship Monitor*
GNI	gross national income
GNP	gross national product
GPT	general purpose technologies
GSE	government-sponsored enterprise
GSP	generalized system of preferences
HDI	Human Development Index
HIPC	Heavily Indebted Poor Countries (Initiative)
IBRD	International Bank for Reconstruction and Development
ICA	International Co-operative Alliance
ICSID	International Center for Settlement of Investment Disputes
ICTs	information and communication technologies
IDA	International Development Association
IDB	Inter-American Development Bank
IFC	International Finance Corporation
ILD	Institute for Liberty and Democracy
ILO	International Labor Organization
IMF	International Monetary Fund
IPO	initial public offering
IRA	individual retirement account
IRS	Internal Revenue Service
IT	information technology
ITA	International Trade Administration
IWW	Industrial Workers of the World
JV	joint venture
LLC	limited liability company
M&As	mergers and acquisitions
MDG	Millennium Development Goals
MERCOSUR	Common Market of the South
MFN	most favored nation (status)
MIGA	Multilateral Investment Guarantee Agency
MMDA	money market deposit account
MNC	multinational corporation

Common Abbreviations in Economics

M1	money supply 1 (measurement 1)
M2	money supply 2 (measurement 2)
M3	money supply 3 (measurement 3)
MTN	multilateral trade negotiations
MU	marginal utility
NABE	National Association for Business Economics
NAFTA	North American Free Trade Agreement
NASDAQ	North American Stock Dealers Automated Quotations
NBER	National Bureau of Economic Research
NCL	National Consumers League
NCUA	National Credit Union Administration
NCUSIF	National Credit Union Share Insurance Fund
NEP	New Economic Program
NGO	nongovernmental organization
NLRB	National Labor Relations Board
NLU	National Labor Union
NOW	negotiable order of withdrawal
NPL	nonperforming loan
NYSE	New York Stock Exchange
OCDs	other checkable deposits
ODA	official development assistance
OECD	Organization for Economic Cooperation and Development
OMB	Office of Management and Budget
OPEC	Organization of Petroleum Exporting Countries
OSHA	Occupational Safety and Health Administration
OTC	over-the-counter
OTS	Office of Thrift Supervision
PIRG	Public Interest Research Group
PPC	production possibilities curve
PPI	producer price index
PPP	purchasing power parity
PRB	Population Reference Bureau
PRC	People's Republic of China
PRGF	Poverty Reduction and Growth Facility
PRWORA	Personal Responsibility and Work Opportunity Act
PTA	preferential trade agreement
PTO	Patent and Trademark Office
R&D	research and development
RDB	regional development bank

RTA	regional trade agreement
S&L	savings and loan association
SAIF	Savings Association Insurance Fund
SAR	special administrative region
SBA	Small Business Administration
SEC	Securities and Exchange Commission
SME	small and medium-sized enterprises
SOE	state-owned enterprise
SRO	self-regulating organization
TC	total cost
TEA	total entrepreneurial activity
TIIS	Treasury Inflation-Indexed Securities
TNC	transnational corporation
TVE	township and village enterprise
UAW	United Auto Workers
UFW	United Farm Workers
UMW	United Mine Workers
UN	United Nations
UNCTAD	United Nations Conference on Trade and Development
UNDP	United Nations Development Program
UNEP	United Nations Environmental Program
UNESCO	United Nations Educational, Scientific, and Cultural Organization
UNFPA	United Nations Population Fund
USAID	U.S. Agency for International Development
USSR	Union of Soviet Socialist Republics
VC	variable costs
WHO	World Health Organization
WOFE	wholly-owned foreign enterprise
WPA	Works Progress Administration
WRI	World Resources Institute
WTO	World Trade Organization
WWW	World Wide Web

Timeline of Key Economic Events of the Modern Era: 1750 to 2005

1760s The physiocratic school of economic thought emerges in France under François Quesnay, establishing the basis for laissez-faire economics

1770s The classical school of economic thought emerges in Britain under Adam Smith, author of *An Inquiry into the Nature and Causes of the Wealth of Nations* (1776)

1791 The First Bank of the United States receives a 20-year charter to support and strengthen America's monetary system and credit in global markets

1798 Thomas Malthus publishes *An Essay on the Principle of Population as It Affects the Future Improvement of Society,* causing some to proclaim economics as the "dismal science"

1803 Jean Baptiste Say publishes his *Treatise on Political Economy,* which popularizes laissez-faire capitalism and the law of markets, also called Say's Law

1816 The Second Bank of the United States receives a 20-year charter to stabilize the money and credit systems of America

1817 David Ricardo publishes *Principles of Political Economy,* defending free trade based on the theory of comparative advantage

1832 President Andrew Jackson vetoes legislation that would have extended the charter of the Second Bank of the United States for another 20 years

1848 Karl Marx and Friedrich Engels publish *The Communist Manifesto,* a fundamental treatise of the Marxist school of economic thought

John Stuart Mill writes *Principles of Political Economy,* which serves as the basic economics textbook for the English-speaking world for a generation

1860s Futures contracts for agricultural products are traded at the Chicago Board of Trade

1867 The first of three volumes of Marx's *Das Kapital* is published

1869 The Knights of Labor is founded by Uriah H. Stephens as a secret society of workers

Timeline of Key Economic Events of the Modern Era

1870s The marginalist school of economic thought rises under William S. Jevons (UK), Karl Menger (Austria), Leon Walras (France/Switzerland), and Knut Wicksell (Sweden)

1876 Thomas A. Edison establishes the world's first private research laboratory, then called an invention factory, in Menlo Park, New Jersey

1883 The socialist Fabian Society is founded in Britain; early leaders include Beatrice and Sidney Webb and George Bernard Shaw

1886 The American Federation of Labor is founded by Samuel Gompers; the AFL replaces the Knights of Labor as America's top labor union

1890 Alfred Marshall publishes *Principles of Economics,* which becomes the most widely recognized economics textbook in the world

The Sherman Antitrust Act is enacted to oppose the formation of monopolies and other restraints on competition

1896 Charles H. Dow creates the Dow Jones Industrial Average, an index of stock performance based on price fluctuations of a dozen key stocks

1899 The National Consumers League, America's first national consumer organization, is founded

1900 The term *economics* replaces *political economy* in common usage

1903 Mary (Mother) Jones leads the march of the mill children to bring national attention to the plight of child labor in America's textile mills

1905 The Industrial Workers of the World is founded under the slogan "One Big Union" and openly challenges the capitalist system in the United States

1911 Frederick Winslow Taylor's book, *Principles of Scientific Management,* revolutionizes management practices around time and motion principles

1913 The Ford Motor Company introduces the moving assembly line to the production of automobiles

The Federal Reserve Act establishes the Federal Reserve System, America's central bank

The Sixteenth Amendment to the U.S. Constitution establishes the national income tax

1914 The Clayton Antitrust Act and the Federal Trade Commission Act outlaw anti-competitive business practices

World War I erupts in Europe, ending the first great age of globalization

1917 Russian Bolsheviks stage a successful communist revolution in Russia under the leadership of Vladimir I. Lenin

1919 The International Labor Organization is founded to advocate for labor's rights in the global economy

1920 Arthur C. Pigou writes *The Economics of Welfare,* a book that gives birth to a new branch of economics called *welfare economics*

1922 The Union of Soviet Socialist Republics (USSR) is formally established as the world's first communist country

Benito Mussolini takes control of Italy under the banner of fascism and reorganizes the economy under the corporate state concept

1928 Joseph Stalin introduces the five-year plan in the Soviet Union, which solidifies the Communist Party's primacy in economic decision making

1929 The stock market crash signals the beginning of the Great Depression in the United States

1933 U.S. President Franklin D. Roosevelt introduces New Deal legislation to address the hardships caused by the Great Depression

The Glass-Steagall Banking Act of 1933 separates commercial and investment banking, and creates the Federal Deposit Insurance Corporation

Frances Perkins is appointed secretary of labor, becoming the first woman cabinet appointee in U.S. history

Joan Robinson publishes *The Economics of Imperfect Competition,* which introduces monopolistic competition as a market structure

1935 The Social Security Act provides income security for the nation's elderly and aids other economically distressed groups

The Wagner Act guarantees workers' right to form unions and bargain collectively with management

1936 John Maynard Keynes publishes *The General Theory of Employment, Interest, and Money,* which launches the Keynesian school of economic thought

The Consumers Union, which publishes *Consumer Reports,* is founded in the United States

1938 The Fair Labor Standards Act creates America's first national minimum wage of $0.25 per hour, a maximum workweek of 44 hours, and overtime pay

The Congress of Industrial Organizations is founded as a rival union to the American Federation of Labor; the CIO promotes industrial organization

1941 Simon Kuznets, the father of the gross domestic product, publishes the classic *National Income and Its Composition, 1919–1938*

1942 Joseph A. Schumpeter publishes *Capitalism, Socialism, and Democracy,* stressing the role of innovation and creative destruction in economic growth

1944 The Bretton Woods Conference creates the World Bank and the International Monetary Fund

The fixed exchange rate system is established

Friedrich August von Hayek publishes *The Road to Serfdom,* a passionate defense of capitalism and laissez-faire economics

1945 The United Nations is founded at the San Francisco Conference

A second great age of globalization begins at the close of World War II

1946 The invention of the electronic numerical integrator and calculator (ENIAC) launches the computer revolution

The Employment Act of 1946 expands the U.S. government's role in promoting full employment, production, and purchasing power

1947 The General Agreement on Tariffs and Trade is created to foster global trade

1949 The People's Republic of China is founded under the communist leadership of Mao Zedong and the principles of Maoism

1954 Peter F. Drucker's book, *The Practice of Management,* introduces management by objectives; this book is recognized as the country's first management textbook

1955 The American Federation of Labor (AFL) and the Congress of Industrial Organizations (CIO) merge to form the nation's largest union, the AFL-CIO

1957 The Rome treaties create the European Economic Community

1960 The International Organization of Consumers Unions, now Consumers International, is founded to press for consumer rights in the global economy

The Organization of Petroleum Exporting Counties, a producer cartel, is founded

1962 President John F. Kennedy identifies four basic consumer rights: the right to safety, to be informed, to choose, and to be heard

1964 The Civil Rights Act of 1964 provides protections against job and wage discrimination based on race, color, religion, gender, or national origin

President Lyndon Johnson initiates a series of Great Society programs to guarantee people's civil rights and expand social programs for the nation's needy

1966 Cesar Chavez founds the United Farm Workers, a union that represents agricultural workers, including migrant farmworkers

1967 President Julius Nyerere of Tanzania introduces *ujamaa,* a type of African socialism based on traditional tribal communalism

1969 The Internet (originally called ARPANET) is invented by the U.S. Department of Defense

1970s Stagflation, the simultaneous occurrence of stagnant growth and rising inflation, complicates government stabilization policies

1970 Paul A. Samuelson is the first American economist to receive the Nobel Prize in Economic Science

1971 Ralph Nader founds Public Citizen and is recognized as the chief spokesperson for the American consumer movement

1973 The flexible exchange rate system replaces the fixed exchange rate system

E. F. Schumacher publishes *Small Is Beautiful: Economics as if People Mattered,* which supports appropriate technology as a means to economic growth

1974 The United States dips into a severe recession

1976 Mao Zedong, father of the People's Republic of China, dies; Mao's death opens the doors for economic reformers to introduce market-oriented policies

1977 Fiber optics technology vastly expands communications potential

1978 Deng Xiaoping adopts a gradualist approach to initiating market-oriented economic reforms in China

The Full Employment and Balanced Growth Act of 1978, also called the Humphrey-Hawkins Act, strengthens the Full Employment Act of 1946

1981 The Economic Recovery Act of 1981, the centerpiece of the supply-side revolution during the Reagan administration, reduces taxes by 25 percent between 1982 and 1984

1983 Paul M. Romer introduces the new growth theory, which stresses the role of knowledge in promoting economic growth

1985 Soviet Premier Mikhail Gorbachev introduces economic and political reforms under the banner of *perestroika* and *glasnost*, respectively

Paul R. Krugman and Elhanan Helpman publish *Market Structure and Foreign Trade,* which introduces the new trade theory

1986 Alice M. Rivlin, a prominent government economist, is the first woman to serve as president of the American Economic Association

1987 Alan Greenspan is appointed chairman of the Federal Reserve System and serves under the presidential administrations of Ronald Reagan, George H. W. Bush, Bill Clinton, and George W. Bush

The Montreal Protocol, a multilateral environmental treaty, targets ozone-depleting substances in the atmosphere

1989 Tim Berners-Lee invents the World Wide Web

1990 A Human Development Index is introduced by the United Nations Development Program to measure progress towards sustainable economic development

1991 The Union of Soviet Socialist Republics formally dissolves

The United States slips into a recession after a prolonged expansion during the 1980s

1992 Russia and other transition countries begin the epic transition from communism to capitalism, and from totalitarianism to democracy

The Rio Earth Summit generates *Agenda 21,* a comprehensive plan for global economic development

1993 The Maastricht Treaty creates the European Union

1994 The North American Free Trade Agreement takes effect

The Common Market of the South, or MERCOSUR, is formed

The eighth and final GATT trade round concludes at Marrakesh with the creation of the World Trade Organization

1995 The World Trade Organization officially replaces the General Agreement on Tariffs and Trade

1996 The Temporary Assistance for Needy Families program limits welfare benefits in the United States and encourages productive employment

1997 Hong Kong is transformed from a British colony to a Special Administrative Region of China

The East Asian financial crisis destabilizes the global economy, which illustrates the danger of financial contagion

The U.S. minimum wage is increased for the twentieth time since 1938, from $4.75 to $5.15

1998 A flurry of mega-mergers and acquisitions bring major corporations, such as Chrysler (U.S.) and Daimler-Benz (Germany), under single ownership

1999 The World Trade Organization's Millennium Round of trade negotiations flops in Seattle, amid massive protests by civil society organizations

The euro begins its phase-in as the European Union's common currency

The World Bank reports that 46 developing countries were involved in conflicts, mainly civil wars and domestic violence, during the 1990s, disrupting their path toward economic development

2000 The Dow Jones Industrial Average peaks at 11,723

The World Resources Institute publishes *World Resources: 2000–2001,* which warns against continued abuse of natural ecosystems by human populations

World population hits 6 billion people

The World Bank introduces a new measurement of economic well-being, the gross national income (GNI) per capita

The United Nations estimates that 37,000 nongovernmental organizations operate globally

The United Nations issues its Millennium Development Goals to guide and measure progress toward sustainable economic development

Hernando de Soto publishes *The Mystery of Capital: Why Capitalism Triumphs in the West and Fails Everywhere Else,* which emphasizes policies of inclusion to promote sustainable economic development

2001 The Summit of the Americas held in Quebec City lays the groundwork for the creation of a 34 nation Free Trade Area of the Americas

The U.S. economy slips into a recession after a prolonged expansion during the 1990s

Terrorist attacks on New York City and Washington, D.C., slow international trade and foreign direct investment

About 13,400 economists were employed in the U.S. economy, earning an average wage of $72,350, about double the average wage of all U.S. workers

2002 The euro officially replaces the national currencies of 12 of the 15 European Union member nations, thus creating the European Monetary Union (euro zone)

The NASDAQ Stock Market, America's largest stock exchange, lists 4,100 companies; the New York Stock exchange, the nation's second largest stock exchange, lists 2,783 companies

The Dow Jones Industrial Average troughs at 7,286 in October

The Freedom House reports that about 4 billion people live in countries that are free or partly free, and about 2 billion live in not free countries

Foreign direct investment dips to $651 billion in inflows, a drop of nearly 50 percent from the 2000 peak of $1,271 billion

The number of bilateral investment treaties increases to 2,200

Official development assistance to poorer countries totals $57 billion

2003 Officers of several large U.S. corporations, such as Enron and Tyco, are indicted for financial crimes and corporate corruption

A record 1.65 million personal and business bankruptcies are filed in the United States

Wal-Mart is the world's largest corporation, earning $259 billion in revenues and employing 1.3 million workers

Subway is America's top-ranked franchise

The Jobs and Growth Tax Relief Reconciliation Act of 2003 reduces income tax rates, and tax obligations, to stimulate economic growth

The World Bank identifies 50 severely indebted countries

The nominal GDP in the United States hits $11 trillion

The American labor force hits 146 million

The U.S. merchandise trade deficit tops $500 billion

2004 The European Union's fifth enlargement adds 10 countries

The International Monetary Fund estimates a global GDP of $37 trillion

Membership in the World Trade Organization is 147 countries

U.S. federal budget deficit tops $500 billion

The foreign debt of developing and transition countries hits $2.7 trillion

2005 The United Nations proclaims 2005 as the International Year of Microcredit

CHAPTER 1

Economics as a Social Science

Chapter 1 introduces economics as a field of study within the social sciences. While people have made economic decisions since the beginning of humankind, the formal study of economics has only recently emerged. Its origins can be traced back to the sixteenth and seventeenth centuries as the fledgling nation-states of Europe grappled with the basic economic questions of what, how, and for whom to produce. Chapter 1 explores the content and methodology of economics, introduces the main types of economic systems, and explores the limitations of economic science—including why economists so often disagree about economic theories, policies, and programs.

THE UNIVERSAL ECONOMIC PROBLEM OF SCARCITY

Scarcity is the universal economic problem. Scarcity exists because people have unlimited wants or needs, but limited resources to satisfy their material desires. Scarcity is called the universal economic problem because it affects all people in all societies, and has done so throughout history.

Economics Defined

Economics is the study of how people choose to use their scarce resources in order to satisfy their wants or needs. Thus, economics deals with the production and distribution of goods and services. The term *economics* comes from *oikonomikos*, which means skilled in household management.[1] It wasn't until the early twentieth century that *economics* came into common usage, replacing the more familiar *political economy*—a term that was introduced in the early 1600s and popularized during the 1700s. As the study of economics evolved over time, increased attention was given to how people used scarce resources, often referred to as the **factors of production** or productive resources, to produce goods and services. The three main factors of production are natural resources, or land; human resources, or labor; and capital goods, or capital. **Natural resources** are the gifts of nature, such as rivers, sunlight, fish and other animals, natural forests, and soil. **Human resources** are the people who are involved in production, including teachers, carpenters, electricians, custodians, and economists. **Capital goods** are items that are designed to produce other products, including cement mixers, shopping malls, business computers, delivery trucks, and office buildings. Many economists include entrepreneurship as a fourth factor of production. **Entrepreneurship** features the risk-taking and innovation of entrepreneurs—people who create new products, innovative production methods, or businesses. How people use the factors of production to produce goods and services to satisfy society's needs is a major component of economics.

Like the other social sciences, economics studies human relationships and behaviors of people. The most important units of study in economics are the behaviors of households, businesses, and government. Economics and the other social sciences—anthropology, human geography, psychology, and sociology—are not exact sciences, however. Why is this so? First, the social sciences deal with human behaviors, and people sometimes behave in unpredictable ways. In this respect, the social sciences are different from the physical sciences, which investigate inorganic matter. In the study of chemistry, for example, chemical reactions between certain compounds are predictable and exact. Second, the social sciences study human behaviors in the real world, not in a laboratory or other controlled environment. Thus, the social scientist is unable to isolate or account for all of the variables that affect the actions of individuals or groups. Despite these limitations, social scientists, including economists, have studied and drawn conclusions about people's economic behaviors. The two main branches of economics are microeconomics and macroeconomics.

Branches of Economics

Microeconomics is the branch of economics that focuses on the interactions among the individual decision-making units within an economy. Microeconomics is the older of the two branches of economics, occupying much of the attention of the early schools of economic thought. The most important participants in the microeconomy are households, business firms, and the government. The **private sector,** or nongovernmental sector of the economy, consists of households and firms. Households, for example, consume the lion's share of all goods and services produced in the U.S. economy. Hence, one important microeconomic topic analyzes consumer demand, why people choose to buy certain goods or services and not others. The behaviors and decisions of other household units including savers, investors, workers, and entrepreneurs are also critical elements in this study. Businesses, the other decision makers in the private sector, supply goods and services in an economy. Economists who study the microeconomy are concerned with how firms make pricing, output, hiring, and other production decisions. These business decisions are guided by the desire to maximize profits in a market economy—another major topic in the field of microeconomics.

Microeconomics is also interested in certain roles of government, or the **public sector** of the economy. Local, state, and national governments make a variety of consumption and production decisions and thus influence the conduct of business in an economy. The federal government, for example, purchases military goods such as submarines and aircraft from individual firms and is also a major employer of workers. Hence, government influences what goods firms will produce as well as the amount of income certain households will receive. In fact, by 2003, 22 million workers were employed by the government at the local, state, and national levels.[2] In the United States, the role of government in the microeconomy is to provide people with public goods and services, establish regulations to protect people from market failures such as pollution and unfair business practices, provide economic security for people, and ensure that all individuals and firms have a fair chance to succeed in the economy.

Macroeconomics is the branch of economics that deals with the economic performance of the entire economy. Macroeconomics, as a broad field of study, arose during the twentieth century, largely in response to the global depression of the 1930s. Macroeconomics focuses on economic growth and economic stability in a nation. Economic growth is often measured by tracking a nation's real gross domestic product over time. The **real gross domestic product** (GDP) is the dollar value of all newly produced goods and services in an economy in a given year, adjusted for inflation. Economic stability refers to maintaining stable price levels for consumer and producer goods, and a fully employed labor force. In short, macroeconomics is concerned with aggregates such as national output, national income, national savings rates, and the national unemployment rate, rather than with the behaviors of individuals or firms.

Government is also a major player in the realm of macroeconomics. This is because the federal government devises policies that affect the economy as a whole. The two most important government policies that influence a nation's economic performance are fiscal policy and monetary policy. Fiscal policy involves changes in taxes and government spending, while monetary policy involves changes in the money supply and cost of credit. For example, if the government wants to jump-start a sluggish economy, it could lower taxes and increase government spending. The government could also increase the money supply and make credit easier to come by. Combined, these policies would increase aggregate (total) demand in the economy and thus stimulate production, create jobs, and encourage new investment. In the U.S. economy, Congress and the president are mainly responsible for forming an effective fiscal policy for the nation, while an independent Federal Reserve System (the Fed) devises the nation's monetary policy (see chapter 10 for more on monetary and fiscal policy).

ECONOMICS: THE SCIENCE OF CHOICE

Economic choice is a conscious decision to use scarce resources in one manner rather than another. Because of scarcity, people simply cannot have everything they may want. Scarcity takes many forms. Scarce financial resources limit a consumer's ability to purchase products. Scarce natural resources limit a producer's ability to supply products. Scarce human or capital resources limit a nation's progress toward economic development. Students often experience a scarcity of time—for homework, athletics, jobs, and recreation. Because people live in a world of unlimited wants and finite resources, they must choose wisely among competing wants or needs. The study of economics helps people determine how to use their scarce resources.

Recognizing Opportunity Costs

The most basic understanding about economic choice is that all choices have a cost. Ordinarily, people tend to equate the cost of a good with its price. That is, if the price of a cup of coffee is $1.50, most people express the cost of that cup of coffee in monetary terms—one dollar and fifty cents. Economists, however, tend to measure the true cost of the choices people make through a different lens. Economists see the real cost, or opportunity cost, of any decision in terms of what was foregone, or given up, if resources were used in one way rather than another. That is, the **opportunity cost** of a choice represents the second-best use of scarce resources. Once again, consider the purchase of a $1.50 cup of coffee. If the buyer was both thirsty and hungry but had just $1.50 to spend, the opportunity cost may well have been the lost opportunity to consume a $1.50 pastry.

Illustrating Choices with Production Possibilities Curves

On a larger scale, nations also make choices about how to use scarce resources to satisfy people's needs. The production choices that nations make also involve opportunity costs. A **production possibilities curve** (PPC) shows the range of possible production choices for two products at a moment in time. It also shows the opportunity costs that a nation might incur at any point along its PPC. Economists make two main assumptions about PPCs. First, resources are fully employed at all points on the PPC. Thus, all points along the existing PPC represent technical efficiency, or efficient production methods. Society's decision to produce at a certain point along its PPC may result in allocative inefficiency, however, if the production decision does not mesh with society's wants or needs. The second assumption is that the nation's resources and technology are fixed at this moment in time.

The PPC shown in Figure 1.1 illustrates the range of production possibilities for nation X for two broad categories of goods, investment goods and consumption goods. **Investment goods** are goods not designed for present con-

Figure 1.1
Production Possibilities Curve for Nation X

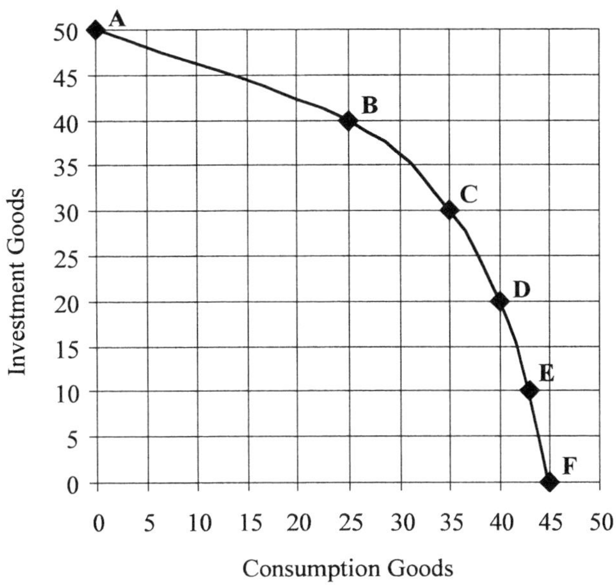

sumption, such as capital goods, business inventories, and residential housing. Investment goods are shown on the vertical axis. **Consumption goods** are goods and services designed for immediate use by consumers, such as food, clothing, automobiles, and medical services. Consumption goods are shown on the horizontal axis. A PPC tells the reader two things—the amount of each good that can be produced at each point along the curve, and the opportunity cost of each possible production decision. In Figure 1.1 all of nation X's resources are devoted to the production of investment goods at point A; thus 50 million units of investment goods are produced, and 0 units of consumption goods are produced. The opportunity cost of production at point A is 45 million units of consumption goods. This is because nation X sacrificed the 45 million units of consumption goods so that all of its resources could be used to produce investment goods. Point F represents the opposite extreme, where all of nation X's resources are devoted to the production of consumption goods. Thus, at point F, 45 million units of consumption goods are produced, and 0 units of investment goods are produced. The specific opportunity cost at point F, as measured by what was given up by nation X, is 50 million units of investment goods.

Rarely does a nation produce at either of these extremes. Instead, nations typically produce at a point somewhere along the PPC. For example, if nation X chose to produce at point B, 40 million units of investment goods and 25 million units of consumption goods are produced. How could opportunity cost be expressed in this situation? In terms of investment goods, the opportunity cost of producing at point B is 10 million units (50–40 million = 10 million) because nation X chooses to sacrifice these 10 million units of investment goods in order to use some of its resources to produce consumption goods. In terms of consumption goods, the opportunity cost of producing at point B is 20 million units (45–25 million = 20 million) because nation X chooses not to produce 20 million units of consumption goods. PPCs are a visual representation of a key understanding in economics: every decision involves a cost.

ECONOMIC SYSTEMS ORGANIZE ECONOMIC ACTIVITY

Scarcity forces people to make economic choices about how to use their resources. Throughout history, people working alone or in groups have come to grips with this reality by organizing economic systems. An **economic system** is the sum total of all economic activity that takes place within a society. That is, economic systems are composed not only of the tangible economic institutions such as business firms, banks, and stock exchanges, but also the more subtle nuances that underlie business activity such as values, practices, customs, or traditions. Economic systems also answer the three **basic economic questions.** What goods and services should be produced and in what quantity? How should these products be produced? For whom should these products be produced? The responses to the basic economic questions help distinguish the three main types of economic systems: traditional economies, command economies, and market economies.

Traditional Economies

A **traditional economy** is a type of economic system that relies on custom or tradition to answer the basic economic questions. That is, society's blueprint for economic activity is written by previous generations. Traditional economies produce goods that satisfy basic survival needs for food, clothing, and shelter. These isolated peoples produce few surpluses; as a result, there is little trade. The how-to-produce question is likewise dictated by tradition, as production methods vary little from one generation to the next. The economic status quo is reinforced by the use of primitive capital goods and the absence of technology and entrepreneurship. Further, a rigid division of labor often uses gender, age, and skills to define a person's status and role in society. Finally, the for-whom-to-produce question often centers on a primitive communalism, where community needs and kinship ties bind people together in the common cause of survival. Today, there are few traditional economies. Small enclaves of people living in remote regions of Africa, Asia, Latin America, and the Arctic have many of the characteristics of traditional economies. These peoples have maintained many of their cultural and economic institutions, apart from the nation in which they reside. Examples include the Mbuti Pygmies of Central Africa, the Kavango tribes of Namibia, the Nigritos of the Philippines, and the Saharias of central India.

The Mbuti Pygmies have lived in the Ituri Forest for thousands of years. The Ituri is a rain forest in the present-day Democratic Republic of Congo (formerly Zaire), but Pygmy bands also inhabit regions that straddle neighboring Congo Republic and Cameroon. The Mbuti live in small bands or groups, are nomadic, and are well acquainted with the bounty of the forest, which provides them with food, clothing, and shelter. The Mbuti, who number 70,000 to 80,000 people, are mainly hunters and gatherers. The simple division of labor that has been passed from generation to generation is determined mainly by gender and age. Men lead the hunts, using primitive capital such as the bow and arrow. Women have primary responsibility for cooking and maintaining the temporary campsites. Both men and women gather edible plants, such as fruits, mushrooms, and roots. The entire Mbuti community takes part in fishing, which typically involves corralling fish into nets. Hence, the needs of the community are met through collective action. Today, the Mbuti have some economic contact with the outside world. For instance, they trade with nearby Bantu tribes. Other contacts have not been as beneficial. Government outreach programs to teach farming techniques to the Mbuti have proven largely unsuccessful. Aggressive timbering and other development projects have also cast a shadow on Mbuti lifestyles (see chapter 2 for more on primitive hunting and gathering societies).

Command Economies

A **command economy** is a type of economic system in which the government dictates the answers to the basic economic questions. That is, economic decision making is highly centralized in the hands of a central authority. During the twentieth century, the communist nations of eastern and central Europe and East Asia created a type of command economy. In these nations, the Communist Party and an elite corps of central planners dictated the use of society's resources by devising and enforcing five-year plans. Central planning dominated economic activity in the Soviet Union beginning in the late 1920s, in the Eastern-bloc nations (Bulgaria, Czechoslovakia, East Germany, Hungary, Poland, and Romania) in the mid-1940s, and in the People's Republic of China in the 1950s. By owning and controlling all of the factors of production, the cumbersome communist planning bureaucracies discouraged entrepreneurship, individual initiative, and product innovation. The collapse of communism in most of the world during the late 1980s and early 1990s dismantled much of the state planning apparatus in these economies. Today, elements of a command economy can still be found in Cuba and North Korea (see chapter 4 for more on communist economies).

Command economies were the norm in different parts of the world for thousands of years. In northern Africa, the Old Kingdom in Egypt (2660 B.C. to 2180 B.C.) employed a command economy with a pharaoh as the undisputed central authority. The pharaoh owned all land and collected taxes from peasants who farmed it. The pharaoh also required peasants to work on public projects such as temples, canals, and pyramids, and to serve in the army. In Asia, the Zhou Dynasty in China (1122 B.C. to 256 B.C.) established a complex feudal economy. Under Chinese feudalism, the emperor owned the land but appointed trusted nobles to govern large portions of the empire. In exchange for these grants of land, a noble owed his allegiance and tribute payments to the emperor. Nobles, in turn, permitted peasants to use plots of land in exchange for their allegiance and tribute. During the first couple of centuries of the Zhou Dynasty, this hierarchical system permitted strong emperors to maintain peace throughout the sprawling empire; build magnificent palaces, canals, and roads; and otherwise tend to the empire's needs. A similar feudal system was established in Europe in the eighth century A.D. As this feudal system evolved over the next few centuries, kings granted tracts of land called fiefs to trusted nobles called vassals in exchange for their loyalty, military service, and tax payments. In theory the king owned all the land, but in reality each vassal (called a lord) commanded his own fief, built his own manor, and dictated the conditions of life to the peasants (called serfs) who were typically tied to the land. Hence, each vassal commanded a self-sufficient manor, giving birth to the manorial system that dominated the Middle Ages. The command economies in ancient Egypt and China and in medieval Europe severely restricted the economic freedom of individuals but created some order under which society could marshal its resources.

Market Economies

A **market economy** is a type of economy that relies on the private sector to answer the basic economic questions and to own and control the factors of production. In a market economy, decentralized decision making by individuals and firms determines what, how, and for whom to produce. At the heart of a market economy are private property and the economic freedoms of the marketplace. An invisible price system, rather than a central authority or custom, allocates resources in market economies. For example, consumers enjoy **freedom of choice**—the ability to spend their money as they wish. In doing so, consumers answer the basic question of what to produce. Producers, in turn, have **freedom of enterprise,** which allows firms to use scarce resources in the most profitable ways. Workers enjoy the freedom to prepare for a variety of occupations, choose a career, and negotiate wages with employers. The **market mechanism,** which Adam Smith called the "invisible hand," permits the forces of supply and demand to determine prices and allocate resources in free and competitive markets.

Over the past few decades, the former British colony of Hong Kong was arguably the freest market economy in the world. Established as a free port by the British in the early 1840s, Hong Kong attracted foreign trade and investment during the nineteenth and twentieth centuries. The influx of aspiring entrepreneurs and foreign capital accelerated during the early twentieth century as people fled the chaos of war and revolution in neighboring China, including the devastating civil war between the Nationalists and the Communists—a conflict that raged until the victorious Communists created the People's Republic of China in 1949. British policies in Hong Kong created free markets and profit incentives, and few government regulations on business activities. The British also invested heavily in the development of a modern infrastructure, including an electrified railroad, a subway system, and an international airport. In 1997 Hong Kong was made a Special Administrative Region (SAR) of the People's Republic of China and is now called Hong Kong SAR. It retains a privileged position within China, however. In fact, according to *Economic Freedom of the World: 2003 Annual Report,* the Hong Kong SAR enjoyed the most economic freedom of any economy in the world in 2001.[3]

THE METHODOLOGY OF ECONOMICS

In its *Occupational Outlook Handbook,* the U.S. Department of Labor defines economists as people who "study how society distributes scarce resources such as land, labor, raw materials, and machinery to produce goods and services."[4] Traditionally, economists are categorized under one of three broad headings—academic economists, business economists, or government economists (see chapter 13 for more on economists). An introduction to the methodology of economics begins by distinguishing positive economics from normative economics.

Positive and Normative Economics

Positive economics, sometimes called descriptive economics, is concerned with what is. That is, it deals with economic relationships that can be objectively tested with data. Consider the following positive statement: If interest rates fall, more people will buy houses. To test this statement, economists would collect statistical data on the number of houses that were purchased as interest rates in the economy changed. If the data verified that house sales increased as interest rates declined, the economist could confirm a relationship between prevailing interest rates and housing sales. Economists are mindful that other variables, such as changes in income levels or consumer confidence, might also influence home purchases. Economic behaviors and relationships might also change over time and, therefore, must be tested and retested.

Normative economics presents a viewpoint on an economic topic or issue. Normative statements comment on policies, programs, or other actions that should or should not happen. Consider the following normative statement: The government should force banks to lower interest rates so that more people can buy houses. This statement offers an opinion, or a subjective view of what ought to be. The viewpoint can be discussed and debated endlessly, but it cannot be verified by objective data as an accurate or inaccurate statement because it is based on the economist's values. Values and other factors sometimes color economists' view of the world, which helps explain why economists often disagree.

An Economic Way of Thinking

An *economic way of thinking* refers to ideas and understandings that guide economic inquiries. The phrase conjures up many images. Some may view an economic way of thinking as a complex set of mathematical formulas, while others may see it as a simple checklist of dos and don'ts in this field of study. In reality, an economic way of thinking encompasses an approach to the study of economics. It also provides some common ground upon which economic topics can be critically examined. While most economists share a common perspective on how to approach a problem or issue, there are no guarantees that they will draw the same conclusions from data. In fact, skeptics sometimes quip that if you linked every economist in the world hand to hand, they still couldn't reach a conclusion. Several key understandings typically shape an economist's perspective.

One understanding that underlies the study of economics is that all decisions involve costs. Scarcity forces people to make choices in the items consumers purchase, in the products firms produce, in the public goods and services government provides, and so on. Economists often remind us that there's no such thing as a free lunch. Whenever a choice is made, an opportunity cost results. The classic choice between economic development and wilderness preservation illustrates how opportunity costs occur in the economy. In 1980, for example, the U.S. Congress passed the Alaska National Interest Lands Conservation Act, which set aside millions of acres of Alaskan wilderness as a national park. This act was widely supported by environmental groups and others. Critics of the Alaska Lands Act pointed to the opportunity cost of wilderness preservation, however. In this case, the opportunity cost was the vast quantities of mineral resources that could not be mined from the wilderness refuge. In essence, Congress declared that the first-best use of this tract of land was the national park, and that the second-best use was mineral development.

A second understanding is that people tend to make rational economic decisions. Rational decision making occurs when people use scarce resources effectively to achieve their goals. Consumers, for example, are rational decision makers when they comparison shop and buy goods that bring them the greatest personal satisfaction at the lowest possible price. Similarly, businesses express their rationality when they employ production techniques that reduce their costs of production. In many respects rational decision making is based on the pursuit of self-interest by individuals and firms. This is because individuals are in the best position to determine their own wants or needs. Adam Smith, the founder of modern economics, wrote about the importance of self- interest in *An Inquiry into the Nature and Causes of the Wealth of Nations* (1776). In this landmark book, Smith argued that both the individual and society benefit when people are given the freedom to work in their own self-interest.

A third understanding is that economic decisions sometimes have unintended consequences. Often these unintended consequences, sometimes called **secondary effects,** occur in the future rather than in the present. For example, in the mid-1970s the government imposed a price ceiling, or maximum price, on petroleum produced in the United States. The goal of the price ceiling was to hold the price of this valuable resource steady to slow the price spiral of related products, such as gasoline and home heating oil. The secondary effects of the

Alaska Peninsula National Wildlife Refuge, Alaska. © U.S. Fish and Wildlife Service. Photograph by Mark Emery.

price ceiling soon rocked the U.S. economy, however. Low oil prices acted as a disincentive for oil companies to explore for new sources of oil. Some companies even capped existing oil wells. As a result, shortages of gasoline, home heating oil, and other petroleum-based products occurred. American consumers were introduced to a new pastime—queuing at gas stations—as well as sorting out a variety of rationing schemes that were enacted to deal with the chaos caused by petroleum shortages. The phase-out of the price ceiling on domestically produced petroleum in the late 1970s restored incentives for U.S. firms to resume oil exploration and drilling.

A fourth understanding is that most economic decisions are made at the margin. The term *margin* in this context means the next, or additional, unit. **Marginalism** is a type of analysis that weighs the additional costs of an economic policy or decision against the additional benefits that might be derived. Economists are involved in many types of marginal analyses. This is especially true in the study of microeconomics, which studies the behaviors of individual consumption and production units. Consumers, for example, consider the marginal utility, or additional satisfaction, that they might receive from the purchase of a second or third pastry before buying additional pastries. The consumer would continue to buy additional pastries as long as the marginal benefit outweighed the marginal cost. Likewise, firms consider the marginal cost of hiring an additional laborer against the marginal revenue that would be derived from employing this worker. The firm would hire an additional worker if this worker contributed more to the firm's revenues than it cost to hire the worker. Economists tend to reject most all-or-nothing decisions, preferring the rationality of making decisions at the margin (see chapter 6 for more on marginal utility).

A fifth understanding is that economic thinking is scientific thinking. Economists approach economics in much the same manner as chemists approach chemistry and physicists approach physics. That is, the social and physical sciences share a common approach to organizing, analyzing, and explaining information. Economists often use an inductive or deductive approach to forming generalizations, economic theories and laws, solutions to problems, and so on. The **inductive approach** begins by identifying a problem and then collecting and organizing relevant data. From these data, the economist forms one or more generalizations to note general tendencies about the problem or issue. A generalization may be prefaced with phrases such as *in most cases* or *rarely* to indicate that there may be exceptions to the general rule. Finally, the economist tests the generalization in a real-world setting. The **deductive approach,** on the other hand, begins the scientific inquiry by forming a hypothesis about a topic using just general observations or impressions about an economic issue or problem. The economist then collects, organizes, and analyzes data related to the topic. Before the hypothesis can be validated, it must withstand the scrutiny of testing in the real world. A generalization or a hypothesis that survives repeated testing over time earns the title of **economic law** or **economic principle.** For example, the most famous economic law, the law of demand, states that consumers buy more of a good when its price is low and lesser amounts when its price is high. While the law of demand seems to be little more than a statement of common sense, it wasn't until the nineteenth century that economists were able to devise a demand curve to illustrate the relationship between price and the quantity demanded of a good.

ECONOMISTS: WHY THEY DISAGREE

There's an old joke that if you put two economists in a room to discuss an issue they will invariably offer three different viewpoints on the topic. Why economists disagree about the causes of or solutions to economic problems may perplex noneconomists. After all, economists tend to agree on the basic language of economics and share many common understandings about the methodology of this social science. So why do economists so often arrive at different conclusions?

Imperfect Information and the Limits of Economic Models

Economic science is the science of predicting the economic behaviors of people—individuals, firms, even nations. Economists, unlike their cousins in the physical sciences, cannot limit or control all of the variables in a laboratory setting, however. The economist's laboratory is the world of economic activity and the countless decisions that are made by individuals, firms, and other groups. Predicting human behaviors in a turbulent sea of economic data is a complex process. Consider the problem of data collection, an important feature of scientific inquiry. Economists must determine which data are relevant to a problem or issue, as well as which are reliable enough to include in the study.

Economists also understand that the volume and complexity of data necessitate some simplification. To help narrow the study, economists often construct an **economic model,** a simplification of reality to focus attention on a specific relationship between two or more variables. For example, the law of demand is an economic model that illustrates how a change in price influences the quantity demanded of a good. Even this simple model has its limitations, however. For instance, to arrive at this cause-and-effect relationship between price and the quantity demanded, all other variables in the economy are momentarily held constant—a commonly used technique called the ***ceteris paribus*** assumption. Economists employ the *ceteris paribus* assumption to study specific economic relationships, knowing that in reality many variables in the economy are in flux. Today, many economists use highly sophisticated mathematical models so that more data and more variables can be used to predict or explain economic behaviors, a practice that is commonly referred to as **econometrics.** With the aid of sophisticated computer technologies, economic forecasters use econometrics to input, analyze, and draw conclusions from vast quantities of data—and still they often arrive at different conclusions.

Schools of Economic Thought: A Matter of Perspective

Economists' assumptions, values, or biases may also color their methodology or conclusions. For example, economists from the different schools of economic thought are predisposed to view an economic problem through a certain lens. Consider the responses of different schools of economic thought to the most serious downturn in U.S. history—the Great Depression of the 1930s. During the Great Depression, the gross national product (GNP) plummeted, the unemployment rate skyrocketed, and many businesses failed. The Keynesian school of economic thought, also called the Keynesians, supported government policies to "prime the pump," or jump-start the sluggish economy. The Keynesians believed that higher government spending and lower taxes would increase aggregate (total) demand in the economy. Higher aggregate demand, in turn, would stimulate business investment, employment, and economic growth. The Keynesian response to the Great Depression was at odds with policies proposed by the more established classical school of economic thought, however. The beliefs of the classical economists were rooted in **laissez-faire capitalism,** a doctrine that opposed government intervention in the economy. Classical economists held firm to the idea that periodic downturns in an economy, even downturns as severe as the Great Depression, would self-correct over time without unwelcome interference by the government. Meanwhile, some within the Marxist school of economic thought saw the global economic downturn of the 1930s as a sign of the inherent weaknesses of capitalism, perhaps even a precursor to capitalism's collapse and the triumph of centrally planned economies (see chapter 2 for more on schools of economic thought).

Economic Fallacies

Disagreements among economists can occur when research is marred by fallacies. A **fallacy** is an error in one's research or reasoning that, in turn, results in erroneous conclusions. There are several types of fallacies that plague the study of economics and the other social sciences.

- **Cause-effect fallacies**. Cause-effect fallacies occur when an incorrect or incomplete relationship is drawn between one event and another. One type of cause-effect fallacy is the **single-cause fallacy,** which identifies just one cause of, or one solution to, a complex problem, when in reality there are multiple causes or solutions. The single-cause fallacy is often called *oversimplification* because the economist's reasoning excludes key variables related to the problem. A second type of cause-effect fallacy is the **correlation-as-cause fallacy,** which assumes that because two events occur at about the same time one must have caused the other. In reality, at any moment in time many events occur, some of which are related and some of which are not.
- **Evidence fallacies.** Evidence fallacies occur when an economist's conclusions are based on insufficient, irrelevant, or inaccurate information. Evidence fallacies may be intentional, to promote a certain position or policy, or unintentional. In either case, the economist's conclusion is tainted by faulty evidence.
- **Fallacy of composition.** The fallacy of composition assumes that what is true or proper for a piece is true or proper for the whole. In the study of economics, what is good or appropriate behavior for an individual (the piece) is not necessarily the proper behavior for the entire society (the whole). For instance, it is commonly agreed that monthly household budgets should be balanced to ensure that all bills are paid. That is, people should live within their budget constraints. On the national level, however, budgetary deficits are sometimes viewed as necessary to moderate downturns in the economy, as was the case during the Great Depression.

BIOGRAPHIES: SHAPERS OF ECONOMIC THOUGHT

Plato and *The Republic*

Plato (428 B.C.–347 B.C.) is among the most important philosophers in the history of Western culture. Born to an established aristocratic family in Athens, the young Plato enjoyed the pursuit of knowledge, often in the company of his older friend and mentor Socrates. Socrates was viewed as a pesky gadfly, however, because of his incessant questioning of Athenian democracy, which he sometimes equated with mob rule. Powerful enemies soon brought Socrates to trial for his heresies, and he was executed in 399 B.C. The death of Socrates had a profound impact on Plato. He traveled in Italy, Sicily, and Egypt, but eventually returned to Athens where in 387 B.C. he founded the Academy, an institution that is often viewed as the first European university. Among Plato's more accomplished students was Aristotle. Plato also devoted himself to study and to writing during this period, authoring numerous dialogues and a book, *The Republic.* In *The Republic,* Plato described an ideal society, including the components of an ideal economy. While it is clear that Plato did not believe that such a society could be built, the ideas in Plato's masterpiece influenced later philosophers, statesmen, reformers, and economists.

In *The Republic,* Plato envisioned a society composed of three distinct classes of people—a ruling class, a warrior class, and a working class. In Plato's view, this broad division of labor attended to the requirements of any civilization, namely good governance, protection from external enemies, and the production of goods and services. Plato also identified specific virtues for each class of citizens—wisdom for the rulers, courage for the warriors, and temperance for the workers. Uniting the entire society was a fourth virtue, justice. An important feature of justice was that each class must be diligent in its own perfection, without meddling in the affairs of the other classes. For workers, contentment would be derived from perfection of their crafts and from the worldly comforts they earned from their labor. For the two upper classes, rulers and warriors, contentment would come from a different source, a selfless pursuit of society's goals. In Plato's ideal society, rulers and warriors were prohibited from owning private property, which was viewed as a source of greed and corruption. Indeed, to prevent the warrior class from becoming "savage tyrants instead of friends and allies," Plato wrote, they should receive just "a fixed rate of pay, enough to meet the expenses of the year and no more," and they should "go to mess and live together like soldiers in a camp."[5]

In many respects, Plato's ideal society, which is outlined elegantly in *The Republic,* was a prototype for enlightened socialist thought 2,000 years later. The influence of Plato's work cannot be overestimated in this respect, having influenced prominent thinkers from Thomas More, to utopian socialists, to Karl Marx. Plato emphasized restrictions on private property and excessive wealth, and the nobility of communal effort to achieve social goals. Further, Plato's discourse in *The Republic* justified the division of labor for an entire society and for common workers as "all things are produced more plentifully and easily and of a better quality when one man does one thing which is natural to him, and does it at the right time, and leaves other things."[6] In his work, Plato also condemned poverty as an avoidable social ill, a problem that is alleviated by a fair distribution of society's wealth.

Sir Thomas More and *Utopia*

Sir Thomas More (1478–1535) was a scholar, a lawyer, a statesman, and an author. More was born the son of a judge in London, England. His formal education included studies at Oxford and at the Inns of Court in London, from which he earned his law degree. More's scholarship did not go unnoticed, and his career profited from close associations with leading intellects of the period and officials in the English court. He was elected to Parliament in 1504, knighted in 1521, elected Speaker of the House of Commons in 1523, and appointed Lord Chancellor of all England by King Henry VIII in 1529. It is not for his ascendancy to a position of authority that Sir Thomas More is best known, however. Instead, More's fame in the field of economic history is derived from his insights about the economic injustices of his times. In his most famous book, *Utopia* (1516), More criticized the excesses of the rising capitalist and commercial classes and their shameless exploitation of common workers.

Utopia, which translates as "nowhere," described the society of a mythical island inhabited by a people called Utopians. Utopian society was built on the principles of justice and communal effort. People were employed in agriculture and useful trades, such as blacksmith, carpenter, or stonemason. They ate in communal dining halls, wore plain clothing, and shunned all luxuries. Specie (gold and silver), so precious to the monarchs of Europe, got "no more respect from anyone than their intrinsic value deserves—which is obviously far less than that of iron."[7] In fact, the Utopians abolished the use of money for transactions on the island, preferring a system of distribution based on need. On the island of Utopia, communal effort, which rarely meant more than six hours of work per day, and a fair distribution of society's output guaranteed prosperity for all. "Under such a system, there's bound to be plenty of everything, and, as everything is divided among the entire population, there obviously can't be any poor people or beggars."[8] More, who was careful to speak through his fictitious acquaintance, Raphael Hythloday, in *Utopia,* saved his most severe criticism for rising capitalists who suffered from the disease called "pride." As Hythloday remarked, "For pride's criterion of prosperity is not what you've got yourself, but what other people haven't got."[9]

Thomas More's *Utopia* was not only a widely read critique of economic injustice in England and other European nations during the 1500s, but also influenced the thinking of socialists and other reformers centuries later. A novel aspect of More's island paradise is that scarcity, the universal economic problem, is so minimal as to hardly be noticed at all. Yet the Utopians did not eliminate scarcity through mass production of goods or the hoarding of specie. Instead, through education they learned to use their resources wisely and to limit their wants and needs.

Adam Smith: Founder of Modern Economics

Adam Smith (1723–1790) was a prominent Scottish economist and philosopher, and is commonly recognized as the founder of modern economics. Smith was born in Kirkcaldy, Scotland, and received a quality education at Glasgow University in Scotland and Oxford University in England. After six years in England, Smith returned to his native Scotland, first as lecturer at Edinburgh University and later as a professor of philosophy at Glasgow University. From 1762 to 1766 Smith tutored the Duke of Buccleuch, traveling extensively with the young duke in Europe. During these travels, Smith met some of the greatest intellects of his time, including François Quesnay, the leader of the physiocrats in France. With a sizable annual stipend from the appreciative duke, Smith was able to devote the next 10 years to writing his provocative book, *An Inquiry into the Nature and Causes of the Wealth of Nations* (1776). The publication of this

Adam Smith, author of *The Wealth of Nations*. Engraving by John Kay, 1790. © Library of Congress.

book marks the birth of the classical school of economics and, in some economists' minds, the creation of economic science.

The Wealth of Nations, as Smith's revolutionary book is often called, openly challenged the powerful mercantilists, who clung to the belief that government regulation of business activity encouraged a favorable balance of trade and the inflow of specie into the nation. Smith countered that free markets, which encouraged individuals to pursue their own self-interest, created the right business climate for a prosperous society. He believed that government should dismantle its web of special privileges and restraints on commerce and permit the "invisible hand" of competitive markets to allocate resources. In *The Wealth of Nations,* Smith described how free markets operate: "It is not from the benevolence of the butcher, the brewer, or the baker, that we expect our dinner, but from their regard to their own interest. We address ourselves, not to their humanity but to their self-love, and never talk to them of our own necessities but of their advantages."[10] Not surprisingly, much of *The Wealth of Nations* is devoted to the benefits of economic freedom in domestic markets and international trade, and to the techniques that support economic growth, including specialization and the division of labor (see chapter 2 for more on the classical school of economic thought).

The impact of Adam Smith's work in the field of economics is incalculable. He, more than any other economist, elevated the study of economics into an academic discipline, separate and distinct from its earlier status as a subset of philosophy or politics. Smith helped redirect the economic thinking of nations and empires, including Great Britain, to unchain the power of free markets. In doing so, he helped unleash a wave of entrepreneurship and technology that fueled the Industrial Revolution. Smith's commitment to laissez-faire, which he borrowed from the physiocrats in France, helped define the rightful role of political institutions in business activity for the next century and a half. In many respects, the pillars of capitalism itself rest squarely on the foundation laid by *The Wealth of Nations.*

Alfred Marshall: An Economic Way of Thinking

Alfred Marshall (1842–1924) was a British economist and mathematician whose theories and approach to economic inquiry contributed significantly to the science of economics. Marshall was born in London and educated at a number of schools, including St. John's College in Cambridge. Originally a mathematician, his interests soon shifted to political economy, as economics was then called. In 1885 he accepted the position as chair of political economy at Cambridge University, where he spent the next 23 years. While at Cambridge, Marshall authored a number of books, but none had as much impact on economic thought as his first, *Principles of Economics* (1890). By the turn of the twentieth century, Marshall was regarded as among the most important economists in the world.

In *Principles of Economics* Marshall expanded on the work of the earlier economists in the realm of supply and demand theory. Marshall brought earlier analyses of supply and demand together onto the same graph, noting that free markets balance the interests of suppliers of goods and demanders of goods at an equilibrium price and quantity. When asked whether supply or demand was the more dominant determinant of the good's price, Marshall compared supply and demand to the blades of a pair of scissors. Just as both blades are needed to cut a piece of paper, both supply and demand are needed to establish a market equilibrium. In *Principles,* he also made further refinements in demand theory by introducing the concept of elasticity of demand, and distinguishing between normal goods and inferior goods (see chapter 6 for more on supply and demand).

Marshall's emphasis on systematic economic analysis solidified people's confidence in the scientific nature of economics, and revolutionized the methodology employed by economists—a methodology that exists to this day. He championed the view that economic models, hypotheses, and even long-established economic laws or principles had to be tested and retested with evidence from the real world. It is precisely for this reason that economics is considered an *empirical science*—a science based on the use of statistical data and other evidence to confirm or refute a model, theory, or proposition.

NOTES

1. Federal Reserve Bank of San Francisco, "Major Schools of Economic Theory," www.frbsf.org/publications/education/greateconomists/grtchls.html.
2. U.S. Bureau of Labor Statistics, "Table B-1. Employees on Nonfarm Payrolls by Industry Sector and Selected Industry Detail" (Washington, DC: U.S. Department of Labor, October 2003). Available at www.bls.gov/news.release/empsit.t14.htm.
3. James Gwartney, Robert Lawson, and Neil Emerick, *Economic Freedom of the World: 2003 Annual Report* (Vancouver, Canada: The Fraser Institute, 2003), 11.
4. U.S. Department of Labor, *Occupational Outlook Handbook: 2002–03 Edition* (Chicago: VGM Career Books, 2002), 239.
5. Plato, *The Republic and Other Works,* trans. B. Jowett (Garden City, NJ: Dolphin Books, 1960), 106–107.
6. Ibid., 54.
7. Thomas More, *Utopia* (New York: Penguin Books, 1965), 86.
8. Ibid., 84.
9. Ibid., 131.
10. Adam Smith, *An Inquiry into the Nature and Causes of the Wealth of Nations* (Chicago: Henry Regnery Company, 1953), 25.

SELECTED READINGS

Bannock, Graham, R. E. Baxter, and Evan Davis. *The Penguin Dictionary of Economics.* New York: Penguin USA, 2004.
Black, John. *A Dictionary of Economics.* 2nd ed. New York: Oxford University Press, 2003.
Buchholz, Todd G. *From Here to Economy: A Short Cut to Economic Literacy.* New York: Plume, 1996.
Canterbury, E. Ray. *The Making of Economics.* 4th ed. London: World Scientific Publishing Company, 2003.
Gwartney, James, Robert Lawson, and Neil Emerick. *Economic Freedom of the World: 2003 Annual Report.* Vancouver, Canada: The Fraser Institute, 2003.
Hazlitt, Henry. *Economics in One Lesson.* Three Rivers, MI: Three Rivers Press, 1988.
Heilbroner, Robert L. *The Worldly Philosophers: The Lives, Times and Ideas of the Great Economic Thinkers.* 7th ed. Carmichael, CA: Touchstone Books, 1999.
Landsbury, Steven E. *The Armchair Economist: Economics and Everyday Life.* New York: Free Press, 1995.
Marshall, Alfred. *Principles of Economics.* Abridged. Amherst, NY: Prometheus Books, 1997.
More, Thomas. *Utopia.* New York: Penguin Books, 1965.
O'Connor, David E., and Christopher Faille. *Basic Economic Principles: A Guide for Students.* Westport, CT: Greenwood Publishing Group, 2000.
Plato. *The Republic and Other Works.* Translated by B. Jowett. Garden City, NY: Dolphin Books, 1960.

Prychitko, David L., ed. *Why Economists Disagree: An Introduction to the Alternative Schools of Thought.* Albany, NY: State University of New York Press, 1998.

Sowell, Thomas. *Basic Economics: A Citizen's Guide to the Economy.* New York: Basic Books, 2000.

Wheelan, Charles. *Naked Economics: Undressing the Dismal Science.* New York: W.W. Norton & Company, 2003.

CHAPTER 2

A Survey of Economic History and Economic Thought

Chapter 2 surveys the epic stages of economic history and the evolution of modern economic thought. Economic history can be divided many different ways. This chapter identifies the sweeping transformation through four stages: primitive food gathering and hunting, permanent agricultural, the industrial age, and the information age. Significant developments within these stages, such as the rise of trade and the use of money, are examined. The chapter also explores the development of new economic ideas and schools of economic thought during the modern era.

THE STAGES OF ECONOMIC HISTORY

Economic history is often divided into four stages: primitive food gathering and hunting, permanent agriculture and animal domestication, the industrial age, and the information age. The progression from one economic stage to the next has not been accomplished in regular intervals, however. Even today, where information and communications technologies have opened pathways to nearly infinite amounts of information, significant portions of the world's population—mainly in the developing world—have not yet embraced the emerging information age. The following sketch of economic history presents a snapshot of how people lived and worked throughout the millennia.

Food Gathering and Hunting Societies

The earliest stage of economic history was the time of the primitive food gathering and hunting societies, which existed throughout the Old Stone Age, or Paleolithic Age (500,000 B.C. to 10,000 B.C.). Small nomadic tribes, perhaps as few as 30 people per tribe, met their survival needs by following the food. These tribes were scattered throughout the world, with concentrations in China and Southeast Asia, Europe, East Africa, and other regions. Tribes were well organized, with a division of labor determined mainly by gender and physical strength. Men made weapons of stone, bone, and wood and hunted animals such as the mammoth and bison. The hunters were skilled in the art of hunting and fishing. They used their extensive knowledge of the natural environment, including the migratory patterns of animals, to their advantage. A man also led the tribe, providing a central authority figure within the context of normal kinship ties of the nuclear and extended families.

Women were assigned to other roles necessary for the tribe's survival. They gathered food, collecting nuts, berries, seeds, wild grains, fruits, roots, shellfish, and other foodstuffs available from the natural environment. Women were responsible for maintaining the campsite, which might consist of caves or of temporary shelters made of branches, straw, or even animal hides. At the campsite, women tended the tribe's fire, which was vital to the group's survival. Fire was necessary for cooking, heat, and protection from predatory animals. For much of the Paleolithic Age, live embers, coal, or torches were carried from place to place to ensure that the tribe's fire was not extinguished. Women also tended the children. While the division of labor in food gathering and hunting societies was simple and rigid, the gender-based roles enabled these primitive communities to survive in an environment that was often inhospitable.

Over time, the food gathering and hunting societies of the Paleolithic Age developed additional skills to cope with their environment. It was during the Paleolithic Age that many peoples developed language, thus enabling them to better communicate ideas from generation to generation. The creation of new and better tools and weapons was another feature of the period, as stone, bone, and wood were transformed from crude blunt instruments to more finely shaped cutting tools. More sophisticated tools were used to prepare animal hides and make arrowheads, spearheads, harpoons, needles, and other items. Technological advances in the production of tools and weapons accelerated in the later stages of the Paleolithic Age. Evidence suggests that communications among nomadic tribes increased during the reign of the Cro-Magnons (35,000 B.C.), spreading new ideas and technologies.

Permanent Agriculture and Animal Domestication

The second stage of economic history—permanent agriculture and animal domestication—occurred during the New Stone Age, or Neolithic Age (10,000 B.C. to 3500 B.C.). The term **agricultural revolution** is used to describe the momentous shift from a nomadic lifestyle during the Paleolithic Age to a more sedentary lifestyle on farms and in permanent settlements during the Neolithic Age. The term *revolution* might be misleading in this context, as it spanned thousands of years and was far from universally accepted. In fact, nomadic and agricultural societies coexisted throughout the Neolithic Age and beyond. Some of the regions that were earliest to embrace the agricultural revolution were located in the Middle East, northeastern China, Central and South America, and eastern Africa. Agriculture and animal domestication remained the dominant feature in the economic landscape of the world until the birth of the industrial age in the 1700s. The agricultural revolution affected the course of economic history in significant ways.

One effect of the agricultural revolution was the rise of permanent settlements—first villages, then towns and cities. Many early settlements were established on fertile territories near rivers, such as the Tigris and Euphrates in the Middle East, the Nile in northeastern Africa, the Indus in India, and the Yellow River in China. Rivers were reliable sources of water for farming and also deposited nutrients in the soil during periodic floods. Early agricultural communities harvested wheat, barley, oats, rice, corn, millet, beans, yams, squash, and other staples, depending on the world region. These communities also domesticated, or tamed, animals. Some animals, such as sheep, goats, pigs, and cattle were raised mainly for food. Others, such as oxen, were trained as draft animals to assist farmers in the fields. Having secured a reliable food supply, towns and cities experienced population growth. The first civilizations were born in the cities. In fact, the term *civilization* is derived from the Latin word *civis,* or citizens of a city.

A second important consequence of the agricultural revolution was specialization. **Specialization** occurs when individuals produce a specific product, a narrow range of products, or a service. The rise of cities encouraged a far more sophisticated division of labor than had existed in the primitive food gathering and hunting societies. In the cities, skilled artisans specialized in the production of farm tools, weapons, jewelry, household items, pottery, baskets, clothing, and other items. Merchants specialized in the business of commerce. Merchants grew in importance as profits from the sale of agricultural surpluses and output from the cities increased. These goods satisfied people's basic survival needs and, later, catered to the more exotic wants and needs of the wealthy classes. The use of nearby rivers to transport goods also increased the ease of commerce. Political and religious leadership became highly specialized as cities grew larger and more complex. Leaders such kings, emperors, and pharaohs relied on the specialized services of engineers, who designed irrigation systems, temples, city walls, and other structures; priests, who attended to society's spiritual needs; artists and sculptors, who decorated monuments and public buildings; tax collectors, who filled government treasuries; and so on.

A third effect of the agricultural revolution was expanded trade over land and water routes. The surpluses of food, luxury items, natural resources, and other items provided incentives for civilizations to aggressively seek out new markets for their output. In the Mediterranean region, a series of powerful states prospered from sea trade. The Minoans (2000 B.C. to 1400 B.C.), located on the island of Crete, conducted profitable trade with Egypt and Phoenicia, exchanging olive oil, wine, and other foods for precious stones, gold, and luxury goods. By 1400 B.C. the Phoenicians, located in present-day Lebanon, had established port cities such as Beirut and Byblos. From 1100 B.C. to 800 B.C. the Phoenician economy centered on a lively sea trade in items such as olive oil, glass, timber from cedar trees, and a prized purple dye that was extracted from a certain marine snail. The Phoenicians planted colonies throughout the Mediterranean region, in locations as distant as North Africa and Spain, to strengthen trade routes and increase profits. Civilizations in other parts of the world also used water routes for trade. The Indus Valley peoples (2500 B.C.) navigated the Indus River to establish profitable trade in items such as fine jewelry, metals, timber, and ivory with settlements along the coasts of the Arabian Sea and Persian Gulf. The African kingdom of Kush became an important trading center along the Nile as early as 1800 B.C. and profited from trade with neighboring Egypt in items such as ivory, granite, ebony wood, gold, and perfume. Trade over land routes also expanded. The Chinese opened trade with peoples in western Asia and the Middle East on a land route commonly known as the Silk Road during the Han Dynasty (202 B.C. to 220 A.D.). In northern Africa numerous trade routes crossed the Sahara Desert in caravans as early as the first or second century A.D. Camels were domesticated to carry the merchants' wares. By the 700s the desert trade included many precious items, including silk, ivory, gold, jewelry, slaves, and salt.

A fourth impact of the agricultural revolution was technological advance. The origins of numerous technologies are traced to the late Neolithic and early Bronze Age (which began about 3500 B.C.). The Middle East was an early wellspring for inventions. The wheel and the sail, for example, revolutionized the transport of goods, people, and ideas. By 3500 B.C. the Egyptians used sailing ships for trade, a technique that later civilizations such as the Phoenicians, Greeks, Romans, and African kingdoms of Kush and Aksum would also profit from. At about the same time, these early civilizations learned to use metals, such as copper and bronze, to produce tools, ornaments, and weapons. Economic historians often view the use of metals as the close of the Stone Age and the beginning of the Metal Age, which included a Bronze Age and an Iron Age. Furnaces were necessary to melt and separate these metals from the worthless ore, thus giving rise to metallurgy—a science that in later years included making alloys such as brass and steel. Technology also made its mark on agriculture as plows, drawn by oxen or horses, vastly increased the number of acres under cultivation. Wheeled wagons, again powered by draft animals, likewise improved the ability to transport larger quantities of output to markets.

Finally, the expanded commercial contacts and wealth that resulted from the agricultural revolution led to the creation of money. **Money** is any item that is commonly accepted in payment for goods or services or in payment of debts. The introduction of money progressed in fits and starts over thousands of years. Slowly, money came to replace **barter,** a system in which one good is exchanged for a second good. The convenience of money over barter became more apparent as civilizations grew and trade expanded. Ancient civilizations used different items for money. In the Americas, the Maya and the Aztecs used cloth and cocoa beans as money. Some West African kingdoms used cowrie shells; China used silk and Egypt wheat. Much later in history, American colonists in Maryland and

Delaware used tobacco as money. The most significant breakthrough in the development of money was the introduction of coins. Over a thousand years B.C. the Chinese used spade coins, which resembled a plow blade, to facilitate transactions. In the seventh century B.C. the Lydians minted the stater, a coin originally made of a gold and silver mixture. About a century later the Athenians introduced the tetradrachma, ushering in an era of coin use by the Greek city-states. Other civilizations, including the Romans, soon adopted the idea of using of coins in domestic and global markets.

The Industrial Age and Factory System

The Industrial Revolution ushered in the third stage in economic history, that of industrialization. **Industrialization** refers to the economic transition from small-scale, labor-intensive production to large-scale, capital-intensive production in factories and mills. Like the agricultural revolution, the Industrial Revolution did not occur in all regions of the world simultaneously. Even today industrialization has eluded many developing nations, and thus many people in these regions remain dependent on subsistence agriculture. The Industrial Revolution began in Great Britain in the 1700s and spread to other European countries and the United States during the 1800s. Industrialization not only changed the nature of business activity, but also reshaped the entire social fabric of nations.

Great Britain was the catalyst for the epic economic and social changes brought about by industrialization. Why was Great Britain in the vanguard of the Industrial Revolution? Economic historians have different viewpoints on this question, but most agree on the following explanations. First, Great Britain was blessed with a wide variety of resources. Some of these resources came from within the country, such as navigable rivers and deep harbors, minerals such as iron ore and coal, and an abundance of inexpensive labor. Other resources, such as timber and cotton, could be imported at low cost from Britain's colonial possessions in North America, Africa, and Asia. Second, Britain's government was stable and, in many respects, farsighted. For example, the British took a leadership role in the **Commercial Revolution** (late 1400s to mid-1700s), which established profitable trade relationships and colonial empires that spanned the globe. During this period, Britain invested heavily in a navy to protect its growing empire and the profitable trade and investment opportunities that were created. Later, Britain also encouraged freer trade by repealing the Corn Laws (1846), which had restricted grain imports. By the mid-1800s the doctrine of free trade was firmly entrenched, and Great Britain was the world's most powerful trading nation. Third, Britain had a budding capitalist economy. **Capitalism** is a type of economic system in which the private sector, individuals and firms, owns and controls the factors of production. Capitalism applies market principles, including private property rights and the profit incentive, to all aspects of economic activity. The lure of profits motivated entrepreneurs to start new businesses, invest in new technologies, negotiate new trade arrangements, and otherwise promote innovation and economic growth. Sound capital markets, including a stable banking system, supplied sufficient money for business investment.

The Industrial Revolution matured in Great Britain with each technological advance. During the first phase of the Industrial Revolution, from the 1700s to the mid-1800s, the factory system took hold in certain heavy industries such as textiles and iron. In Britain, the invention of the flying shuttle in 1733 and the spinning jenny in 1764 increased productivity in textile mills. The cotton gin, invented by American Eli Whitney in 1794, complemented the earlier technologies. The invention of the steam engine revolutionized production in many industries, and it is often viewed as the most important invention of the industrial age. Thomas Newcomen pioneered steam-powered engines to pump air into underground coal mines in the early 1700s. About 60 years later, James Watt's improvements on Newcomen's designs create capital goods capable of draining mines of excess water and powering textile mills, iron mills, and other industries. Steam engines were also adapted to improve transportation, most notably steamships and locomotives. In communications, American Samuel F. B. Morse invented the telegraph by devising an electromagnetic receiver in 1838 and a communications code, called Morse code, to speed messages across great distances. By 1866 a transatlantic telegraph cable linked the United States and Europe. The early Industrial Revolution also sparked inventions in agriculture, including the McCormick reaper in 1834 and John Deere's steel plow in 1837.

During the second phase of the Industrial Revolution, which occurred after 1850, the United States, Germany, and other Western countries rushed to join the mass production bandwagon. In America in the mid-1850s, the Bessemer process enabled the mass production of inexpensive high-grade steel. By 1901 the United States Steel Corporation was the largest steel producer in the world. In communications, American Alexander Graham Bell invented the telephone in 1876, and in 1895 Italian Gugliemo Marconi successfully experimented with wireless communication—the precursor of the radio. Michael Faraday's pioneering work in the field of generating electricity in the early 1830s laid the groundwork for numerous applications of electrical power. During the second phase of the Industrial Revolution, electric power was pivotal in telephone communications, lighting systems, consumer durables, and transportation systems such as tramways, subways, and railways. German inventors, led by Nikolaus Otto, developed the first gasoline-powered internal combustion engine in 1876, a technology that countrymen Gottleib Daimler and Karl Benz soon applied to the production of automobiles.

The Industrial Revolution radically changed the way goods were produced. In the preindustrial economy of Great Britain, for example, many people were part of the domestic system. Under the **domestic system,** sometimes called the cottage system, people worked in their homes to produce cloth, shoes, baskets, and many other items. A businessman delivered the necessary materials and tools to workers' homes, collected the finished product, and paid the workers according to how many items were produced. Under the domestic system, skilled artisans, craftsmen, and even peasants set their own work schedules.

The Industrial Revolution established a new model for producing goods, however, based on the factory system. Under the **factory system,** large factory buildings were constructed, heavy machinery installed, and wage laborers recruited to work in the factories. The new division of labor was highly specialized, with each worker expected to perform a specific task in a larger production process, whether in nineteenth-century British textile mills or twentieth-century American automobile plants. The factory system increased national output and laid the foundation for a rising middle class of industrial workers. In many cases, it also dehumanized the production process, forcing men, women, and children to endure sweatshop conditions in the factories, mills, and mines. A **sweatshop** is any industrial workplace characterized by poor working conditions, excessive hours, and low pay. But as populations increased, farmland became more scarce, and craftsmanship was replaced by mass production, factory work in the fast-growing urban centers was sometimes the only viable alternative for workers in search of jobs.

The spread of the Industrial Revolution to other European powers and to the United States proceeded slowly during the 1700s and early 1800s, but accelerated during the second half of the nineteenth century. Why did it take a century for the Industrial Revolution to take hold outside of Britain? One reason was that Great Britain jealously guarded its technology and for a time prohibited the export of its advanced capital or the emigration of its most skilled technicians to other countries. These policies inhibited the flow of technology beyond the bor-

Sweatshop in a New York City tenement, 1889. Photograph by Jacob A. Riis. © Library of Congress.

ders of Britain. Another factor was the disruptive effect of constant warfare and social upheavals that plagued the European continent during the early Industrial Revolution. For example, the French Revolution (1789–1791), the Napoleonic Wars (1803–1815), the widespread revolutions of 1848, and other conflicts had crippling effects on economic development. By the mid-1800s, however, the United States, Germany, and other nations were aggressively challenging Great Britain's industrial leadership in the world. As the pace of technological development accelerated around the world and Britain removed its restrictions on cross-border flows of technological information, other countries latched onto and adapted these technologies to meet the needs of business. In fact, by the mid-1800s the industrialized countries were nurturing the first great age of globalization. Globalization forged strong economic networks that linked world economies mainly through international trade and foreign investment. Underlying this complex web of economic relationships was the unifying idea of global capitalism, an economic system that allowed the lure of profits to guide business decisions.

The Information Age

The fourth stage of economic history is often called the information age due to the rapid infusion of information and communications technologies into the production process. **Information and communications technologies** (ICTs) are the technological advances that increase people's ability to collect, store, retrieve, and share information. Economists are still split on whether to categorize the information revolution as the dawn of an entirely new stage in economic history or just an important appendage to an evolving industrial age. This book treats the information age as the start of a fourth stage of economic history, a stage that began during the final quarter of the twentieth century. Its roots are firmly planted in the technologies of the industrial age. Electricity, the telephone, early computers, mass production techniques, and other technologies all contributed to the rise of the information age. What is radically new about today's ICTs is the degree to which they are integrated and mutually supporting, an indicator that the rapidly evolving information revolution is still in its infancy.

The information age is grounded in several key technologies. The first is computer technology, which has progressed with lightning speed since World War II. In 1946 the Electronic Numerical Integrator and Calculator (ENIAC), the world's first functional electronic computer, was invented by Americans John W. Mauchly and John P. Eckert, Jr. Since then, technological advances have allowed the computer industry to evolve from the use of vacuum tubes, to transistors, to integrated circuits, to the microprocessor. Technology also broadened the appeal of computers by expanding the market from large mainframe computers that were mainly used by big businesses, the government, and universities to user-friendly personal computers. Second, the production of sophisticated software has complemented advances in computer technology, encouraging computer applications in homes, schools, and smaller businesses. Third, the invention of the Internet in 1969 by the U.S. Department of Defense spawned an international web of computer networks. The use of the Internet, or "internetworking of networks," expanded during the 1970s and 1980s when a basic infrastructure was developed and conveniences such as e-mail were added. But it was the invention of the World Wide Web by Tim Berners-Lee in 1989 that opened the floodgates to Internet use. Through the World Wide Web, the information revolution exploded as people were able to communicate and share information through a global network that was both easy to use and inexpensive. By 2002 an estimated 600 million people had ready access to the Internet.[1] Fourth, communications technologies kept pace with the computer revolution. The launch of Telstar in 1966 into Earth's orbit gave birth to satellite communications. Microwave technology, which was well established by the 1980s, paved the way for widespread wireless telephone service. In 1977 fiber optics also increased the information flows. By 2001 advances in fiber optics technology allowed more information to be sent over a single cable in one second than was possible across the entire Internet in 1997.[2] Modems and facsimile (fax) machines have complemented other ICTs in the mutually supporting ICT infrastructure.

ICTs have transformed the conduct of business in today's fast-paced global economy. Consider how ICTs have already been woven into the fabric of economic life in the richer, developed countries. Over the Internet, businesses can advertise their products and scan the planet for low-cost factors of production and obtain information about new markets and new business opportunities. Advanced ICTs also open the doors to individualized marketing and distribution of goods. When consumers' purchases are received and executed electronically, record keeping becomes faster and more accurate, and layers of corporate bureaucracy are stripped away. The **virtual firm,** a firm that conducts its business over the Internet, reduces many of the brick-and-mortar costs of production such as the construction of retail or storage buildings and the storage of inventories. The growth of business-to-business (B2B) and business-to-consumer (B2C) electronic commerce in the global economy hit $2.3 trillion in 2002.[3] Further, high-tech industries such as pharmaceuticals have benefited from the streamlined research and development (R&D) and testing of goods via ICTs. ICTs have likewise made significant inroads into many services-producing industries such as insurance, banking and financial services, and retail and wholesale trade. The fact the services-producing industries account for the lion's share of output in the developed countries—more than three-quarters of the total output and 78 percent of all jobs in the United States in the early 2000s—is yet another reminder of the growing importance of ICTs.[4]

The information age, like the Industrial Revolution before it, has progressed unevenly throughout the global economy. The resulting ICT chasm between the richer developed countries of the global north and the poorer developing countries of the global south is often referred to as the **digital divide.** In 2001 there were just 6 Internet users for every 1,000 people in the low-income developing countries, compared to 397 Internet users per 1,000 people in the high-income countries. In the United States, there were about 500 Internet users per 1,000 people, roughly half of the entire population of the country.[5] The digital divide has become one of the most important economic issues in today's global economy because it influences the pace of economic development, including people's quality of life, throughout the world. Economies of the global north are well connected through ICTs; hence, they have numerous business advantages over competing firms in the global south. By the early 2000s many developing economies had not only been bypassed by industrialization but also were in danger of becoming further marginalized, or excluded from the economic opportunities offered in the digital economy (see chapter 12 for more on sustainable economic development).

SCHOOLS OF ECONOMIC THOUGHT

A **school of economic thought** consists of economists who share common ideas about how scarce resources should be used to achieve society's goals. Numerous schools of economic thought have arisen since the 1700s. Some have focused on the goal of economic freedom, stressing the value of private incentives and unfettered markets to allocate society's resources. Others have advocated the abolition of private property and profits as a means of creating economic equity and justice. Competing schools of thought have evolved over time, have challenged well-established economic doctrines, and have instigated monumental changes in how societies answer the basic economic questions of what, how, and for whom to produce.

Mercantilism

Mercantilism is the belief that a country's wealth is derived from its ability to accumulate specie—mainly gold and silver. Mercantilism is not a school of economic thought in the traditional sense, mainly because there is no unified body of writings that mercantilists accept. Instead, the viewpoints expressed by the mercantilists represented the interests of the merchant class during the sixteenth, seventeenth, and eighteenth centuries. The origin of mercantilism dates back to the mid-1500s, when a group called the bullionists formed in England. The bullionists were uncompromising in their belief that bullion in the form of gold and silver should remain within the borders of the country at all costs. The bullionists argued that the acquisition of bullion was the surest route to national wealth and power. The grandeur of Spain, which built its prosperity on precious metals looted from its New World colonies during the 1500s, was cited as proof that gold and silver created national wealth. Bullion gathered from the colonial possessions of the other European nations did not match the bounty that Spain enjoyed, however. By the early 1600s a related theory, later called mercantilism by Adam Smith, was born. The most eloquent mercantilist spokesman of the era was Thomas Mun (1571–1641), a merchant from

London, England (see the biography of Thomas Mun). The mercantilists generally agreed that accumulating bullion was vital to the survival of the nation, but stressed the value of international trade as the means to acquire these riches.

The mercantilists drew much of their support from the rising merchant and business classes. They encouraged the government to create trade policies that would result in a **favorable balance of trade,** a condition in which the value of a nation's exports is greater than the value of its imports. A favorable balance of trade ensured that more wealth, including specie, flowed into the nation than flowed out. Several leading European nations including Great Britain, France, Spain, and Prussia adopted mercantilist ideas during the 1600s and 1700s and created a business climate that supported a favorable balance of trade. How was this accomplished? First, governments created **trade barriers,** such as import tariffs and quotas, to discourage or prohibit certain foreign imports. Second, governments subsidized domestic industries and granted trade monopolies to encourage exports and the inflow of bullion. Third, governments built vast colonial empires, and restricted trade and business activity to favor the mother country. Under mercantilism, colonies were expected to supply the mother country with inexpensive raw materials and then purchase finished products exported by the mother country. In the 1600s and 1700s, for example, Britain's Navigation Acts restricted American trade to benefit the mother country.

History has shown that the mercantilists viewed the world through a selective lens, one that invariably focused on the narrow interests of the commercial class and the monarchy. The mercantilist approach to creating national wealth, which equated wealth with treasuries filled with specie, failed to give proper attention to other growth factors such as agricultural production, the quality of the labor force, technological advances, and so on. In addition, the financial rewards generated by mercantilism favored wealthy merchants and businesses. The common people, on the other hand, were often viewed as little more than cheap labor, a market for industrial output, and an endless supply of soldiers to carry out the monarch's global ambitions. The mercantilists also embraced a narrow view of trade, seeing exchanges in terms of winners and losers rather than as business transactions from which both parties could benefit. Still, the mercantilists were in the vanguard of the commercial revolution that swept across the European continent during the seventeenth and eighteenth centuries. They strengthened the global economic network and nurtured early capitalist ideas such as the sanctity of private property and the importance of profit incentives.

The Physiocratic School

The **physiocratic school,** or physiocracy, is generally viewed by economists as the first true school of economic thought. The physiocrats emerged in 1760s France, drawing their economic theories from François Quesnay and their political clout from allies in the royal court of King Louis XIV and King Louis

XV (see the biography of François Quesnay). Quesnay's *The Economic Table* laid the philosophical foundations of the physiocratic school. This book proclaimed the existence of a natural order in the economic life of nations that stressed the primacy of agriculture and the agricultural class over the less-productive classes of proprietors, craftsmen, industrialists, and merchants. To the physiocrats, agricultural land enabled farmers to produce enough output to satisfy domestic and foreign demand. The central goal of economic activity was to increase the nation's net product (*produit net*), which was measured by the value of agricultural output above and beyond the costs of production. Given the physiocratic school's emphasis on a natural economic order, it is appropriate that this economic school of thought took its name from the term *physiocracy*, or rule of nature.

Laissez-faire was another important feature of the physiocrats' natural order. **Laissez-faire** is the belief that market forces should determine the use of society's scarce resources, and that the government should not interfere in business activities. Laissez-faire was a direct attack on prevailing mercantilist doctrine, which favored many types of government intervention in business activity, including the use of trade barriers to restrict free trade, subsidies to protect weak businesses, and state monopolies to bolster business profits. The laissez-faire doctrine also brought the physiocrats into conflict with time-honored traditions in the countryside. For example, in France the physiocrats opposed traditional restrictions on farmers such as the *corvee,* which required peasants to work for the state for a period of time each year; internal tariffs, which limited the flow of agricultural output within the nation; and restrictions on the free movement of workers from region to region. To the physiocrats, government interference in the economy disrupted the natural order because it distorted the orderly functioning of domestic and international markets. The physiocrats believed that the government's role should be limited to national defense and the nation's internal security.

The rise of the physiocrats was an important step in the development of economic science. This early school of economic thought recognized that the various pieces of an economy—farmers, merchants, manufacturers, and others—functioned in an interdependent system. For instance, the physiocrats saw that firms incurred costs when they employed resources, which describes exchanges in factor markets. The physiocrats also favored economic freedom for enterprising businesses to sell their wares in competitive markets, which describes exchanges in the product market. These understandings established a foundation for later academic study in the circular flow of goods, resources, and money in the economy (see chapter 3 for more on the circular flow model). The doctrine of laissez-faire, which was popularized by the physiocrats, also influenced later economists, including the founder of modern economics, Adam Smith. The physiocrats had powerful enemies, however. Despite its splash in academic circles and at the French royal court, the physiocratic school had little impact on government policies in France or elsewhere. Their preoccupation with the land led the physiocrats to insupportable conclusions, including the notion that merchants, manufacturers, and other producers were incapable of contributing to the nation's net product.

The Classical School

The **classical school** of economics emerged during the 1770s and for nearly a century influenced economic thinking and economic policies in Europe and the Americas. Some of the most widely read economists of all time are classical economists, including Jean Baptiste Say, David Ricardo, Thomas Malthus, John Stuart Mill, and Adam Smith—who is widely held to be the founder of modern economics (see the biography in chapter 1). The publication of Adam Smith's *An Inquiry into the Nature and Causes of the Wealth of Nations* in 1776 is often cited as the beginning of the classical school.

While the classical economists wrote about a variety of topics, there was a clear undercurrent of commonly held principles. These principles included a conviction that free markets allocate resources in the fairest and most efficient manner, that government intervention in the economy obstructs prosperity, and that competition creates opportunities for enterprising businesses and individuals. These principles put the classical economists into conflict with the mercantilists and their allies, who clung tenaciously the prevailing system of government preferences and regulations designed to benefit the wealthy classes. The American rebellion against the British crown in 1776, the same year *The Wealth of Nations* was published, caused many people to question the wisdom of mercantilism and sparked interest in Smith's alternative route to national wealth.

The classical economists believed that self-regulating markets, rather than government intervention, was the most rational path to national wealth. A **market** is any situation in which a voluntary exchange occurs. Classical economists argued that market prices signal people about how to use their scarce resources. Consumers, for example, respond to price signals by increasing their consumption of certain goods when the price is low, and decreasing their consumption when the price is high. Producers minimize their costs of production by employing the lowest-cost resources. Workers consider price, in the form of wages, when comparing job opportunities. In short, free markets, coupled with individual self-interest, are able to coordinate millions of daily economic decisions in an economy. It is not surprising that the classical school adopted the laissez-faire doctrine from the physiocrats—a doctrine that opposed most forms of government interference in business activity and supported economic freedom in competitive markets.

Classical economists also supported free trade in international markets. **Free trade** occurs when trade barriers such as import tariffs and quotas are eliminated. In addition, free trade requires removing government subsidies to domestic industries and other assistance to domestic firms so that cross-border exchanges of goods are fair. The economic advantages of free trade seemed clear to Smith, Ricardo, and others. Smith argued that competitive international markets would stimulate business activity and production efficiency as firms sought new and profitable markets. The less coddling of firms by the government, the more productive they would necessarily become. Later, David Ricardo expanded on Smith's support of free trade by introducing the theory of comparative advantage, which encouraged nations or regions to specialize in the production of goods best suited to their resources. Ricardo argued that regional specialization would not only allow regions to make the best uses of their scarce resources, but also would necessitate cooperative trade relationships among nations (see chapter 11 for more on the theory of comparative advantage).

Classical economists were also concerned about the role and condition of labor in the economy. For example, Smith argued that people's standard of living would rise as their productivity improved. Higher worker **productivity,** or output per worker, could be accomplished through a division of labor, particularly in manufacturing enterprises. A division of labor requires breaking down the tasks workers perform into smaller, more specialized functions within a plant. It is also dependent on the use of advanced capital goods and the effective management of wage laborers. In *The Wealth of Nations,* Smith explained the benefits of a division of labor in the production of pins, as shown in Figure 2.1.[6]

Some classical economists shunned Smith's optimism and took a dimmer view of the world's economic future. Thomas Malthus, for example, argued that population growth would soon outpace economic growth and food production, a situation later economists referred to as the Malthusian trap (see the biography of Thomas Malthus). Later classical economists, such as John Stuart Mill, even questioned the fairness of free markets in distributing income. By the mid-1800s, Mill and others observed the inhumanity of sweatshop conditions for the growing urban working class, and concluded that some government intervention might be required to correct economic injustices.

The Marginalist School

The **marginalist school** of economic thought was founded in the 1870s by William S. Jevons (United Kingdom), Karl Menger (Austria), Leon Walras (France/Switzerland), and Knut Wicksell (Sweden). By the turn of the century, the marginalists had more fully explored the process of rational decision making on both sides of the market, demand and supply. Economic decisions, they argued, were typically made at the margin. In economics *margin* refers to the next unit or the additional unit. The groundbreaking work of the marginalists soon dominated supply and demand analyses, the theory of value, and other elements in the realm of microeconomics:

On the demand side of the market, the marginalists developed the concept of utility, and how changes in utility affect the price people are willing to pay for goods or services. **Utility** refers to the usefulness or satisfaction a consumer derives from the purchase of an item. In the early 1870s marginalists such as Jevons, Menger, and Walras had developed the law of **diminishing marginal utility.** This economic law states that, as a consumer purchases additional units

Figure 2.1
Adam Smith Describes the Division of Labor

> [I]n the way in which this business [the production of pins] is now carried on, not only the whole work is a peculiar trade, but it is divided into a number of branches, of which the greater part are likewise peculiar trades. One man draws out the wire, another straights it, a third cuts it, a fourth points it, a fifth grinds it at the top for receiving the head; to make the head requires two or three distinct operations; to put it on, is a peculiar business, to whiten the pins is another; it is even a trade by itself to put them into the paper; and the important business of making a pin is, in this manner, divided into about eighteen distinct operations, which, in some manufactories, are all performed by distinct hands. . . . I have seen a small manufactory of this kind where ten men only were employed. . . . Those ten persons . . . could make among them upwards of forty-eight thousand pins each day. . . . But if they had all wrought separately and independently, and without any of them having been educated to this peculiar business, they certainly could not each of them have made twenty, perhaps not one pin in a day.
>
> In every other art and manufacture, the effects of the division of labour are similar to what they are in this very trifling one.
>
> *An Inquiry Into the Nature and Causes of the Wealth of Nations,*
> Adam Smith

of the same item in a given period of time, the marginal utility falls. Today, this observation seems self-evident. Consider your consumption of slices of pizza at a local restaurant. The first slice of pizza offers you high utility because it satisfies a basic need. But your satisfaction tends to decline as you consume the second, third, fourth, or fifth slice. Diminishing marginal utility was used by the marginalists to explain rational consumer decision making. That is, to maximize satisfaction the rational consumer would stop buying one item—additional slices of pizza in this case—if the same money could be spent on another item that offered higher marginal utility. Diminishing marginal utility also helped explain how the price or value of a good is determined. Goods with higher marginal utility command a higher price, while goods with lower marginal utility command a lower price (see the biography of William Stanley Jevons).

On the supply side of the market, the marginalists built on earlier work by the classical economists to more fully examine the value of resources used in production. The supply side of the market deals with the perspective of the producer. In the 1890s Swedish economist Knut Wicksell developed the marginal productivity theory (see the biography of Knut Wicksell). According to this theory, firms should employ additional resources in production only when the additional (marginal) revenues were equal to or greater than the additional (marginal) costs for these resources. After all, if the marginal costs were greater than the marginal revenues, the firm would incur a loss. Meanwhile, in Austria Karl Menger developed the concept of **derived demand,** a theory of production that stated that the demand for resources was derived from the demand for the final goods that these resources produced. In other words, resources, including human labor, have value only when they can be used to produce goods that people are willing to buy.

The marginalists added significantly to economic science during the late nineteenth century. Indeed, much of the groundwork for contemporary studies in microeconomics is rooted in the work of marginalists such as Jevons, Menger, and Walras. The marginalists broke with the classical tradition by stating that price is determined not just by the costs of production, as the classical economists had theorized, but also by the market demand for goods or resources.

Marxism and the Marxist School

Marxism is a school of economic thought grounded in socialist principles, dedicated to the overthrow of capitalism, and committed to the creation of a perfected form of socialism called communism. It includes a vast body of economic, political, and social thought. Marxism originated in the mid-nineteenth century, when German-born Karl Marx teamed with English businessman Friedrich Engels to write a pamphlet entitled *The Communist Manifesto* (1848). In this brief treatise, Marx and Engels examined the nature of class conflict throughout history, concluding that communism would inevitably replace the oppressive capitalist system. Marxism has sometimes been called *scientific socialism* to reflect the depth of Marx's examination of capitalism, its weaknesses, and reasons for its eventual collapse. Much of the theory of the Marxist school of economic thought is presented in *The Communist Manifesto* and *Das Kapital* (1867).

European socialism, which appeared in the late 1700s and early 1800s, was in large measure a reaction to the economic hardships that workers endured during the Industrial Revolution. The socialists generally supported public ownership of the key means of production such as factories, a more equitable distribution of income and wealth, and equal opportunities for all people in society. Karl Marx and Friedrich Engels expanded on these principles, calling for the complete abolition of private property, which they believed was the root cause of injustice, oppression, and class conflict. They also expanded on earlier theories by the classical economists, including Adam Smith and David Ricardo, in the realm of labor theory of value. The classical economists had widely acknowledged that labor was an important factor of production and, therefore, a key determinant in the price of a firm's output. Marx observed that under capitalism there was a growing gap between the monetary value of workers' contribution to production and the monetary value of their wages—a gap that Marx referred to as **surplus value.** In Marx's view, the surplus value rightfully belonged to the workers who produced the output, not to the capitalists who dehumanized laborers in sweatshops. The capitalists, on the other hand, viewed surplus value as legitimate profits to which they were entitled under capitalism.

Marx theorized that human history was evolutionary and that class conflict would inevitably result in the overthrow of capitalism. The process of change from one stage of history to the next was dictated by **dialectical materialism,** an ongoing clash between an oppressed class and an oppressor class. In Marx's view, class conflict was necessary to progress from one stage of history to the next. For instance, the conflict during the feudal stage of history pitted the dominant landed aristocracy against the rising capitalists—such as merchants, manufacturers, and other entrepreneurs. The result of this conflict was the birth of a new stage of history called capitalism. Under capitalism, Marx witnessed a clear division between the class of wage laborers, which he called the proletariat, and the class of factory owners and other capitalists called the bourgeoisie. In *The Communist Manifesto* he wrote: "Our epoch, the epoch of the bourgeoisie, shows, however, this distinctive feature: it has simplified the class antagonism. Society as a whole is more and more splitting up into two great hostile camps, into two great classes directly facing each other: *bourgeoisie* and *proletariat.*"[7] He theorized that the conflict between proletariat and bourgeoisie would result in a new and final stage of history called socialism. Marx's vision of socialism included the complete abolition of private property, which was viewed as the dominant cause of class conflict. He also theorized that the state would eventually wither away, thus removing another agent of exploitation.

Marxism drew its inspiration from the writings of Karl Marx, but the Marxian school of thought splintered into a number of directions soon after his death in 1883. One early debate within the Marxist camp concerned the inevitability of capitalism's breakdown and the triumph of socialism. This basic tenet of Marxism was challenged by Eduard Bernstein, but was vigorously defended by those closest to Marx, including Friedrich Engels and Karl Kautsky. During the twentieth century, Marxist views have been also been adapted. For example, in the early 1900s Russian revolutionary Vladimir Ilyich Lenin abandoned the Marxian notion that the proletarian revolution would begin in an industrialized country with a large urban proletariat, such as Germany or Great Britain. He eventually led a successful communist revolution in Russia, and, under the banner of Marxism-Leninism, established the Union of Soviet Socialist Republics in 1922. Similarly, Mao Zedong adapted Marxism by tapping the revolutionary fervor of China's rural peasantry, rather than an urban proletariat, to topple the Nationalist government of Chiang Kai-shek and establish the People's Republic of China in 1949 (see chapter 4 for more on communism).

The Keynesian School

The **Keynesian school** of economic thought, or the Keynesians, provided the theoretical foundations for greater government intervention in promoting economic growth and stability. British economist John Maynard Keynes founded the Keynesian school in the 1930s. During the 1930s a global depression resulted in declining national output, low investment, high unemployment, and a general pessimism about the future. In his landmark book, *The General Theory of Employment, Interest, and Money* (1936), Keynes recommended that governments intervene in the economy to stimulate aggregate (total) demand, create jobs, and boost economic growth. Keynes's proposals were viewed as heresy by mainstream economists, many of whom were disciples of the classical laissez-faire doctrine. As the worldwide depression lingered during the 1930s, the influence of laissez-faire economists diminished.

Keynes focused on changing aggregate demand to promote economic growth and stability. **Aggregate demand** is the total demand for all goods in an economy. During the Great Depression (the name given to the global depression in the United States), aggregate demand in the United States was low due to massive unemployment, an epidemic of bank failures, and low consumer confidence. Keynes believed that the federal government should increase aggregate demand by pumping more money into the economy. To achieve this end, he proposed the implementation of an expansionary fiscal policy that included tax reductions and increased government spending. Keynes theorized that a rebound in aggregate demand would cause businesses to increase production, employ additional workers, and invest in new capital goods. Governments from around the world, including the administration of Franklin Delano Roosevelt (FDR) in the United States, latched onto the Keynesian solution during the 1930s. In the United States, FDR

President Franklin D. Roosevelt, Fireside Chat, 1937. © Library of Congress.

and Congress approved an avalanche of new programs, collectively called the New Deal, to bolster consumer confidence and aggregate demand. FDR also provided moral support to the shaken American people with regular radio addresses called "fireside chats" during the dark days of the Great Depression.

The Keynesians ushered in a new era in economic thinking, particularly with respect to expanded government responsibilities in the economy. They opened new discussions and debate in the field of macroeconomics, especially problems related to economic growth, unemployment, and inflation. The passage of the Employment Act of 1946, which made it national policy to "promote maximum employment, production, and purchasing power,"[8] formalized a new era of government responsibility in supporting the nation's macroeconomic goals (see chapter 10 for more on stabilization policies).

BIOGRAPHIES: THE SHAPERS OF ECONOMIC THOUGHT

Thomas Mun and the Mercantilists

Thomas Mun (1571–1641) was a prominent merchant and defender of mercantilism in the late sixteenth and early seventeenth centuries. Mun was born to a wealthy merchant family in England and thus enjoyed the advantages of education and position. He also gained a wealth of hands-on experience in the art of commerce by involving himself in commercial ventures in Italy, Turkey, and elsewhere. Mun was convinced that international trade could result in handsome profits for the merchant class and could enrich England—a goal that was important to the nationalistic Mun. As his reputation grew during the early 1600s, Mun's influence increased. In 1615 he was elected a director of the East India Company, a private corporation to which the English government granted monopoly power in certain traded commodities.

Mun's most famous book, *Discourse on England's Treasure by Foreign Trade,* was published in 1664, more than 20 years after his death. In this book, Mun closely examined the qualities and responsibilities of the perfect merchant, which included excellence in all aspects of accounting, currency conversion, and shipping and navigation. Mun also believed that merchants should be well acquainted with foreign laws, cultures, and languages. In his book, Mun also vigorously supported the monopoly status of the East India Company, trade restrictions on certain imports, and government subsidies to export industries. The most controversial aspect of his book was his break with the powerful bullionists, who advocated the accumulation of specie in the form of gold and silver as the sole path to national wealth.

Mun favored trade policies to create a favorable balance of trade for England. He proposed that English merchants use some of the nation's specie to purchase inexpensive resources from foreign lands, resources that could be processed and reexported to other nations at a higher price. Mun reasoned that the value of England's relatively expensive exports would far outweigh the value of cheap imported resources, a circumstance that would guarantee a favorable balance of trade and the inflow of additional specie into England. Mun's unorthodox views put him at odds with diehard bullionists, however, who preferred to hoard England's specie within national borders.

The views of Thomas Mun, Antonio Serra (Italy), Jean-Baptiste Colbert (France), and other mercantilists influenced government policies across Europe during the 1600s, 1700s, and early 1800s. In fact, it wasn't until the birth of the classical school of economic thought in the 1770s that a competing theory—that of free trade—seriously challenged the worldview of the mercantilists.

François Quesnay: Father of the Physiocrats

François Quesnay (1694–1774) was born to parents of humble origin in Mere, France. Quesnay had few natural advantages in his early life. His primary education was spotty; his parents were common laborers; and he was orphaned by age 13. But what Quesnay lacked in wealth and social status he more than compensated for in intellect and ambition. Through disciplined self-education, he progressed from country barber, to surgeon (barbers and surgeons were often one and the same in seventeenth- and eighteenth-century France), to personal physician of Madame de Pompadour, the mistress of King Louis XV. While Quesnay's dabbling in the study of economics began after his sixtieth birthday, his groundbreaking theories soon made him one of the preeminent economic thinkers of his time and the undisputed father of the physiocrats.

It was with the publication of *The Economic Table* (*Tableau Economique*) in 1758 that Quesnay built a solid reputation as an economic thinker. This epic book followed a few articles penned by Quesnay on farming and the value of agriculture in France, which appeared in the *Encyclopedia* in 1756 and 1757. These articles, along with his favored position at the royal court of King Louis XV, created a powerful audience for Quesnay's ideas.

A central theme in *Tableau Economique* was that agriculture was the only truly productive sector of the economy. In Quesnay's view, this division between productive and sterile sectors of the economy was based on a natural order. One fundamental principle in this natural order was that agriculture alone resulted in a net product (*produit net*). The net product was the value of output above and beyond the costs of production. Using this reasoning, it followed that farmers and landowners represented the only truly productive class within the economy. By producing surpluses, the productive agricultural class not only supplied enough output to feed itself but also was able to meet the needs of people in the nonagricultural sectors. From Quesnay's perspective, the most appropriate goal for the national economy was obvious—to increase the net product of agricultural goods. Quesnay's arrogance offended the sterile classes, including proprietors, merchants, craftsmen, and industrialists.

François Quesnay continued to write about economic topics until the late 1760s, building both an international reputation and a devoted core of disciples in France. Contemporaries simply referred to Quesnay and his followers as "the economists." By the early 1800s, however, the term *physiocracy*, or rule of nature, came into common usage to denote the importance of natural laws in the theories of the physiocrats.

Thomas Malthus and the Dismal Science

Thomas Robert Malthus (1766–1834) was among the foremost English economists in the classical school. Malthus, who preferred the name *Robert* to *Thomas*, was well educated first by private tutors and later at Jesus College in Cambridge, England. In 1797 Malthus rejected his father's utopian beliefs and theorized that humankind was doomed to a future of poverty and misery as the growth of human population outpaced society's ability to produce food. With the support of his father, the younger Malthus formalized his thoughts in a book, *An Essay on the Principle of Population as It Affects the Future Improvement of Society* (1798). The book's pessimistic view of the future was a departure from the optimism of Adam Smith, who believed that free markets would fuel economic growth and create a prosperous society. Malthus's gloomy predictions also ran contrary to beliefs of the small but growing circle of utopians and other visionaries. His insights on population caused many people to perceive economics as the dismal science.

An Essay on the Principle of Population, which evolved into a lengthier and more sophisticated treatise by its sixth edition in 1826, was based on two main propositions. First, Malthus theorized that population, if unchecked by conscious actions or other circumstances, would double every 25 years. Hence, population growth would occur in geometrical progression—1, 2, 4, 8, 16, 32, 64, and so on. Second, he believed that the growth in food production would increase only in arithmetical progression—1, 2, 3, 4, 5, 6, and so on. Malthus's inescapable conclusion was "that the power of population is indefinitely greater than the power of the earth to produce subsistence for man."[9] In other words, the human condition would be poverty and misery—pitted by war, famine, and plague—with little chance for people to progress beyond mere subsistence.

Malthus's famous essay, which was published at the outset of the Industrial Revolution, did not anticipate the enormous technological advances in agriculture and industry that would soon occur. Over time, industrialization promoted economic growth and a higher standard of living for many people. While the doomsday predictions of Malthus were largely dispelled by the rising tide of wealth and prosperity, especially during the twentieth century, the specter of overpopulation still haunts a planet that expects an additional 3 billion mouths to feed by 2050.[10]

William Stanley Jevons and the Marginalist Revolution

William Stanley Jevons (1835–1882) was a prominent scientist, mathematician, logician, and economist—and a founder of the marginalist school of economic thought. Jevons was born in Liverpool, England, and received his early education at the Liverpool Mechanics Institute. In 1852 he enrolled in University College, London, but cut his studies short to accept a position as an assayer in Sydney, Australia. During his leisure time in Australia, Jevons applied his mathematics background to economics. He returned to London in 1859 and completed his bachelor of arts degree (1860) and his master of arts degree (1862) at University College. Teaching positions followed, first at Owens College (later called the University of Manchester) in 1866, and then at University College (1876), where he remained until 1880. While still in Manchester Jevons published his most famous book, *Theory of Political Economy* (1871), which explored the concept of marginal utility. In the process, he laid the groundwork for the marginalist school of economic thought.

In *Theory of Political Economy* Jevons examined the utility or satisfaction people derived from the consumption of goods. This book expanded on his earlier analyses of marginal utility, which first appeared in an academic paper entitled "General Mathematical Theory of Political Economy" that was presented to the British Association in 1862 and published in 1866. Jevons assumed that consumers could measure the utility they received from the consumption of different goods and services. Hence, to maximize total utility (total satisfaction) from a consumer's limited income, the rational consumer must assess the marginal utility (additional satisfaction) gained from each item consumed. Further, Jevons concluded that the marginal utility decreased as additional units of the same item were consumed in a given span of time, an observation known as the **law of diminishing marginal utility.** This economic law explained that people were willing to pay a higher price for a good when it was scarce because each unit consumed offered higher marginal utility, and that people were willing to pay a lower price when the same good was in abundant supply because additional units consumed offered lower marginal utility. Jevons's groundbreaking work in utility theory gave life to the marginalist revolution that, quite independently, was also occurring in Austria (Karl Menger) and France (Leon Walras). The fact that prominent economists from different countries had come to similar conclusions increased the legitimacy of Jevons's work and the momentum of the early marginalist thinking.

The marginalist revolution represented yet another step in the development of economic science. The law of diminishing marginal utility advanced the concept of rational decision making by noting that economic decisions are not all or nothing propositions. By linking marginal utility to the price consumers were willing to pay for a good, Jevons and the marginalists made significant contributions to demand theory. Today, marginal analyses extend into virtually every area of decision making—by households, businesses, and the government.

Knut Wicksell and Marginal Productivity

Johann Gustav Knut Wicksell (1851–1926), better known as Knut Wicksell, was a controversial Swedish economist and reformer who made significant contributions to both microeconomic and macroeconomic theory during his checkered career. Wicksell was born in Stockholm to a middle-class Swedish family. He was well educated, earning his bachelor of science degree magna cum laude from the University of Uppsala. In his youth, Wicksell was much influenced by the writings of Robert Malthus. Wicksell spoke and wrote freely on topics such as prostitution, poverty, overpopulation, and the general deterioration of the human condition. His radical positions, including support for legalized abortions, earned Wicksell condemnation from professors at Uppsala. In 1886 Wicksell received a travel grant to continue his university studies in London, Paris, Vienna, Strasbourg, and Berlin. After returning to Sweden in 1890 and adding a law degree to his credentials, Wicksell was finally invited to teach economics at the University of Lund in 1900. He was often praised by his students, and sometimes criticized by his peers, until his retirement in 1916.

Wicksell is sometimes called "the economist's economist" because of his ability to distill economic thought and communicate conclusions with clarity. In his book, *Value, Capital, and Rent* (1893), Wicksell introduced the marginal productivity theory of distribution. This theory established that a firm's payment for any factor of production cannot exceed the revenue derived from the additional output, or marginal product. For instance, if the value of the marginal product of the last worker hired was $10 per day, then the most the firm could offer in wages was $10, assuming all other costs were constant. In the language of economists, the marginal factor cost cannot be greater than the marginal revenue product. By analyzing the marginal product that resulted from hiring each worker or other input, Wicksell argued that firms could determine the most efficient amount of each factor to employ in production.

The enormity of Wicksell's work in marginal analysis and other areas of economics cannot be overstated. His 1890s marginal productivity theory revolutionized thinking on the supply side of the market, much like the marginal utility theory of Jevons, Menger, and Walrus had altered economic thinking on the demand side of the market a couple of decades earlier. Another of Wicksell's books, *Theory of Public Finance* (1896), supported cost-benefit analyses in the public sector. A cost-benefit analysis weighs the marginal costs against the marginal benefits of certain public programs or policies. Today, cost-benefit analyses are required in many types of public policy decisions.

NOTES

1. United Nations Conference on Trade and Development (UNCTAD), *E-Commerce and Development Report 2002* (New York: United Nations, 2002), 1, 7–8.
2. The World Bank, *World Development Report 2000/2001* (New York: Oxford University Press, 2000), 310–11.
3. UNCTAD, *E-Commerce and Development Report 2002*, 1, 7–8 and *Economic Report of the President: 2000* (Washington, DC: United States Government Printing Office, 2000), 116.
4. Bureau of Economic Analysis (BEA), "Table B.8. Employment by Industry," *Survey of Current Business*. 83 (March 2003).
5. United Nations Development Program (UNDP), "Table 11. Technology: Diffusion and Creation," in *The Human Development Report 2003, Summary* (New York: Oxford University Press, 2003), 274–77.

6. Adam Smith, *An Inquiry into the Nature and Causes of the Wealth of Nations* (Chicago: Henry Regnery Company, 1953), 9–10.

7. Karl Marx and Friedrich Engels, *The Communist Manifesto* (New York: Washington Square Press, 1964), 58–59.

8. "The Employment Act of 1946," in *Documents in American History,* 7th ed., ed. Henry S. Commager (New York: Appleton-Century-Crofts, 1963), 514–15.

9. Thomas Robert Malthus, *An Essay on the Principle of Population* (New York: W. W. Norton, 1976), 20.

10. Alene Gelbard, Carl Haub, and Mary M. Kent, "World Population Beyond Six Billion," *Population Bulletin* 54 (March 1999): 27.

SELECTED READINGS

Backhouse, Roger. *The Ordinary Business Life: A History of Economics from the Ancient World to the Twenty-First Century.* Princeton, NJ: Princeton University Press, 2002.

Buchholz, Todd G., and Martin Feldstein. *New Ideas from Dead Economists: An Introduction to Modern Economic Thought,* rev. ed. New York: Penguin USA, 1999.

Coleman, D. C. *Myth, History and the Industrial Revolution.* Rio Grande, OH: Hambledon Press, 2003.

Cortada, James W. *The Digital Hand: How Computers Changed the Work of American Manufacturing, Transportation, and Retail Industries.* New York: Oxford University Press, 2003.

Earle, Thomas. *Bronze Age Economics: The First Political Economies.* Boulder, CO: Westview Press, 2002.

Easterlin, Richard A. *The Reluctant Economist: Perspectives on Economics, Economic History, and Demography.* New York: Cambridge University Press, 2004.

Force, Pierre. *Self-Interest before Adam Smith: A Genealogy of Economic Science.* New York: Cambridge University Press, 2004.

Freeman, Chris, and Francisco Lonca. *As Time Goes By: From the Industrial Revolution to the Information Revolution.* New York: Oxford University Press, 2002.

Friedman, Milton, and Rose Friedman. *Free to Choose: A Personal Statement.* New York: Avon Books, 1979.

Gowdy, John M. *Limited Wants, Unlimited Means: A Reader on Hunter-Gatherer Economics and the Environment.* Washington, DC: Island Press, 1998.

Keynes, John M. *The General Theory of Employment, Interest, and Money.* Amherst, NY: Prometheus Books, 1997.

King, J. E. *A History of Post Keynesian Economics since 1936.* Northampton, MA: Edward Elgar Publishers, 2003.

Malthus, Thomas R. *An Essay on the Principle of Population.* Reissue Edition. New York: W.W. Norton, 1976.

Marx, Karl, and Friedrich Engels. *The Communist Manifesto.* New York: Washington Square Press, 1964.

Meek, Ronald L. *The Economics of Physiocracy: Essays and Translations.* New York: Augustus M. Kelly Publishers, 1993.

Mun, Thomas. *England's Treasure by Foreign Trade.* New York: Augustus M. Kelly Publishers, 1986.

Quinn, Daniel. *Beyond Civilization: Humanity's Next Great Adventure.* Three Rivers, MI: Three Rivers Press, 2000.

Ruccio, David F., and Jack Amariglio. *Postmodern Moments in Modern Economics.* Princeton, NJ: Princeton University Press, 2003.

Sargent, Thomas J., and François R. Velde. *The Big Problem of Small Change.* Princeton, NJ: Princeton University Press, 2002.

Schwartz, Glenn M., and Steven E. Falconer, eds. *Archaeological Views from the Countryside: Village Communities in Early Complex Societies.* Washington, DC: Smithsonian Institution Press, 1994.

Wallerstein, Immanuel M. *Modern World System II: Mercantilism and the Consolidation of the European World-Economy, 1600–1750.* San Diego, CA: Academic Press, 1997.

CHAPTER 3

The Rise of Modern Capitalism: The Power of the Market

Chapter 3 examines capitalism, an economic system that relies on decentralized private-sector decision making in free markets. The roots of European capitalism date back to the twelfth and thirteenth centuries, when trading cities such as Florence and Ghent spearheaded lively trade in the Mediterranean region—the first serious challenge to Europe's parochial feudal system, a type of command economy. Over the next few centuries, capitalism gradually expanded to regions in western and northern Europe, fed by economic revolutions in commerce and industry and radical changes in people's worldview. As capitalism evolved, it both shaped and was shaped by prevailing economic conditions. Societies tussled over issues such as income distribution, the exploitation of human and natural resources, and the legitimate role of government in the economy. In recent years global capitalism has come to dominate the economic landscape of the world. Channeling the power of free markets to create a prosperous and just global economy remains an elusive goal, however.

THE ORIGINS OF CAPITALISM

Capitalism is a type of economic system based on the private ownership and control of the factors of production—natural resources, human resources, capital resources, and entrepreneurship. In a capitalist economy, the private sector—individuals and firms—are mainly responsible for answering the basic economic questions of what, how, and for whom to produce. Over the past five centuries, the institutions and practices of capitalism have evolved. Among its key underpinnings are private property rights, profit incentives, competition, and economic freedom. Capitalism is often referred to as the free enterprise system to emphasize the importance of marketplace freedoms. Five key events contributed to the rise of European capitalism from the 1100s to 1900: the commercial revolution, the Protestant Reformation, mercantilism, the Industrial Revolution, and the publication of Adam Smith's *The Wealth of Nations.*

The Commercial Revolution and Foreign Trade

One factor that contributed to the rise of modern capitalism was the commercial revolution. The term **commercial revolution** refers to the dramatic increase in international trade, and the underlying forces that supported these commercial relationships, from the late fifteenth through the eighteenth centuries. The seeds of the commercial revolution were planted as early as the twelfth and thirteenth centuries, however. Its infancy was marked by the rise of an urban merchant class, which profited handsomely from foreign trade. Trade brought wealth, power, and prestige to trading cities such as Venice and Florence in Italy, Bruges and Antwerp in Flanders, Lubeck and Hamburg in Germany, and London in England. During the fourteenth and fifteenth centuries, many European towns joined the Hanseatic League, an organization dedicated to mutual protection and profitable trade in items such as grains, timber, precious metals, furs, and cloth. The Hanseatic League supported trade fairs as a means of expanding its growing web of commercial contacts. Predictably, important European trade fairs emerged in existing trading cities, which stretched from London to Novgorod, Russia. Trade fairs remained an important conduit for international commerce in raw materials, intermediate goods, and finished products from the thirteenth to seventeenth centuries.

European exploration and subsequent conquest of Asia, Africa, and the Americas from the late 1400s to the 1800s added fuel to the commercial revolution. During this period, European nations competed for profitable overseas markets, expanded their colonial empires, and looted established civilizations. The growth of commercial contacts increased the wealth and power of the commercial class, a development that intensified their ongoing power struggle with the feudal aristocracy—the traditional ruling elite whose wealth and position were tied to the land. The commercial revolution strengthened the pillars of capitalism, including private property rights, profit incentives, competition, and economic freedom.

- *Private property rights.* The commercial revolution relied on the ability of people to own and control private property. Individual ownership of property encouraged entrepreneurs to start new businesses to produce and transport goods for sale in distant markets.
- *Profit incentives.* The commercial revolution stimulated business activity by supporting private profits. In the process, it rejected entrenched teachings of the Catholic Church, which, during the Middle Ages, had condemned most types of profits as sinful.
- *Competition.* The commercial revolution created an environment in which competitive markets flourished. This competition among merchants occurred within and between trading towns and cities and at the seasonal trade fairs. Pockets of merchants scattered

across Europe were protected within walled cities, by mutual protection pacts, and later by powerful monarchs.

- *Economic freedom.* The commercial revolution expanded the choices available to individuals and firms. Businesses were allowed greater freedom to decide how to produce goods and conduct commerce, and how to accumulate and reinvest their profits. Expanded foreign trade increased consumer choice by increasing the variety of goods in the marketplace. Even serfs, who for centuries had been the muscle of the feudal system, gradually left the farms to seek opportunities in the bustling towns and cities.

The economic rivalries that existed among the merchants of Europe were tempered by their need to cooperate and to live by some commonly accepted rules. By the early 1500s, merchants had created money exchanges to facilitate international trade. A money exchange converted one currency into an equivalent amount of a second currency, a prerequisite for an orderly trading system. Letters of credit also came into common usage during the commercial revolution. Letters of credit enabled merchants to purchase goods or settle debts with a written promise of payment. Letters of credit were easier to transport than bulky coins, and reduced the danger of theft by highwaymen or warring princes. The establishment of money exchanges and letters of credit illustrate the resourcefulness of the budding commercial class in Europe. These business practices also had a positive impact on creating free markets built on the principle of voluntary exchange, another foundation of modern capitalism.

The Protestant Reformation and Profit Incentives

A second factor that contributed to the rise of modern capitalism was the Protestant Reformation, which swept across large segments of northern and western Europe during the sixteenth and seventeen centuries. The Protestant Reformation challenged many of the ideas and practices of the Roman Catholic Church, including Catholic restrictions on private profits and other worldly rewards for business activity. In the realm of economics, the early Protestant leaders, such as Martin Luther in Germany and John Calvin in France, reformed religious doctrines to support the economic virtues of hard work, thrift, productive enterprise, and the accumulation of wealth. Combined, these virtues are often referred to as the *Protestant ethic*—a worldview that Europeans transplanted throughout their growing empires during the 1600s and 1700s.

The Protestant ethic embraced many of the capitalist ideas and practices spawned by the commercial revolution. For instance, Protestantism was comfortable with using private property to create profitable businesses in commerce, industry, and other endeavors. This belief encouraged entrepreneurship, technological innovations, and aggressive investment in business enterprises. Protestantism condoned banking, including the right of banks to charge interest on loans, a practice that was roundly condemned as usury by Catholicism. In fact, for a time the Catholic Church viewed money lending as so sinful that only non-Christians could become moneylenders. Protestantism also valued individual initiative and the efficient use of workers' natural talents and skills in production. It accepted the premise that, while all work was noble, some workers were more productive and, hence, more valuable to society. It stood to reason that workers with greater talents should be entitled to greater financial rewards than workers with lesser talents, a logical argument that linked wages with worker productivity. In addition, poverty was often associated with moral corruption and personal weaknesses. The Protestant ethic made people mindful that hard work was not only pleasing to God, but also profitable for people with superior abilities.

Mercantilism and the Modern Nation-State

A third factor that contributed to the rise of modern capitalism was mercantilism, which dominated European economic thought for much of the sixteenth, seventeenth, and eighteenth centuries. Mercantilism, or the mercantile system, assumed that national wealth and global power were best achieved by the accumulation of specie (gold and silver). The mercantilists, mainly merchants and manufacturers, favored national policies to encourage exports and restrict imports in order to obtain a favorable balance of trade. Some European nations, especially Spain, were further enriched by vast quantities of precious metals looted from their colonial possessions, mainly in the Americas. A symbiotic relationship soon developed between the wealthy commercial and manufacturing classes on the one hand and European monarchs on the other. That is, taxes levied on commercial and industrial enterprises swelled the treasuries of kingdoms, and thereby helped monarchs solidify control over their countries. In return, monarchs were entrusted with building and maintaining a social infrastructure to nurture infant capitalist enterprises. The components of an economic and social infrastructure created a more predictable and stable business climate. Major infrastructure components included:

- *Stable political institutions.* Stability was best measured by the government's ability to protect its citizens from foreign invasion and domestic unrest. Hence, a strong central government and a strong military were essential.
- *Public goods.* Public goods such as highways, bridges, canals, harbors, postal systems, and naval fleets to protect the nation's business interests abroad facilitated domestic production as well as international trade.
- *Legal codes.* Laws supportive of capitalism included private property rights, including the right to accumulate wealth and earn profits from business activity. Other rules and procedures governed credit, internal commerce, and enforcement of contracts.
- *National currencies.* National currencies facilitated all financial transactions within and between nations. National currencies had clear advantages over traditional barter, which was time-consuming and required a double coincidence of wants. They also simplified accounting procedures and currency conversion at the money exchanges.

The new alliance between the mercantile class and monarchs changed the balance of power in much of western and northern Europe during the seventeenth and eighteenth centuries. This alliance wrested authority from the landed aristocracy, which had dominated the feudal economies of the continent since the eighth century. The transfer of power also brought a new, forward-looking class of entrepreneurs into positions of power.

The Industrial Revolution and the Entrepreneurial Spirit

The Industrial Revolution, which established the primacy of mechanized production over hand labor in the eighteenth and nineteenth centuries, was a fourth factor that contributed to the rise of modern capitalism. The Industrial Revolution was born in England, where, by the 1700s, conditions were ripe for an epic economic transition toward industrialization (see chapter 2 for more on the Industrial Revolution). Entrepreneurs during the industrial age strengthened the pillars of capitalism, including private property rights, profit incentives, competition, and marketplace freedoms. They also expanded the productive capacity of business enterprises and nations through ingenious technological advances, sophisticated capital markets, and the rise of the modern corporation.

Technology, which applies scientific discoveries to production, created numerous business opportunities for capitalist entrepreneurs. In Great Britain, for example, inventors James Hargreaves and Richard Arkwright not only profited handsomely from their invention of improved spinning machines, but also transformed the cotton textile industry from a cottage industry to factory production during the late 1700s. Similarly, inventors Thomas Newcomen, James Watt, and John Wilkinson pioneered steam engines that, during the eighteenth and nineteenth centuries, were adapted to power textile and steel mills, locomotives, and ships. In short, profit incentives harnessed the talents of inventors and entrepreneurs alike, and created the momentum for further technological innovation.

A financial revolution, which spawned sophisticated capital markets, also fanned the fires of capitalism during the Industrial Revolution. **Capital markets,** broadly defined, are the financial institutions in a nation that channel savings from households to business firms for the purpose of productive investment. By the mid-1800s, Great Britain's capital markets included insurance companies, an active stock exchange, and a sound banking system supported by the Bank of England (England's central bank). Not surprisingly, London was viewed as the financial capital of the world, a position it enjoyed for about a century. Other industrializing countries including Belgium, Germany, France, and the United States saw the benefits of capital markets and followed Britain's lead in developing their own institutions as they trekked toward the twentieth century. The importance of stable capital markets cannot be overestimated. These financial institutions harnessed society's wealth and channeled it into productive and profitable areas (see chapter 8 for more on financial markets).

The rise of the modern business corporation also supported the triumph of capitalism during the Industrial Revolution. A **corporation** is a firm that is owned by stockholders but typically run by professional managers. A business corporation is also a legal entity in itself. Thus, it can acquire property or other wealth, earn and distribute profits to shareholders, and sue or be sued. The origin of the business corporation dates back to the trading companies of the 1500s. These businesses sold shares, or stock in the firm, to spread the financial risk over a larger number of investors. Early business corporations were often granted monopoly status by governments, a practice that the mercantilists of the 1600s and 1700s defended as a way to increase the monopolist's profits and strengthen colonial empires. The modern business corporation became a dominant feature of capitalist economies during the nineteenth and twentieth centuries. Through the sale of stock, business corporations accumulated sufficient money to build factories, develop new technologies, and otherwise transform the dreams of entrepreneurs into profitable business enterprises. The financial success of modern business corporations was, in large measure, responsible for the rapid industrialization of the developed nations of the world. It was also the wellspring of rising living standards for many people in the industrialized nations (see chapter 5 for more on corporations).

Adam Smith and the Laissez-Faire Doctrine

A fifth factor that contributed to the rise of modern capitalism was Adam Smith's book, *An Inquiry into the Nature and Causes of the Wealth of Nations* (1776). In this landmark book, Smith recorded the benefits of a free market economy based on decentralized decision making. In Smith's view, individuals and firms were best able to determine how to allocate scarce resources to satisfy their consumption or production needs. Smith also observed that, when individuals and firms pursued their own self-interest, they also contributed to the general welfare of society.

In *The Wealth of Nations,* Adam Smith popularized the concept of laissez-faire capitalism. **Laissez-faire capitalism** was a strand of capitalism that rejected most types of government intervention in the economy and supported decentralized private-sector decision making. The laissez-faire philosophy did not originate with Adam Smith, however. Instead, Smith popularized the laissez-faire doctrines of François Quesnay, the prominent French economist and undisputed leader of the physiocrats. In *The Wealth of Nations,* Smith expanded on and adapted laissez-faire principles to support marketplace freedoms, including free trade in global markets. He also outlined the legitimate role of government in the economy, a role that prohibited government intervention in many marketplace activities. Smith acknowledged the need for government to protect its people from foreign invasion or civil unrest. He also believed that the government should maintain a stable business climate by protecting private property rights, the enforcement of contracts, and other formal and informal institutions of the free enterprise system. Smith opposed most types of government regulation of business activity, government restraints on external and internal trade, central planning of economic activity, costly government bureaucracies, and the use of public money to support the poor. He also opposed excessive taxation to finance these unwelcome government intrusions in the free market. Smith believed that an "invisible hand," which he equated with the informal operations of free and competitive markets, would guide society's use of scarce resources in a manner that was both efficient and fair.

TWENTIETH-CENTURY CAPITALISM: NEW DIRECTIONS

At the dawn of the twentieth century, laissez-faire capitalism dominated the global economy. Rapid industrialization in developed nations such as the United Kingdom, Germany, the United States, and Japan had not only increased per capita national output but had also improved the standard of living for millions of people. In addition, capitalism's success in creating national wealth increased the power of industrial and commercial interests within the political systems of nations during the nineteenth and early twentieth centuries. Predictably, government legislation supported capitalism and the accumulation of wealth by the capitalists. The ability to acquire vast fortunes reinforced profit incentives for entrepreneurs. These large stores of wealth also provided the financial fuel for economic development in the industrialized nations.

Partitioning the Planet: Capitalism and Imperialism

By the early 1900s, the triumph of laissez-faire capitalism had created domestic markets unfettered by government regulations. It had also resulted in international markets where free trade, exuberant foreign direct investment, and investment in capital markets had stitched together a highly interdependent global economy. Capitalism's ascendancy was hastened by the imperialist policies of the world's major powers. Imperialism is a process by which one country wrests political power away from another country, kingdom, tribe, or other political entity. Imperialism was driven by a number of forces. Through conquest, nations expanded their military power and national prestige. There were also economic motives for imperialism, which included the profits that could be made from the global exploitation of natural and human resources, the creation of new trade routes and markets for national output, and other entrepreneurial business activities. By the turn of the century, about 30 percent of the world's population lived under colonial rule, and an additional 37 percent lived under the thumb of absolute monarchs—some within the sprawling European empires (see chapter 9 for more on the relationship between democracy and capitalism).[1]

Imperialism brought many of the poorer regions of the world under the control of the industrialized nations, mainly the major European powers. The scramble to expand colonial empires, and thereby control key resources and markets, intensified during the late 1800s and early 1900s. By the outbreak of World War I in 1914, virtually all of Africa and much of Asia had been absorbed into the empires of the major powers. Leading the charge to partition the planet were Great Britain, which controlled significant territories in the Middle East, southern and eastern Africa, western Asia (including India), and eastern Asia;

the Netherlands in the Dutch East Indies (Indonesia); the Japanese in Korea and some Pacific islands such as Formosa (Taiwan); and France in northern and western Africa and Indochina. Germany, Italy, Belgium, Russia, and the United States also joined the imperialist bandwagon during the period. By the start of World War I, much of the world was marching to the beat of a capitalist drum, a circumstance that was viewed by the developed countries as both desirable and irreversible.

Laissez-Faire Capitalism and the Circular Flow Model

Laissez-faire capitalism is based on the free flow of products and resources in competitive markets. A simplified **circular flow model** illustrates how goods and services are exchanged in free markets. Like any economic model, the circular flow model is a simplification of reality. The circular flow model shown in Figure 3.1 illustrates exchanges in two markets, the product market and the factor market. The **product market** represents all purchases of finished goods and services in an economy. Households are the basic consumption unit, and businesses are the basic production unit. In the U.S. economy, millions of transactions are made in the product market every day. The **factor market,** sometimes called the resource market, represents all purchase of resources in an economy. Households provide the factors of production to business firms. Businesses, in turn, pay for these resources. The payments made by businesses to households are called the costs of production: wages in exchange for labor, interest in exchange for capital, rent in exchange for land, and profits in exchange for entrepreneurship (see chapter 5 for more on production and the costs of production). These same payments are types of household income.

The circular flow model also shows the two other flows—the flow of resources, goods, and services on the outer circle, and the flow of money on the inner circle. The outer circle shows that households willingly supply resources to businesses in the factor market. Businesses, in turn, transform these resources into finished goods and services for sale in the product market. The inner circle

Figure 3.1
The Circular Flow Model

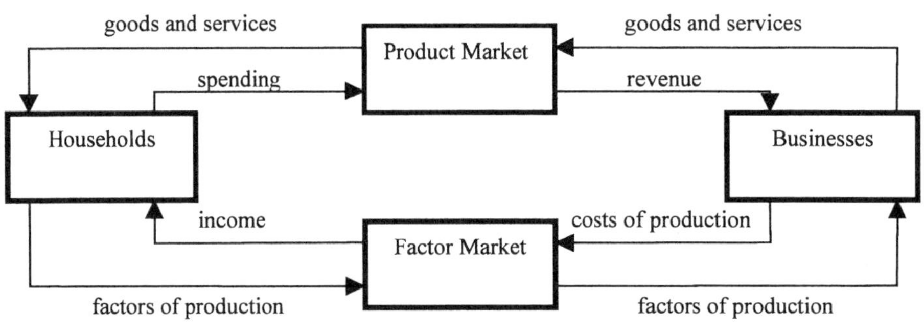

The Nanjing Road in Shanghai, China, 2002. Consumer buying in retail shops along the Nanjing Road is another type of business activity in a nation's product market. © Changing China Fulbright-Hays Group Projects Abroad, 2002. Photograph by Todd Wisdom Jarvis.

shows that businesses make money payments to households in the factor market. These money payments represent income for households, which enable households to buy finished goods and services in the product market. Under laissez-faire capitalism, the flows in both the product market and the factor market are free from most types of government regulation.

A Changing Role for Government: Amending the Model

Laissez-faire capitalism, which seemed so secure during the pre-World War I era, was severely shaken by this global conflict. Europe, the epicenter of the capitalist revolution during the nineteenth and early twentieth centuries, was ravaged by the war. The global economic web that the Europeans had painstakingly woven, a web rooted in international trade and foreign investment, began to unravel. Indigenous peoples in Africa and Asia intensified their cries for independence and openly challenged their European overlords. Some nations, including the United States, retreated into isolationism during the 1920s and 1930s. Isolationist policies often resulted in higher protective tariffs, restrictions on foreign investment, strict limits on immigration, and other barriers to the free flow of resources, goods and services, people, and money across national borders. In addition, the future of capitalism was threatened by the creation of the world's first communist nation, the Union of Soviet Socialist Republics (USSR), at the close of World War I and by a general deterioration of capitalism in much of eastern and central Europe during the postwar years. These cracks in laissez-faire capitalism expanded into wide fissures during the global depression of the 1930s. During this depression, the weaknesses inherent in laissez-faire capitalism were exposed as unemployment rates rose, businesses failed, nations' gross national product plummeted, and despair reigned. The prolonged depression intensified the call for a more activist role for government in the economy, and a radical change in the thinking of many economists and government leaders.

A **mixed economy** is a strand of capitalism that combines features from both the market model and the command model. Mixed economies stress decentralized private-sector economic decision making. That is, individuals and firms own and control most of the factors of production and are responsible for answering the basic economic questions of what, how, and for whom to produce. Mixed economies also borrow features from the command model, especially in the realms of business regulation, the provision of social programs, and stabilization policy. Technically, all economies are mixed economies, some leaning toward the market model and some leaning toward the command model. In common usage, however, the term *mixed economy* refers to economies that are primarily market oriented, or capitalist, but that have increased the role of government in the economy. In the U.S. economy, the government is a major player in both the product market, where it buys large quantities of goods and services, and the resource market, where it purchases large amounts of resources. Big government also provides a wide variety of public goods and services, redistributes income and wealth, regulates business activity, and stabilizes the macroeconomy. To finance these activities, government also collects taxes from households and businesses. Since the Great Depression, the United States has been the world's largest mixed economy.

CAPITALISM IN THE UNITED STATES

The Great Depression, which began in the United States in 1929, resulted in unparalleled economic hardships for Americans during the 1930s. At its outset, Republican president Herbert Hoover and his advisers believed that the economic downturn was just another **recession,** a short-lived economic downturn not unlike the postwar recession of the early 1920s or the Panic of 1907. Hoover held fast to the laissez-faire principles that had guided the U.S. economy over the previous century. The president was not blind to the dangers of recessions, however. He made personal appeals to business leaders not to cut workers' wages, and to union leaders not to demand pay increases. He also appealed to local charities and local government to provide assistance to people who had lost their jobs, savings, and homes. Hoover created the President's Organization on Unemployment Relief (POUR) to support the efforts of local charities. As the severity of Great Depression deepened, Hoover even agreed to the creation of a new federal agency, the Reconstruction Finance Corporation (1932), to make loans to failing businesses and to the financially distressed states. The resounding victory of Democratic candidate Franklin Delano Roosevelt over Hoover in the presidential election of 1932 expressed most Americans' preference for a more aggressive approach to ending the economic nightmare, however. The policies and programs initiated by the Roosevelt administration throughout the 1930s ended laissez-faire capitalism in the United States and ushered in a new era in capitalism's evolution.

The New Deal: A Turning Point in American Capitalism

By the time Franklin D. Roosevelt (FDR) was inaugurated as president on March 4, 1933, the foundations of the U.S. economy were crumbling. One-quarter of the American labor force was unemployed, and wage cuts affected millions of additional workers. Bank failures closed more than 10,000 banks, causing millions of people to lose their savings. Foreclosures on mortgages took homes from hundreds of thousands of families. Business bankruptcies disrupted business activity. And while the gross national product (GNP) continued in its tailspin, endless bread lines twisted through city streets. The highly anticipated New Deal program of the Roosevelt administration brought the federal government out of the shadows and made it a prominent player in the national economy.

Under FDR's leadership, the basic institutions of capitalism, such as private property rights, profit incentives, and competitive markets, were protected. Yet, New Deal legislation also set the stage for an expanded role for the government in four key areas: providing public goods, promoting economic well-being, regulating business activity, and stabilizing the economy.

- *Providing public goods*. Government public works jobs such as the Public Works Administration (1933), Civilian Conservation Corps (1933), and Works Progress Administration (1935) not only created employment for millions of workers but also expanded the nation's role as provider of public goods. These public goods expanded the nation's infrastructure through the construction of highways and bridges, sewage systems, dams, national parks and recreation areas, public buildings, and so on. The Tennessee Valley Authority (1933) was created as a government-owned energy corporation to supply electricity to the Southeast.
- *Promoting economic well-being*. Direct government financial assistance to Americans was a prominent feature of the New Deal. For example, government mortgage assistance programs such the Home Owners Loan Corporation (1933) and the Farm Credit Administration (1933) helped homeowners in urban and rural areas refinance mortgages. The Social Security Act (1935) created additional financial security for the elderly, single mothers with dependent children, and the blind.

Apple seller in Washington, D.C. symbolizes the plight of the unemployed during the Great Depression, 1930. © Library of Congress.

- *Regulating business activity*. The government's regulatory role expanded to correct market failures in the U.S. economy. For example, the Securities Act (1933) and Securities Exchange Act (1934) were created to prevent fraud in the issuance of securities (stocks, bonds, or other securities) by corporations and in the trading of securities by brokers on the nation's stock and bond markets. The Glass-Steagall Banking Act (1933) separated commercial banking from investment banking, thus prohibiting commercial banks from making speculative investments in the stock market. The Fair Labor Standards Act (1938) established the first national minimum wage of $0.25 per hour, a maximum workweek of 44 hours, and time-and-a-half pay for hours worked beyond 44 hours.
- *Stabilizing the economy*. The government's stabilization efforts used monetary and fiscal policies to increase aggregate demand in the economy. Fiscal policies decreased taxes and increased government spending during the Great Depression. Monetary policies increased the money supply and reduced the costs associated with borrowing money. By increasing aggregate demand, the Roosevelt administration worked to

jump-start production in the sluggish U.S. economy. These stabilization policies were given a theoretical boost with the publication of *The General Theory of Employment, Interest, and Money* (1936) by the British economist John Maynard Keynes (see chapter 10 for more on stabilization policies).

Economic Goals: Guiding American Capitalism in the Postwar Years

The unprecedented government intervention in the U.S. economy during the 1930s, coupled with the rapid growth in government during World War II from 1941 to 1945, were turning points in the development of American capitalism. Much reform legislation passed during the depression years remained intact or was expanded in the post–World War II era. Setting the stage for a more activist role for government in postwar America was the Employment Act of 1946, which stated:

> The Congress hereby declares that it is the continuing policy and responsibility of the federal government to use all practicable means consistent with its needs and obligations to foster and promote free competitive enterprise and the general welfare, conditions under which there will be afforded useful employment opportunities, including self-employment, for those able, willing, and seeking to work, and to promote maximum employment, production, and purchasing power.[2]

This historic legislation committed the federal government to take prudent steps to guarantee full employment, economic growth, and price stability within the context of a capitalist economic system.

Since the 1940s, the United States has adopted six broad **economic goals,** which outline the nation's economic objectives and guide the use of society's resources. National economic goals are also useful in evaluating the overall performance of the American economy. These goals include:

- *Economic freedom*. Economic freedom refers to the freedoms of the marketplace. It deals with freedoms guaranteed to consumers, producers, workers, savers and investors, and other participants in the economy to use their resources as they see fit.
- *Economic efficiency*. Economic efficiency refers to maximizing output per unit of input, or increasing productivity. Allocative efficiency evaluates the degree to which national output meets people's wants and needs.
- *Economic equity*. Economic equity refers to society's vision of fairness. The concept of fairness is influenced by personal values. There is considerable debate about what constitutes fairness, especially in the realm of society's distribution of income or wealth.
- *Economic security*. Economic security refers to the protection of people from unforeseen events that are beyond their control. Security is enhanced by federal deposit insurance, unemployment compensation, bankruptcy procedures, and so on.
- *Economic stability*. Economic stability refers to the full employment of society's resources—human, natural, and capital resources—and price stability. Economists generally agree that the labor force experiences full employment when the national

unemployment rate is 5 percent. Price stability occurs when the overall price level is relatively constant, without inflation or deflation.

- *Economic growth*. Economic growth refers to sustained increases in a nation's real GDP per capita. That is, economic growth occurs when the value of a nation's output, per person, increases, even after adjusting annual data for inflation.

Features of American Capitalism Today

Capitalism proved to be a resilient economic system, having weathered the storm of two world wars, a global depression, and the emergence of a major contender—communism—during the twentieth century. In the immediate post–World War II era, some of the nations of the West, such as the United States and later Japan, clung to many of the capitalist principles that had propelled their economies into positions of global dominance during the 1800s and early 1900s. But world events had altered capitalism in significant ways during the global depression of the 1930s and by World War II. In western Europe many countries, including economic powerhouses such as France, Great Britain, and West Germany, adopted democratic socialism to guide society's use of resources. **Democratic socialism** is a type of economic system in which the government owns and controls some of the means of production and provides an extensive array of social welfare programs. In the postwar years, many European countries nationalized the commanding heights of the economy. **Nationalization** occurs when the government takes ownership of a company or an industry, but compensates the previous owner. European nations nationalized industries such as health care, telecommunications, railways, and airlines; energy resources; and a number of heavy industries including steel and automobiles. Still, most business activity remained in the hands of the private sector. The United States and Japan followed a different path during the postwar years, relying on the private ownership of capital and the market mechanism to allocate scarce resources. The **market mechanism** is an informal network of price signals that influence people's production and consumption decisions. In the American mixed economy, the interaction of supply and demand, rather than the government, was allowed to coordinate the distribution of resources (see chapter 6 for more on supply and demand).

What are the essential features of American capitalism today? First, private property is vigorously protected under the law. **Private property** is any good, resource, or other asset that is owned and controlled by an individual or business firm. Legal codes protect people's property rights and their freedom of contract—the right to earn profits from voluntary transactions made with personal or business properties. Enforcement of contracts is a function of the courts. Private property rights also apply to the security of financial assets, such as savings accounts, and securities, such as corporate stocks and bonds. Private property rights support the profit incentives that motivate people to work, save, invest, and produce in a capitalist economy. Second, freedom of choice enables consumers to freely select which goods and services to purchase. That is, consumers are free to cast their "dollar votes" for goods and services that best satisfy their needs. Third, freedom of enterprise permits firms to conduct business operations in a manner consistent with earning profits. Firms are free to choose what products to produce, how to market and advertise their output, and how to minimize their costs of production. Fourth, competition is essential to the dynamic capitalist economy of the United States. **Competition** is the economic rivalry that exists among producers of similar products. Under capitalism, competition drives firms to produce quality products in an efficient manner. As a result, efficient firms tend to survive, while weaker firms fail. Competition also tends to lower prices for consumer goods and producer goods. A fifth feature of American capitalism, limited government, is examined in the upcoming section of this chapter.

American Capitalism and Limited Government

The concept of limited government evolved over the twentieth century. To the laissez-faire capitalists before the Great Depression, the role of government in the economy was severely restricted. Government, for example, provided some public goods, such as school buildings and local roads. The economic well-being of the people was very much the personal responsibility of individuals, however. Government regulation of business activity was spotty and largely ineffective. The Sherman Antitrust Act of 1890 was one noble effort to regulate the power of monopolies. After sparring with the Standard Oil monopoly in the courts for 20 years, the government, under the provisions of the Sherman Act, was finally able to break up the oil giant in 1911. In the realm of macroeconomic stabilization, the government created the Federal Reserve System, or Fed, in 1913 to serve as the nation's central bank. The Fed's main goal was "to maintain a noninflationary, fully-employed, growing economy, and to maintain balance in the nation's trade and financial dealings with other countries."[3] To this end, the Fed was empowered to assist ailing banks and the government in times of financial distress, including recessions and depressions (see chapter 10 for more on the role of the Fed).

Today, the concept of limited government includes a far more comprehensive set of responsibilities for government. Some economists have even labeled the period of time between the close of World War II and the present an era of big government. For example, between 1950 and 2003, the number of government employees at the federal, state, and local levels jumped from about 6.5 million to 22 million, an increase of more than 200 percent, as shown in Figure 3.2.[4] Government intervention in the U.S. economy has been most keenly felt in the areas of providing public goods, supporting the social safety net, business regulation, and macroeconomic stabilization. The growth in the size of government and in its role in the economy reflects the changing attitudes of a growing American population about the need for economic security and economic equity.

The government's first role in the U.S. economy is as a provider of **public goods,** goods provided by the government for use by all members of society.

Figure 3.2
Government Workers by Level of Government: 1950 to 2003 (in millions)

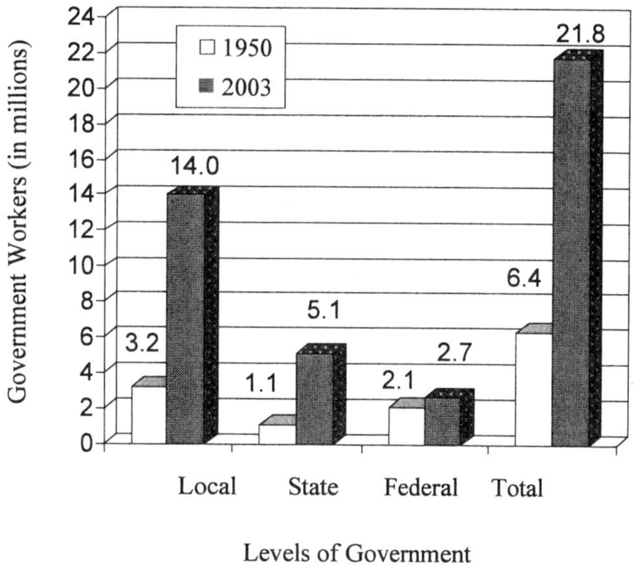

Source: U.S. Bureau of Labor Statistics, "Table B-1," October 2003; *Statistical Abstract of the United States: 2001;* and *The Statistical History of the United States: From Colonial Times to the Present.*

In a pure capitalist economy, public goods such as highways, schools, or submarines would be underproduced by businesses. This is because it would be difficult for a private business to prevent others from benefiting from the use of these goods free of charge—a situation referred to as the **free-rider dilemma.** Yet, certain goods are necessary for the general well-being and security of nations, such as an infrastructure (roads, bridges, seaports, and airports), criminal justice system (police, courts, and prisons), national defense, and so on. Government has endeavored to meet the growing wants and needs of its population by supplying public goods. At times, government produces the good directly, as is the case with the U.S. Postal Service. More commonly, government hires private firms to produce public goods, as is the case with highways, schools, police stations, and military hardware. To pay for public goods, government collects taxes at all three levels—local, state, and federal. In 2004, for example, the federal budget called for the collection of nearly $2 trillion in taxes to pay for public goods and other programs (see chapter 10 for more on taxes).[5]

Government's second role in the U.S. economy is to promote people's economic well-being. Government social programs, which have expanded greatly since the Great Depression, redistribute some of society's wealth from taxpayers to the needy through a system of transfer payments. The two main types of transfer payments are social insurance and public assistance programs. **Social insurance** provides assistance to people who have made a financial contribution to the program. The largest social insurance programs in the United

The F/A-18C Hornet is a public good in the area of national defense. Photograph by PH3 Mark J. Rebilas. © Department of Defense.

States are Social Security and Medicare, which in 2004 provided assistance to more than 45 million Americans and accounted for one-third of all federal expenditures, about $750 billion. Social Security is a form of income assistance, while Medicare is a health insurance program, and each is designed mainly to assist the elderly. **Public assistance** programs provide aid to people in need, but do not require payments by recipients. The largest public assistance program in the United States is Medicaid, a health insurance program for about 34 million Americans who are poor, disabled, or in nursing homes. Medicaid costs are shared between the federal and state governments, and represent an annual expenditure of about $185 billion.[6] Other public assistance programs include Temporary Assistance for Needy Families, food stamps, and Supplemental Security Income (see the biography of Arthur C. Pigou for more on welfare economics).

Government's third role in the U.S. economy is business regulation. Many business regulations were designed to protect people from market failures. A **market failure** occurs when free markets result in inefficient use of resources, negative side effects such as pollution, inadequate or misleading information, or other violations of the public trust. Business regulations define the standards of conduct for business activity and protect workers, consumers, savers, investors, and other stakeholders in the economy. The Occupational Safety and Health Administration (OSHA), which was created in 1970, investigates worker safety issues and is empowered to force compliance with safety regulations in the workplace. The Equal Employment Opportunity Commission (EEOC), which was established under the historic Civil Rights Act of 1964, protects workers against discrimination on the job. The Consumer Product Safety Commission (CPSC) has served as a consumer watchdog since 1972, and is empowered to issue product warnings and recalls. The Federal Deposit Insurance Corporation (FDIC), which was launched during the Great Depression to insure depositors' savings, also monitors banks' business practices. The Securities and Exchange Commission (SEC), also created during the 1930s, guards investors from fraud and other illegal practices such as insider trading. The Environmental Protection Agency (EPA), which was founded in 1970, regulates the handling of hazardous wastes and monitors firms' compliance with environmental regulations. Aggressive enforcement of antitrust legislation by the Justice Department, which resulted in the breakup of AT&T in 1982 and a decision against the Microsoft monopoly in the early 2000s, illustrates the government's commitment to competitive markets.

The government's fourth role in the U.S. economy is macroeconomic stabilization. FDR's aggressive New Deal programs and policies, including a willingness to incur budget deficits during economic downturns, opened the door to future interventions. For example, during the early 1960s President John F. Kennedy supported tax cuts and increased federal spending to combat a lingering recession. These fiscal policies were supported by the Federal Reserve System, which initiated its own assault on the recession, mainly by increasing the money supply and reducing the cost of borrowing. Combined, these policies increased aggregate demand in the economy and helped reverse the economic downturn. Similarly, in May 2003 President George W. Bush signed into law the Jobs and Growth Act of 2003, which used tax cuts to jump-start business activity (see chapter 10 for more on stabilization policy).

GLOBAL CAPITALISM IN THE TWENTY-FIRST CENTURY

Capitalism evolved in fits and starts as it progressed through the commercial, industrial, and information revolutions. Capitalism also was forced to acknowledge its own inherent weaknesses, however, such as recurring recessions, inflation, market failures such as pollution and monopoly power, and poverty at the national and international levels. Yet its core principles—private property, profit incentives, competitive markets, and economic freedom—have withstood the test of time. Global economic conditions at the dawn of the third millennium present additional opportunities, and significant challenges, to global capitalism. The direction of global capitalism during the twenty-first century will likely be influenced by a number of factors, including technological advance, globalization, and transnational organizations.

Information and Communications Technologies

Technological advance will continue to play a key role in the evolution of capitalism. New technologies during the Industrial Revolution redirected production from cottage industries to the factory system during the eighteenth and nineteenth centuries—a tiny speck of time in the economic history of humankind. Today, technological advance, particularly in information and communications technologies (ICTs), is transforming the economies of nations at an even quicker pace. ICTs permit the transfer of resources from traditional manufacturing to services-producing industries and offer almost limitless business opportunities for existing firms and aspiring entrepreneurs. ICTs, along with advances in transportation, have freed businesses from traditional geographic constraints by enabling ideas, information, goods, services, money, and people to effortlessly traverse the globe in search of profits. Yet, new technologies can also heighten tensions among nations. For instance, during the 1990s and early 2000s the digital divide—the ICT gap between richer and poorer nations—widened the income gap between the nations of the global north and the global south. One challenge for capitalism in the twenty-first century is to reduce the digital divide by making technology more available to developing regions.

Globalization

A second force that will influence the direction of capitalism in the twenty-first century is economic globalization. **Globalization** is an intentional movement by individuals, businesses, transnational organizations, and governments to encourage cross-border flows of goods and services, people, real capital, and money. Globalization creates a more integrated and interdependent world economy based on free markets. It expands economic opportunities in the three main areas of international trade, foreign direct investment (FDI), and investment in international capital markets. Yet, the potential pitfalls of economic globalization cannot be ignored. Will the global trading system be receptive to the poorer nations' demands for inclusion? Will multinational corporations work toward sustainable economic development by protecting the rights of labor, preserving the environment, and respecting cultural diversity? Will business conduct in global financial markets strengthen or destabilize the global financial system? To fulfill the promise of global capitalism, all nations must be invited to the global picnic (see chapters 11 and 12 for more on globalization).

Transnational Organizations

A third factor that will influence the direction of global capitalism is the growth of transnational organizations. A **transnational organization** is a formal group or institution designed to address global issues through collective action. Broad-based membership in transnational organizations increases the power of these groups to establish and enforce the rules under which global capitalism operates. Today, important transnational organizations include the United Nations, which supports economic well-being and sustainable economic development; the World Bank, which finances development projects; the International Monetary Fund, which promotes financial stability; the World Trade Organization, which promotes freer trade; and regional development banks, which finance sustainable development projects in Africa, Asia, Eastern Europe, and Latin America. On a more grassroots level, the conduct of business in the global arena has also been influenced by **nongovernmental organizations** (NGOs), which gather and share information and instigate reforms. NGOs and other broad-based civil society organizations (CSOs) are society's gadflies. They magnify the voices of ordinary citizens and force governments, multinationals, and transnational organizations to reexamine economic and social policies that affect the quality of people's lives.

BIOGRAPHIES: SHAPERS OF ECONOMIC THOUGHT

John Stuart Mill and Economic Liberalism

John Stuart Mill (1806–1873) was a British economist, philosopher, and reformer. While Mill's scholarly work borrowed heavily from the classical economists such as David Ricardo and Adam Smith, he also challenged prevailing economic beliefs and advocated for economic and political reform. Mill was born in London in 1806, the eldest son of James Mill, one of Britain's leading intellects. By his early teens, Mill had mastered Latin and Greek, had studied ancient philosophers such as Plato and Aristotle, and was conversant in logic and economics. In 1823 he began a long career in the East India Company and, following in his father's footsteps, eventually earned the highest position in the company's India House (1856). During his employ at the East India Company, Mill wrote his most important book in the field of economics, *Principles of Political Economy* (1848). This book explored many of the central ideas of the classical economists (see chapter 2 for more on the classical school of economics). It also served as the most popular economics textbook for the English-speaking world and contributed to a rising tide of economic liberalism.

Mill's work in the field of economics helped redefine the classical notion of economic liberalism in Europe. *Economic liberalism* in the eighteenth and early nineteenth centuries stressed the primacy of the individual and the importance of economic freedom in domestic and international markets. Consistent with laissez-faire doctrines, it generally opposed government intervention in economic activity. Mill adapted this traditional view of economic liberalism to address the misery and injustices that confronted the working classes during the early Industrial Revolution, however. In *Principles,* Mill questioned the distribution of income and wealth in the industrial nations. He declared that the laws of property "have not held the balance fairly between human beings, but have heaped impediments upon some, to give advantage to others; they have purposely fostered inequalities, and prevented all from starting fair in the race."[7] Thus, Mill challenged the mainstream classical belief that certain natural laws governed the production and distribution of goods. Mill went so far as to recommend reforms in Ireland that would redistribute some land to the peasants.

Yet Mill was not prepared to condemn the basic institutions of capitalism, such as private property and profit incentives. In *Principles* he wrote: "In the present stage of human improvement at least, it is not . . . the subversion of the system of individual property that should be aimed at, but the improvement of it, and the participation of every member of the community in its benefits."[8] While a reformer, Mill understood the importance of profits to business expansion, employment, and economic growth.

Mill's economic liberalism also approached economic issues through a utilitarian lens. **Utilitarianism,** applied to economics, supported economic policies that would do the greatest good for the greatest number of people. For example, Mill favored the repeal of England's Corn Laws in 1846 based on utilitarian principles. The Corn Laws, which severely restricted the import of foreign grains into England, benefited a few landlords and merchants at the expense of the masses who, prior to the repeal, had no recourse but to buy higher-priced domestically grown grains.

The compassion of the reform-minded Mill extended into a number of related issues during the nineteenth century. As a Liberal MP (Member of Parliament) from 1865 to 1868, he championed the rights of women and favored universal suffrage. His sympathy for the working class led him to advocate for workers' rights, unionism, land reform, and worker-owned cooperatives. Mill even qualified his commitment to laissez-faire by stating, "Laisser-faire [sic], in short, should be the general practice: every departure from it, unless required by some great good, is a certain evil."[9] To Mill, the "great good" included additional government assistance to the poor and regulations on monopoly power.

Arthur C. Pigou: Founder of Welfare Economics

Arthur C. Pigou (1877–1959), a British economist and educator, is widely recognized as the founder of welfare economics. Pigou was born on the Island of Wight, England, and received his early education at Harrow and his higher education at King's College, Cambridge. In 1902 Pigou was appointed lecturer at Cambridge, a position that required him to teach economics. His fascination with the subject grew, and in 1908 he succeeded the venerable Alfred Marshall as chair of political economy at the college, a position he held until his retirement in 1943. While chair of the political economy department, Pigou wrote *Wealth and Welfare* (1912), which, in an expanded form, reappeared as his most famous book, *The Economics of Welfare* (1920).

In *The Economics of Welfare,* Pigou supported additional government intervention in the economy to relieve the human suffering of the poor. He reasoned that, under capitalism, self-interest guided the allocation of resources by individuals and firms. He also recognized that the winners in a capitalist economy were rewarded lavishly, while the less fortunate were left to fend for themselves. Pigou concluded that, because society sanctioned certain economic inequities, the government should assume some responsibility for the plight of the poor. He also reasoned that the redistribution of some wealth from the rich to the poor would increase the well-being of society. In *The Economics of Welfare,* he argued, "it is evident that any transference of income from a relatively rich man to a relatively poor man of similar temperament, since it enables more intense wants to be satisfied at the expense of less intense wants, must increase the aggregate sum of satisfaction."[10] To meet the most basic needs of the poor, Pigou proposed public assistance in providing housing, health care, and other necessities. Economists often look to *The Economics of Welfare* as the birth of **welfare economics**—a branch of economics that deals with the redistribution of society's income and wealth to promote people's economic well-being.

By the 1920s Pigou's groundbreaking work in the field of welfare economics represented a direct challenge to entrenched laissez-faire doctrines, which viewed government intervention in the economy as unwarranted and counterproductive. Pigou's work also laid the philosophical foundation for the creation of the welfare state. In a welfare state, the government assumes a central role in promoting the general well-being of citizens through extensive social insurance and public assistance programs, free public education, and other programs for the needy. Since World War II, Sweden, Norway, and other nations in western Europe have supported the concept of the welfare state, mainly on the grounds of economic equity and security. Opponents of the welfare state argue that cradle-to-grave security destroys the incentive to work and, thus, retards economic efficiency and growth.

Friedrich A. Hayek: In Defense of Economic Freedom

Friedrich August Hayek (1899–1992) was an Austrian-born economist and a consistent champion of economic freedom throughout the turbulent twentieth century. Hayek was born to an intellectual family in Vienna, Austria, in 1899. His university studies first brought him to the University of Vienna, where he earned two doctorates in the early 1920s, and then to New York University in the United States. While Hayek served as an economics professor at the prestigious London School of Economics (1931–1950), he authored his best-known and most controversial book, *The Road to Serfdom* (1944). Since the 1940s, this book has been viewed as one of the most compelling defenses of capitalism and laissez-faire economics. Hayek also taught at the University of Chicago (1950–1962) and the University of Freiburg (1962–1968) in Germany. In 1974, 30 years after the publication of *The Road to Serfdom,* Hayek was honored as a corecipient of the Nobel Prize in Economic Science.

Two dominant themes pervade *The Road to Serfdom* and most of Hayek's other books. The first theme defends free markets as the most efficient means of allocating scarce resources. Central to Hayek's argument was that no one could pretend to know what was best for all participants in a society. This is because knowledge is fragmented and dispersed among the general population. For example, consumers know what goods or services best satisfy their individual needs, while firms know the proper mix of resources in a production process. It followed that individuals and firms, guided by price signals and self-interest, were best able to answer the basic economic questions of what, how, and for whom to produce.

Hayek's second theme warned of the dangers of government intervention in the economy. Hayek believed that an expanded role for government would inevitably lead to central economic planning and a total disruption of the market mechanism. That is, government bureaucrats would inevitably make poor choices for society and set the conditions for economic chaos. In addition, Hayek argued that central planners and others in government would soon abuse their power to increase their own wealth and political clout. In Hayek's view, this centralization of economic and political power in the hands of a small minority could end in just one way—totalitarianism. In his book, *The Fatal Conceit: The Errors of Socialism* (1988), Hayek echoed his earlier objections to central planning by critiquing the crumbling Soviet economy. He stated:

> At least before the obvious failure of Eastern European socialism, it was widely thought . . . that a centrally planned economy would deliver not only "social justice," . . . but also a more efficient use of economic resources. This notion appears eminently sensible at first glance. But . . . the totality of resources that one could employ in such a plan is simply not knowable to anybody, and therefore can hardly be centrally controlled.[11]

Hayek was horrified by the shift in the intellectual and political climate of many Western democracies during the 1930s and 1940s toward government planning, the welfare state, and socialism. To counter this unwelcome swing in the global economic pendulum, Hayek, along with his friend and colleague Ludwig von Mises founded the Mont Pelerin Society in 1947. The Mont Pelerin Society brought people from academia and business together to support private property rights and free market economies and to oppose the socialist alternative.

Keith S. Joseph: Reversing the Dependency Culture

Keith S. Joseph (1918–1994) was a leading British economist and political leader who championed the virtues of free enterprise as the surest path to individual and national wealth. Joseph was born to a wealthy London family, the son of Sir Samuel Joseph, who ran the family construction firm, Bovis. The younger Joseph graduated from Oxford College shortly before Great Britain entered World War II. After the war, Joseph's interest in social issues and economic conditions motivated him to enter politics. He was elected to London's common council and in 1956 won a seat in Parliament as a Conservative. It was during the 1970s that Joseph's conservatism gained national and international attention. Teaming with another rising star, Margaret Thatcher, Joseph founded a free-enterprise think tank called the Centre for Policy Studies (CPS) in 1974. Its central mission was to expose the inherent weaknesses of Britain's socialist policies and to advocate for a capitalist solution to the nation's growing economic problems. The election of Margaret Thatcher to the position of prime minister (1979) and the subsequent capitalist counterrevolution in Britain were largely built on Joseph's ideas and powers of persuasion.

Through the CPS, Joseph worked tirelessly to change public opinion and public policy. Joseph's first obstacle was to overcome three decades of statism, which he believed was Britain's chief economic problem. **Statism,** an economic philosophy that supports aggressive government intervention in the economy, had been the cornerstone of the Labour Party's political agenda since the close of World War II. In postwar Britain, statism included the nationalization of key industries such as health care, steel, energy, transportation, and telecommunications. It also included costly cradle-to-grave public welfare programs, a dependency culture, and an extensive public sector to implement economic and social policies. By the mid-1970s, Joseph, Thatcher, and other Conservatives openly challenged Labour's economic policies and the oppressive tax system that was necessary to finance these programs. Joseph's campaign to change people's attitudes was aided significantly by worsening economic conditions in Britain, which by the late 1970s included paralyzing labor strikes, double-digit inflation, massive unemployment, and a generalized despair.

Joseph's free enterprise alternative to statism centered on instituting policies to promote entrepreneurship and enhance production, the British version of supply-side economics. In a CPS pamphlet, *Conditions for Fuller Employment* (1978), Joseph wrote, "The market creates the framework: but it is people who act within it. . . . Resources do not allocate themselves: they have to be organized by people, above all the entrepreneur."[12] Supply-side theories became the centerpiece of Margaret Thatcher's reform package, and when she became prime minister in 1979, she aggressively pursued a supply-side agenda.

The supply-siders believed that national wealth and prosperity were best achieved by increasing national output. Joseph reasoned that increased production creates additional jobs, higher incomes for workers, and more profits for prudent investors. To jump-start production, several important policy changes were required. The first was government downsizing, which required smaller government bureaucracies, a reduction in business subsidies, and stricter limits on the public dole. In other words, Joseph proposed dismantling the welfare state and reversing the dependency culture. The second was tax cuts, a natural consequence of smaller government. The third was privatization of state-owned industries, which were often plagued by chronic inefficiencies and debt. The fourth was the containment of powerful labor unions, which had dominated public policy for decades. Combined, Joseph believed that these policies would encourage entrepreneurship and restore incentives to work, save, invest, and produce. These ideas transformed economic thought in Great Britain. Commenting on "the revival of the philosophy and principles of a free society" in Great Britain, Margaret Thatcher stated that "History will accord a very great place to Keith Joseph in that accomplishment. A tremendous place."[13] Joseph's supply-side ideas also influenced economic policies in the United States during the 1980s under the banner of Reaganomics.

Walter E. Williams: No Free Lunch

Walter E. Williams (1936–) is a prominent American free market economist and columnist. Williams's controversial views on a variety of contemporary issues—including environmentalism, affirmative action, taxation, and the legitimate role of government in the economy—have stoked the fires of debate for decades. Williams was born in Philadelphia. His professional training occurred at a number of schools, including UCLA, where he earned his doctorate in economics, and Washington and Jefferson College, where he earned his doctor of laws degree. Williams currently teaches at George Mason University in Fairfax, Virginia, where he served as economics department chair from 1995 to 2001. In his most recent book, *More Liberty Means Less Government: Our Founders Knew This Well* (1999), Williams defended a strict interpretation of the U.S. Constitution and a reduction in government controls on individuals' personal freedoms.

Williams' believes that the Constitution of the United States set narrow parameters for government intervention in the American economy. In *More Liberty Means Less Government,* he argued that the original intent of the Constitution has been perverted, especially during the twentieth century. Williams was highly critical of excessive government regulations, including many health and safety standards in the workplace, the minimum wage, most environmental regulations, and the labyrinth of agencies and departments at all levels of government. In *All It Takes Is Guts: A Minority View* (1987), Williams stated: "On top of government's limited ability to do good, is government's inability to regulate economic activity. . . . No government agency has the ability to coordinate the private plans of millions upon millions of decision-makers making billions upon billions of daily decisions."[14]

Williams opposed other government interventions in the economy. He opposed most forms of business regulations, mainly because regulations put American firms at a competitive disadvantage with foreign competitors. Williams opposed the "legalized plunder" of the American people, including costly public transfer payments to the poor and elderly, subsidies to businesses, and trade barriers that limit consumer choice and increase prices. He opposed affirmative action, a government policy that extends certain preferences to minorities and women mainly in the workplace and higher education. In Williams's view, affirmative action is unfair, tarnishes the achievements of African Americans and women at work or school, and masks the deeper problem of unequal opportunities in the public education system.

Williams sings a familiar free market refrain that "there is no such thing as a free lunch" in the economic lives of people. He offered free market economics as the centerpiece for the reform of the American economy, an initiative that would downsize the federal bureaucracy, streamline businesses regulations, promote free trade, abolish the minimum wage and affirmative action, and institute tax cuts. Under this package, Williams has predicted an improved business climate, vigorous entrepreneurship, and healthy incentives to work, invest, and produce goods and services.

NOTES

1. Freedom House, *Democracy's Century: A Survey of Global Political Change in the 20th Century* (New York: Author, 1999), 1–4.
2. "The Employment Act of 1946," in *Documents in American History,* 7th ed., ed. Henry S. Commager (New York: Appleton-Century-Crofts, 1963), 514–15.
3. C. J. Parnow, *A Day at the Fed* (New York: Federal Reserve Bank of New York, Public Information Department, 1977), 4.
4. Bureau of Labor Statistics (BLS), "Table B-1. Employees on Nonfarm Payrolls by Industry Sector and Selected Industry Detail" (Washington, DC: U.S. Department of Labor, October 2003). Available at www.bls.gov/newsrelease/empsit.t14.htm; *Statistical Abstract of the United States: 2001*, 121st Edition, "Table No. 609" (Washington, DC: U.S. Census Bureau, 2001), 395; U.S. Census Bureau, *The Statistical History of the United States: From Colonial Times to the Present* (New York: Basic Books, Inc., 1976), 1100.
5. Office of Management and Budget (OMB), "Table 7. Budget Totals," *Budget of the United States Government: Fiscal Year 2004, Mid-Session Review*, Summary Tables (www.whitehouse.gov/omb/budget/fy2004/summarytables.html) and Executive Office of the President/OMB, "Table S-2. Budget Summary by Category," *Budget of the United States Government: FY 2004* (Washington, DC: U.S. Government Printing Office, 2003), 312.
6. Ibid.
7. John S. Mill, *Principles of Political Economy,* Vol. I, 2nd ed. (London: John W. Parker, West Strand, 1949), 265.
8. Ibid.
9. John S. Mill, *Principles of Political Economy,* Vol. II, 2nd ed. (London: John W. Parker, West Strand, 1949), 518–19.
10. Arthur C. Pigou, *The Economics of Welfare,* 4th ed. (London: MacMillan and Co., 1932), 89.
11. Friedrich A. Hayek, *The Fatal Conceit: The Errors of Socialism,* W. W. Bartley, ed. (Chicago: University of Chicago Press, 1988), 85.
12. Keith Joseph, *Conditions for Fuller Employment* (London: Centre for Policy Studies Publication, 1978), cited in "New Labour's Secret Godfather," *New Statesmen,* www.newstatesman.co.uk.
13. Margaret Thatcher, "CPS Mission Statement," Centre for Policy Studies, www.cps.org.uk/mission.htm.
14. Walter E. Williams, *All It Takes Is Guts: A Minority View* (Washington, DC: Regnery Books, 1987), 91.

SELECTED READINGS

Baumol, William J. *Free Market Innovation Machine: Analyzing the Growth Miracle of Capitalism.* Princeton, NJ: Princeton University Press, 2002.

Brink, Lindsey. *Against the Dead Hand: The Uncertain Struggle for Global Capitalism.* New York: John Wiley & Sons, 2001.

Denham, Andrew, and Mark Garnett. *Keith Joseph*. Chesham, UK: Acumen, 2001.

De Soto, Hernando. *The Mystery of Capital: Why Capitalism Triumphs in the West and Fails Everywhere Else.* New York: Basic Books, 2000.

Ebenstein, Alan. *Friedrich Hayek: A Biography.* New York: St. Martin's Press, 2001.

Ebenstein, William, Edwin Fogelman, and Alan Ebenstein. *Today's ISMS: Socialism, Capitalism, Fascism, Communism, and Libertarianism.* 11th ed. Paramus, NJ: Prentice Hall, 1999.

Friedman, David D. *The Machinery of Freedom: A Guide to Radical Capitalism.* 2nd ed. Chicago: Open Court Publishing Company, 1989.

Friedman, Milton. *Capitalism and Freedom.* Chicago: University of Chicago Press, 1963.

Friedman, Milton, and Rose D. Friedman. *Free to Choose: A Personal Statement.* reprint ed. Orlando, FL: Harvest Books, 1990.

Fulcher, James. *Capitalism: A Very Short Introduction.* New York: Oxford University Press, 2004.

Grant, R. W. *The Incredible Bread Machine: A Study of Capitalism, Freedom, and the State.* 2nd ed. San Francisco: Fox & Wilkes, 1999.

Hawken, Paul, Amory Lovins, and L. Hunter Lovins. *Natural Capitalism: Creating the Next Industrial Revolution.* Newport Beach, CA: Back Bay Books, 2000.

Hayek, Friedrich A. *Individualism and Economic Order.* reissue ed. Chicago: University of Chicago Press, 1996.

———. *The Road to Serfdom.* 50th anniv. ed. Chicago: University of Chicago Press, 1994.

Hayek, Friedrich A., ed. *Capitalism and the Historians.* Chicago: University of Chicago Press, 1963.

Heilbroner, Robert L. *21st Century Capitalism.* reprint ed. New York: W.W. Norton & Company, 1994.

Hirschman, Albert O., and Amartya Sen. *The Passions and the Interests.* 20th anniv. ed. Princeton, NJ: Princeton University Press, 1997.

Kaplow, Louis, and Steven Shavell. *Fairness versus Welfare.* Cambridge, MA: Harvard University Press, 2002.

Lindblom, Charles E. *The Market System: What It Is, How It Works, and What to Make of It.* New Haven, CT: Yale University Press, 2001.

McCraw, Thomas K., ed. *Creating Modern Capitalism: How Entrepreneurs, Companies, and Countries Triumphed in Three Industrial Revolutions.* Cambridge, MA: Harvard University Press, 1999.

McMillan, John. *Reinventing the Bazaar: A Natural History of Markets.* New York: W. W. Norton & Company, 2003.

Mill, John Stuart. *Principles of Political Economy: And Chapters on Socialism*, ed. Jonathon Riley. New York: Oxford University Press, 1999.

Muller, Jerry Z. *The Mind and the Market: Capitalism in Western Thought.* New York: Anchor, 2003.

Northrop, Cynthia C. , ed. *The American Economy: A Historical Encyclopedia.* Santa Barbara, CA: ABC-CLIO, 2003.

Perelman, Michael. *The Invention of Capitalism: Classical Political Economy and the Secret History of Primitive Accumulation.* Durham, NC: Duke University Press, 2000.

Pigou, Arthur C. *The Economics of Welfare.* Piscataway, NJ: Transaction Publishers, 2002.

Pryor, Frederic. *The Future of U.S. Capitalism.* New York: Cambridge University Press, 2002.

Trentmann, Frank. *Markets in Historical Contexts: Ideas and Politics in the Modern World,* ed. Mark Bevir. Cambridge, UK: Cambridge University Press, 2004.

Williams, Walter E. *More Liberty Means Less Government: Our Founders Knew This Well.* Stanford, CA: Hoover Institution Press, 1999.

Wood, Ellen M. *The Origin of Capitalism: A Longer View.* New York: Verso Books, 2002.

CHAPTER 4

The Other Isms: Socialism, Communism, and Fascism

Chapter 4 examines socialism, communism, and fascism—each of which offers an alternative way to organize economic activity in a nation (see chapter 3 for more on capitalism). The oldest of the three, socialism, dates back to the early nineteenth century. The socialists often disagreed about specific policies to address the excesses of capitalism, but were linked by their support for a more equitable distribution of society's income and wealth. Socialism gained a foothold in many of the advanced countries of Europe and in developing nations after World War II. The second ism, communism, was born with the publication of *The Communist Manifesto* in 1848. During the twentieth century, communism was adapted to address unique economic conditions in the Soviet Union, the People's Republic of China, Cuba, and other nations. The third ism, fascism, arose in Europe after World War I. Private enterprise survived under fascism, but only under the watchful eye and oppressive thumb of a totalitarian government. Fascism dominated Italy and Germany between World War I and World War II.

THE THEORY AND PRACTICE OF SOCIALISM

Socialism is a type of economic system based on public ownership and control of key factors of production, mainly natural and capital resources. Under socialism, the government owns key natural resources, such as coal and oil, and capital resources, such as large factories and mines. Socialism, in its many forms, also stresses the rights of labor, which include fair compensation and favorable working conditions for the employed and a safety net of social programs for the needy. Hence, socialists believe that the most important goal of economic activity is the social welfare of the people rather than the individual profits of firms, entrepreneurs, or investors. Many forms of socialism have emerged over the past two centuries, each offering remedies to the perceived injustices spawned by capitalism and the industrial age.

Early Socialists in the Nineteenth Century

Modern socialism first appeared in western Europe in the early 1800s, with many of the most influential socialist thinkers hailing from France and Britain. The French philosopher Comte Henri de Saint-Simon (1760–1825), the founder of French socialism, was an early champion of the anticapitalist crusade in Europe. Saint-Simon believed that capitalism's reliance on individual self-interest encouraged social disorganization, injustice, and exploitation. As an alternative to capitalism, Saint-Simon favored the creation of a society administered by experts, such as scientists, engineers, artists, and industrialists—people who were best able to combine the technological marvels of the day with the emerging industrialism. Further, Saint-Simon supported equal opportunity for workers. He believed that people should be able to elevate their social and economic status based on merit rather than on inherited wealth or other entrenched privileges of a ruling class. Saint-Simon's social ideas were widely disseminated throughout Europe by his disciples, mainly through the posthumous publication of the *Doctrine de Saint-Simon* and the creation of the Saint-Simonian movement.

In Great Britain, Robert Owen (1771–1858), a Welsh-born industrialist and social reformer, pioneered new methods of organizing industrial production centered on humanizing people's workplace and community. Owen believed that workers' welfare and the success of a commercial enterprise were mutually supporting. In 1799, after several successful business ventures in Manchester, England, Owen and his partners purchased New Lanark Mills in Scotland. Owen improved the plant's real capital, as well as housing and sanitation in New Lanark, a town of 2,000 people. In 1816 he also established a privately funded school in New Lanark to instill proper attitudes and behaviors in the town's youth. In *A New View of Society* (1813), Owen described his social beliefs. This book, along with the success of the New Lanark Mills, brought reformers from around the world to his utopian community.

Soon thereafter, Owen proposed the establishment of self-contained villages, or villages of cooperation, to deal with the ever-present problems of pauperism and unemployment. He proposed that villages be structured around a common residence hall and cafeteria, and that workers be employed in a communal effort to achieve production goals. The first Owenite community based on communal principles was established in the United States (1825) at New Harmony, Indiana. The failure of the New Harmony experiment in 1828 didn't prevent the founding of several similar communities in Great Britain, however. In the 1830s Owen turned his attention to other social movements, including trade unionism and the cooperative movement. Producer cooperatives are businesses that are owned and operated collectively by workers. Owen's social experiments influenced reformers and labor activists on both sides of the Atlantic Ocean for decades to come.

The Fabian Society, which was founded in 1883–1884, also had a profound impact on the course of socialism in Great Britain and other European nations. The Fabian Society was organized by a small group of British intellectuals, including George Bernard Shaw and Beatrice and Sidney Webb (see the biography of Beatrice and Sidney Webb). The Fabians, who were viewed as radicals, favored the creation of a democratic socialist state in Great Britain. They favored a gradualist approach to achieving social reform, however. This approach favored the power of persuasion, rather than violent revolution, to influence public opinion and government policies. True to the socialist tradition, the Fabians opposed gross disparities in income and wealth between the rich and the poor, inhumane working conditions, the dearth of social programs, and the absence of personal freedoms. In *The Decay of Capitalist Civilization* (1923), Beatrice and Sidney Webb offer a biting critique of capitalism. They argue:

> It is therefore clear that a nation, in deciding to establish or to continue the private ownership of land and capital as the basis of the industrial organization of its people, deliberately chooses inequality. We must face this now with our eyes open. The outrageous disparity in capitalist countries between one man and another, and between one class and another, independently of their merits . . . is not produced by any defect in the working of capitalism, but is inherent in its very nature. It is not a transient phenomenon, but a permanent feature.[1]

Throughout its history, the Fabian Society remained an organization of intellectuals, rather than a mass movement. The society's non-Marxist orientation also permitted Fabians to participate constructively within Great Britain's political system. In fact, the Fabians were influential in establishing Britain's Labour Party in 1906, and over the years many Fabians were elected to Parliament.

Socialist political parties and labor organizations also sprang up in many other European countries and in the United States during the late nineteenth and early twentieth centuries. In Germany, the socialists established the Social Democratic Party in 1869, a party that vacillated between the revolutionary and the gradualist approaches to social reform well into the twentieth century. Similarly, strong socialist or labor parties arose in Scandinavia and in neighboring nations to the south, such as Austria, Belgium, France, and the Netherlands, during the final quarter of the nineteenth century. Power struggles flared between Marxist and non-Marxist socialists in each of these countries, but socialist candidates continued to win seats in national and local legislatures throughout the period.

The socialist movement in the United States remained relatively weak. The Socialist Labor Party, established in 1877, floundered for a quarter century. It remained a poor cousin to the more powerful nonsocialist American Federation of Labor (AFL)—a labor union that had become the most important voice for workers in the nation. The creation of the Socialist Party in 1901 briefly brought the socialists out of the shadows. In fact, Eugene V. Debs, the five-time socialist candidate for president between 1900 and 1920, garnered close to 1 million votes in the presidential elections of 1912 and 1920. The Socialist Party's opposition to America's involvement in World War I, and the imprisonment of Debs for his outspoken criticism of the government during the war, irreparably weakened the Socialist Party.

Democratic Socialism in the Developed World

Socialism in the developed world—the highly industrialized nations—adopted a distinctively non-Marxist and gradualist tenor during the post–World War II era. Its stronghold was Scandinavia, Western Europe, and several regions of the British Commonwealth such as Australia, Canada, and New Zealand. Socialism failed to attract a significant constituency in the United States, however. Over the past half century, European socialism has often been referred to as democratic socialism. **Democratic socialism** is a type of socialism that embraces limited government ownership and control of the means of production, indicative planning, and comprehensive social welfare programs to promote the public good. Further, democratic socialism favors democratic political institutions that invite open discussion of economic and political issues, guarantee free elections, and protect the civil and human rights of citizens. Conspicuously absent from the platform of democratic socialists in the postwar era was the radical rhetoric that, in earlier years, had supported the abolition of private property, class consciousness, class struggle, and the eventual toppling of capitalism.

The first feature of democratic socialism, limited government ownership and control of productive enterprises, was achieved through the process of nationalization. **Nationalization** occurs when the government assumes ownership of an important firm or an entire industry, but compensates the previous owner. Nationalized businesses are organized and managed in different ways. Most are restructured as public corporations. Under this model, the government appoints a board of directors to operate the industry, but the decisions of this appointed board are made independently from the government. A second management model brings the nationalized industry under the direct control of an existing government agency or department. Hence, the government makes all decisions that affect the company or companies in the industry. A third model creates joint ownership of a corporation, with some shares of stock owned by the government and some by private investors. Joint ownership requires collaboration between the public and private sectors to make corporate decisions.

Democratic socialists supported nationalization to guarantee an adequate quality and availability of essential goods and services. Government ownership of key industries, called the "commanding heights," also gave the government some control over prices and employment. The postwar Labour government of British Prime Minister Clement Attlee nationalized the coal and steel industries, the railways, the docks and harbors, some public utilities, and the health care system. Similarly, in the postwar period French socialists were instrumental in nationalizing public utilities such as gas and electricity, mining, banking, and insurance. Later, France nationalized the railways, airlines, and a number of major corporations such as the auto manufacturer Renault.

By the late 1970s and 1980s, many governments moved to denationalize, or privatize, state-owned businesses. **Privatization** is the process of selling state-owned enterprises to individuals or firms. In the vanguard of privatization was Britain's Conservative prime minister Margaret Thatcher. From 1979 to 1990, the Thatcher administration's aggressive privatization policies denationalized telecommunications, the coal industry, and some railway operations. Privatization also complemented other market reforms, effectively dismantling the welfare state. In France Prime Minister Jacques Chirac initiated privatization in many large industrial corporations, banks, and insurance companies by the late 1980s. From 1990 to 2000 privatization in the 15 European Union (EU) countries alone had generated $421 billion in new government revenues, with Italy ($109 billion), France ($75 billion), and the United Kingdom ($63 billion) leading the way. From a global perspective, 45 percent of all privatization revenues in the world were generated by EU nations during this period.[2]

A second feature of democratic socialism in the postwar period was indicative planning. **Indicative planning** is a collaborative, inclusive economic planning process. Under this planning model, representatives from the public and private sectors devise a set of recommendations to guide society's use of resources. Hence, government officials, business leaders, academicians, and workers have a voice in the process. Indicative plans typically established national targets for economic growth, investment, inflation, unemployment, government expenditures, international trade, and so on. Where appropriate, these plans also attempted to boost prosperity in lesser-developed regions within countries. The overriding goal was to improve the standard of living and quality of life for the people, rather than meddle in the business operations of private firms.

France pioneered indicative planning at the close of World War II. Its main goal was to channel scarce resources into areas most critical to the nation's postwar reconstruction. By the 1960s, most other European countries, socialist and nonsocialist alike, adopted some form of economic planning. In most, cases these four- or five-year plans responded to a specific economic problem or crisis. By the 1980s, however, the enthusiasm for economic planning had waned. Led by the United States and Great Britain, most developed countries shifted toward market-oriented solutions to economic problems. Government involvement in economic planning was viewed as incompatible with the efficient functioning of free markets. By the early 2000s, the importance of economic planning in the developed countries had diminished significantly.

The third, and most visible feature of democratic socialism in the postwar world was the creation of the welfare state. In a **welfare state,** the government plays a major role in promoting the economic well-being of its people. The main goals of the welfare state were to ensure a minimal standard of living for the people and to reduce glaring gaps in income or wealth between different income groups. To achieve these goals, the state invested heavily in public education, guaranteed equal opportunities for success, and provided cradle-to-grave security for its people through a vast array of social programs. During the final half of the twentieth century, many of the countries of Western Europe embraced the welfare state concept. By the 1950s, Sweden had become the world's pre-eminent welfare state. It created an extensive network of mutually supporting social welfare programs that, over time, were woven into the fabric of Swedish society. These programs include national health care, national accident insurance, unemployment insurance (usually provided through labor unions and supplemented by the state), job-retaining programs, generous paid leaves of absence from work for childbearing and child rearing, subsidized higher education and housing, tax-free monetary allowances for children, paid vacations, retirement pensions, and pensions for widows, orphans, and children who had lost a parent.

Challenges to democratic socialism have stiffened over the past quarter century. Even in Sweden, critics argued that heavy taxes, which financed the welfare state, were a disincentive to productive work and investment. In 1991 Swedish voters opted for a change in policy by ousting the Social Democrats and electing a Conservative government headed by Carl Bildt. Bildt's reform package included a tax cap on wages, capital gains, dividends, interest income, and corporate profits. He also encouraged limited privatization and entrepreneurial activity. Through a series of governments from the 1990s to early 2000s, Sweden enacted policies supportive of private enterprise and entrepreneurship while maintaining important features of the social safety net. The pendulum in most other European nations swung more decisively toward the free market.

Socialism in the Developing World

The heyday of Third World socialism spanned the 40-year period between the mid-1940s and the mid-1980s. The road to socialism in the developing world was pitted with a variety of economic, political, and cultural potholes, however. Economically, developing countries lacked an adequate infrastructure in areas such as transportation, communications, education, health services, and sanitation. In addition, the still underdeveloped factors of production—human, natural, and capital resources—were incapable of supporting modernization. Politically, developing countries lacked a tradition of representative government and the rule of law, factors that invited political instability and corruption. Culturally, the poorer nations often faced internal conflicts on issues ranging from overpopulation to tribal or clan warfare. Internal conflicts resulted in the waste or destruction of society's scarce resources. Layered on top of these inherent disadvantages was a profound distrust of foreigners, a by-product of colonial rule, and inadequate mechanisms to devise and implement development plans. Third World socialists typically offered programs of land reform, nationalization, and central planning to promote sustainable development.

Land reform was the starting point for most socialist movements in the developing world. It involved a change in ownership or control of productive farmland from a landed aristocracy to village groups. Land reform was viewed as pivotal to the socialist agenda due to the centrality of agriculture in developing economies. Tanzanian president Julius Nyerere initiated one bold experiment in land reform in the late 1960s when he introduced the villagization process, called *ujamaa,* in his East African country. Under *ujamaa,* tracts of land were transformed into community-based farming collectives. Clusters of families jointly worked the collectives and shared the output. Under the banner of African socialism, Tanzania and other African countries sought to capitalize on the traditional, communal concept of land tenure that had existed in some precolonial African societies. Unfortunately, in Tanzania and elsewhere, collectivized agriculture failed to increase crop yields or the self-reliance of the people (see the biography of Julius K. Nyerere).

At the same moment in time, a similar socialist experiment was underway in the South American country of Chile. Under legislation sponsored by the Socialist and Communist Parties, the Chilean government expropriated uncultivated lands and established peasant cooperatives to work them. **Expropriation** occurs when the government seizes private property, but offers no compensation to the previous owner. Plans to expand Chile's agrarian reform during the early 1970s were cut short when, in 1973, Socialist president Salvador Allende was killed in a coup d'état. The military junta that replaced the socialist government halted land redistribution and set the country on a more market-oriented development path. Agrarian reform involving the redistribution of land was commonplace, but largely unsuccessful, in Third World socialist economies during the postwar period.

A second feature of the socialist agenda was the seizure of the economy's commanding heights. Government seizures of property, through nationalization or expropriation, were intended to foster greater fairness and stability in nations. After India gained its independence from Great Britain in 1947, the newly elected government of socialist Prime Minister Jawaharlal Nehru instituted large-scale nationalization of mining, heavy industries, transportation, communications, and financial services. Egypt, under the leadership of Gamal Abdel Nasser, undertook an aggressive program of nationalization during the 1950s and 1960s. Nasser brought most major industrial and financial enterprises under the control of the government. Similar government seizures occurred in the North African nations of Tunisia and Algeria during the 1950s, Chile in the early 1970s, and dozens of other countries during the postcolonial era. The state-owned enterprises in the developing countries encountered predictable problems, such as poor work incentives, distorted price signals, and bloated bureaucracies.

Third, socialists in the developing countries adopted central economic planning. The main goal of economic planning was to allocate society's resources in a manner that fostered economic development and equity. The scope and rigidity of economic plans varied. For example, India's indicative plans guided the nation's economic development, but did not dictate production quotas or resource use for all industries. In fact, Indian five-year plans barely touched the agricultural sector, which remained in private hands and employed the vast majority of workers in the country. More rigid five-year plans were formed in the one-party states and in the states run by military dictatorships. Socialist planning in these states more closely resembled that of the authoritarian socialist regimes in the Soviet Union. In the poorer nations, the central plans, usually called development plans, stressed the collectivization of agriculture and large-scale nationalization or expropriation of major industries to jump-start modernization. Economic planning was also a tool to maintain the government's control over a country. One-party or military governments in the socialist camp were led by President Julius Nyerere in Tanzania, President Kwame Nkrumah in Ghana, President Gamal Abdel Nasser in Egypt, President Sekou Toure in Guinea, and others.

Socialist economic planning was largely unsuccessful in the developing world. It was plagued by inaccurate or unreliable economic data, poor coordination of programs, and unrealistic expectations for progress. Inexperienced government bureaucracies and corrupt officials squandered scarce resources. Even India, which had nurtured democratic institutions since its independence, suffered the stifling effects of socialist economic planning from 1947 to 1991. India's indicative plans influenced many aspects of industrial production by limiting firms' output, controlling prices, rationing resources, discouraging entrepreneurship and the use of new technologies, and limiting foreign trade. While economic planning is still a feature of India's economy, economic reforms since 1991 have stressed the role of the market in allocating society's resources. Interestingly, India's privately run agricultural sector successfully employed the innovative agricultural techniques of the green revolution—the use of hybrid and genetically engineered seeds, fertilizers, and pesticides, and advanced capital goods—to achieve food self-sufficiency by the 1960s.

THE RISE OF COMMUNISM IN THE TWENTIETH CENTURY

Communism is a type of command economy in which the government owns and controls the great majority of the means of production, such as factories, farms, and other businesses. Public ownership and control of the factors of production permit the government to dictate society's answers to the basic economic questions of what, how, and for whom to produce. In ancient times, some primitive agricultural communities practiced a form of communism. These ancient economies were based on common ownership of the land and an equitable distribution of output. Since the mid-1800s, however, communism has been associated with the theories of Karl Marx and Friedrich Engels and with the application of these theories in the former Soviet Union, the People's Republic of China, Cuba, and elsewhere.

Marxism: The Basis of Modern Communism

Marxism, the theoretical basis for modern communism, emerged as a distinct school of economic thought during the mid-1800s (see the discussion of Marxism in chapter 2). The main ideas expressed in Marxism stem from writings of Karl Marx and his lifelong collaborator and friend Friedrich Engels. Together, they wrote *The Communist Manifesto* in 1848. Later, after Marx's death in 1883, Engels edited and published the second and third volumes of Marx's *Das Kapital.* Marxism is built largely on an economic interpretation of history, often called *scientific socialism*. Key Marxist ideas revolve around his view of surplus value, dialectical materialism, and the inevitability of communism.

Surplus value is the gap between the monetary value of the worker's output and the monetary value of the worker's wage. In Marx's view, capitalist owners of the means of production confiscate this surplus value to enrich themselves and thus relegate common workers to lives of poverty and misery. To Marx, the deepening chasm between the rich and the poor would lead to class consciousness, the recognition by the toiling masses that they, as a group, were being exploited by the propertied capitalist class.

Dialectical materialism is manifest in the historical clash between exploited and exploiter classes. In Marx's view, history had progressed through a series of stages, from primitive tribal, to ancient slave-owning, to feudalism, and to capitalism, each marked by conflict between an exploited and exploiter class. In *The Communist Manifesto,* Marx boldly asserted: "The history of all hitherto existing society is the history of class struggles."[3] Marx predicted that the injustices of capitalism would instigate yet another conflict, this time between the exploited class of industrial workers, the proletariat, and the class of capitalist exploiters, the bourgeoisie. This class conflict would create a new stage in humankind's evolutionary history called socialism.

Marx viewed communism, a perfected form of socialism, as the final and inevitable stage of history. Under communism, all private property would be abolished. The abolition of private property, in turn, would eliminate class distinctions and end the class conflicts that had dominated earlier stages of history. Marx prophesized that progress toward communism would be achieved gradually and would be marked by people's willingness to work for the common good and to distribute society's output according to need. In the meantime, the people would govern in a dictatorship of the proletariat. The government, itself viewed as an instrument of oppression, would also wither away during the transition, until it disappeared completely.

Marxism was interpreted and revised by European theorists during the late nineteenth and early twentieth centuries. It was also adapted to better serve the needs, or justify the practices, of revolutionaries and governments. The application of Marxism by the Soviet Union, the People's Republic of China, and Cuba illustrate different forms of Marxism during the twentieth century.

Communism in the Soviet Union: 1917–1991

In the October Revolution of 1917, the Bolsheviks (also called the Reds), under the leadership of Vladimir I. Lenin and Leon Trotsky, brought communism to Russia. The Bolsheviks had long favored violent revolution as a means of creating a communist state in Russia. As a tight-knit band of professional revolutionaries, they were also quick to seize opportunities. In the fall of

1917 Lenin and Trotsky pounced on the teetering Russian provisional government that had just formed in the spring of that year. The provisional government was unable to bring victory against Germany in World War I or quell the chaos caused by wartime shortages of food and other essential goods. A disciplined Bolshevik assault on the weakened provisional government put the Bolsheviks in the driver's seat and permitted Lenin to steer the economy. Communism had arrived, but with a Leninist twist. While Lenin accepted the traditional Marxist proposition that the urban proletariat would be in the vanguard of the revolution, he also stressed the importance of the peasantry in transforming the agricultural sector along communist lines, and their inclusion in the dictatorship of the proletariat. Lenin stressed the central role of a small, disciplined cadre of professional revolutionaries in creating class consciousness, initiating revolution, and subsequently ruling the country. By the fall of 1917, Lenin applied his version of Marxism to a nation already crippled by the devastation of World War I and wracked by a civil war that would drag on until 1921.

Lenin immediately embarked on an economic program called war communism. Under **war communism,** Russia's resources were mobilized to defeat the Bolsheviks' conservative foes, called the Whites, in a fierce civil war that raged until 1921. The communist government expropriated virtually all domestic- and foreign-owned banks, manufacturers, mines, railroads, and other industries. To feed the Red Army and urban labor force, the government confiscated the crops of peasants and rationed essential goods. Even human resources were corralled by the government, and forced labor became commonplace. Predictably, by the end of the civil war Russia's economy was in shambles.

In 1921 Lenin introduced the **New Economic Policy** (NEP), a program of small-scale private enterprise designed to spark production and employment. Under the NEP, the government permitted peasants to own and farm private plots of land and to sell their surpluses—the amount left over after an assigned quota had been delivered to the government—on the open market. Lenin also returned many smaller enterprises to private hands, while retaining control over the major industries. The positive results of the NEP were felt almost immediately. Production of most goods and services rose to prewar levels, and the economy stabilized under the watchful eye of the Bolshevik leadership, the Red Army, and the Cheka (secret police). In 1922 the Union of Soviet Socialist Republics (USSR) was formally established, proclaiming the creation of the world's first communist nation. Lenin's untimely death in 1924 led to a power struggle among the Bolshevik elite, and by 1927 Joseph Stalin held the reigns of power.

Stalin's tyrannical rule of the USSR stretched from 1927 to 1953. He created a command economy built on a foundation of public ownership of the means of production and central planning. Upon Lenin's death in 1924, Stalin, Trotsky, and other Soviet leaders were content to stay the course, permitting the NEP and commercial relationships with the capitalist nations of the West to stabilize the battered Soviet economy. When Stalin solidified his claim to power in 1927, however, he abruptly changed direction. He abandoned private enterprise in the countryside by collectivizing agriculture. Entire villages were absorbed into massive state-owned farms. Millions of rich peasants, or kulaks, were slaughtered, many dying of famine or disease in the countryside or in Siberian slave labor camps. Smaller industries were again expropriated. Stalin also introduced the five-year plan to the Soviet economy. **Five-year plans,** which began in 1928, established priorities for national production and set specific production targets, called production quotas, for state-owned industries. Gosplan, the state planning agency, was responsible for devising and implementing the five-year plans. During the Stalinist era, successive five-year plans emphasized the production of industrial and military goods at the expense of agricultural and consumer goods. The concept of centralized decision making was transplanted by the Soviet Union into the communist-occupied countries of Eastern Europe after World War II. These occupied countries, collectively called the Eastern bloc, included Bulgaria, Czechoslovakia, East Germany, Hungary, Poland, and Romania. While there was some room for adapting production methods in these occupied lands, the Communist Party's monopoly on power was not questioned. The Soviet economy began to unravel by the late 1960s and 1970s. By the mid-1980s, the Soviet economy was in crisis.

Premier Mikhail Gorbachev attempted to rescue the faltering economy with a series of economic and political reforms during the mid-1980s. Economic reforms were packaged under the banner of *perestroika*. **Perestroika** restructured the Soviet economy along more market-oriented lines to promote economic growth and modernization. Limited private enterprise was encouraged; many wage and price controls were lifted; subsidies to state-owned firms were reduced; commercial contacts in the global economy were expanded; and individual plant managers were empowered to make many production decisions. Gorbachev also introduced national campaigns to reduce corruption, alcoholism, and other drags on the fragile economy. Political reforms, under the heading of *glasnost*, were also instituted to support economic reforms and individual freedoms. **Glasnost** created a new atmosphere of openness in the political arena, a national mood that encouraged discussion and debate of economic and political issues.

The inherent weaknesses of the communist system overwhelmed the Soviet Union, however. Bloated and corrupt government bureaucracies, obsolete capital goods, low worker productivity, weak incentives, and the lack of entrepreneurial skills and business expertise severely limited the effectiveness of Gorbachev's reforms. International pressures added to the nation's economic woes. Government coffers were drained by the unsuccessful Soviet invasion of Afghanistan from 1980 to 1989 and by an ongoing arms race with the United States. Festering resentments by people in certain Soviet republics and in the Soviet-occupied Eastern bloc nations also boiled over into the streets. By 1991, the Baltic republics of Lithuania, Latvia, and Estonia had declared their independence from the Soviet Union. Poland, under the leadership of Lech Walesa and the Solidarity Movement, led the charge to end the communists' monopoly on political power in the Eastern bloc. By the early 1990s, communism in the Soviet Union and Eastern Europe had collapsed. The Soviet Union was formally dissolved on December 26, 1991, and the 15 former Soviet republics became independent countries soon thereafter.

Communism in the People's Republic of China: 1949–1978

The communist takeover of China in 1949 was the result of decades of armed struggle between the Chinese Communist Party (CCP), headed by Mao Zedong, and the Kuomintang Party (KMT), headed by Chiang Kai-shek. During the bloody Chinese civil war, Mao skillfully built alliances, especially with the peasantry, explaining that "revolutionary war is a war of the masses; it can be waged only by mobilizing the masses and relying on them."[4] Mao promised land reform to the peasants, an attractive pledge in a country where large landlords dominated the agricultural sector and dictated the conditions of life for millions of tenant farmers. In 1949 the KMT or Nationalists, weakened by corruption, military defeats, and sagging popular support, fled to the island of Taiwan, where Chiang Kai-shek established a separate Republic of China. Meanwhile, on the Chinese mainland, Mao and the CCP triumphantly established the People's Republic of China in October 1949, thus creating a communist government in the world's most populous country. Marshalling the efforts of China's 500 to 600 million people behind the new communist regime remained a daunting task.

Chinese communism, referred to as Maoism, wavered between the pragmatic and the dogmatic from 1949 to Mao's death in 1976. Under Maoism, the CCP held a monopoly on political power and permitted no opposition to any policies emanating from Beijing, the nation's capital. Under its people's democratic dictatorship, which was modeled on Lenin's dictatorship of the proletariat, the CCP controlled the government and dictated China's economic course. The path toward communism was pitted with unrealistic leaps and painful retrenchments throughout the 1950s, 1960s, and 1970s, however, which disrupted production in agriculture, industry, and commerce.

Collectivization was the centerpiece of the government's agricultural policy from the 1950s to the 1970s. The first step in the collectivization process was to rid the countryside of rich landlords and to redistribute land to the peasants in small private plots. This goal was achieved between 1949 and 1952. The second step was to introduce cooperative enterprise into the countryside. In 1953 small collective farms were created by government decree. The land on these collectives was still privately owned, but it was worked by several families called mutual-aid teams. Soon, larger cooperatives were formed, with land, tools, draft animals, and other possessions owned by the cooperative enterprise rather than by individual peasants. Finally, in 1958, the people's communes were introduced, marking a radical leap toward communism. With lightning speed, over 100 million households were absorbed into people's communes, an action that restructured virtually every aspect of village life. Now, the CCP leadership in each commune dictated the allocation of resources, including labor, to build the region's infrastructure, work the farms, and attend to other business activity in industry and commerce. Communes also controlled education and law enforcement and administered punishments for counterrevolutionary activity or dissent. All private property and private incentives were banned.

The negative reaction to the communes in the countryside was swift. Some peasants refused to plant or harvest crops without an incentive system, while others sabotaged farms and other businesses, destroyed their herds, or otherwise disrupted production. Widespread opposition by the peasants and a serious drought reduced crop yields. Faced with the specter of famine, the government restored limited incentives, including small private plots of land, to the peasantry from 1959 to 1961. The functioning of the commune system, with its limited and uncertain incentive system, fluctuated greatly during the 1960s and 1970s. Selective implementation of government policies by local CCP officials, the economic chaos caused by the Great Proletarian Cultural Revolution during the 1960s and early 1970s, and internal power struggles added to the confused state of Chinese agriculture and industry during the period.

Reform in China's industrial sector followed a similar course during the Maoist era. The 1950s witnessed the systematic dismantling of private enterprise and the rapid rise of state-owned enterprises (SOEs). To coordinate the government's expropriation of private firms in industry and commerce, China embarked on its first five-year plan in 1953. By the end of this plan in 1957, virtually all of the country's industrial and commercial firms were in the government's hands. Buoyed by its success in reigning in privately owned firms, the government's second five-year plan (1958–1962) promised a **Great Leap Forward** to double the nation's industrial production. Under this plan, peasants in the people's communes were expected to contribute to China's rapid industrialization by constructing and operating backyard furnaces to increase China's production of steel and other heavy industrial products.

Inadequate capital goods, the lack of technical expertise, and nonexistent private incentives transformed the Great Leap into an economic free fall. By the early 1960s, the government was forced to retrench in the industrial sector, just as it had already done in agriculture. The crippled Chinese economy was given another negative jolt by the excesses of the Great Proletarian Cultural Revolution in the 1960s and 1970s. The Cultural Revolution was meant to be a purification campaign to identify and punish counterrevolutionaries. Youthful militants, called the Red Guard, purged scientists, engineers, party officials, and other well-educated professionals to stamp out lingering capitalist ideas among China's elite. These purges stamped out important elements of China's human capital, however, a tragedy that rippled through China's already stumbling economy.

Communism in Cuba: 1959–Present

Under the leadership of Fidel Castro, communism was brought to Cuba in 1959. Castro's violent revolution toppled Cuba's dictatorship, headed by Fulgencio Batista, and established the Republic of Cuba. Castro immediately instituted a series of socialist reforms, including the expropriation of virtually all private enterprises and the elimination of all dissent. He also introduced Soviet-style central planning to dictate the use of Cuba's resources. In response to Premier Castro's aggressive seizure of private assets, including American-owned plantations and other businesses, the United States slapped a total embargo on Cuba in the early 1960s. This embargo banned trade, foreign investment, and travel to or from Cuba. Castro turned to the Soviet Union for economic and military assistance, which the USSR generously supplied to its new friend in the Western Hemisphere.

Cuba instituted significant economic reforms during the 1990s, particularly after the collapse of its most important benefactor, the Soviet Union, in 1991. In 1993 the Castro dictatorship dismantled its cumbersome central planning agency, the Central Planning Board, in favor of more specialized planning

Labor-intensive agricultural production in Cuba, processing tobacco, 2002. © U.S. Department of Agriculture. Photograph by Peter Manzelli.

ministries, which promote tourism, industrial development, agricultural development, foreign direct investment, and other areas of economic activity. During the 1990s Castro also legalized many small-scale private enterprises, mainly in the services-producing sector. In agriculture, some large state-owned farms were divided into smaller producer cooperatives. These cooperatives were required to sell a portion of their output to the state for a set price, but were encouraged to sell the remainder for profit in farmers' markets. Agricultural production continued to rely on human labor rather than mechanization. In recent years the Cuban government also courted foreign investment and legalized the use of the U.S. dollar in most types of transactions. While these reforms recognized the value of private incentives, the vast majority of Cuba's human, capital, and natural resources remained firmly under the thumb of Castro during the early 2000s. In addition, the communists retained a monopoly on political power, ruthlessly suppressing dissenting viewpoints and coping with the economic stresses found in most other developing countries.

TRANSITION ECONOMIES: THE FALL OF COMMUNISM

The inherent weaknesses of communism in the Soviet Union, China, Cuba, and elsewhere were evident by the final quarter of the twentieth century. These economies quaked under the pressure of sluggish economic growth, stifling bureaucracies, low productivity, and a host of other economic problems. In addition, the people's standard of living continued to lag farther and farther behind that of the Western capitalist countries. In response, most communist countries sought a new path to economic prosperity, one based on free market principles rather than Marxist doctrine. National strategies to achieve a transition toward free market economies differed, however. Russia adopted shock therapy in the early 1990s to jump-start its transition to capitalism. The People's Republic of China, on the other hand, opted for a gradual introduction of market reforms.

The Economic Transition in Russia: Shock Therapy

The dissolution of the Soviet Union in December 1991 signaled the collapse of communism in central and eastern Europe and central Asia. It also signaled the beginning of an epic transition in the region, as 28 formerly communist countries adopted strategies to establish market economies and democratic governments. Collectively, these 28 countries were called the **transition economies,** or transition countries. Twelve of the 15 former Soviet republics, now independent countries, joined together into a loose confederation called the Commonwealth of Independent States (CIS) to ease the transition process. CIS members were Armenia, Azerbaijan, Belarus, Georgia, Kazakhstan, Kyrgyz Republic, Moldova, Russia, Tajikistan, Turkmenistan, Ukraine, and Uzbekistan. The 16 transition countries of central and eastern Europe and central Asia were Albania, Bosnia and Herzegovina, Bulgaria, Croatia, the Czech Republic, Estonia, Hungary, Latvia, Lithuanian, the former Yugoslav republic of Macedonia, Poland, Romania, Serbia and Montenegro, the Slovak Republic, and Slovenia. Russia is the largest transition economy in the region.

Since 1992, Russia's shock therapy approach to economic and political transition has generated mixed results. In the realm of economic reform, Russia's **shock therapy** relied on the implementation of aggressive government policies designed to rid the country of communist-era baggage and to institute new practices based on market principles. Under the leadership of Boris Yeltsin from 1992 to 1999 and Vladimir Putin since 2000, Russia's brand of shock therapy rested on four pillars: mass privatization, limited government, competitive markets, and global connections.

The first pillar, massive privatization, transferred state-owned productive properties, such as farms, factories, mines, retail stores, and so on, to the private sector. Privatization occurred through the distribution of ownership vouchers, the sale of stocks, public auctions, and other means. Privatization was most successful in the small- and medium-sized enterprises (SMEs), mainly in light industries, services, construction, and retail trade. During the 1990s, private-sector output climbed from 5 percent to 70 percent of national output in Russia.[5] More problematic was privatization of large state-owned enterprises (SOEs) and the collective farms, each stuck in the mire of outdated capital, mismanagement, and endless subsidies that rewarded inefficiency. Adding some momentum to Russia's privatization efforts in the late 1990s was the largely successful transfer of the country's coal industry into private hands.[6] In the early 2000s, the Putin administration also rekindled the sputtering movement toward privatization. Putin identified hundreds of additional SOEs for privatization and explored larger-scale privatization in major industries such as railways and electrical generation. The blossoming of the Russian stock market in the early 2000s reflected greater public confidence in the economy's shift toward private enterprise.

Second, the concept of limited government curtailed government intervention in resource allocation, pricing, and output decisions. Gosplan, the state planning agency, was disbanded. Reforms targeted the building of a legal framework to guide and protect private property rights, profits, and business activity—including the policies to ensure compliance with contracts, clarify bankruptcy codes, adopt standardized accounting procedures, deregulate industries, reduce licensing restrictions on businesses, and reduce business subsidies. In the early 2000s a new land code permitted private ownership of land in the cities, while a new labor code expanded firms' freedom to hire and fire workers. Tax reforms, which simplified the tax system and broadened the tax base, reduced the overall tax burden and strengthened the government's hand in collecting taxes. Challenges remained, however. High on the reform agenda for the twenty-first century were strengthening the rule of law, overcoming vested interests, reigning in unreported business activity from the large informal sector, guaranteeing macroeconomic stability, and expanding the social safety net for the unemployed, the elderly, the sick, and others in need. Russia's economic performance in promoting economic growth and price stability is shown in Table 4.1.[7]

Third, the government laid the groundwork for competitive markets based on the principle of voluntary exchange rather than government decree. Under competitive markets, individuals and firms were expected to respond to the invisible signals of the price system, signals that influenced both consumption and production decisions. Russia's shock therapy eliminated most government controls on prices in 1992–1993 to stimulate market activity and bury the archaic central planning apparatus. The predictable short-term result was **hyperinflation,** as the inflation rate soared to nearly 2000 percent in 1992 and nearly 900 percent in 1993.[8] As the economy adjusted to market-determined prices, inflationary pressures eased, as shown in Table 4.1. Russia also deregulated and liberalized business activity and privatized thousands of firms to promote competition. Russia carried communist-era baggage into the twenty-first century, however, including thousands of inefficient SOEs, costly subsidies to inefficient businesses, and nagging resistance to reform by vested interests—including the rich and well-connected oligarchs, who connived to reap the most lucrative deals during the early phases of privatization.

The fourth pillar in Russia's transition was to rejoin the global economy. Under communism, the Soviet economy had few economic ties to the capitalist nations of the West, preferring to develop trade and investment opportunities within the Eastern bloc. Since 1992, the Russian economy has made progress, in fits and starts, toward integrating its economy within the global network. For most of the 1990s, Russia's international trade was hampered by its nonconvertible currency, the ruble. A **nonconvertible currency** is one that cannot be exchanged for another currency due to its uncertain value. The fluctuating value of the ruble, coupled with the poor quality of Russian output, caused trade to flounder. Foreign direct investment (FDI) by outside firms was also hindered by the confused investment climate in Russia. Unclear property rights, excessive business regulations, government corruption, cronyism, and organized crime were a few main concerns that kept many foreign investors out of Russian markets. By the late 1990s and early 2000s, government stabilization policies and market-oriented reforms had made Russia's business climate more hospitable for trade and FDI. Russia recorded trade surpluses in excess of $50 billion per year from 2000 to 2003, built largely on oil exports.[9] In addition, Russia attracted more

Table 4.1
Russia's Performance Indicators: 1995–2004 (measured in percent)

Indicators	1995	1996	1997	1998	1999	2000	2001	2002	2003	2004
Real GDP	-4.2	1.0	1.8	-4.9	5.4	9.0	5.0	4.3	4.0	3.5
Inflation rate	198.0	47.9	14.7	27.8	85.7	20.8	20.7	16.0	13.4	9.7

Source: International Monetary Fund, *World Economic Outlook, April 2003,* 181, 189

than twice as much FDI from 1996 to 1999 ($8.4 billion) as it did in the early transition years from 1992 to 1995 ($4 billion).[10] Also important was Russia's willingness to involve international organizations in its transition process. Russia solicited development loans from the European Bank for Reconstruction and Development (EBRD) and the World Bank, foreign aid from the Development Assistance Committee (DAC), and technical and other financial assistance from the International Monetary Fund (IMF). Russia is currently jockeying for accession to the World Trade Organization (WTO), a move that would necessarily result in greater liberalization in the country's trade and cross-border investments.

While the Russian transition is far from complete, many signs point to continued progress. By the early 2000s, Russia had achieved real economic growth, rising real incomes, a stable stock market, and trade surpluses. At the same time, Russia experienced steady declines in inflation, unemployment, capital flight, and poverty.[11] The Russian economy had rebounded from its financial quagmire of the late 1990s, and had done so within the context of a program of market reforms. In recognition of the progress Russia made during the first decade of its transition, the U.S. Department of Commerce officially designated Russia a market economy in 2002.

China's Transition: Crossing the River by Feeling the Stones

Soon after Mao's death in 1976, China took its first cautious steps toward economic reform. The Chinese Communist Party (CCP) viewed market-oriented reforms as essential to China's modernization. Under the leadership of Deng Xiaoping, a policy of gradualism was adopted to methodically explore market-oriented alternatives to central planning and government control over the economy. Deng referred to this gradualist approach as "crossing the river by feeling the stones." Gradualism produced a dual-track economic system. One track, considered the economic mainstream during the late 1970s and 1980s, consisted of China's existing planned economy. The second track consisted of a series of market-oriented experiments.

The most significant of these early experiments was the **household responsibility system,** which encouraged peasants to lease agricultural land from the government. Peasants were required to work the land and sell a certain amount of their output to the state at a fixed price. They were free to sell the remainder of their crops on the open market for a profit. Market incentives increased the productivity of labor and encouraged the CCP to proceed to the next stone, the expansion of **township and village enterprises** (TVEs). TVEs are profit-making firms in rural regions that are owned or financed by the local government or, in special cases, by individuals. The number of TVEs in rural China grew from 1.5 million in the late 1970s to 25 million by the mid-1990s. They created 120 million jobs in industry, agriculture, construction, transportation, and commercial and catering services. By the late 1990s, TVEs accounted for 30 percent of China's GDP. TVEs were also an important feature in China's rural

The Pudong New Area skyline at night, Shanghai/Pudong, China, 2000. © Changing China Fulbright-Hays Group Projects Abroad, 2002. Photograph by Todd Wisdom Jarvis.

poverty reduction plan. From 1978 to 1997, rural poverty dropped from 250 million people to 50 million. During the 1980s, China also created its first free trade zones (FTZs), which were small capitalist enclaves located mainly in eastern cities. FTZs encouraged international trade by reducing or eliminating trade barriers. The initial success of early free trade zones also laid the groundwork for the explosion of Chinese exports during the 1990s and early 2000s. Much of China's most promising business activity and entrepreneurial experience stemmed from the efforts of individuals and firms involved in the household responsibility system, TVEs, and free trade zones.[12]

China's reform package expanded during the 1990s and early 2000s to strengthen market institutions, private-sector business activity, and the country's position within the global economy. The founding of the Shanghai and Shenzhen Stock Exchanges in 1990 represented a major step in institution-building. By 2001 over 100 securities firms used these highly computerized stock exchanges to link buyers and sellers of stock in 1,100 listed companies. The Shanghai Stock Exchange (SSE) became the dominant stock market in China in the early 2000s, with 646 listed companies and 34 million investors holding RMB 2.7 trillion (2.7 trillion renminbi) in traded securities.[13]

Private-sector business activity accelerated during the 1990s and early 2000s in several ways. First, many maturing TVEs were privatized. Second, government regulations were eased on private firms, joint ventures (JVs), and wholly owned foreign enterprises (WOFEs). Third, many SOEs were streamlined. Nonessential services were spun off, creating business opportunities for aspiring entrepreneurs. The share of industrial output produced by SOEs fell from 78 percent to just 23.5 percent between 1978 and 2000. During the same period of time, the percent of all urban workers employed by SOEs shrank from 78 percent to just 38 percent.[14] Fourth, regional development zones were created. Since the early 1990s, these zones have sparked modernization. By the early 2000s, there were over 80 regional development zones operating in China, over half of which were classified as high-tech areas. The most spectacular of these zones is the Pudong New Area, as shown in Figure 4.1. Fifth, in 2004 the government amended China's Constitution to permit private ownership of land in the countryside and in the cities, a major step toward guaranteeing private property rights, freedom of enterprise, and profit incentives.

International connections, mainly through trade and foreign direct investment (FDI), have also supported China's transition. During the 1990s and early 2000s, China aggressively courted multinational investment and consistently attracted more FDI than any other developing country in the world, about $41 billion in 2000 alone.[15] In addition, China became one of the largest participants in the global trading system. The value of China's exports, excluding exports from the Hong Kong special administrative region (SAR), totaled $363 billion in 2002, making it the sixth largest exporting nation in the world.[16] Additional trade liberalization was scheduled in the early 2000s to comply with World Trade Organization (WTO) guidelines. China's Tenth Five-Year Plan (2001–2005), which was approved by the National People's Congress in spring 2001, pledged continued support for economic reforms as a means to improve living standards and promote continued economic growth.

Significant obstacles to China's successful transition remain. Key challenges include

- *Widening income gap.* The income gap between China's haves and have nots is growing. The haves are concentrated in urban areas, mainly in the eastern portion of the country. They are typically more educated and better connected to the opportunities that resulted from China's opening to the West. The have nots are concentrated in rural areas, where the bulk of China's 1.3 billion people live. These regions rely heavily on small-scale agriculture for their income. Complicating the picture is a large floating population of surplus agricultural workers, numbering in excess of 100 million people. The floating population migrates between the countryside and the cities in search of employment and other economic opportunities.
- *Uneven development.* Despite the government's plans for western development, most of China's limited tax revenues are invested in the east, in regions such as the Pudong New Area and in Beijing (as it prepares for the 2008 Summer Olympics). Most FDI is also centered in the eastern cities.
- *Inadequate safety net.* There are gaping holes in China's safety net of social programs. While government workers are entitled to pension plans and the urban poor have access to some public transfer payments and medical assistance, the vast majority of

Figure 4.1
The Pudong New Area

The Pudong New Area, China's preeminent high-tech development region, is located in the east coast city of Shanghai. It covers 533 square kilometers and has a population of 1.6 million people. Pudong is often referred to as the dragon head of China's modernization and is a widely recognized symbol of China's economic transformation.

The Pudong New Area is composed of several key development zones, including: the Zhangjiang High-Tech Park, the Jinqiao Export Processing Zone, the Waigaoqiao Free Trade Zone, and the Lujiazui Finance and Trade Zone. Some of these development zones, in turn, have specialized parks or bases to cluster similar types of businesses into a single location. For example, located within the Zhangjiang High-Tech Park is the Pudong Software Park, the Technology Innovation Park, the National Biopharmaceutical Base, and the Microelectronics Base. Other zones were designed to create a twenty-first century living and working environment for Pudong's 1.6 million residents and for the millions of foreigners who visit each year.

In its 2001–2005 development plan, the Pudong New Area stressed ongoing improvements in the region's physical and information infrastructure, a hospitable business climate, and fair and efficient government. The plan called for the government to invest an additional RMB 200 billion (nearly $25 billion) in the area over the five-year period. Indicators of past successes abound. For example, the Pudong New Area attracted 7,700 projects from 70 countries and regions by the early 2000s, causing total investment in the region to jump from $1.5 billion in 1992 to $38 billion in 2001. About half of all investment was derived from three sources: the Hong Kong SAR (21%), the United States (18%), and Japan (11%). During the same period of time, the value of Pudong's GDP, or total output, increased about tenfold, from RMB 104 billion to more than RMB 1 trillion.

China's population is not covered by health insurance, minimum income programs, or other types of assistance. In addition, little has been done to address the needs of the huge floating population, which is often denied basic social services due to residency requirements. The outbreak of SARS (serious acute respiratory syndrome) in 2003 underscored the need for additional medical services in the country.

- *Insolvent financial institutions*. For many years China's state-owned banking system was required to make unwise loans to the large, inefficient state-owned enterprises (SOEs). The banking system is currently dominated by the Big Four: Bank of China, Industrial and Commercial Bank of China, China Construction Bank, and Agricultural

Bank of China. Today, many experts believe that 50 percent to 60 percent of all loans are nonperforming loans (NPLs), or loans that SOEs and others will never repay (the government estimates that just 25 percent of all loans are NPLs). Recently, some of these NPLs have been transferred to asset management companies (AMCs) to relieve the stress on the banking system. The scope of AMC activity is woefully inadequate, however. In addition, banks continue to make noncommercial loans based on poor credit risk management to the SOEs.

- *Inefficient state-owned enterprises*. All major industries are controlled by SOEs. Most SOEs are inefficient, and many continue to rely government subsidies and loans from the state-owned banks to maintain production and employment levels. Further liberalization of trade and investment will inevitably create additional stresses on inefficient SOEs.
- *Corruption*. Government corruption is epidemic. Corruption is a way of life in the gray economy, or informal sector of the economy. Bribes often supplement the incomes of those wielding power. Corruption creates an unfair playing field in business activity, discourages FDI, and robs the government of tax revenues that might have been generated by legitimate businesses. In recent years, severe punishments, including the death penalty, have been used to deter corruption.
- *Authoritarian political system*. China's gradual movement toward economic freedom has not been accompanied by a corresponding shift toward political freedom. Currently, the CCP's monopoly on political power remains intact, as demonstrated by the harsh repression of free speech at Tiananmen Square in the spring of 1989. The unsettled question is whether an economic system striving to become more open and free can peacefully coexist with a political system bent on maintaining its monopoly on political power.

FASCISM

Fascism is a totalitarian system of government in which a single political party, typically headed by a charismatic leader, dictates the political, economic, and social beliefs of society. During the twentieth century, fascist political doctrine embraced the superiority of the state over the individual, rabid nationalism, unquestioned obedience to authority, and the use of force to gain political and military objectives. Fascist economic doctrine was based on centralized decision making within the context of private ownership. Fascist systems briefly governed Italy (1922–1943) and Germany (1933–1945) during the twentieth century, with tragic consequences for humanity. While fascism was mainly a European ism, it attracted some adherents in Latin America and Asia during the 1920s, 1930s, and 1940s. Today, fascism is relegated to the fringes of political thought, an unpleasant memory of a failed experiment in tyranny.

Fascism in Italy: 1922–1943

Fascism first took hold in Italy in the early 1920s. The architect of Italian fascism was Benito Mussolini, also called Il Duce (the leader). Mussolini appealed to Italian nationalism, and later militarism, to stamp out democratic

The Beijing Yanshan Petrochemical Company, a division of Sinopec, a major state-owned enterprise in China, 2002. © Changing China Fulbright-Hays Group Projects Abroad, 2002. Photograph by Todd Wisdom Jarvis.

sentiments and to create a totalitarian government. He also reorganized Italy's economy around the concept of the corporate state. The **corporate state,** or corporativism, brought the many components of the Italian economy under the government's control.

Mussolini methodically chipped away at the power of workers and business enterprises in Italy during the 1920s. In 1927 the Charter of Labor firmly established the fascist government at the head of the economy. Under this charter, businesses, laborers, and others were placed under the watchful eye of corporations, government agencies designed to monitor and direct business activity. Corporations were organized by industry and were designed to unify employers and employees in a common mission—to serve the state. Naturally, all of these government corporations were placed under the thumb of Il Duce and the Fascist Party. Workers immediately lost all rights, including the right to strike. Businesses also lost some freedoms, but, working in partnership with the government, were guaranteed profits. In 1939 Italy's national legislature, the Chamber of Deputies, was even replaced by a Chamber of Fasci and Corporations. From 1927 to the collapse of the Italian fascist regime during World War II, the corporate state emphasized the interests of the state over the welfare of the individual.

Fascism in Germany: 1933–1945

Fascists controlled Germany from 1933 to the close of World War II in 1945. Under the direction of Adolf Hitler, the self-proclaimed Führer (leader) of the National Socialist German Workers' Party (Nazi Party), the fascists quickly and violently crushed opposition groups within the country. This created a Nazi stranglehold on all aspects of German life, including economic activity.

Hitler ruthlessly usurped power in Germany during the mid-1930s. Germany's Charter of Labor, which was enacted in 1934, adapted the Italian corporate state model. It wrested economic decision making power from the private sector and placed it squarely in the hands of the federal bureaucracy. For instance, the highly centralized German corporate state not only prevented union activity and strikes, but also dictated where people worked and how they spent their leisure time. The German version of the corporate state was influenced by intense nationalism and militarism. Its nationalist war economy during the 1930s and 1940s favored economic self-reliance for the German nation, a policy that rejected many types of commercial contacts with other nations. Further, by the late 1930s, massive public spending on military rearmament demonstrated the government's power to dictate society's production priorities. Soon, these tools of war would be used to validate Hitler's claim that only force rules. The horrific consequences of Germany's one-party totalitarian rule during the 1930s and 1940s discredited the corporate state model during the post–World War II era.

BIOGRAPHIES: SHAPERS OF ECONOMIC THOUGHT

Beatrice and Sidney Webb: The Fabian Society

Beatrice Webb (1858–1943) and **Sidney Webb** (1859–1947) were English social reformers and among the most influential members of the socialist Fabian Society. Beatrice (Potter) Webb was born to a prosperous family and enjoyed the benefits of wealth, including contacts with leading business and political figures. Her interests turned to social work during the 1880s, which brought her face-to-face with London's wretched poverty. The misery of the poor fueled her disenchantment with capitalism. Soon she authored articles critical of the exploitation of laborers. In 1891 she published her first book, *The Co-operative Movement in Great Britain.* Sidney Webb was born to a lower-middle-class London family. He left school by age 16 to become a clerk for the City of London and by the late 1870s was employed in London's civil service. He continued his education through evening classes and extensive outside reading. By the mid-1880s he earned his law degree from London University. Known for his keen mind, Sidney was courted by the newly formed Fabian Society, which he joined in 1885. Two years later, he published the classic *Facts for Socialists,* a concise book that clearly outlined the beliefs of the Fabians. Beatrice Potter and Sidney Webb, who were introduced to one another in 1890, shared a passion for social justice. In 1892 they were married, thus beginning a half-century of combined effort to advance the Fabians' socialist agenda.

After their marriage, Beatrice and Sidney Webb collaborated on numerous projects while supporting one another's careers. Beatrice Webb was a pivotal member of the Royal Commission on the Poor Law from 1905 to 1909. Her proposals, including universal social insurance, were ahead of her time but influenced the ideas of later reformers. Sidney Webb founded the London School of Economics and Political Science in 1895 and, decades later, served as a Member of Parliament (1922–1929). The complementary relationship that developed between Beatrice and Sidney Webb resulted in a lifetime of activism on behalf of the poor and the needy. Their activism took many forms, as authors, lobbyists, and public servants. Viewed as radicals in their day, the Webbs became the conscience of society and champion of the common person. In *The Decay of Capitalist Civilization,* which they co-authored in 1923, the Webbs derided the blatant inequalities that stemmed from capitalism. They reported:

> Any poor man has a very limited freedom. To the propertyless wage-earner freedom may mean nothing more than the freedom, by dint of perpetual toil, to continue to exist on the very brink of starvation. Hence inequality in income in itself entails inequality in personal freedom.[17]

The many books authored by the Webbs also provided a philosophical foundation on which later Labour governments built Britain's welfare state.

Julius Nyerere and *Ujamaa* Socialism

Julius K. Nyerere (1922–1999) was a prominent Tanzanian educator, political leader, and idealist. He also founded the most widely recognized form of African socialism, called *ujamaa.* Nyerere was born the son of a Zanaki chief in the former British colony of Tanganyika. He earned his teaching certificate in 1945 at Makerere University in Kampala, Uganda, and a master of arts degree in the early 1950s at the University of Edinburgh, Scotland. While studying in Edinburgh, Nyerere's interest in socialism grew, as did his resolve to free his native land from foreign control. In 1952 he returned to Tanganyika, where two years later he helped found the Tanganyika African National Union (TANU), an organization he would head for more than two decades. He also provided leadership for the country in its largely peaceful transition from British colony to independent nation, a process that was completed in 1961. He was elected president of Tanganyika in 1962. Two years later, after successful negotiations unified Tanganyika and Zanzibar into the United Republic of Tanzania, Nyerere was elected the new nation's first president. As president of Tanzania from 1964 to his retirement in 1985, Nyerere remained committed to the concept of *ujamaa* socialism, a largely unsuccessful experiment in social organization.

Nyerere's vision of *ujamaa* socialism was based on traditional African communalism and a doctrine of self-reliance. In his *Arusha Declaration* (1967), Nyerere eloquently defended *ujamaa,* a term that is often translated as familyhood. He argued that cooperative enterprise would improve the quality of people's lives. He believed that communal effort, modeled on the structures of the traditional extended family, was the fairest way to share the workload and distribute society's output. Nyerere was particularly concerned about the disproportionate amount of work required of women in the countryside. To achieve his ideal society, Nyerere aggressively relocated millions of peasants from private plots to village cooperatives, often called *ujamaa* villages, during the late 1960s and early 1970s. By the mid-1970s, about 70 percent of the entire population had been uprooted, most against their will, and resettled in rural *ujamaa* villages.

The economic consequences of this forced relocation to *ujamaa* villages were disastrous. Lacking individual incentives, peasants refused to work the long hours that Nyerere proposed. In addition, the government's central planning apparatus was woefully inadequate. Poorly planned *ujamaa* villages were often located on land unsuitable for permanent agriculture. At the government's insistence, the production of cash crops such as tobacco also cut deeply into the nation's production of food staples. Not surprisingly, the state's production targets were rarely met, and the people languished in a country that remained among the poorest in the world. Even billions of dollars in foreign aid during the 1970s and 1980s, mainly from sympathetic Scandinavian nations, was insufficient to reverse the economic downturn that accompanied *ujamaa* socialism.

After Julius Nyerere stepped down from the presidency in the mid-1980s, Tanzania adopted a more capitalist approach to its economic development. Hence, for a decade prior to his death the former president witnessed the dismantling of central planning, price controls, and other features of *ujamaa* socialism. During the 1990s and early 2000s, Tanzania also instituted policies to privatize state-owned enterprises, liberalize trade and investment, and restore profit incentives in economic activity.

Karl Marx and Scientific Socialism

Karl Marx (1818–1883) was a German-born historian, economist, philosopher, and revolutionary. His father was a successful lawyer in the city of Trier, where Marx attended secondary school during the early 1830s. He entered the University of Berlin in 1936, where he studied history, law, and philosophy. In 1841 Marx earned a doctorate in philosophy from the University of Jena. It was in Berlin that Marx was introduced to the philosophy of Georg Wilhelm Hegel and to a number of radical thinkers and groups. Hegel's doctrine explained that conflict between older ideas created new ideas, a process he called the dialectic. Hence, change was born from conflict. Marx later used the same reasoning to explain the progression of human history from one stage to the next. According to Marx, all history was a history of conflict between an exploited class and an exploiter class, a process he called dialectical materialism. Marx, working in collaboration with his friend Friedrich Engels, made this interpretation of history a centerpiece of *The Communist Manifesto* (1848) and the foundation of scientific socialism.

Marx's radicalism often brought him into conflict with the authorities. During the 1840s, he contributed articles and editorials to newspapers, wrote inflammatory pamphlets, and joined secret organizations such as the Communist League. In fact, it was the Communist League that commissioned Marx and Engels to co-author the *Communist Manifesto* in the winter of 1847–1848. Marx's revolutionary activities did not go unnoticed, however. He was banished from a number of countries, including France, Belgium, and Prussia (now Germany). He, his wife Jenny, and his growing family took refuge in London, England, in 1849. While in London, Marx lived in poverty for much of the 1850s and 1860s. During this period of time, three of his six children died. His most steady employment was as a foreign correspondent for the *New York Daily Tribune,* a leading American newspaper. Engels also contributed funds to supplement his friend's income over the years.

While in London, Marx also acquired an international reputation. In the mid-1860s he assumed a leadership role in the Communist International, an organization dedicated to the advancement of communism worldwide. Meanwhile, he labored on his most important work, *Das Kapital,* or *Capital.* Volume I of *Das Kapital* was published in 1867. Hailed as the bible of the laboring classes, *Das Kapital* grew to three volumes. Volumes II and III were edited by Engels and published after Marx's death. In *Das Kapital,* Marx vigorously critiqued the brutality of capitalist production. He predicted that competition among the capitalists would result in even lower wages for workers, who had nothing to sell except their labor. He believed that intense competition would also encourage capitalists to invest in labor-saving equipment, causing massive unemployment for wage laborers as well as economic instability. He concluded that intolerable economic conditions would inevitably spark a bloody proletarian revolution to topple capitalism and create a new economic system called socialism.

At the time of Marx's death in 1883, his ideas were narrowly circulated among radical groups, mainly in Europe. During the twentieth century, however, Marxism was adapted by Lenin, Mao Zedong, and other revolutionaries, changing the course of world history.

Deng Xiaoping: Market Socialism, with Chinese Characteristics

Deng Xiaoping (1904–1997) was an important government leader and reformer in the People's Republic of China. Deng was born in Paifang Village, which is located in Sichuan Province, and was educated in local schools until age 16. In 1920 Deng was selected to participate in a work-study program in France. The goal of this program was to train Chinese youth in key industrial skills necessary for China's economic development. Deng's interests soon shifted from industrial skills to Marxist thought and labor activism, however. By 1924 Deng was an active member of the Chinese Social Youth League in Europe and the Chinese Communist Party (CCP). Deng's revolutionary fervor was stoked by additional studies in Marxist-Leninist theory while a student in the Soviet Union from 1925 to 1926. Upon his return to China in the late 1920s, Deng became absorbed in the work of the CCP. His next 20 years were devoted to wresting political power away from the opposition party, the Kuomintang. After Japan's defeat in World War II removed the external threat to China, the festering distrust between the communists and the KMT erupted into a full-scale civil war. In 1949 the communists were victorious, and Deng assumed a number of key leadership roles in the newly formed People's Republic of China.

Political turbulence during the 1950s, 1960s, and 1970s tossed the Chinese economy in irrational directions. Deng, always the pragmatist, was often caught in the whirlwind. For instance, during the mid-1950s Deng sat comfortably as the secretary-general of the CCP and a member of the ruling Politburo. A decade later, during the Great Proletarian Cultural Revolution, he was dismissed from all CCP positions and disgraced as a revisionist and an agent of creeping capitalism. For a portion of his exile from the CCP, Deng worked as a manual laborer. Even after Deng was returned to a position of authority in 1973, he was forced to deflect attacks by hard-line conservative forces, including the Gang of Four, of which Mao's wife Jiang Qing was a member.

In 1978, two years after Mao's death, Deng emerged as the most important leader in China. In that same year, Deng set a new course for China's economic development. He immediately threw his support behind the Four Modernizations, which loosened some government controls over the economy. The Four Modernizations stressed the need to upgrade industry, agriculture, science and technology, and national defense. Deng also introduced policies to restore private incentives, encourage individual initiative and entrepreneurship, and rejoin the global economy. To pacify conservative elements in government, Deng reiterated support for the Four Cardinal Principles, which included continued support for socialism, the dictatorship of the proletariat, the CCP's monopoly on power, and Maoist thought. Deng's gradualist approach to economic reform created a hybrid economy that, by the 1990s, the Chinese labeled a "socialist market economy with Chinese characteristics." Deng's chosen successor, Jiang Zemin, continued the gradualist strategy for China's economic transformation into the early 2000s, a process Deng referred to as "crossing the river by feeling the stones."

It is difficult to determine Deng's most enduring legacy. Will he be remembered for the brutal suppression of prodemocracy demonstrators at Tiananmen Square in 1989? Or will he be honored as the person who loosed the chains on the Chinese economy, creating a freer, more prosperous country?

NOTES

1. Sidney Webb and Beatrice Webb, *The Decay of Capitalist Civilization* (New York: Harcourt, Brace and Company, 1923), 17–18.
2. Ladan Mahboobi and Ayse Bertrand, "Recent Privatization Trends, Table 1. Country Breakdown of Global Amount Raised from Privatization," *Financial Market Trends* 79 (June 2001): 44.
3. Karl Marx and Friedrich Engels, *The Communist Manifesto* (New York: Washington Square Press, 1964), 57.

4. Mao Zedong, *Quotations from Chairman Mao Tse-tung* (New York: Bantam Books, 1967), 48.

5. The World Bank, "Table 1.3. Private Sector Growth, 1990s," in *Transition: The First Ten Years: Analysis and Lessons for Eastern Europe and the Former Soviet Union* (Washington, DC: The World Bank, 2002), 6.

6. Igor Artemiev and Michael Haney, *The Privatization of the Russian Coal Industry: Policies and Process in the Transformation of a Major Industry,* The Policy Research Working Papers Series (The World Bank Group, April 2002), 1–2, 14, 23–24.

7. International Monetary Fund (IMF), "Table 7. Countries in Transition: Real GDP" and "Table 13. Countries in Transition: Consumer Prices," *World Economic Outlook, April 2003* (Washington, DC: IMF Publications, 2003), 181, 189.

8. IMF, "Table 13. Countries in Transition: Consumer Prices," *World Economic Outlook, May 2000* (Washington, DC: IMF Publications, 2000), 215.

9. The World Bank, "Table 5. Main Macroeconomic Indicators," *Russian Economic Report* 6 (August 2003): 20.

10. The World Bank, "What Can Transition Economies Learn from the First Ten Years? A New World Bank Report," *Transition Newsletter* 13 (January-February 2002): 14. Available at www.worldbank.org/transitionnewsletter.

11. The World Bank, "Table 5. Main Macroeconomic Indicators," 20.

12. International Labour Organization (ILO), "Development of Township and Village Enterprises," in *China: Promoting Safety and Health in Township and Village Enterprises* (Bangkok, Thailand: ILO Regional Office for Asia and the Pacific, 1998), 6–8; Richard Hirschler, "China's Experience with Transition: What Is Behind Its Stunning Success?" *Transition Newsletter* 13(May-June 2002): 5–7 (www.worldbank.org/transitionnewsletter); and Embassy of the People's Republic of China in the United Kingdom, "The Development of China's Agriculture," www.chinese-embassy.org.uk/eng/14053.html.

13. Shanghai Stock Exchange, *Shanghai Stock Exchange* (Shanghai/Pudong, China: Author, 2002), 4, 10, 14–15.

14. Hirschler, "China's Experience with Transition," 7.

15. National Bureau of Statistics, People's Republic of China, "Statistical Communique of the People's Republic of China on the 2000 National Economic and Social Development,"www.stats.gov.cn/english/newsrelease/statisticalreports/200203290018.htm.

16. World Trade Organization (WTO), "Appendix Table 1A.1. Leading Exporters and Importers in World Merchandise Trade, 2002" and "Appendix Table 1A.3. Leading Exporters and Importers in World Trade in Commercial Services, 2002," in *World Trade Report 2003* (Geneva, Switzerland: WTO Publications, 2003), 68, 70.

17. Webb and Webb, *The Decay of Capitalist Civilization,* 55.

SELECTED READINGS

Aslund, Anders. *Building Capitalism: The Transformation of the Former Soviet Bloc.* New York: Cambridge University Press, 2001.

Busky, Donald. *From Utopian Socialism to the Rise and Fall of the Soviet Union: Communism in History and Theory.* Westport, CT: Praeger, 2002.

Dawson, Doyne. *Cities of the Gods: Communistic Utopias in Greek Thought.* New York: Oxford University Press, 1997.

Ebenstein, William, Edwin Fogelman, and Alan O. Ebenstein. *Today's ISMS: Socialism, Capitalism, Fascism, Communism, and Libertarianism.* 11th ed. Paramus, NJ: Prentice Hall, 1999.

Fitzpatrick, Tony. *After the New Social Democracy: Social Welfare for the 21st Century.* Manchester, UK: Manchester University Press, 2003.

Harrison, J. F. C. *Robert Owen and the Owenites in Britain and America: The Quest for the New Moral World.* Brookfield, VT: Ashgate Publishing Company, 1993.

Hoffman, David E. *The New Oligarchs: Wealth and Power in the New Russia.* Oxford, UK: Public Affairs, Ltd., 2002.

International Monetary Fund, ed. *World Economic Outlook, October 2000: Focus on Transition Economies.* Washington, DC: IMF Publications, 2001.

Lenin, Vladimir I. *Essential Works of Lenin: "What Is to Be Done?" and Other Writings*, ed. Henry M. Christman. Mineola, NY: Dover, 1987.

Mao Zedong. *Quotations from Chairman Mao Tse-tung.* New York: Bantam Books, 1967.

Marti, Michael E. *China and the Legacy of Deng Xiaoping: From Communist Revolution to Capitalist Evolution.* Dulles, VA: Brasseys, Inc., 2002.

Marx, Karl, and Friedrich Engels. *The Communist Manifesto.* New York: Washington Square Press, 1964.

Marx, Karl. *Das Kapital: A Critique of Political Economy,* ed. Friedrich Engels. San Francisco: Regnery Publishing, Inc., 1996.

Misra, Kalpana. *From Post-Maoism to Post-Marxism: The Erosion of Official Ideology in Deng's China.* New York: Routledge, 1998.

Mosse, George L. *The Fascist Revolution: Toward a General Theory of Fascism.* New York: Howard Fertig, 2000.

Muravchik, Joshua. *Heaven on Earth: The Rise and Fall of Socialism.* San Francisco: Encounter Books, 2002.

Nyerere, Julius Kambarage. *Freedom and Development.* New York: Oxford University Press, 1985.

Owen, Robert. *A New View of Society, 1816,* ed. Jeffrey Stern. New York: Thoemmes Press, 1996.

Pendergast, Sara, and Tom Pendergast, eds. *Worldmark Encyclopedia of National Economies.* Vols. 1–4. Farmington Hills, MI: Gale Group, 2002.

Pierson, Paul, ed. *The New Politics of the Welfare State.* New York: Oxford University Press, 2001.

Pipes, Richard. *Communism: A History*. New York: Modern Library, 2001.

Radice, Lisanne. *Beatrice and Sydney Webb: Fabian Socialists.* New York: St. Martin's Press, 1984.

Ryner, J. Magnus. *Capitalist Restructuring, Globalization and the Third Way: Lessons from the Swedish Model.* New York: Routledge, 2002.

Service, Robert. *Lenin: A Biography.* Cambridge, MA: Belknap Press, 2002.

Wang Mengkui, ed. *China's Economic Transformation over 20 Years.* Beijing, China: Foreign Languages Press, 2000.

Webb, Sidney, and Beatrice Webb. *The Decay of Capitalist Civilization.* New York: Harcourt, Brace and Company, 1923.

CHAPTER 5

Business Firms: The Basic Production Unit

Chapter 5 explores the structure and operation of business firms in the U.S. economy. The firm is the basic production unit in an economy. As such, firms produce the great majority of all goods and services used by individuals, other firms, and government. Firms operate within three broad economic sectors: the services-producing sector, the goods-producing sector, and the agricultural sector. The three main types of firms are sole proprietorships, partnerships, and corporations. Several other forms of business organization also contribute to economic activity, including limited liability companies, joint ventures, producer cooperatives, and nonprofit organizations. Firms compete for customers' dollar votes in different types of competitive environments, or market structures. The four types of market structure are perfect competition, monopolistic competition, oligopoly, and monopoly. Over time, some industries have consolidated through mergers and acquisitions. The government has kept a watchful eye on business consolidations over the past century. Antitrust legislation has been enacted to protect competitive markets in the U.S. economy.

PRODUCTION: FIRMS MOBILIZE THE FACTORS OF PRODUCTION

A **firm** is a business entity that produces a good or service. Firms are often called businesses, or business firms. Firms use the four factors of production—natural resources, human resources, capital resources, and entrepreneurship—to produce outputs. Outputs are typically categorized by the degree of processing that has gone into the product. For example, the output of a logging firm is cut trees. Economists view unprocessed trees as raw materials. The output of a sawmill is board lumber, a semi-finished or intermediate good. The output of a furniture manufacturer might be wooden tables and chairs, a final good. A firm usually produces one type of good or service. For example, General Motors produces motor vehicles; Nike produces athletic wear; and Merrill Lynch produces financial services. An **industry** represents all of the firms that produce a similar product. For example, in the early 2000s General Mills, Kellogg, Kraft Foods, and Quaker Oats were the four largest firms in the breakfast cereal industry. The Small Business Administration (SBA) reported that there were 22.9 million firms operating in the U.S. economy in 2002.

The Role of Management

Management is a process that coordinates the use of resources to achieve an organization's goals. Management is crucial to attaining production efficiency in all types of business firms and in other organizations such as government agencies and private charities. The four main functions of management are

- Planning—determining the goals and direction for an organization
- Organizing—arranging resources to achieve the organization's plan
- Implementing—using resources to produce a good or service
- Controlling—assessing the results of the production process

Effective business management is based on the decisions of a firm's manager or managers. In a smaller firm, such as a sole proprietorship, the owner is usually the lone manager. Hence, this manager is responsible for planning, organizing, implementing, and controlling production. In larger corporations, however, several layers of managers attend to business operations. Senior managers often collaborate with the corporation's board of directors to formulate the company's goals. They also make most of the day-to-day production decisions related to the four management functions. Senior management is composed of the chief executive officer (CEO), the chief financial officer (CFO), the company's president and vice presidents, and other top executives. Middle managers represent a management level beneath the senior managers in the corporate hierarchy. Middle managers tend to have more specialized responsibilities within the corporation. They also implement policies devised by senior management. Supervisors occupy the final tier of management. Supervisors are an important link between upper management and the workers. They instruct, evaluate, and motivate employees. An effective management team is based on clear communication and respect (see the biographies of Frederick W. Taylor and Peter F. Drucker for more on management).

Large Firms and Small Firms

There are many ways to classify firms. One of the most common is by number of employees. A small firm, usually called a **small business,** employs fewer than 500 workers. In 2002, 22.9 million firms operated in the U.S. economy, 99.7 percent of which were classified as small businesses. By the early 2000s, small businesses accounted for about half of all private-sector jobs and produced about half of all private-sector output. In addition, between two-thirds and three-quarters of all new jobs in the U.S. economy were created by small businesses. The 17,000 large firms, with 500 or more employees, comprised less than 1 percent of all firms in the U.S. economy. Yet, this tiny percentage of U.S. firms accounted for the remaining half of all private-sector jobs and output in the economy.[1] In addition, major U.S. firms were dominant players in the global economy. Ranked by total revenues, 35 of the top 100 firms in the world were American-based enterprises in 2002. Most of the other top 100 corporations were also headquartered in the highly industrialized nations of the global north, including Japan (20 ranked corporations), Germany (13), France (10), and the United Kingdom (7). The largest U.S. corporations in 2003 are shown in Table 5.1.[2] (See chapters 11 and 12 for more on multinational corporations and foreign direct investment.)

Economic Sectors

Firms are also grouped by economic sector. All economies have three economic sectors, which divides a country's output into the main areas of production—services-producing, goods-producing, and agricultural. The **services-producing sector** consists of firms that supply productive activities in the economy in areas such as transportation and communications, wholesale and retail trade, and finance and insurance, and a wide variety of services related to business operations, health care, social welfare, and so on. Government services at the federal, state, and local levels are also included in the services-producing sector. In the highly developed countries, most jobs and national output stem

Table 5.1
Top 10 U.S. Corporations: 2003

Rank	Corporation	Headquarters	Total Revenues ($ billions)
1	Wal-Mart Stores	Bentonville, Arkansas	$259
2	Exxon Mobil	Irving, Texas	$213
3	General Motors	Detroit, Michigan	$196
4	Ford Motor	Dearborn, Michigan	$164
5	General Electric	Fairfield, Connecticut	$132
6	ChevronTexaco	San Ramon, California	$113
7	ConocoPhillips	Houston, Texas	$99
8	Citigroup	New York, New York	$95
9	International Business Machines	Armonk, New York	$89
10	American International Group	New York, New York	$81

Source: "Fortune 500 Largest U.S. Corporations," *Fortune*, April 5, 2004, F–1 from the services-producing sector. For example, in 2003 the services-producing sector accounted for 108 million jobs in the United States, 78 percent of all jobs in the economy. At the same time, about 77 percent of all national output was services related.[3] Services constitute a far smaller segment of national output in the less-developed countries, such as Albania (21%), Burundi (30%), Central African Republic (25%), and the Lao People's Democratic Republic (25%).[4]

The **goods-producing sector** consists of firms that supply tangible items such as final goods, intermediate goods, and resources. The three main components of the goods-producing sector are manufacturing, construction, and mining. In a highly developed industrialized country like the United States, the goods-producing sector is capital-intensive. That is, production is heavily reliant on the use of sophisticated capital goods, a factor that dramatically increases the productivity of labor. In 2003 firms in the goods-producing sector of the U.S. economy employed 28 million workers, or 20 percent of employed workers in the civilian labor force. In the early 2000s, the goods-producing sector produced roughly 20 percent of the total national output.[5] In developing countries, the goods-producing sector is mainly labor-intensive, a method of production that relies on physical labor rather than real capital. The lack of capital goods helps explain why national output and the productivity of labor are relatively low in the poorer regions of the world.

Robotics illustrates capital-intensive production at a U.S. Chevrolet plant, 1999. © General Motors PhotoStore.

The **agricultural sector** of an economy is composed mainly of farms, dairies, poultry and livestock farms, forestry, and the fishing and shellfish industries. In most highly industrialized countries, production in the agricultural sector is high mechanized and efficient. Hence, most developed countries employ only a small percentage of their workforce in agriculture to achieve food self-sufficiency. In 2003 only 2.6 million workers were employed in the agricultural sector of the U.S. economy, and during the early 2000s the agricultural sector accounted for less than 2 percent of the national output.[6] Still, high productivity in the agricultural sector not only enabled U.S. firms to feed a domestic population of over 290 million people, but also permitted firms to export massive agricultural surpluses to other world regions. The situation is quite different in the developing world, however. Productivity in the labor-intensive agricultural sector of many developing countries is relatively low. As a consequence, more than half of the labor force in some developing countries is still employed in agriculture, and national output is skewed to the production of basic foodstuffs or unstable cash crops.

Business Profits and Business Losses

Most firms in a market economy produce products in order to earn profits. In fact, economists typically make the assumption that all firms in competitive markets are profit maximizers. That is, firms make business decisions based on anticipated profits. A firm earns a profit when its total revenues are greater than its total costs. The **costs of production** are the payments made by firms in exchange for the factors of production (see the circular flow model in Chapter 3 for more on factor-market exchanges). There are four main costs of production. For the typical firm, the largest cost of production is wages and salaries, which are exchanged for workers' labor. Other costs of production include rents, in exchange for natural resources; interest, in exchange for the money borrowed to purchase capital goods; and profits, in exchange for the risk-taking and innovation of entrepreneurs.

Firms divide their costs into two main categories, fixed costs and variable costs. **Fixed costs** (FC) are business costs that do not change when the firm's rate of output changes. That is, whether a firm produces 10 items or 100 items per day has no impact on its FC. Typical fixed costs include monthly rents on property, long-term leases on plant or equipment, insurance premiums on a facility, local property taxes, and interest payments to creditors. **Variable costs** (VC) are business costs that increase when production rises and decrease when production falls. The two most significant VC are wages or salaries and payments for raw materials and intermediate goods. When the firm's rate of output climbs, more workers and materials are needed in production. Conversely, when the firm's rate of output falls, fewer workers and materials are required. A firm's **total cost** (TC) is the sum of all FC and VC. In a market economy, firms that are able to earn consistent profits in competitive markets survive, while firms that incur consistent losses tend to fail.

Bankruptcy is the legal recognition that a business or an individual cannot repay its debts. In the U.S. economy, a bankruptcy code identifies the requirements and procedures for declaring bankruptcy. In 2003 the Administrative Office of the U.S. Courts reported the filing of a record 1.65 million business and nonbusiness bankruptcy cases for the 12-month period between July 1, 2002, and June 30, 2003. Of this figure, just 37,182, about 2 percent of the total, were filings for business bankruptcies. The remaining 98 percent of filings were for personal bankruptcies.[7]

Many firms opt to file under Chapter 11 of the bankruptcy code. Under Chapter 11, a firm is protected from its creditors, in some cases for years, while it restructures its operations. The goal of a Chapter 11 filing is to give the firm time to return to profitability and to make good on some or all of its past debts. The firm's creditors, in the meantime, are able to ask the courts to monitor the firm's business activities or investigate mismanagement or wrongdoing. In December 2001 Texas-based Enron filed for bankruptcy protection under Chapter 11. This was the largest Chapter 11 bankruptcy filing in U.S. history. Attention soon turned to charges of corporate fraud against Enron executives and its accounting firm. These charges centered on the nondisclosure of massive debts, insider trading, and subsequent financial hardships incurred by Enron investors and employees. The bankruptcy proceedings and the related criminal investigations of Enron executives by the Securities and Exchange Commission (SEC), the U.S. Justice Department, and other federal agencies will likely take years to complete (see chapter 6 for more on nonbusiness, or personal, bankruptcies).

FORMS OF BUSINESS ORGANIZATION

Firms produce or provide goods and services to consumers, and hence represent the supply side of a market. By the early 2000s, firms in the United States supplied about $20 trillion worth of products to households, other firms, and the government. Ranked by total sales or receipts the top six sectors in the American economy were wholesale trade ($4.4 trillion in receipts), manufacturing ($3.8 trillion), retail sales ($3.2 trillion), finance and insurance ($2.6 trillion), health care and social assistance ($1.2 trillion), and construction ($1.1 trillion). In addition, business firms pumped over $4 trillion in wages and salaries into workers' pockets.[8] The three main forms of business organization are sole proprietorships, partnerships, and corporations.

Sole Proprietorships

A **sole proprietorship** is a firm that is owned by one person, the proprietor. In some instances, the proprietor is the only paid worker employed in the business. In other cases, the proprietor hires employees to help run the business. Sole proprietorships are the most numerous form of business organization in the U.S. economy, totaling 15.1 million, nearly three-quarters of all firms. Sole proprietorships accounted for just 4.7 percent of all business receipts, however.[9]

Proprietors often operate businesses such as small retail shops, restaurants, auto service stations, and personal care services.

There are a number of advantages and disadvantages of running a sole proprietorship. One advantage is the ease of forming and dissolving the firm. While a proprietor must abide by local zoning regulations, obtain necessary permits or licenses, and comply with health and safety standards, there are no significant obstacles to starting the firm. Similarly, the proprietor is able to dissolve or sell the business at his or her own discretion, without the hassle of consulting partners, stockholders, or other stakeholders in the company. Second, the proprietor is the boss. Thus, he or she is free to make all decisions necessary to the operation of the business, including production methods, hiring, inventory, and so on. As the sole decision maker, the proprietor also enjoys psychological rewards, such as pride and prestige, associated with running a successful firm. Third, the proprietor is entitled to all profits generated by the firm. In addition, the proprietor's profits are taxed only once as personal income, thus avoiding the double taxation that plagues corporations.

There are disadvantages of sole proprietorships, however. First, the sole proprietor's decision making is the least expert of any form of business organization. This is because the proprietor is personally responsible for a myriad of business decisions connected with the production and distribution of the firm's output. Second, proprietors must accept unlimited liability for all business debts. This means that the personal assets of the proprietor, and his or her spouse, could be tapped to pay debts incurred by the firm. Third, credit is often difficult to come by for proprietorships. Financial institutions view proprietorships as less creditworthy than other forms of business organization because business operations rely on the good judgment, skills, and good health of a single individual—the proprietor. Proprietorships also lack sufficient collateral to guarantee the safety of borrowed money should the business go bust. Proprietors are often obliged to dip into personal savings or tap into the resources of family or friends to finance business start-up costs.

Partnerships

A **partnership** is a firm that is owned by two or more people, called partners, each of whom has a financial interest in the company. Like sole proprietorships, most partnerships are small businesses. The two main types of partnerships are general partnerships and limited partnerships. In a general partnership, the partners operate the business together, sharing decision making and other responsibilities. In a limited partnership, one or more of the partners run the business while other partners simply invest money in the firm—mainly to finance start-up costs. The partners who invest money but do not get involved in the day-to-day operation of the business are called silent partners. There are fewer partnerships in the U.S. economy than any other type of business organization. The 1.2 million partnerships in the United States accounted for 5.9 percent of all firms and 3.4 percent of all business receipts.[10] Partnerships are common in the professions, such as law, medicine, and engineering, and in the skilled trades, such as construction and home repair services.

The advantages of operating a partnership are similar to those of a sole proprietorship. First, partnerships are fairly easy to organize. Like sole proprietorships, partnerships must comply with local regulations regarding zoning, licensing, and so on. In addition, partners should draft a partnership contract to specify the roles and responsibilities of each partner in running the firm, how profits are to be distributed, and how to dissolve the firm should one or more partners want to exit it. Second, decision making in partnerships is more specialized and, therefore, more expert than in sole proprietorships. Third, general partners are also able to improve the quality of services by consulting with one another and doing internal evaluations of colleagues' performance. Fourth, partners connected with the day-to-day operation of the business enjoy the psychological rewards of business success. Fifth, partners share business profits according to the terms of the partnership contract. For the general partners, profits directly connect success in the workplace with financial gain, a significant incentive to work up to potential. For silent partners, profits ensure a payoff as prescribed in the partnership contract. These profits might take the form of interest payments, lump sum payments, a percentage of the firm's profits, or other compensation. Sixth, like a proprietor's profits, the profits of partners are taxed just once as personal income.

There are also disadvantages of partnerships. First, decision making among two or more general partners is sometimes a source of conflict. Even with a clearly defined process for making decisions, conflicts can be time-consuming, costly, and demoralizing. Second, general partners must accept unlimited liability for business losses, obligations, or debts incurred by any of the partners. Thus, a poor business decision, an expensive legal suit, a product recall, or other financial disaster can sap the personal assets of all general partners. Silent partners, however, have limited liability, and, thus, their financial loss is limited to the amount of money invested in the partnership. Third, access to credit is often limited. Like sole proprietorships, partnerships generally rely on the talents and health of a few people. In addition, partnerships often lack the collateral to back large loans from banks. Thus, partnerships lack access to the types of financial capital that are more readily available to larger, more stable corporations.

Corporations

A **corporation** is a firm that is a legal entity in itself. A corporation is able to conduct business in its own name in much the same way that an individual does. As a legal entity, the corporation's ownership is separate and distinct from the operation of the firm. The owners of a corporation are its shareholders, who purchase certificates of ownership called shares or **stocks.** Shareholders, in turn, elect a board of directors to make important policies and set goals. The board of directors also hires professional managers to conduct the day-to-day operations of the firm. Officers usually include a chief executive officer (CEO), a chief financial officer (CFO), a president, vice presidents, and others who may be deemed necessary by the board of directors. There are 4.4 million corporations operating in the U.S. economy, about 21 percent of all business firms. Corporations generated $16.9 trillion in business receipts, about 91 percent of the national total.[11] Thus, measured by level of business activity, corporations are the dominant form of business organization in the U.S. economy. Corporations exist in all three sectors of the economy: services-producing, which includes retail and wholesale trade, banking and financial services, communications and transportation; goods-producing, which includes manufacturing, construction, and mining; and agriculture, which includes food crops, forestry, and fishing. Most well-known corporations are public corporations, in which stock is widely traded on a stock exchange. Closed corporations, on the other hand, restrict stock ownership to a small group, perhaps family members or company employees. Examples of closed corporations, also called private companies, are Koch Industries, Mars, Enterprise Rent-a-Car, Levi Strauss, and Hallmark Cards.

There are several advantages to the corporate business structure. First, the owners, or shareholders, enjoy limited liability. Thus, the maximum amount of money shareholders could lose is the amount invested in the corporation. Second, corporations have the most expert management of any type of business organization. The professional management of most corporations is highly educated and highly specialized. Third, corporations are the most stable form of business organization. This stability is derived from the ease in which ownership is transferred from one shareholder to another. Hence, frequent changes in ownership do not interrupt business activity within the corporation. Fourth, corporations have the greatest capacity to raise financial capital for business investment. This is because corporations are the only form of business organization that can raise money by issuing bonds and stocks. Corporate bonds represent debt, a type of IOU to investors. Investors expect to earn annual interest payments on this IOU until the bond matures, at which time the final interest payment and the entire principal is repaid to the investor. Corporate stocks are issued through an initial public offering (IPO). Corporate stocks represent ownership, called equity in the firm. Investors expect to earn regular dividends from their investment in stocks and, over time, expect the value of the stock to appreciate. Investors earn capital gains when a stock is sold for more than its purchase price, but incur capital losses when the stock's selling price is lower than its original purchase price (see chapter 8 for more on trading stocks).

Disadvantages of corporations also exist. First, there is a sharp division between those who own the corporation and those who are involved in its business operations. There is potential for conflict between the owners, who want a fair return on their investment, and management, which is concerned with using profits to maintain or upgrade production facilities. In addition, there is a greater potential for conflict between workers and management, as each looks to its own self-interest in the workplace. Second, specialized decision making is sometimes a time-consuming and complex process as proposals, changes in policies, and so on pass through layers of management. Third, corporations are the most difficult type of business to form. A corporation must form a board of directors, draft its articles of incorporation, adhere to strict guidelines in the issuance of stock, and so on. The rules and regulations for forming corporations vary from state to state, but most follow the provisions outlined in the Model Business Corporation Act. Fourth, corporations are subject to a double taxation of corporate profits. Corporate profits are first subject to the corporate income tax, a progressive tax on corporate profits. The same money is taxed a second time by the federal income tax when profits are distributed to shareholders in the form of dividends. The Jobs and Growth Tax Relief Reconciliation Act of 2003 tempered this disadvantaged by reducing the maximum tax rate on dividend income from 38.6 percent to 15 percent and also reducing the maximum tax rate on capital gains from 20 percent to 15 percent.

The two main types of corporations are C-corporations and S-corporations. Both types are required to file their articles of incorporation with a state government, select a board of directors, obtain all necessary licenses, and pay required fees as a condition to selling shares of stock and conducting business. The most important difference between the two types of corporations is in the payment of taxes. Profits earned by a C-corporation are subject to double taxation. S-corporations, however, have a special tax status, which allows corporate profits to be ushered through the corporation and reported directly as income for shareholders. Under this arrangement with the Internal Revenue Service (IRS), shareholders in S-corporations pay taxes on corporate profits just once through the personal income tax. There are several other distinctions between C-corporations and S-corporations. For instance, S-corporations are limited to 75 shareholders, all of whom must be U.S. citizens or residents. C-corporations can be organized with as few as one shareholder, and shareholders can be of any nationality. Most corporations are organized as C-corporations, as shown in Table 5.2.[12]

Many major corporations expand production and sales through franchising. A **franchise** is a business consisting of a parent company, called a franchiser, and satellite firms called franchisees. A franchise contract defines the business re-

Table 5.2
Forms of Business Organization: 1997

Business Organization	Number of Firms	Percent of Firms	Total Receipts ($ billions)	Percent of Receipts
Sole proprietorship	15,123	72.6%	$872	4.7%
Partnership	1,226	5.9%	$622	3.4%
C-corporation	2,390	11.5%	$13,892	74.9%
S-corporation	1,979	9.5%	$2,977	16.0%
Other*	103	0.5%	$190	1.0%
All firms	20,821	100%	$18,553	100%

*Other includes cooperatives, estates, and receiverships.
Source: U.S. Census Bureau, *1997 Economic Census.*

lationship between franchiser and franchisee. For example, a franchise contract typically outlines the franchiser's responsibilities in training local managers and employees, connecting its franchisees with suppliers or distributors, and arranging for credit or other financial assistance to defray start-up costs. Also listed in the contract are the franchisee's responsibilities, which often include assurances of quality standards and financial remuneration to the parent company for the use of its brand name and other assistance. Entrepreneurs who become franchisees enjoy many of the psychological and monetary rewards of sole proprietors, but operate under the guidance and supervision of a parent company.

Franchise start-up costs vary widely. Some of the more expensive franchise start-ups are hotels, such as Days Inns, which range from $407,000 to $5.4 million. Some fast-food franchises are also expensive to start, including McDonald's, $490,000 to $1.5 million, and Kentucky Fried Chicken, $1.1 to $1.7 million. There are usually lower average start-up costs for service franchises in fields such as fitness (Curves, Jazzercise), commercial cleaning (Jani-King, CleanNet USA), and real estate (RE/MAX, Century 21, Coldwell Banker). Table 5.3 shows the top 10 franchises in 2003.[13]

Table 5.3
Top 10 Franchises: 2003

Rank	Franchise Name	Product Line	Start-up Costs ($ thousands)
1	Subway	Submarine sandwiches	$86–$213
2	Curves	Fitness and weight loss	$31–$36
3	7-Eleven	Convenience store	Varies
4	McDonald's	Hamburgers, etc.	$490–$1,500
5	Jani-King	Commercial cleaning	$11–$34
6	Taco Bell	Mexican food	$3,000
7	Quizno's	Sandwiches and soups	$208–$244
8	Super 8 Motels	Economy lodging	$291–$2,300
9	Jackson Hewett	Tax preparation	$47-$75
10	Sonic	Drive-in restaurants	$621–$1,200

Source: Entrepreneur.com, *Entrepreneur's 24th Annual Franchise 500.*

OTHER FORMS OF BUSINESS ORGANIZATION

Some businesses do not fit neatly under the traditional headings of sole proprietorships, partnerships, or corporations. Several of the most important alternative forms of business organization include limited liability companies, joint ventures, producer cooperatives, and nonprofit organizations.

Limited Liability Companies

A **limited liability company** (LLC) is a hybrid business organization that combines features from corporations, partnerships, and sole proprietorships.

Like a corporation, an LLC registers with the state by filing articles of organization. Filing this document is relatively easy, as most states supply a fill-in-the-blank form to simplify the task. These articles identify the owner or owners of the LLC, the location of the firm's headquarters, and the name of the business. Many LLCs also create an operating agreement, which outlines the decision-making process, profit distribution, and a dissolution procedure. The limited liability for LLC members, or owners, also resembles that of corporate shareholders. That is, the LLC is responsible for business debts, legal suits, or other liabilities or claims against the business, while the owner's personal assets are protected. Also, because the LLC is not considered a legal entity in itself for tax purposes, business profits are taxed just once as personal income of the owner.

Joint Ventures

A **joint venture** is a short-term business agreement between two or more companies to produce or sell a good or service. Any form of business organization—sole proprietorships, partnerships, or corporations—can enter into a joint venture. In a joint venture, each company is expected to contribute certain physical or financial assets and expertise to the business relationship. Each firm also expects to earn profits from this temporary alliance. In many cases, a joint venture is formed between a foreign firm and a domestic firm for mutual benefit. The foreign firm benefits by gaining access to new markets. The domestic firm benefits by gaining access to new technologies, management techniques, or innovative production techniques. Examples of joint ventures abound. United Technologies (U.S.) teamed with South Korean and Chinese firms to produce elevators, with Japanese firms to produce air conditioning systems, and with Russian firms to produce aircraft and rocket engines. Since the 1990s, numerous joint ventures have also been negotiated between Chinese auto manufacturers and foreign firms including Volkswagen (Germany), General Motors (U.S.), Peugeot (France), and Suzuki (Japan).

Producer Cooperatives

A **producer cooperative** is a business that is owned and operated by the employees or members of the firm. That is, the workers own the shares of the cooperative much like stockholders own shares of a corporation. Members also have limited liability for debts incurred by the co-op. Many producer co-ops are formed to ensure steady employment for workers or to provide essential services to members, rather than to earn profits. Producer cooperatives are typically classified by the size of the area they serve: local, regional, national, or international co-ops.

Producer co-ops exist in many industries in the U.S. economy. For example, in the financial services sector, credit unions are a type of financial co-op that allows members to deposit and borrow money and write checks (called share drafts) on favorable terms. In the agricultural sector, farmer-owned co-ops provide members with a wide variety of services to minimize business costs or increase business receipts. Farmer-owned co-ops purchase farm supplies and equipment. They also market and transport agricultural output to regional markets or processors. Farmer-owned co-ops provide members with low-cost services that might not otherwise be available at a reasonable cost, including electrical and telephone service, insurance and health care, and credit. The U.S. Department of Agriculture reported that the net business volume for 3,229 farmer-owned cooperatives in the United States climbed to $103 billion in 2001. Net business volume measures the receipts from the sale of crops, livestock, production supplies, and services provided by farmer co-ops.[14] (See chapter 6 for more on consumer cooperatives.)

Nonprofit Organizations

A **nonprofit organization** exists to provide goods or services to people, but not to earn profits for shareholders, employees, or other stakeholders. Nonprofit organizations raise money to finance production mainly by soliciting contributions from individuals, firms, or the government. These funds, in turn, are used to support a variety of charitable, humanitarian, educational, scientific, or community programs and services. There are more than 850,000 nonprofit organizations operating in the United States. Many are organized as nonprofit corporations, also called nonstock corporations. Others are organized as unincorporated associations, partnerships, and foundations. Individual states determine many of the conditions under which nonprofit organizations operate. Some states, for example, exempt nonprofit organizations from local and state taxes, and limit their liability in legal cases brought against them. States also set standards for fundraising and may require a variety of permits and licenses. Many nonprofit organizations are household names, such as the Red Cross, the Boy Scouts and Girl Scouts of America, Veterans of Foreign Wars, the Sierra Club Foundation, the American Civil Liberties Union, and the United Way.

TYPES OF MARKET STRUCTURE

U.S. business firms operate within different competitive environments, or market structures. **Market structure** refers to the way industries are organized. The four types of market structure are perfect competition, monopolistic competition, oligopoly, and monopoly. Market structures are compared and contrasted by number of firms, type of product, ease of entry or exit, amount of market power, and level of government intervention.

Perfect Competition

Perfect competition is a type of market structure in which thousands of firms, operating independently, produce an identical (homogeneous) product. Firms are able to enter or exit perfectly competitive industries easily because there are few, if any, **barriers to entry**—factors that discourage or prevent firms from joining or leaving an industry. Perfectly competitive firms have no market power. That is, these firms have no control over the price they charge for their output. Instead, they are obliged to accept the market price for the identical product they produce. In fact, economists call competitive firms "price takers" to emphasize that the forces of supply and demand in the entire market, rather than the pricing decisions of individual firms, determine the price of output. Finally, the role of government in perfectly competitive industries is small, mainly because there is no danger of firms conspiring to raise prices, restrict output, or otherwise engage in anticompetitive practices. In the U.S. economy, perfect competition is best illustrated by business activity in certain agricultural industries, such as wheat and corn, where thousands of firms produce identical products for sale in domestic and international markets.

Monopolistic Competition

Monopolistic competition is a type of market structure in which many firms, perhaps 25, 50, or even 100 or more, produce differentiated products—goods that are similar but not identical. It is relatively easy for firms to enter or exit monopolistically competitive industries due to low barriers to entry. The economic rivalry among competing firms is often intense. Advertising, often confined to local markets, is used to accent the differences between competitors' products, to create customer loyalty, and persuade people to buy certain goods. Brand loyalties give monopolistically competitive firms a small amount of market power, which helps explain the slight differences in the prices of producers' output. Firms' pricing decisions are heavily influenced by the availability of substitute goods, however, preventing competitors from raising prices beyond a narrow range. Because of the high level of competition in monopolistically competitive industries, little government intervention is necessary. In the U.S. economy, the fast-food industry operates within a monopolistically competitive market structure. This industry is characterized by many specialized fast-food restaurants, which produce pizza, hamburgers, submarine sandwiches, tacos, fried chicken, and so on (see the biography of Joan V. Robinson for more on imperfect competition).

Oligopoly

Oligopoly is a type of market structure in which several firms, perhaps 3, 6, or 12, dominate production in the industry. Today, many economists define an oligopoly as any industry in which the four top firms control at least 40 percent of the industry's total output. There are two forms of oligopoly, differentiated and pure. Firms operating in differentiated oligopolies produce similar but not identical products. For example, General Motors, Ford Motor, and Chrysler comprise a differentiated oligopoly because they dominate domestic production of different makes and models of automobiles in the U.S. auto industry. Similarly, four firms—General Mills, Kellogg, Kraft Foods, and Quaker Oats—dominate the breakfast cereal industry. Firms operating in pure oligopolies produce a homogeneous, or identical, product. Most pure oligopolies produce industrial goods such as steel and aluminum. In the U.S. economy, for example, major steel companies include U.S. Steel, Bethlehem Steel and LTV, while in aluminum production Alcoa, Alumax, and Reynolds Metals lead the way. High barriers to entry discourage firms from entering or exiting the industry. Barriers include high costs for real capital, research, and national advertising. In addition, brand loyalties, which are stronger in oligopolies than in other types of market structure, discourage the entry of new firms into an industry. Brand loyalties increase the oligopolist's market power, giving the firm more control over pricing decisions.

Oligopolies are characterized by interdependent pricing, as competing firms necessarily respond to the price changes of rivals. In some cases, interdependent pricing takes the form of price leadership, a legal pricing strategy in which the industry's largest firm initiates a price change with the understanding that other firms in the industry will follow suit. The government monitors oligopolies to prevent illegal, anticompetitive behaviors by large oligopolists, however. For example, the government prevents **collusion,** an illegal conspiracy among competitors designed to fix prices, agree on market share, or otherwise reduce competition. Collusion is an unfair trade practice because it would permit competing firms to act as a single producer and, thus, increase their market power. Federal regulators such as the Federal Trade Commission (FTC) and the Antitrust Division of the Justice Department protect the public interest by guarding against collusion and other anticompetitive business behaviors.

Monopoly

Monopoly is a type of market structure in which one firm is the sole producer of a good or service. Today, many economists define a monopoly as a firm that controls 80 percent to 90 percent of a certain market. Entry into and exit from monopolies is very difficult due to high barriers to entry, which include the high costs of capital, patented technology, or the economies of scale. While a monopolist is the sole producer of a product, its market power is usually restricted by government regulations on product pricing, product quality, and product availability. Government regulation of monopolies is considered necessary because the monopolist's price and profits are not constrained by competing firms. The four main types of monopolies are natural, technological, government, and geographic.

- *Natural monopoly*: A **natural monopoly** exists when a single firm is able to produce a product more efficiently than could a larger number of competing firms. The natural monopolist's advantage is its ability to benefit from the **economies of scale**—the decline in average costs of production as more units of output are produced. For example, from the 1920s to the 1980s, American Telephone and Telegraph's (AT&T) natural monopoly on telephone service in the United States was justified by the economies of scale argument. Today, many state and local governments allow natural monopolies to supply local goods and services ranging from electrical power to trash collection.

- *Technological monopoly*: A **technological monopoly** exists when a firm develops a new technology that it alone can use to produce a new product or production method. New technologies are protected by patents, which grant an inventor exclusive rights to produce or use an invention for a period of time of up to 20 years. For example, for a time patents protected the technologies used in Polariod's instant photography film and in Xerox's photocopiers. The federal Patent and Trademark Office (PTO) administers patent laws in the United States. In 2002 about 350,000 patent applications were filed with the PTO. Americans also filed 45,000 patents with the World Intellectual Property Organization (WIPO) in 2002 to protect their research.[15]
- *Government monopoly*: A **government monopoly** exists when any level of government becomes the sole producer of a good or service. On the local level, towns and cities are often the sole producers of some basic services, such as water and sewerage services. Typically, these types of services would not ordinarily be supplied in sufficient quantity, or at a reasonable price, by smaller competitive firms in the private sector. The largest government monopoly at the national level is the U.S. Postal Service (USPS), which maintains its monopoly on first-class mail delivery. The USPS employs about 800,000 workers and competes with private mail delivery firms in other markets, such as overnight delivery service.
- *Geographic monopoly*: A **geographic monopoly** exists when one producer provides a good or service to a geographic region. Geographic monopolies generally appear in remote locations that, at most, can support just one supplier. For instance, a general store in a small community may be able to survive if it is the only shop providing essential goods. The opening of a second general store may drive both shops out of business due to the limited size of the market. Today, geographic monopolies are less important due to widespread use of electronic commerce over the Internet, mail-order shopping, and access to modern transportation systems.

MERGERS AND ACQUISITIONS

Business firms expand their operations in two ways. One is by building new production facilities, such as a factory, office building, or farm. A second way is through mergers and acquisitions (M&As). A **merger** occurs when two or more firms combine their assets, or equity, to form a larger firm. Typically, mergers result in a larger ownership base because investors from each formerly independent firm now share in the ownership of the new company. The merger between Exxon and Mobil to form the Exxon Mobil corporation in 1999 illustrates this process. **Acquisitions** occur when one firm buys some or all of the ownership in a second firm. In many cases, one firm can acquire a second firm by purchasing as little as 10 percent of its shares of stock. As a result, the acquiring firm wrests ownership and control from the previous owners of the acquired firm, or target company. One recent acquisition was the purchase of Pharmacia Corporation by pharmaceutical giant Pfizer in 2003, a deal that cost Pfizer $63 billion in acquisition and related fees. Today, Pfizer is the world's largest pharmaceutical company.

Reasons for Mergers and Acquisitions

The primary motive for negotiating M&As is to generate additional business profits. There are a number of ways this goal might be achieved. First, M&As can reduce production costs. Through corporate downsizing, superfluous employees are laid off, and less efficient production facilities are closed as production is consolidated in newer plants. Second, an acquiring firm's output expands immediately. M&As transfer ownership of productive facilities without interrupting the production process. In fact, M&As often diversify a firm's product line by adding recognizable brand name products to the enlarged firm's mix of output. Third, M&As provide instant access to the research and technology, patents and copyrights, and managerial expertise of the acquired firm. These technology transfers and infusion of new resources jump-start innovation and the production of new and profitable products. Fourth, M&As reduce production bottlenecks by bringing different phases of a larger production process under the control of a single management. Fifth, M&As provide access to new domestic or international markets. Cross-border M&As, for example, allow multinational corporations to build on acquired firms' business relationships, customer bases, and channels of distribution. Multinationals also circumvent existing trade barriers by producing and selling goods in their foreign production facilities (see chapter 11 for more on cross-border M&As and foreign direct investment).

Types of Corporate Combinations

There are three main types of mergers and acquisitions, each reflecting a different corporate strategy to increase the size and profitability of a firm. These types of M&As are horizontal mergers, vertical mergers, and conglomerate mergers. A **horizontal merger** combines competitors that sell similar products in the same market. The aggressive combination of oil refineries by John D. Rockefeller in the late 1800s, which resulted in the creation of the Standard Oil monopoly, illustrates this process. By consolidating the refining stage in the U.S. oil industry, Standard Oil eliminated competition in one critical phase of oil production. A **vertical merger** combines firms that produce goods or raw materials used at the different stages in the production of a final good. The combination of about 180 firms to create the U.S. Steel Corporation in 1901 was based on gaining control of production facilities at each phase in the production of steel, from the mining of iron ore to the manufacture and distribution of finished steel. A **conglomerate merger** combines unrelated firms from different industries into a single business enterprise. International Telephone and Telegraph (ITT) was the world's most recognized conglomerate during the post–World War II era. Founded as a telecommunications company in 1920, ITT combined some 350 companies under its corporate umbrella, mostly during the 1960s and 1970s. Within the ITT empire were Aetna, the Hartford Insurance Company, Avis Rent-A-Car, and Sheraton Hotels. ITT unraveled during the

1980s and 1990s, however, and the streamlined company was itself acquired by the Starwood Lodging Trust in 1998.

PROTECTING COMPETITIVE MARKETS

The rise of monopolies, trusts, and other business combinations during the late 1800s and early 1900s concentrated more wealth into the hands of fewer people. As a result, competition in mining, manufacturing, transportation, and other key industries declined. Monopolies were formed by combining firms under a single ownership through mergers and acquisitions. Trusts also arose during the period. A **trust** was an association of corporations whose stock was held by a single board of trustees. The growing power of monopolies, trusts, and other consolidations of wealth and power provided sufficient justification for government intervention by the 1890s.

Over the past century, the government has passed a series of antitrust laws to prevent business consolidations that would substantially reduce competition. In doing so, the government reaffirmed its commitment to protecting competitive markets, the wellspring of economic freedom, individual opportunity, and technological innovation in a dynamic economic system. Listed below are several key laws designed to preserve competitive markets in the United States.

- *Sherman Antitrust Act.* The Sherman Act of 1890 outlawed trusts and other business combinations that attempted to limit competition or restrain interstate commerce. Restraints on trade included price fixing by rival firms and agreements to divide market share among competing firms.

"Next!" Standard Oil's power over private businesses and the government, 1904. J. Ottmann Lith, Company. Illustration by Udo J. Keppler. © Library of Congress.

- *Clayton Antitrust Act.* The Clayton Antitrust Act of 1914 strengthened and expanded the scope of the Sherman Act by outlawing certain anticompetitive business practices such as tying agreements and interlocking directorates. A **tying agreement** stipulates that, in order to purchase one item, a buyer must also purchase other goods, usually complementary goods, exclusively from the same seller. In an **interlocking directorate,** some of the same people sit on the boards of directors of rival corporations. The act also prohibits one firm from purchasing stocks in a competing firm if the result is to reduce competition.
- *Federal Trade Commission Act.* The Federal Trade Commission Act of 1914 created the Federal Trade Commission (FTC) to enforce the Clayton Act. Later, the FTC took a leadership role in monitoring truth in advertising. The FTC is empowered to issue cease-and-desist orders to halt anticompetitive practices.
- *Robinson-Patman Act.* The Robinson-Patman Act of 1936 prevents discriminatory pricing, especially pricing schemes to benefit large buyers over smaller ones.
- *Wheeler-Lea Act.* The Wheeler-Lea Act of 1938 prohibits business deception, including false or misleading advertising. The act also created an antitrust agency within the U.S. Department of Justice, which shares responsibility for the enforcement of antitrust laws with the FTC.
- *Celler-Kefauver Antimerger Act.* The Celler-Kefauver Antimerger Act of 1950 prohibits firms from buying the assets of another firm if the result is to substantially reduce competition in an industry. This act expanded on the Clayton Act, which only prohibited a firm from buying the stocks of a rival firm.

BIOGRAPHIES: SHAPERS OF ECONOMIC THOUGHT

Frederick Winslow Taylor and Scientific Management

Frederick Winslow Taylor (1856–1915) was an American industrial engineer and consultant who, through his time-and-motion studies in the industrial workplace, became the father of scientific management. Taylor was born in Germantown, Pennsylvania, to a prosperous professional family. He earned an engineering degree at the Stevens Institute of Technology, but accepted entry-level employment in a number of industrial firms in Philadelphia. In the early 1880s, Taylor took a job as a common laborer at the Midvale Steel Company. As he rose to the position of chief engineer over the next several years, he introduced production techniques designed to reduce the inefficient use of time and resources. In 1893 Taylor launched a new career as an engineering and management consultant, helping firms such as Bethlehem Iron Company, later called Bethlehem Steel, apply his time-and-motion studies to increase industrial efficiency and profits. Taylor's theories on scientific management, soon referred to as Taylorism, gained him an international reputation. His book, *The Principles of Scientific Management* (1911), influenced management techniques for generations.

The Principles of Scientific Management is a collection of Taylor's conclusions about effective management practices. According to Taylor: "The principal object of management should be to secure the maximum prosperity for the employer, coupled with the maximum prosperity for each employé."[16] To achieve these goals, Taylor believed that capital, workers, and materials must be organized in a manner consistent with efficient production. At the heart of scientific management was the specialization of tasks. He supported a complex division of labor based on highly specialized jobs. Under Taylorism, each worker was trained for a specific job suited to the worker's abilities. He supported the use of sophisticated capital within a plant to replace the traditional rule of thumb, a method of production that often relied on the individual craftsmanship of workers and the use of nonstandard tools. Taylor also believed that workers who met production expectations, which were sometimes measured by daily production quotas, should be rewarded for their efficiency. Thus, Taylor supported higher wages for workers whose productivity was high, and lower wages for less productive workers. Finally, Taylor believed that a complementary relationship should exist among all of the factors of production. That is, the success of the firm's organizational structure depended on mutually supporting, albeit impersonal, relationships between employees, management, and the carefully arranged real capital at their disposal. In *Principles of Scientific Management,* Taylor argued:

> It is no single element, but rather this whole combination, that constitutes scientific management, which may be summarized as:
>
> Science, not rule of thumb.
> Harmony, not discord.
> Cooperation, not individualism.
> Maximum output, in place of restricted output.
> The development of each man to his greatest efficiency and prosperity.[17]

The ideas of Frederick Winslow Taylor influenced management strategies in the United States and other industrialized countries during the late nineteenth century and much of the twentieth century. Yet, opposition to scientific management developed almost immediately after Taylor applied his revolutionary thinking to the production process. Entrenched managers were reluctant to alter traditional management models. Workers were angered over the loss of jobs at the streamlined, more efficient plants. Unions, which Taylor viewed as unnecessary, were skeptical that a cooperative spirit could exist in a workplace where the pace of production was dictated by the ticks of a stopwatch. By the 1960s and 1970s, workers in many American factories balked at the dull and repetitious production routines that typified assembly-line production, and they demanded more participation in the decisions that affected working conditions. Workplace reforms over the past quarter century have significantly altered the methods of production in the U.S. economy. Yet Taylor's pioneering studies made work and job design, quality control, cost-efficiency, and productivity front-burner concerns for the modern manager.

Peter F. Drucker: The Practice of Management

Peter F. Drucker (1909–) is an American economist, consultant, and management expert whose ideas on management shaped the organizational structures of U.S. businesses, nonprofit organizations, and government agencies.

Drucker was born in Vienna, Austria, and received his first doctoral degree in public and international law from Frankfort University in Germany. Drucker's career as an educator, author, and consultant spanned more than half a century, during which he earned numerous honorary doctorates from prestigious colleges and universities in Europe, North America, and Asia. Much of his teaching career was spent as a professor of management at the Graduate Business School of New York University (1950–1971), and, since the early 1970s, as a professor of social science and management at Claremont Graduate University in California. In *The Frontiers of Management* (1986), Drucker described management as "the specific practice that converts a mob into an effective, purposeful, and productive group."[18] Drucker is often referred to as the guru of modern management.

Drucker's contributions to the field of management studies are recorded in the 30 books he has written since the 1930s. In *The Practice of Management* (1954), he introduced the theory of management by objectives (MBO), a central theme in many of his works. MBO stresses management's central role in setting organizational goals, communicating these goals and more specific performance targets to subordinates, and measuring outcomes. Under MBO, the manager is also the linchpin in motivating workers and in instilling a sense of personal responsibility for meeting performance standards.

Another recurring theme in Drucker's work is the reality of social and economic change, and the need for management to initiate dynamic, innovative responses to these inevitable changes. In *The Age of Discontinuity* (1969), for example, Drucker observed the dawn of an epic change from a manufacturing-based economy to one based on knowledge. He emphasized the need for lifelong learning to enable the knowledge worker to adapt to the new technologies of the information age. He also formulated a famous set of dos and don'ts for innovators. He advised managers to seek out and aggressively develop new opportunities, but cautioned them to avoid unwieldy investments that might do little more than open doors for rival firms. By the early 2000s, Drucker had contempt for self-serving managers whose unethical and illegal business decisions drove a number of major U.S. corporations into bankruptcy.

Drucker's productive career created the modern discipline of management, its theory and its practice. In fact, many experts in the field insist that *The Practice of Management* (1954) was the country's first management textbook. Drucker believed that the study of management was neither an art nor a science. Instead, he labeled management a practice that "feeds off" a number of related disciplines including "economics, psychology, mathematics, political theory, history, and philosophy."[19] In 1987 the Claremont Graduate University named its Graduate Management Center after Drucker, and in 2002 President George W. Bush honored him with the Presidential Medal of Freedom.

Samuel M. Walton: Entrepreneurship and Building a Business

Samuel M. Walton (1918–1992) was an American businessman, entrepreneur, and founder of the Wal-Mart Stores, Inc., the world's largest corporation.

Walton was born in the small town of Kingfish, Oklahoma, and had an ordinary childhood first in Oklahoma and later in Missouri. After graduating from the University of Missouri, Walton worked in retailing, and in 1962 he opened the first Wal-Mart store in Rogers, Arkansas. Walton's entrepreneurial vision was to create a chain of discount retail stores based on low prices, high-quality merchandise and service to customers. In the fall of 1969, Wal-Mart incorporated, and in 1970 the first shares of Wal-Mart stock were traded. Walton remained the president and chief executive officer of Wal-Mart until 1988, and he continued on as chairman of the board until his death in 1992. Under his leadership, Wal-Mart surpassed Sears as the largest retailer in the United States in 1991. In 2003, Wal-Mart Stores, Inc., was the largest corporation in the world, with sales receipts of $259 billion.

Walton combined entrepreneurial skills with effective management techniques to build the Wal-Mart discount retail empire. As an entrepreneur, Walton was an innovator and a risk-taker. Like most entrepreneurs, he was able to see a business opportunity, one based on low-margin, high-volume retailing. At about the same time, other discount retailers were also established, including K-Mart (S.S. Kresge Company) and Target (Dayton Hudson Company). Since the early 1960s, Walton strove to lower prices and honor his three basic beliefs, which promised respect, service, and excellence. Walton's management skills were another important feature in the rise of Wal-Mart. As a skillful manager, Walton was a master of planning, organizing, implementing, and controlling business operations. For example, in the mid-1960s he was among the first business leaders in the country to computerize business operations to keep track of costs, revenues, inventories, and so on. The use of early information technologies was one way Wal-Mart was able to cut production costs and maintain its competitive advantage over other discount retailers.

Walton's life was consumed with transforming a vision into a thriving business. By 2003 Wal-Mart Stores, Inc., was composed of four retail divisions in the United States: Wal-Mart Stores (1,494 stores), Wal-Mart Supercenters (1,386 stores), SAM's Clubs (532), and Wal-Mart Neighborhood Markets (56). Combined with Wal-Mart International (1,309 stores in eight foreign countries and Puerto Rico), Walton's retail empire totaled 4,777 outlets. In addition, ranked by total revenues ($259 billion) and number of employees (1.3 million), Wal-Mart was the world's largest corporation by the early 2000s.[20] In the process of building a business, Walton transformed retailing in the world's largest consumer society. Not surprisingly, Walton's business successes were controversial, even scorned by some. Smaller retailers in both rural and urban America have closed their doors, unable to match Wal-Mart's low prices. Others decry Wal-Mart's role in altering neighborhoods and communities. Still, consumers in the United States and other countries, about 100 million customers per week, express their freedom of choice by purchasing goods under the banner of "Every Day Low Prices."

Joan V. Robinson: Imperfect Competition

Joan V. Robinson (1903–1983) was a prominent British economist who explored the operation of imperfectly competitive industries—industries that fell between the extremes of perfect competition and monopoly. Robinson was born in Surrey, England, received a top-notch early education, and studied economics at Girtin College, Cambridge University, from which she graduated in 1925. In 1931 she accepted a teaching position at Cambridge, where she taught economics for the next four decades. Early in her academic career, she penned her most famous book, *The Economics of Imperfect Competition* (1933). A socialist and active member of the Labour Party, Robinson also explored many other topics during her career, including income distribution, labor and employment, comparative economic systems, growth theory, and economic development in the poorer regions of the world.

In *The Economics of Imperfect Competition,* Robinson examined the functioning of industries that followed neither of the traditional models of perfect competition and pure monopoly. Robinson viewed each producer in a monopolistically competitive industry as a partial monopolist. Thus, each firm had a degree of market power: the ability to raise the price without losing all the demand for the product. Robinson argued that market power was derived from each firm's ability to create some consumer loyalty. The existence of market power distinguished monopolistically competitive firms from perfectly competitive firms, which were price takers with no market power.

Robinson also stressed that firms operating within a monopolistically competitive industry were interdependent. That is, pricing and production decisions made by one firm affected the business decisions of competitors. American economist Edward H. Chamberlain came to many of the same conclusions regarding the operation of imperfectly competitive industries in *The Theory of Monopolistic Competition,* which was published just a few months prior to Robinson's book. Chamberlain argued that firms within monopolistically competitive industries possessed some market power by virtue of product differentiation, the ability to ascribe unique features or benefits to distinguish one similar product from another. Product differentiation was achieved by creating brand names and brand loyalties, a solid reputation of service to customers, or other factors. The work of Robinson and Chamberlain laid the foundation for future studies of the two main forms of imperfect competition, monopolistic competition and oligopoly. Robinson also observed that other groups in the economy possessed market power. For example, a large buyer of a product could influence the product's price. Hence, large buyers exercised "monopsony" power in certain markets, just as large producers exercised monopoly power.

Throughout her career, Robinson continued to explore the interplay of market forces, including the struggles between groups with market power, such as big business and labor unions. She also studied the consequences of these struggles on economic growth, inflation, and employment. Robinson was controversial, as her socialist views were often critical of capitalism. She critiqued the glaring disparities in income and wealth among people in the industrialized world, and the development gap between richer and poorer countries. She also examined the market failures spawned by capitalism, including pollution, misleading product information, and anticompetitive business practices. Economists generally agree that Robinson was among the preeminent economic theorists of the twentieth century.

NOTES

1. Small Business Administration (SBA), "Small Business by the Numbers," May 2003, 1. Available at www.sba.gov.
2. "The Global 5 Hundred: The World's Largest Corporations," *Fortune,* July 21, 2003, 106.
3. Bureau of Labor Statistics (BLS), "Table A-21. Employed Persons by Industry and Occupation," October 2002, www.bls.gov/pub/suppl/empsit.cpseea21.txt; and U.S. Department of Commerce, *Survey of Current Business* 83 (October 2003): D-31.
4. The World Bank, "Table 12. Structure of Output," *World Development Report 2000/2001: Attacking Poverty* (New York: Oxford University Press, 2000), 296–97.
5. BLS, "Table A-21," D-31.
6. Ibid.
7. Administrative Office of the U.S. Courts, "Bankruptcy Cases Continue to Break Federal Court Caseload Records," www.uscourts.gov.
8. U.S. Census Bureau, "Table 1: Advance Summary Statistics for the United States," *2002 Economic Census,* www.census.gov/econ/census02/advance/TABLE1.htm; and U.S. Census Bureau, "Table 2a: Employment Size of Employer Firms, 2001," statistics about business sizes (including small businesses) from the U.S. Census Bureau, www.census.gov/epcd/www/smallbus.html.
9. U.S. Census Bureau, "Table 4: Employer and Nonemployer Firms by Legal Form of Organization, 1997," statistics about business size (including small businesses) from the U.S. Census Bureau, www.census.gov/epcd/www/smallbus.html.
10. Ibid.
11. Ibid.
12. Ibid.
13. "Entrepreneur's 24th Annual Franchise 500," *Franchise Zone, Entrepreneur.com, 2003,* www.entrepreneur.com/franzone/listing/fran500/o,5831,,00.html.
14. U.S. Department of Agriculture (USDA), "Farmer Co-op Sales, Income Climb in 2001," October 2002, www.rurdev.usda/rd/newsroom/2002/2001coopwrap,html.
15. World Intellectual Property Organization (WIPO), "10% Increase in International Patent Applications Filings in 2002," February 18, 2003, www.wipo.org/pressroom/en/releases/2033/p338.htm.
16. Frederick Winslow Taylor, *The Principles of Scientific Management* (New York: W. W. Norton & Company, 1947), 9.
17. Ibid., 140.
18. Peter F. Drucker, *The Frontiers of Management* (New York: E. P. Dutton, 1986), 351.
19. Ibid., 227.
20. Wal-Mart Stores, "Wal-Mart Announces Expansion Plans for FYE 2005," www.walmartstores.com; "The Global 5 Hundred: The World's Largest Corporations," *Fortune,* July 21, 2003, 106, 119; and "Fortune 500 Largest Corporations," *Fortune,* April 5, 2004, F–1.

SELECTED READINGS

Bannock, Graham, Evan Davis, Paul Trott, and Mark Uncles, eds. *Dictionary of Business.* Princeton, NJ: Bloomberg Press, 2003.

Birkeland, Peter M. *Franchising Dreams: The Lure of Entrepreneurship in America.* Chicago: University of Chicago Press, 2002.

Brakeman, Steven, and Ben J. Heijdra, eds. *The Monopolistic Competition Revolution in Retrospect.* Cambridge, UK: Cambridge University Press, 2003.

Caffey, Andrew A. *Franchises and Business Opportunities.* Irvine, CA: Entrepreneur Media Inc., 2002.

Davis, Michael H., and Arthur Raphael Miller. *Intellectual Property: Patents, Trademarks, and Copyright.* 3rd ed. Belmont, CA: West Wadsworth, 2000.

Dees, J. Gregory, Jed Emerson, and Peter Economy. *Enterprising Nonprofits: A Toolkit for Social Entrepreneurs.* New York: John Wiley & Sons, 2001.

Drucker, Peter F. *The Essential Drucker: In One Volume the Best Sixty Years of Peter Drucker's Essential Writings on Management.* New York: HarperBusiness, 2001.

Geisst, Charles R. *Monopolies in America: Empire Builders and Their Enemies from Jay Gould to Bill Gates.* New York: Oxford University Press, 1999.

Goleman, Daniel. *Business: The Ultimate Resource.* Cambridge, MA: Perseus Publishing, 2002.

Gove, John. *Made in America: The True Stories behind the Brand Names That Built a Nation.* New York: Berkley Books, 2001.

Jacobs, Sanford. *The Greatest Business Stories Ever Told.* New York: The Lyons Press, 2003.

Klein, Maury. *The Change Makers: From Carnegie to Gates, How the Great Entrepreneurs Transformed Ideas into Industries.* Philadelphia: Owl Books, 2004.

Magretta, Joan, and Nan Stone. *What Management Is: How It Works and Why It's Everyone's Business.* New York: Free Press, 2002.

Pallister, John, and Alan Isaacs. *A Dictionary of Business.* New York: Oxford University Press, 2003.

Posner, Richard A. *Antitrust Law.* 2nd ed. Chicago: University of Chicago Press, 2001.

Robinson, Joan. *The Economics of Imperfect Competition.* New York: St. Martin's Press, 1969.

Skeel, David A., Jr. *Debt's Dominion: A History of Bankruptcy Law in America.* Princeton, NJ: Princeton University Press, 2003.

Sutton, John. *Technology and Market Structure: Theory and History.* Cambridge, MA: MIT Press, 2001.

Tabarrok, Alexander, ed. *Entrepreneurial Economics: Bright Ideas from the Dismal Science.* New York: Oxford University Press, 2002.

Taylor, Frederick Winslow. *The Principles of Scientific Management.* New York: W. W. Norton & Company, 1947.

CHAPTER 6

Consumers Organize: Consumer Behavior and Consumer Power

Chapter 6 examines consumers and their role in the American mixed economy. Consumers represent the basic consumption unit in the economy. In 2004 there were more than 290 million consumers in the U.S. economy. Consumer behavior is influenced by a number of factors, including the perceived utility of goods, the availability of substitutes, and the prices of goods and services. The interplay between consumer demand and the supply of goods and services offered by producers is pivotal to product pricing. Over the past century, consumer power has grown in fits and starts. In part, the growth in consumer power is the result of an active consumer movement on the state, national, and international levels. Significant support for consumer rights has also come from government, business leaders, and international organizations.

CONSUMERS AND CONSUMER BEHAVIOR

Consumers buy goods and services to satisfy personal wants or needs. As the basic consumption unit in the American economy, consumers represent the demand side of a market. **Producers** make or sell goods and services to earn profits. Producers, usually called businesses or firms, represent the supply side of a market. Combined, consumers and producers comprise the private sector of the economy. Decentralized private-sector decision making is a foundation of the American economy.

Consumers in the American Economy

People's consumption of goods and services is directly related to their household income. In 2003, $9.2 trillion in personal income poured into American households. **Personal income** is the sum total of all earned income and transfer payments that households receive after social insurance contributions have been deducted but before personal taxes have been paid. *Earned income* refers to money earned by an individual in exchange for a productive activity or investment. Most of the earned income in the American economy is derived from wages and salaries, interest and dividend payments, and proprietors' profits, as shown in Figure 6.1. Government transfer payments also generate income for households. Government *transfer payments* are payments of money, goods, or services that are financed with tax dollars and distributed to other groups that do not offer productive services in return. The largest public transfer program in the American economy is Social Security, a social insurance program for the nation's elderly. Other transfer payments offer income or other assistance to the poor, the unemployed, and others in need. Often, households have multiple sources of income, perhaps collecting a wage or salary from a job, interest from a savings account, and dividends from stocks. Even after taxes and social insurance contributions were deducted from household income, Americans' total disposable personal income in 2003 was $8.2 trillion, of which 98 percent was spent and 2 percent was saved.[1]

Consumer spending drives most economic activity in the American economy. In 2001 the average American household spent $39,518 on consumer goods and services. Over the years, housing has been the largest category of consumer spending. Housing includes mortgage or rent payments, utilities, furniture and appliances, and other household needs. In 2001 housing accounted for nearly one-third of all consumer spending. Other major categories of consumer

Figure 6.1
Sources of Household Income: 2003*

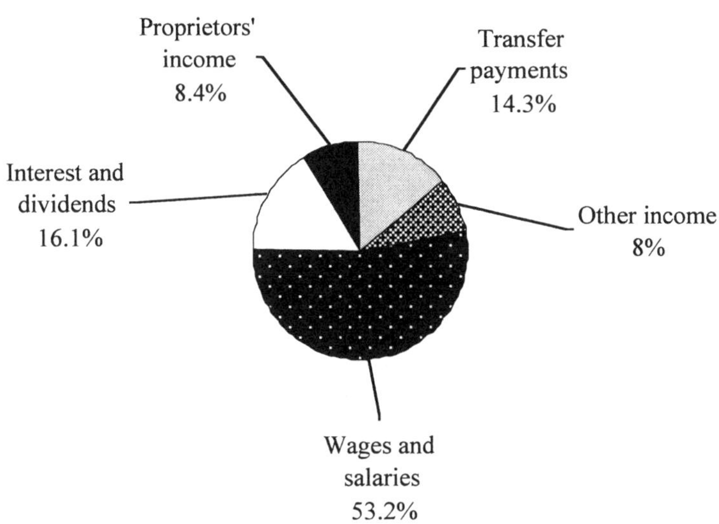

*Data based on second quarter, 2003.
Source: U.S. Commerce Department, Bureau of Economic Analysis, "Personal Income and Its Disposition," News Release, September 26, 2003.

Figure 6.2
Household Spending: 2001

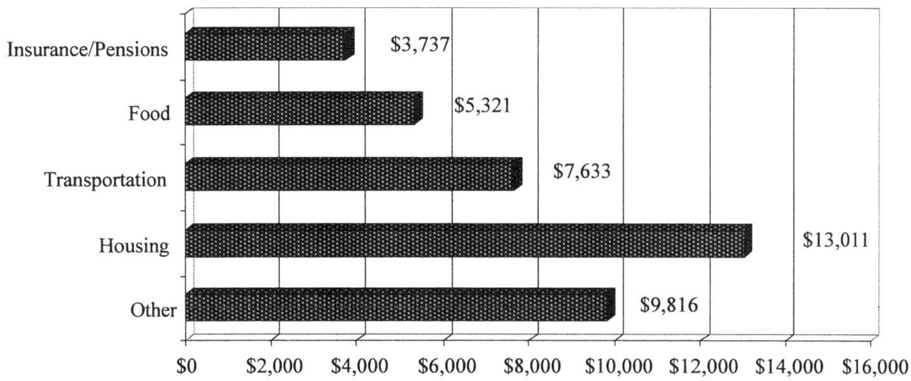

Source: U.S. Department of Labor, Bureau of Labor Statistics, "Consumer expenditures in 2001," *BLS News* December 3, 2002.

spending included transportation (19.3% of consumer spending), food (13.5% of consumer spending), and insurance and pensions (10% of consumer spending). Figure 6.2 shows the average consumer expenditures for a typical household in 2001.[2]

Consumer Behavior in the American Economy

Consumer behavior deals with people's buying decisions in an economy. In the American mixed economy, consumers are free to choose which goods and services to purchase. This freedom of choice is best demonstrated when consumers cast their dollar votes for or against products. Naturally, consumers are not financially able to buy unlimited quantities of products. Instead, consumer choice is influenced by budget constraints. **Budget constraints** include a household's income and wealth, along with the prices of products in the economy. In addition to budget constraints, three other factors affect consumer behavior—the utility of a good, the income effect of a price change, and the substitution effect of a price change. An understanding of these factors enables businesses, the government, and others to better predict consumer behavior.

Utility reflects the amount of satisfaction a person derives from the consumption of a good or service. Economists measure the utility of a purchase in *utils*, or units of satisfaction. In reality, people's tastes and preferences for products vary, and, therefore, precise comparisons of the utility of one product against a second product are impossible. Yet, as a general principle, people tend to buy goods and services that offer them the highest utility, or satisfaction, per dollar spent. Pivotal to consumers' buying decisions is the **law of diminishing marginal utility,** which states that as additional units of the same product are consumed in a given period of time, the amount of additional satisfaction, or

Table 6.1
Jeremy's Diminishing Marginal Utility

Number of Slices of Pizza	Total Utility (in utils)	Marginal Utility (in utils)
0	0	0
1	15	+15
2	25	+10
3	30	+5
4	30	0
5	25	-5

marginal utility, will decline. Consider the utility for slices of pizza shown in Table 6.1. In this hypothetical situation, Jeremy derives the greatest utility, 15 utils, from the first piece of pizza. Total utility rises when the second and third pieces of pizza are consumed because each slice results in some additional satisfaction. Note that the marginal utility falls as additional slices are consumed, however, from 15 utils for the first slice, to 10 utils for the second slice, to 5 utils for the third slice, and so on. This diminishing marginal utility reflects the incremental reduction in satisfaction for slices of pizza consumed in a certain time period. In fact, by stuffing himself with the fourth and fifth slices of pizza, Jeremy encounters zero and then negative marginal utility.

A second factor that affects consumers' buying decisions is the income effect of a price change. The **income effect of a price change** states that as the price of a product falls consumers are financially better off, and when the price of a product rises consumers are financially worse off. Note that the income effect has nothing to do with a change in a household's income. Instead, the income effect deals with the impact of price changes on the amount of goods and services people are able to purchase. For example, if the Jones household typically buys 10 gallons of milk each month at a price of $4 per gallon, its monthly expenditure for milk is $40. If the price of milk falls to just $3 per gallon, the household's monthly expenditure for 10 gallons of milk will fall to just $30. The Jones household is financially better off due to the drop in the price of milk because the extra $10 can be spent on milk or other products. If, on the other hand, the price of milk increases from $4 per gallon to $5 per gallon, the Jones household will be financially worse off because it will have to reduce its consumption of milk or some other good or service.

A third factor that influences consumers' buying decisions is the substitution effect of a price change. The **substitution effect of a price change** states that, if the price of a product falls, consumers will buy more of the product and less of the higher-priced substitute goods. Conversely, if the price of a product rises, consumers will buy less of it and more of the lower-priced substitutes. Consider the Jones household's monthly milk expenditures once again. According to the substitution effect of a price change, a decrease in the price of milk from $4 per gallon to $3 per gallon would likely result in the purchase of additional gallons of milk and of fewer units of substitute goods such as soft drinks or bottled water. If, on the other hand, the price of milk jumped from $4 per gallon to $5 per gallon, the Jones household would likely respond by purchasing fewer gallons of milk and more units of substitutes such as soft drinks, bottled water, or fruit juice.

Advertising and Consumer Behavior

In an economic context, **advertising** is a paid announcement by a business designed to inform consumers about a good or service, and to persuade people to buy the product. Advertising is also used for purposes other than selling products. For instance, political candidates advertise to influence voters' electoral decisions, while charitable and other nonprofit organizations advertise to bring attention to issues or raise funds. Advertising by business firms strives to differentiate between competing goods, accentuating unique features or benefits of the advertised product. The features of a product represent its composition, design, ingredients, components, or other physical attributes. The benefits highlight what the product can do for the buyer, including ways to improve health, appearance, comfort, and so on.

Advertising can be local, national, or international in scope. In the United States, advertising agencies are often used to devise advertising campaigns for large firms. Ad agencies employ a number of advertising appeals and techniques to garner the consumer's attention, to create brand loyalties, and to shape tastes and preferences. An advertising appeal represents the general direction of an advertisement or an ad campaign. Leading ad appeals include humor, sex appeal, rational appeal, and a variety of emotional appeals. Several important ad techniques are

- Bandwagon, which asks consumers to join the crowd by purchasing a good
- Card-stacking, which list the positive features or benefits of a good
- Demonstration, which shows how a good works or how it meets a need
- Product comparison, which shows the superiority of one good over a substitute
- Testimonial, which relies on a personal endorsement of a good

Over the past century, the growth of America's consumer society and the growth of advertising have proceeded hand in hand. According to *Advertising Age,* U.S. advertising spending on different media was $237 billion in 2002. Roughly half represented measured media, while the remainder was based on estimates. Of the measured media spending in 2002, the top spot was occupied by television (43%), followed by newspapers (19%), magazines (16%), the Yellow Pages (12%), and other (10%)—the Internet, outdoor ads, and radio. The estimated, or unmeasured, ad spending includes direct mailings, catalogs, and others.[3] Predictably, fierce competition in America's consumer-oriented industries

Table 6.2
Domestic Advertising Spending: 2002 Rankings

Rank	Industry	Spending ($ millions)	Rank	Corporation	Spending ($ millions)
1	Automotive	$16,365	1	General Motors	$3,652
2	Retail stores	$13,528	2	AOL Time Warner	$2,923
3	Movies, media	$6,024	3	Procter & Gamble	$2,673
4	Food, beverage	$6,015	4	Pfizer	$2,566
5	Medicines	$5,445	5	Ford Motor	$2,252

Source: 100 Leading National Advertisers: 48th Annual Advertiser Profile Edition, Advertising Age; and "Domestic Advertising Spending by Category."

generated significant spending on advertising in the United States, as shown in Table 6.2. In 2002 the top five advertising spenders in the global economy were Procter & Gamble, Unilever, General Motors, Toyota Motor, and Ford Motor, respectively.[4]

Consumers and the National Economy

Consumer spending on final goods and services is the largest component of spending in the U.S. gross domestic product (GDP). The GDP is the nation's most reliable measurement of total output of goods and services in a given year. In 2002, total consumer spending on final products, called *personal consumption expenditures*, represented 66.6 percent of the GDP. The other major types of spending calculated into the nation's GDP accounted for smaller percentages of national output—government consumption expenditures (17.3%) and investment expenditures (16.1%).[5] (See chapter 9 for more on GDP.)

Because consumer spending represents two-thirds of all expenditures in the American economy, consumers' willingness and ability to purchase products is vital to the nation's economic performance. When consumers' incomes rise and people feel confident about spending money, **aggregate demand**—the total demand for goods and services in an economy—tends to rise. An increase in aggregate demand stimulates economic activity and thus contributes to economic expansions. When people's incomes and confidence fall, however, aggregate demand likewise falls. Sagging consumer demand discourages production and investment and contributes to economic downturns.

Consumer behavior in the American economy is influenced by present economic conditions and by expectations of future economic conditions. One of the most recognized gauges of consumer confidence is the Consumer Confidence Index (CCI). The Conference Board, a respected nonprofit economic research organization, publishes the CCI every month. The CCI reports on consumers' attitudes and buying intentions, which in turn influence business decisions concerning production, hiring, and so on. Consumer confidence can swing rapidly in the American economy in response to national or international events. For instance, in 2002–2003 news of sluggish economic growth, rising unemployment, and preparations for war against Iraq resulted in a steep decline in the CCI from 111 in March 2002 to just 64 in February 2003. By January 2004 the CCI had risen to 97, largely in response to an improved employment picture. The base year for the index is 1985 (1985 = 100).[6]

DEMAND, SUPPLY, AND PRICE DETERMINATION

A central feature of capitalism is the efficient operation of free markets. A **market** occurs whenever two or more parties freely exchange goods or services. Recall from chapter 3, Figure 3.1, that there are two primary types of markets, a product market where final goods and services are exchanged, and a factor market where resources are exchanged. Countless exchanges take place in U.S. product and factor markets every day. But how are the prices for goods, services, and resources determined? Under capitalism, the impersonal forces of demand and supply establish most prices and, in doing so, bring order to the seeming chaos of the marketplace.

Demand in the Marketplace

Demand is the amount of a good, service, or resource that people are willing and able to buy at a series of prices at a moment in time. The demand for a product or resource is illustrated in tabular form by a demand schedule, or with a demand curve, as shown in Figure 6.3. The demand curve slopes downward, reflecting the most famous of all economic laws, the law of demand. According to the **law of demand,** there is an inverse relationship between price and quantity demanded. That is, if the price of a good increases, the quantity demanded will decrease. Conversely, if the price of a good decreases, the quantity demanded will increase. To construct an initial demand curve for a product, economists employ the *ceteris paribus* assumption. Under the *ceteris paribus* assumption, all external factors that might affect the demand for the product, except price, are temporarily held constant. In the product market, the demand curve typically represents the viewpoint of the consumer, who buys final goods or services from businesses. In the factor market, the demand curve typically represents the viewpoint of the producer, who buys resources from households.

The demand curve shown in Figure 6.3 represents the demand for product X at this moment in time. Hence, a change in the price of product X causes a change in the quantity demanded, not a change in the overall demand for the product. Speaking precisely, economists say that a change in price causes a movement along an existing demand curve. In Figure 6.3, for example, if the price of product X decreases from $6 to $4, there is a downward movement along the existing demand curve. In this case, the $2 change in price caused the quantity demanded to increase from 6,000 items to 8,000 items, but had no impact on the overall demand for product X.

Figure 6.3
Illustrating the Demand for Product X

Demand Schedule for Product X

Price	Quantity Demanded (in thousands)
$10	2
$8	4
$6	6
$4	8
$2	10

Demand Curve for Product X

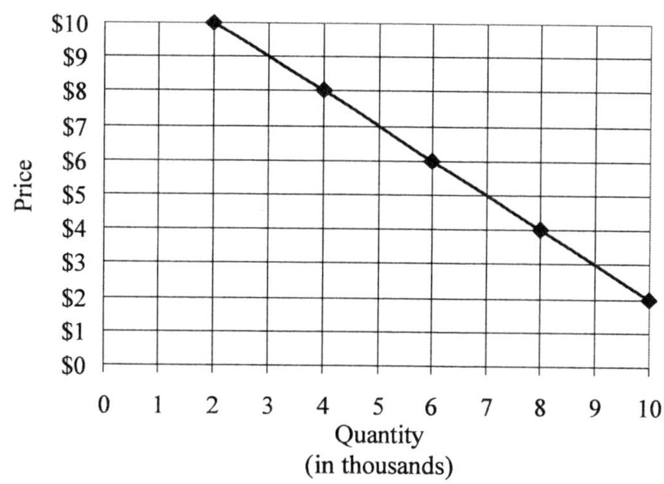

So how does a change in the overall demand for a good occur? To change the demand for a good, the *ceteris paribus* assumption is lifted, allowing other factors, called determinants of demand, to enter the picture. A change in one or more of the determinants of demand causes buyers to want more or less of a good at each and every price. There are six main determinants of demand: people's tastes and preferences, income level, market size, price of substitute goods, price of complementary goods, and expectations. Suppose, for example, that a successful television commercial favorably affected people's tastes and preferences for product X. The likely result is that buyers would purchase more of product X at each and every price. Perhaps buyers would be willing to purchase 4,000 items at a price of $10; at $8 they would buy 6,000 items; at $6 they would buy 8,000 items; at $4 they would buy 10,000 items; and at $2 they would buy 12,000 items. Hence, a change in tastes and preferences, a determinant of demand, causes the entire demand curve to shift to the right (a positive shift). The new demand curve represents the new reality of the marketplace, so the original demand curve disappears. Of course, people's tastes and preferences can also work against a product or service, as is often the case with fads or products that have become obsolete, such as typewriters or record albums. A decline in people's tastes and preferences causes a shift of the entire demand curve to the left to show that people are willing to buy less of the product at each and every price. In addition to tastes and preferences, the other determinants of demand include

- *Income level.* An increase in people's incomes will cause the demand for most goods to increase, and vice versa.
- *Market size.* An increase in market size (a larger number of potential buyers) will cause the demand for most goods to increase, and vice versa.
- *Price of a substitute good.* An increase in the price of a substitute good will cause an increase in the demand for the related product, and vice versa. A **substitute good** is a product that can be used in place of a similar good. For instance, some buyers will switch from the higher-priced substitute good, and cast their dollar votes instead for the less expensive related product.
- *Price of a complementary good.* A decrease in the price of a complementary good will cause an increase in demand for the related good, and vice versa. A **complementary good** is a product that is used in conjunction with another product. Lower-priced complementary goods make using the related good less costly.
- *Expectations.* Optimistic views about personal or national prosperity will cause an increase in the demand for most goods, while pessimistic views have the opposite effect.

Supply in the Marketplace

Supply is the amount of a good, service, or resource that producers are willing and able to sell at a series of prices at a moment in time. The supply of a product or resource is illustrated in tabular form by a supply schedule, or with a supply curve, as shown in Figure 6.4. The supply curve slopes upward, reflecting the law of supply. According to the **law of supply**, there is a direct relationship between the price of a good and the quantity supplied. That is, if the price of a good increases, the quantity supplied will also increase. Conversely, if the price of a good decreases, the quantity supplied will also decrease. The *ceteris paribus* assumption is used to construct an initial supply curve, just as it is used to chart an original demand curve. In the product market, the supply curve typically represents the viewpoint of businesses, which produce or sell final goods or services to households. In the resource market, the supply curve represents the viewpoint of households, which sell labor and other resources to businesses.

The supply curve shown in Figure 6.4 represents the initial supply of product X at this moment in time. Thus, a change in the price of product X causes a change in the quantity supplied, not a change in the overall supply of the product. Economists say that a change in price causes a movement along an existing supply curve. In Figure 6.4, if the price of product X increases from $2 to $4, there is an upward movement along the existing supply curve. In this situ-

Figure 6.4
Illustrating the Supply of Product X

Supply Schedule for Product X

Price	Quantity Supplied (in thousands)
$10	10
$8	8
$6	6
$4	4
$2	2

Supply Curve for Product X

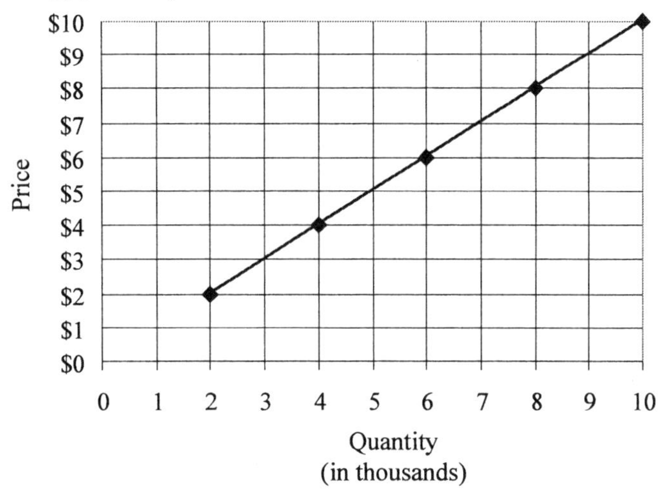

ation, the $2 change in price caused the quantity supplied to increase from 2,000 items to 4,000 items, but had no impact on the overall supply of product X.

The supply of a product changes when the *ceteris paribus* assumption is lifted, and one or more of the determinants of supply changes. A change in a determinant of supply causes the supplier to supply more or less of a good or resource at each and every price. There are five main determinants of supply: resource prices, technological advance, number of firms in an industry, taxes, and expectations. Suppose, for example, that there was a decrease in the price of natural resources used in the production of product X. Reduced costs of production would likely cause producers to supply more of product X at each and every price. At a price of $2, for example, producers would be willing to supply 4,000 items; at $4 they would supply 6,000 items; at $6 they would supply 8,000 items; at $8 they would supply 10,000 items; and at $10 they would supply 12,000 items. Thus, a change in the price of a key resource, a determinant of supply, causes the entire supply curve to shift to the right (a positive shift). The new supply curve represents the new reality of the marketplace, so the original supply curve disappears. Conversely, an increase in the price of key resources used in the production of product X would raise the costs of production and cause producers to supply less at each and every price (a negative shift). In addition to resource prices, the four other determinants of supply are

- *Technological advance.* Improvements in technology allow businesses to improve efficiency and cut production costs, thus encouraging firms to increase the supply of the product. Technological advances in one industry can also negatively affect production in a related industry. For example, technological advances in the computer industry made the typewriter obsolete.
- *Number of firms in an industry.* When additional firms enter an industry, the supply of the product tends to increase. Conversely, when firms exit an industry, the overall supply of the product tends to fall.
- *Taxes.* Higher business taxes tend to increase business costs and thus cause businesses to reduce the supply of goods and services. Lower taxes reduce production costs and encourage businesses to increase the supply of goods.
- *Expectations.* Optimistic expectations about future prosperity in the economy, and about the prospects for high prices and healthy profits within an industry, cause businesses to increase the supply of goods. Pessimistic economic forecasts cause businesses to reduce the supply of goods.

Market Equilibrium: The Interplay of Demand and Supply

Market equilibrium occurs at the point where the market demand and market supply curves intersect. Thus, the market equilibrium is the best compromise between the interests of consumers, represented by the demand curve, and the interests of producers, represented by the supply curve. At the market equilibrium, the product's price and quantity are determined. Figure 6.5 illustrates the demand and supply for product X. At a low price of $2, the quantity demanded is high—10,000 items in this case. Producers, on the other hand, would be willing to produce 10,000 items only if they could charge a high price of $10 per item. The power of the free market is its ability to make the necessary compromises, without decrees or coercion from the government, to balance the interests of consumers and producers. Figure 6.5 shows that, at this moment in time, the equilibrium price for product X is $6 and its equilibrium quantity is 6,000 items. Note that the horizontal axis is now labeled quantity, rather than quantity demanded or quantity supplied, because both the demand curve and the supply curve are shown on the same graph.

The Government and Price Determination

While the forces of supply and demand are responsible for establishing most prices in the U.S. economy, the government sometimes overrides the compromises of the market to set prices for a product or a resource. This type of govern-

Figure 6.5
Market Equilibrium for Product X

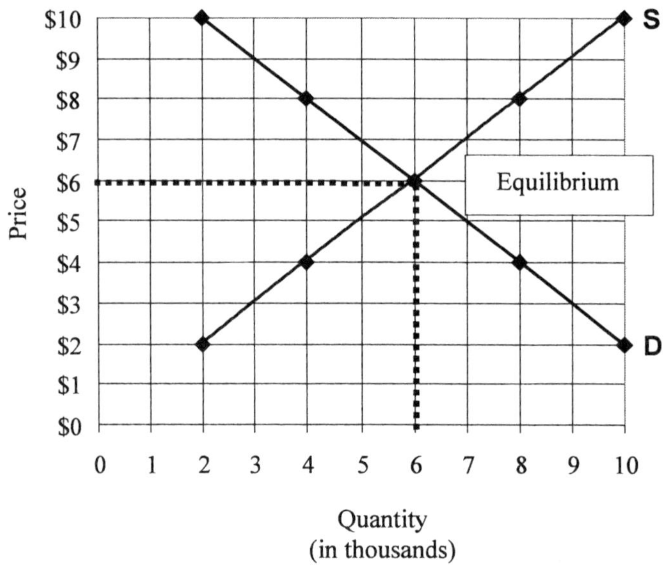

ment intervention in the economy typically occurs when government, at any level, feels that a price is unfairly high for consumers or unfairly low for producers. There are two types of government price controls: price ceilings and price floors.

A **price ceiling** is a government-imposed maximum price that a seller may charge for a good or service. The main goal of a price ceiling is to make a product more affordable to consumers. Rent controls are a common type of price ceiling in the United States. Local governments limit rents at a price below the market equilibrium. In Figure 6.6, for example, the equilibrium price for a rental unit is $500 and the equilibrium quantity is 40,000 rental units. When the govrnment limits rents to $400, the quantity demanded of rental units increases to 50,000, at point B, while the quantity supplied decreases to 30,000, at point A. The result is a shortage of rental units because the quantity demanded is greater than the quantity supplied. Price ceilings have been used sparingly in the U.S. economy during the twentieth century. For example, during World War II the federal government imposed price ceilings on certain consumer goods to hold inflation in check. The government also imposed price ceilings on domestically produced oil during the mid-1970s.

A **price floor** is a government-guaranteed minimum price for a product or a resource. The main goal of a price floor is to provide a higher income for certain suppliers of goods or resources. In the product market, the government has instituted price floors on a number of agricultural products to boost revenues for the nation's farmers. In the factor market, the federal government's price floor on wages, called the minimum wage, has set a minimum price for the services of workers since the late 1930s (see chapter 7 for more on price floors and the minimum wage).

Figure 6.6
Price Ceilings and Shortages

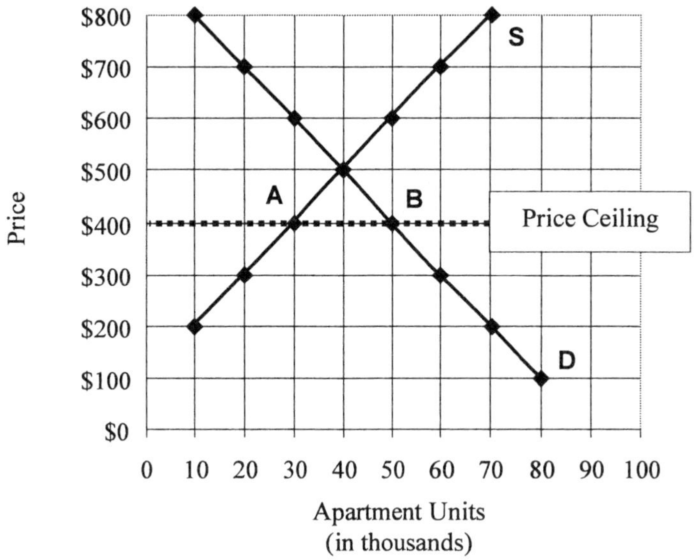

THE CONSUMER MOVEMENT AND CONSUMER POWER

The birth of America's consumer society during the early twentieth century sparked interest in consumerism in the United States. Broadly defined, **consumerism** is the protection of consumer interests. There are many subsets to this definition. For instance, consumerism is directly concerned with protecting consumers' freedom of choice—the right to buy products that are safe and that meet promised quality standards. Consumerism is also related to establishing limits on the freedom of enterprise of businesses by prohibiting business practices that may be unethical, deceptive, or illegal. In its broadest context, consumerism delves into matters of social justice, including issues related to the redistribution of society's wealth, sustainable consumption, and other quality of life concerns. People who actively support the goals of consumerism are called **consumerists.** Consumerists work on behalf of consumer interests individually and as members of organizations or agencies in the private or public sectors. For more than a century, private-sector consumerists have formed a loosely coordinated consumer movement in the United States. More recently, consumerism has gained momentum in the global community.

The National Consumer Movement in the United States

The **consumer movement** is the embodiment of the actions, programs, and other forms of activism of individual consumerists and private consumerist organizations. The movement welcomes the support of public officials, government agencies, and businesses on behalf of consumers, but does not recognize the government or businesses as participants in the movement. The history of the consumer movement in the United States dates back more than 100 years, a period of time in which the movement has made irregular progress.

In the early 1900s, the consumer movement was mainly concerned with overcoming substandard living conditions and the prevailing attitude of caveat emptor (let the buyer beware). Massive immigration at the turn of the twentieth century created a large pool of unskilled labor in many American cities, and wages and the standard of living declined for millions of people. Caveat emptor implied that producers were blameless for products that were unsafe or failed to meet performance standards. Substandard and injurious products, such as unsafe food and medicines, routinely victimized consumers. Under these conditions, people became more suspicious of businesses, prompting consumers to organize.

Early consumerist voices included the muckrakers, aggressive investigative news reporters and authors who researched unfair business practices, unsafe products, and other violations of the public trust. The muckrakers often published their findings in magazines such as *McClure's* and *Puck.* Other muckrakers, including Upton Sinclair, authored novels such as *The Jungle* (1906). *The Jungle* exposed the horrific living conditions of immigrants and the nauseating production techniques employed by Chicago's meat-packing industry. The pub-

Children stuff sausages in a Chicago meatpacking house, 1893. Strohmeyer & Wyman (New York, NY). © Library of Congress.

lic outrage caused by *The Jungle* was instrumental in gaining congressional approval of the Pure Food and Drug Act of 1906. At about the same time, America's first national consumer organization, the National Consumers League (1899), was formed to advocate for improved working and living conditions for the urban poor. Table 6.3 identifies a number of major consumer organizations that strengthened the U.S. consumer movement.

As the consumer movement matured, it became a recognized force for change in the American economy. During the 1950s and 1960s, major national organizations such as the Consumers Union and Consumers' Research expanded

Table 6.3
Major Consumer Organizations

Name of Organization	Established (date)	Mission or Purpose
National Consumers League (NCL)	1899	Founded to improve the quality of life for the urban poor; today its focus has shifted toward a wide range of consumer issues such as food safety and health care
Consumers' Research (CR)	1928	Founded to test consumer goods for safety and quality standards; CR publishes *Consumers' Research* magazine to publicize the results of its product tests
Consumers Union (CU)	1936	Founded to test consumer goods and improve people's standard of living; CU conducts extensive product research, publishes the influential *Consumer Reports*, and lobbies for consumer legislation
Consumers International (CI)	1960	Founded to coordinate global consumer-oriented activities in the developed and developing world and to help create consumer-oriented organizations
Consumer Federation of America (CFA)	1967	Founded to unite various consumer groups in order to support consumer goals before state legislatures, federal regulatory agencies, and Congress; in the early 2000s the CFA was comprised of 285 organizations with a combined membership of 50 million people
Public Citizen	1971	Founded to advocate for political reform and a variety of issues ranging from auto safety to toxic waste cleanup; spawned related local consumer groups such as Congress Watch and Health Research Group

their product research capabilities and became influential voices in shaping public opinion and public policy. Consumer organizations pressed for the enactment of consumer laws and regulations. They also nurtured the rise of a consumer consciousness, an attitude in which people rejected caveat emptor and insisted on honesty and fairness in marketplace transactions. The consumer movement also gained momentum during the 1960s and 1970s through the efforts of individuals. For example, in 1962 President John F. Kennedy announced a Consumer Bill of Rights for Americans, which included the right to product safety, the right to be informed, the right to choose, and the right to be heard. Since then, four additional consumer rights have been added to the list: the right to redress, the right to consumer education, the right to a healthy environment, and the right to satisfaction of basic needs. By the mid-1960s, another individual, Ralph Nader, burst into the national limelight with his book *Unsafe at Any Speed* (1965). In true muckraking tradition, this book exposed engineering and construction defects in certain American automobiles and argued persuasively that many injuries and deaths could be avoided with better auto design. Consumer activism became the trademark of Nader and of the numerous support organizations he founded over the next several decades (see the biography of Ralph Nader).

Since the 1960s, the U.S. consumer movement has helped weave the concept of consumer rights into the economic mainstream. Numerous laws, government regulations, and private and public watchdog agencies and organizations were established to protect consumer interests. What are the main characteristics of today's consumer movement? First, the consumer movement is diverse. Hundreds of specialized consumer groups advocate for improvements in areas such as health care, product and food safety, nutrition and nutrition labeling, truth in advertising, financial services, telemarketing, environmental protection, and others. Specialized consumer groups complement the work of the larger national organizations such as the Consumers Union, Consumers' Research, and the Consumer Federation of America. Second, the consumer movement has clout. The movement's influence increased as it became more professional, better funded, and supported by both public opinion and by law. Today consumer groups employ researchers, scientists, engineers, and other experts, which adds to their legitimacy. Professional lobbyists and lawyers are also employed by consumer groups to support consumers' interests through legislation and litigation. Third, the consumer movement is global. Active consumer movements exist in virtually all developed countries, and, with the support of Consumers International and the United Nations, consumerism has gained momentum in the developing world.

The State and Local Consumer Movement in the United States

The state and local consumer movement dates back to the late nineteenth century. In the 1890s, for example, state consumer leagues were founded to advocate for the poor, particularly women and children who endured sweatshop conditions in factories and mills. Early consumer leagues also recognized the need for a stronger consumer voice to ensure product safety, including the safety of the food supply. To expand the scope and influence of this consumer voice, state consumer leagues established the nation's first national consumer organization, the National Consumers League (NCL), in 1899. Since then, state and local consumer groups have provided grassroots support for consumer-oriented legislation and have complemented the work of the national consumer organizations such as Consumers' Research, the Consumers Union, and the Consumer Federation of America. During the 1960s, state and local consumer groups blossomed, and over the past quarter century, hundreds of them have been established to serve consumer interests in areas such as public utilities, housing, health care, energy, and personal finance.

Today, state and local consumer groups generally share a number of characteristics. First, they tend to focus their attention on local issues, such as deceptive advertising, shoddy goods or services, and other business abuses. Larger issues, such as global environmental degradation and substandard living standards, are generally left to national organizations. Second, state and local consumer groups tend to be highly specialized. That is, these groups form to deal with a narrow range of consumer issues, such as energy production and consumption, or health care reform, or quality housing for people. They often employ or rely on volunteer services of experts in these specialized fields. Third, state and local consumer groups normally conduct their operations independently. They establish their own goals, raise funds, and implement policies—including consumer education programs—without significant intervention by other consumer groups. The Consumer Federation of America (CFA) and Consumers International (CI) coordinate some state and local consumer activities with those of the national or international movements, however. Finally, state and local consumer groups work within existing political institutions to address local consumer problems. They often employ skilled lobbyists and experts to influence the decisions of town or county officials or policy boards, state regulatory agencies, and state legislatures. The CFA's eleventh annual consumer complaint survey identified the top areas of consumer dissatisfaction at the state level in 2001. Most consumer complaints centered on everyday consumer problems in the realms of home improvements, consumer durables, auto sales and repair services, and borrowing and credit. By the early 2000s, the Federal Trade Commission (FTC) reported rising numbers of consumer complaints of fraud and identity theft. In 2003 alone the FTC received more than 200,000 identity theft complaints resulting from credit card fraud, phone or utility fraud, bank fraud, and others.[7]

International Consumer Movement

Consumers International coordinates the global consumer movement. CI is an independent nonprofit organization of consumer groups and nongovernmental organizations (NGOs). Originally called the International Organization of Consumers Unions, CI was founded in 1960 to unify the voices of consumers worldwide. By the early 2000s, CI membership included over 250 organizations spread across 115 countries. In its 2002 annual report, CI reaffirmed the importance of consumer organizations "to act as a countervailing power to the influence of business and industry in global debates."[8] CI, in cooperation with the United Nations and numerous nongovernmental organizations, has taken the lead in the global consumer movement. It has endeavored to form consumer organizations to meet growing consumer needs in the poorer world regions. CI also sponsors high-profile annual events such as World Consumer Rights Day, which in 2004 focused on people's right to clean water and adequate sanitation.

Over the past decade, CI has championed a variety of global consumer concerns, many connected with the changing global economy. By the early 2000s, its efforts were focused mainly on food safety, the availability of basic services, health care, environmental protection, consumer education, sustainable consumption, and corporate social responsibility. To these ends, CI not only assisted member organizations to reform national consumer policies, but also participated in the decision making of global institutions, such as the United Nations, and in regional organizations such as the Economic Community for West African States (ECOWAS), the Organization for Economic Development and Cooperation (OECD), and the Association of Southeast Asian Nations (ASEAN). CI helped devise and currently supports the implementation of the United Nations Guidelines for Consumer Protection, originally established in 1985. These UN guidelines expanded on the four consumer rights named by President John F. Kennedy in 1962, and include the right to redress, the right to consumer education, the right to a healthy environment, and the right to the satisfaction of basic needs. At its seventeenth world conference in 2003, CI examined issues such as the growth of e-commerce, cross-border retailing, and corporate power in the global economy (see the biography of Esther Peterson for more on the UN guidelines).

Consumer Cooperatives and Consumer Power

Another source of consumer power in the American and global economies is the consumer cooperative. A **consumer cooperative,** or consumer co-op, is a nonprofit, member-owned business designed to provide goods or services to members. Since the primary reason to form a consumer co-op is to provide members with products, rather than earn business profits, these co-ops are often able to produce or provide products at reasonable prices. In addition to ensuring the availability of essential goods at fair prices, consumer co-ops create more competitive markets. Consumer co-ops in the United States and around the world express their solidarity through shared values, including democratic decision making, business social responsibility, and self-reliance. By the early 2000s, there were 48,000 cooperatives—consumer co-ops, worker co-ops, and producer co-ops—operating in the U.S. economy. They served the needs of 120 million Americans.[9] (See chapter 5 for more on producer co-ops, and chapter 7 for more on worker co-ops.)

Consumer co-ops are an important force in the national and international economy. By the early 2000s, consumer co-ops in the United States provided services in many different industries. According to the Consumer Federation of America, consumer co-ops were especially important in providing financial services, electricity, telecommunications services including Internet access, food, housing, nursery school, childcare, and health care. Other consumer co-ops provided insurance, college book and food services, and even funeral arrangements.[10] In the global economy, the International Co-operative Alliance (ICA) "unites, represents, and serves co-operatives worldwide." The ICA, which represents the interests of 250 consumer, worker, and producer co-ops, serves the needs of 760 million members in agriculture, banking, energy, housing, tourism, and other sectors.[11]

CONSUMER PROTECTION

Consumer protection in the United States is viewed as a shared responsibility involving federal agencies, local authorities, consumer organizations, the business community, and consumers themselves. Over the years, a substantial body of consumer law has also been enacted to support basic consumer rights, especially the rights to safety, to choose, to be informed, to be heard, and to redress of grievances. There is still some debate about the relative power of businesses versus consumers in the American economy. The theory of producer sovereignty, which was popularized in the 1950s and 1960s by economists such as John Kenneth Galbraith, stated that producers manipulated consumer demand through advertising and marketing campaigns (see the biography of John K. Galbraith). Today, however, the theory of consumer sovereignty represents mainstream economic thought. This theory states that knowledgeable, discerning consumers have sufficient information to exercise their freedom of choice, and that consumers are ably protected from business abuses by government agencies, private organizations, and the legal system.

Public and Private Consumer Watchdogs

A variety of agencies and organizations in the public and private sectors of the economy promote the general welfare of consumers in the United States. At the national level, the Federal Trade Commission (FTC), the Consumer Product Safety Commission (CPSC), and the Food and Drug Administration (FDA) provide important safeguards of consumers' rights. The FTC, founded in 1914, enforces many of the nation's consumer protection and antitrust laws by protecting competitive markets and preventing unethical and deceptive business practices. It enforces existing laws and regulations in the realms of advertising, lending practices, credit, domestic and international marketing, and other areas of consumer concern. The FTC also enforces antitrust legislation to prevent anticompetitive mergers and other business practices that serve to substantially restrict competitive markets. The CPSC, founded in 1972, is a federal regulatory agency that protects consumers "against unreasonable risks of injuries associated with consumer products."[12] The CPSC investigates complaints involving product safety and has the power to order product recalls to remove unsafe items from store shelves and showrooms. In 2002 the CPSC initiated nearly 1,000 product recalls or other actions to remove hazardous products from U.S. markets. Other federal regulatory agencies, such as the FDA, are also concerned with consumer safety. At the state level, state consumer affairs departments, credit counseling services, and other agencies provide additional protections for consumers.

Federal consumer law covers a wide variety of protections for U.S. consumers. Some legislation deals with product safety, such as the Pure Food and Drug Act (1906), Flammable Fabrics Act (1953), Hazardous Substances Labeling Act (1960), and Cigarette Labeling Act (1966). Many consumer laws protect fairness in personal finances, such as buying, borrowing, or using credit. For instance, the Fair Housing Credit Act (1968) and the Equal Credit Opportunity Act (1974) prohibit discrimination in credit transactions based on race, national origin, gender, age, or marital status. To guarantee that sufficient information is made available to savers and borrowers, Congress enacted the Truth in Lending Act (1968), the Consumer Leasing Act (1976), the Fair Credit and Charge Card Disclosure Act (1988), and the Truth in Savings Act (1991). The Fair Credit Reporting Act (1970) and the Fair Debt Collection Practices Act (1977) allow consumers to challenge their credit reports and to halt harassment by creditors. Antitrust laws such as the Sherman Act (1890), Clayton Act (1914), and Celler-Kefauver Act (1950) protect competitive markets. From the perspective of consumers, competitive markets represent an important check on firms' market power and help ensure reasonable prices for products.

Business organizations and professional associations also support consumer interests. For example, Better Business Bureaus (BBB) are nonprofit organizations of local businesses that serve business and consumer interests in many regions of the country. BBBs often provide information about area businesses and help reconcile consumer complaints with local business enterprises. A professional association is an organization of people who work in the same field. These associations are designed to maintain the quality of a good or service and to create a positive image for the professional group, so they are sensitive to consumer needs. Professional associations, such as the American Medical Association and the American Advertising Federation, monitor members' business practices and behaviors.

Consumer Responsibilities

With consumer rights come consumer responsibilities. Consumer organizations, business groups, and governments have discussed the topic of consumer responsibility over the years. Today, there is general consensus that consumers should exercise responsibility in their personal buying decisions and in their personal interactions with businesses should disputes arise. Consumers have a responsibility to make informed buying decisions. Consumers should comparison shop, distinguish wants from needs, consider personal budget constraints, obtain product information from a variety of sources, resist hard-sell techniques, and read and comprehend instruction manuals and warrantees. Consumers also have a responsibility to challenge business abuses by retailers and manufacturers. Consumers should respectfully question, discuss, and, if necessary, report instances of unethical or illegal business behaviors to government agencies. Abusive business practices include the use of deceptive advertising, the use of illegal sales techniques such as bait and switch, the marketing of dangerous or defective products, failure to fulfill service contracts, and so on. Consumers should also keep sales receipts, warrantees, and so on to help resolve disputes.

There is also a push to infuse sustainable consumption into the mix of consumer responsibilities. **Sustainable consumption** is a type of consumption based on the efficient purchase and use of resources and products by consumers, government, and businesses. Sustainable consumption was added to the UN Guidelines for Consumer Protection in 1999 as a way to encourage societies to "[meet] the needs of present and future generations for goods and services in ways that are economically, socially and environmentally sustainable."[13] Responsibilities shared by consumers, government, and businesses include the efficient use of resources and goods, the application of environmentally sound technologies, recycling, and the creation of policies to reduce inequalities within and between countries. The responsibilities outlined in sustainable consumption are related to ethical consumption, which challenges consumers to cast their dollar votes based on their values as well as their needs. Ethical consumption challenges the wide disparity between the amount of goods and services consumed in the richer nations versus the poorer nations. It also discourages the consumption of goods produced through the exploitation of natural ecosystems and workers, particularly women and children.

Personal Bankruptcy

Consumer protection, in its broadest sense, extends into helping people cope with traumatic personal financial difficulties. In most cases, consumers who have fallen into debt can be guided out of their financial quagmire with assistance from a state consumer credit counseling service or, perhaps, a nonprofit debt consolidation firm. At other times, personal bankruptcy is necessary to attend to the hopelessness of unsustainable debt. **Bankruptcy** is a formal acknowledgement that an individual or business firm cannot pay its creditors. There are many reasons why people acquire massive debts—sickness or death, credit abuse, or other tragic circumstance. Personal bankruptcy is considered an action of last resort because it often results in the liquidation of personal assets, the loss of future credit, or other limits on the individual's freedom of choice. In 2003 the Administrative Office of the U.S. Courts announced the filing of a record 1.65 million bankruptcies. Of this total, 98 percent were nonbusiness, or personal, bankruptcies, as shown in Table 6.4.[14]

Table 6.4
Bankruptcy Filings: 2000–2003

Year	Personal Bankruptcies	Business Bankruptcies	Total Bankruptcies
2000	1,240,012	36,910	1,276,922
2001	1,349,471	37,135	1,386,606
2002	1,466,105	39,201	1,505,306
2003	1,613,097	37,182	1,650,279

Source: Administrative Office of the U.S. Courts, News Release, August 18, 2003.

Most personal bankruptcies are filed under Chapter 7 and Chapter 13 of the U.S. bankruptcy code. In 2003 about 70 percent of all bankruptcies were filed under Chapter 7 of the code. Chapter 7 bankruptcies permit the courts to sell off most of the person's belongings in an effort to repay a portion of the debts. Taxes owed to the government are paid off first. Typically, there is little money remaining to satisfy other creditors. Some financial obligations cannot be cancelled under Chapter 7, such as alimony payments to a former spouse or student loans. Still, once the court proceedings are concluded, the individual's debt is gone, as is the chance to receive additional credit for a decade or so.[15]

Chapter 13 bankruptcy filings represented nearly 29 percent of the total in 2003. Under Chapter 13 of the bankruptcy code, individuals pay creditors, in full or in part, in installments spanning three to five years. An officer of the court is typically appointed to oversee the individual's compliance with the terms of the bankruptcy. The individual's wages may be tapped to guarantee payments to creditors. The bankruptcy also damages the individual's chance to receive additional credit for a number of years. Still, under Chapter 13, the rescheduled debt is repaid, and the individual's assets, such as house and car, are protected from creditors.[16]

BIOGRAPHIES: SHAPERS OF ECONOMIC THOUGHT

Ralph Nader: Public Citizen

Ralph Nader (1934–) is an American lawyer and social critic, and the nation's foremost consumer advocate. Nader was born to Lebanese immigrant parents in Winsted, Connecticut. His quick mind and insatiable appetite for learning eventually brought him to Princeton, where he earned his bachelor's degree in 1955, and then to Harvard Law School, where he earned his law degree in 1958. In 1963, after a brief teaching stint at the University of Hartford, Nader traveled to Washington, D.C. In 1965 he published, *Unsafe at Any Speed,* a book that attacked the U.S. auto industry for its emphasis on stylish design rather than safety. This scathing critique provoked a consumer outcry for action, and in 1966

Congress passed the National Traffic and Motor Vehicle Safety Act to strengthen auto safety standards.

Propelled by his victory in the realm of auto safety, Ralph Nader became the most recognized voice in the U.S. consumer movement. As a consumer activist, Nader was not content to simply expose business abuses and government corruption. Instead, he advocated for changes in the private and public sectors to guarantee consumers their basic rights to safety, to choose, to be informed, to be heard, and to obtain redress. In 1969 Nader established his first research organization, the Center for Study of Responsive Law. This center was the focal point for early consumer crusades by Nader and a large cadre of supportive college students, who were soon dubbed Nader's Raiders. Under Nader's guidance, student-led public interest research groups (PIRGs) sprang up on college campuses across the nation to press for consumer rights. In 1971 Nader founded Public Citizen, an organization that would eventually spawn Congress Watch, Health Research Group, Critical Mass Energy Project, Global Trade Watch, and the Litigation Group.

Ralph Nader's activism reinvigorated the U.S. movement and brought consumerism into the national spotlight during the 1960s and 1970s. Through his publications and his support organizations, Nader successfully lobbied on behalf of consumer interests at the state and national levels. His relentless and uncompromising assault on unfair, unethical, and deceptive practices by businesses and the government contributed to the creation of new federal watchdog agencies such as the Occupational Safety and Health Administration (OSHA), the Environmental Protection Agency (EPA), and the Consumer Product Safety Commission (CPSC). Nader's activism also pressured business and government leaders to enact laws, regulations, and reforms to protect safety and fairness in many industries, such as insurance, nuclear power, food processing, pharmaceuticals, banking, telecommunications, and automobiles. As the presidential candidate representing the Green Party in the elections of 1992, 1996, and 2000, Nader's far-reaching platform called for consumer rights, environmental protection, social and economic justice, and democratic reforms in the U.S. political system. Many of these themes were echoed in his 2004 presidential bid, and are examined in his more recent books, including *Cutting Corporate Welfare* (2000), and *Crashing the Party: Taking on the Corporate Government in an Age of Surrender* (2002).

Esther Peterson: Consumer Activist

Esther Peterson (1906–1997) was an American social activist and advocate for the rights of women, workers, and consumers. Peterson was born in Provo, Utah, where she received her early education. She earned a bachelor's degree from Brigham Young University in 1927, and a master's degree from Columbia Teachers' College in New York City in 1930. Over the next 60 years, her colorful career as an educator, union organizer, lobbyist, corporate consumer adviser, and consumer advocate allowed Peterson to work with ordinary citizens and U.S. presidents on behalf of people's rights. Peterson's career as a social reformer is told in her autobiography, *Restless: The Memoirs of Labor and Consumer Activist Esther Peterson* (1997).

Peterson is best known for her skillful work on behalf of consumers in America and around the world. During the presidencies of John F. Kennedy and Lyndon B. Johnson, Peterson rose to the position of assistant secretary of labor. As special assistant to the president for consumer affairs from 1964 to 1967, Peterson worked to coordinate the efforts of the splintered consumer movement and to expand the federal government's formal support for the consumerist agenda. To this end, Peterson was instrumental in founding the Consumer Federation of America in 1967, an organization designed to unify the voice of the U.S. consumer movement. During the 1970s, Peterson wore many hats. She advised corporations on consumer policies and, from 1974 to 1976, served as president of the National Consumers League. In 1977 Peterson returned to public service, once again serving as the special assistant to the president for consumer affairs in President Carter's administration. Numerous federal consumer laws were enacted during the 1960s and 1970s to protect consumers from unsafe products, workers from hazardous working conditions, and borrowers from deceptive and unfair lending practices.

Peterson was also an advocate of consumerism in the global economy. Her vision included the creation of universal consumer protection guidelines applicable to all peoples in the global economy. From 1983 to 1993, Peterson represented the International Organization of Consumers Unions, now called Consumers International (CI), at the United Nations. Her efforts paid dividends when, in 1985, the UN's General Assembly adopted the United Nations Guidelines for Consumer Protection. This UN resolution added the weight of the world's most powerful international organization behind a set of universal consumer rights. The UN's consumer guidelines encouraged nations to implement policies that would satisfy people's basic needs, permit the creation of consumer organizations, eliminate abusive business practices, and expand international cooperation. Two years after Peterson's death, these guidelines were expanded to reflect the need for sustainable consumption, a goal supported by the UN, CI, and other groups.

Sylvia Porter: A Trailblazer in the World of Personal Finance

Sylvia Porter (1913–1991) was a prominent American economist, specializing in the field of personal finance. Porter was born in Patchogue, New York, to Russian-Jewish immigrant parents. She earned a bachelor's degree in economics from Hunter College in New York in 1932. During the 1930s, Porter continued her formal education at the New York University School of Business. She also gained valuable experience in the world of finance while employed at a Wall Street investment firm. By the mid-1930s, Porter published her first financial newsletters and newspaper columns, and in 1939 she penned the first of her 30 books, *How to Make Money in Government Bonds.* Porter's reputation grew quickly, and by the late 1930s her syndicated financial columns appeared in hundreds of newspapers around the world. In 1975 she published *Sylvia Porter's Money Book,* a national best-seller.

Sylvia Porter was a trailblazer in the field of personal finance. She pioneered and popularized the topic of personal finance through her publications. Her financial columns, first published by the *New York Post* and later by the *New York Daily News,* helped familiarize consumers with investment strategies and money management. She expanded on her journalistic triumphs with *Sylvia Porter's Money Book: How to Earn It, Spend It, Save It, Invest It, Borrow It, and Use It to Better Your Life* (1975) and with her widely read *Sylvia Porter's Personal Finance Magazine* (1984–1989). These publications expanded consumers' ability to make informed choices in the American marketplace.

Porter was a trailblazer for women who wished to enter the male-dominated world of finance. While writing for the *New York Post,* Porter concealed her gender by signing her popular syndicated column "S. F. Porter." This ploy was deemed necessary to gain entry into the field. In later years, her columns were signed "Sylvia Porter," smoothing the path for other women economists and financial experts. Porter's prolific writings also explored many topics related to the prudent use of money, including investing, paying taxes, and planning for retirement.

John K. Galbraith: Consumer Manipulation in an Affluent Society

John Kenneth Galbraith (1908–) is among the twentieth century's most popular and controversial economists. Much of the controversy relates to Galbraith's theories on the power of advertisers to manipulate consumer demand. Galbraith was born in Ontario, Canada, and earned his bachelor's degree in agricultural economics at the University of Toronto in 1931. He continued his graduate studies in the United States, earning a doctorate in economics from the University of California, Berkeley, in 1934. After Galbraith's brief teaching stints at the University of California and Princeton, President Franklin Roosevelt appointed him to a leadership position in the Office of Price Administration during World War II. After the war, Galbraith accepted an economics professorship at Harvard, a position he held from 1948 until his retirement in 1975. During Galbraith's professional career, he wrote over two dozen books. His views were often provocative. For instance, in *American Capitalism* (1952) and *The New Industrial State* (1967), he supported the growth of consumer groups, labor unions, and big government to balance the power of large corporations, a balancing act he called "countervailing power." He also vigorously challenged traditional views on consumer demand in *The Affluent Society* (1958).

In *The Affluent Society,* Galbraith argued that major manufacturers and skillful advertising firms conspired to create consumers' demand for certain goods and services. He theorized that business firms held the upper hand in market transactions, a belief often referred to as the theory of producer sovereignty. Galbraith contended that the manipulation of consumer tastes and preferences was based on product differentiation, the creation of brand loyalties, and adept persuasion techniques designed to accent differences between similar products. In *The Affluent Society,* Galbraith stated "that wants can be synthesized by advertising, catalyzed by salesmanship, and shaped by the discreet manipulations of the persuaders."[17] Some other prominent authors of the 1950s were in agreement with Galbraith's views on producer sovereignty, most notably sociologist Vance Packard. In his widely read *The Hidden Persuaders* (1957), Packard theorized that even deeper psychological manipulations of consumer preferences were underway. The implications of producer sovereignty were unnerving to many people in the 1950s and 1960s. In effect, the theory of producer sovereignty questioned whether consumers' marketplace freedoms were more myth than reality.

While the theory of producer sovereignty challenged the more mainstream explanations about how free markets function, it has been largely discredited in recent decades. Most economists, sociologists, psychologists, and other social scientists reject the premise that consumers are pawns in a game rigged by producers and advertisers. Today, most economists lean toward the theory of **consumer sovereignty,** which rests on the belief that informed buyers exercise freedom of choice and are capable of making reasoned marketplace decisions. Consumer sovereignty also emphasizes the power of consumers, through individual buying decisions, to guide the production decisions of firms. Galbraith's views have enduring value, however. Even today there is uncertainty about how consumer wants and needs are determined. Economists still debate the impact of advertising spending on consumer preferences, an expenditure that averaged nearly $250 billion per year in the early 2000s.

NOTES

1. U.S. Department of Commerce/Bureau of Economic Analysis (BEA), "Personal Income and Its Disposition," March 26, 2004.
2. U.S. Department of Labor/Bureau of Labor Statistics (BLS), "Consumer Expenditures in 2001, *BLS News* December 3, 2002, www.bls.gov/news.release/cesan.nr0.htm.
3. *100 Leading National Advertisers: 48th Advertiser Profile Edition, Advertising Age*, June 23, 2003, 2.
4. Ibid., 3; "Domestic Advertising Spending by Category (2002)," www.adage.com; and "Top 100 Global Marketers," *Advertising Age's Global Marketing: 2003 Edition,* November 10, 2003, 3.
5. U.S. Department of Commerce/BEA, "Real Gross Domestic Product and Related Measures," February 28, 2003, www.bea.gov/briefrm/tables/ebr1.htm.
6. The Conference Board, "The Conference Board's Consumer Confidence Index Plummets Nearly 15 Points," February 25, 2003, www.consumerrresearchcenter.org/consumer_confidence; The Conference Board, "Consumer Confidence and Job Openings Are Down in All Regions of the Country," March 4, 2003, www.conference-board.org/utilities/pressFriendly.cfm?112501_NACAA.html; and The Conference Board, "Consumer Confidence Index Improves in October, October 28, 2003, www.conference-board.org/economics/consumerConfidence.cfm.

7. Consumer Federation of America (CFA), "Home Improvement Complaints Top NACAA/CFA's Annual Consumer Complain List," November 25, 2002, www.consumerfed.org/112501_NACAA.html; and Federal Trade Commission, *National and State Trends in Fraud and Identity Theft,* January 22, 2004, 2–3.

8. Consumers International, *Annual Report 2002* (London: Author, 2002), 3.

9. National Cooperative Business Association (NCBA), "Co-op Primer," 2003, www.ncba.coop/primer.cfm.

10. Consumer Federation of America (CFA), *The Cooperative Difference: Consumers Helping Themselves to Meet Needs and Save Money* (Washington, DC: Author).

11. International Co-operative Alliance (ICA), "What Is the ICA?" 1997–2003, www.coop.org/welcome.htm.

12. U.S. Consumer Product Safety Commission (CPSC), "Frequently Asked Questions," www.cpsc.gov/about/faq.html.

13. United National Environmental Program (UNEP), "United Nations Guidelines for Consumer Protection (as expanded in 1999)," Section G. 42, www.eptie.org/pc/sustain/guidelines/un-guidelines.htm.

14. Administrative Office of the U.S. Courts, "Bankruptcy Cases Continue to Break Federal Court Caseload Records," August 18, 2003, www.uscourts.gov.

15. Ibid.

16. Ibid.

17. John Kenneth Galbraith, *The Affluent Society* (New York: Mentor Books, 1958), 128.

SELECTED READINGS

Aronson, Brad, and Robbin Lee Zeff. *Advertising on the Internet.* 3rd ed. New York: John Wiley & Sons, 2004.

Berger, Warren. *Advertising Today.* New York: Phaidon Press Inc., 2004.

Brobeck, Stephen, Robert N. Mayer, and Robert O. Herrmann, eds. *Encyclopedia of the Consumer Movement.* Santa Barbara, CA: ABC-CLIO, 1997.

Cohen, Lizabeth. *A Consumers' Republic: The Politics of Mass Consumption in Postwar America.* New York: Knopf, 2003.

Cohen, Maurie J., and Joseph Murphy. *Exploring Sustainable Consumption: Environmental Policy and the Social Sciences.* New York: Pergamon Press, 2001.

Cross, Gary. *An All-Consuming Century.* New York: Columbia University Press, 2002.

Editors of Consumer Reports Magazine. *Consumer Reports Buying Guide: 2003.* Yonkers, NY: Consumer's Union, 2003.

Galbraith, John K. *The Affluent Society.* New York: Mentor Books, 1958.

Gronow, Jukka, and Alan Warde. *Ordinary Consumption.* New York: Routledge, 2003.

Keller, Edward, and Jonathon Berry. *The Influentials: One American in Ten Tells the Other Nine How to Vote, Where to Eat, and What to Buy.* New York: Free Press, 2003.

Lewis, Herschell G., Carol Nelson, and Rance Crain. *Advertising Age Handbook of Advertising.* New York: McGraw-Hill/Contemporary Books, 2000.

Martin, Justin. *Nader: Crusader, Spoiler, Icon.* Cambridge, MA: Perseus Publishing, 2002.

Nader, Ralph. *Crashing the Party: Taking on the Corporate Government in an Age of Surrender.* New York: St. Martin's Press, 2002.

Parisi, Nicolette, and Marc Robinson. *Understanding Consumer Rights (Essential Finance).* New York: DK Publisher, 2001.

Peterson, Esther. *Restless: The Memoirs of Labor and Consumer Activist Esther Peterson.* Washington, DC: Caring Publications, 1997.

Porter, Sylvia F. *Sylvia Porter's Money Book: How to Earn It, Spend It, Save It, Invest It, Borrow It, and Use It to Better Your Life.* New York: Doubleday, 1975.

Snyder, Stephen. *Credit after Bankruptcy: A Step-by-Step Action Plan to Quick and Lasting Recovery after Personal Bankruptcy.* Yonkers, NY: Bellwether, Inc., 2000.

Storrs, Landon R. Y. *Civilizing Capitalism: The National Consumer' League, Women's Activism, and Labor Standards in the New Deal Era.* Chapel Hill: University of North Carolina Press, 2000.

Stearns, Peter N. *Consumerism in World History: The Global Transformation of Desire.* New York: Routledge, 2002.

Zaltman, Gerald. *How Customers Think: Essential Insights into the Mind of the Market.* Boston: Harvard Business School Press, 2003.

Zyman, Sergio, and Armin Brott. *The End of Advertising as We Know It.* New York: John Wiley & Sons, 2002.

CHAPTER 7

Workers Organize: The Labor Force and Labor Power

Chapter 7 deals with workers, the growth of worker power, and the vital role of workers in the American economy. The civilian labor force in the United States is composed of 146 million workers, most employed by business firms or by the government in the services-producing, goods-producing, and agricultural sectors of the economy. The economic behaviors of workers and entrepreneurs are influenced by incentives, including wages and salaries. In the American economy, the forces of supply and demand determine most workers' wages. Government, at the state or national level, also influences some workers' wages. Labor power in the United States has grown significantly over the past century and a half due to labor activism, labor legislation, and changing attitudes about human resources in the American workplace. As a result, workers' wages, fringe benefits, and working conditions have improved steadily over time.

WORKERS AND WORKER BEHAVIOR

Labor, or human resources, represents the human input in production. Labor is generally considered to be the most important input, or factor of production. Without labor, other factors of production, such as capital goods and natural resources, would remain idle and nonproductive. Some labor is mainly manual, including many types of jobs in construction, manufacturing, mining, and agriculture. Other labor is mainly intellectual, including many jobs in education, law, medicine, and engineering. Further, a special category of labor, the entrepreneur, is instrumental in the creation of new businesses. Economists sometimes view entrepreneurship as a fourth factor of production. From an economic perspective, labor mobilizes the other inputs and, in exchange, expects monetary compensation, usually in the form of a wage or salary.

Workers and the American Labor Force

The **labor force** in the United States consists of individuals who are 16 years old or older and are either employed or actively seeking a job. In 2003 the civilian labor force numbered 145.8 million workers, of whom 137.4 million were employed and 8.4 million were unemployed. The **employment rate,** or percentage of the labor force that had a job, was 94.2 percent. The **unemployment rate,** or percentage of the labor force without a job, was 5.8 percent.[1] The U.S. labor force experienced phenomenal growth during the twentieth century, climbing from 28.5 million in 1900 to just under 146 million in 2003. The U.S. Department of Labor predicted that the labor force would climb to 158 million by 2010.[2]

To create a profile of the American labor force, economists often categorize workers by job type, gender, educational background, or other characteristic. One characteristic of the U.S. labor force is the dominant position of service-sector jobs. In 2003 the services-producing sector employed about 78 percent of all workers in the economy. Important job categories within the services-producing sector include transportation and public utilities, wholesale and retail trade, finance and insurance, real estate, government, and a wide variety of other services in the realms of health, entertainment, business maintenance, law, education, auto repair, and so on. In addition, the Labor Department predicted that of the 22 million new jobs created between 2000 and 2010, 20 million would be in services-producing industries. The goods-producing sector accounted for 20 percent of all jobs. The main goods-producing industries are associated with manufacturing, construction, and mining. The agricultural sector employed the remaining 2 percent of the labor force in farming, dairying, fishing, and forestry. This distribution of jobs is in marked contrast to U.S. employment patterns in the early twentieth century, as shown in Figure 7.1.[3]

A second feature of the U.S. labor force is the growing importance of women workers in American labor markets. The expanding role of women in the labor force is best illustrated by comparing the labor force participation rates for men and women over time. The labor force participation rate measures the labor force as a percent of the working-age population. For example, in early 2003 the overall labor force participation rate for all working-age people was 66.2 percent, which meant that about two-thirds of all working-age Americans were in the labor force. Reported by gender, about three out of four men and three out of five women were counted in the U.S. labor force. The participation rate was far different for both men and women in the past, however, as shown in Table 7.1.[4] Note how the gender gap has narrowed over the past century.

A third feature of the U.S. labor force is its high educational level. The educational attainment of American workers increased dramatically over the past century. For example, in 1900 just 6 percent of the general population had earned high school diplomas. In 2000, 84 percent of all Americans were high school graduates, and one-quarter of the adult population had earned four-year college degrees or more.[5] By 2003 about 90 percent of all employed workers aged 25 years or older

Figure 7.1
U.S. Employment by Sector: 1900 and 2003

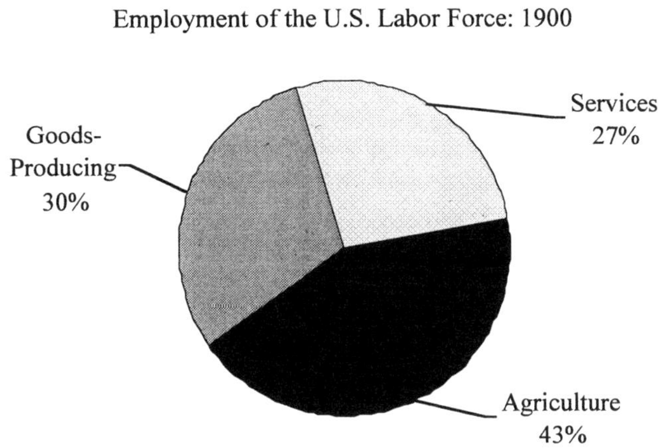

Source: U.S. Bureau of the Census, *The Statistical History of the United States: From Colonial Times to the Present,* 139.

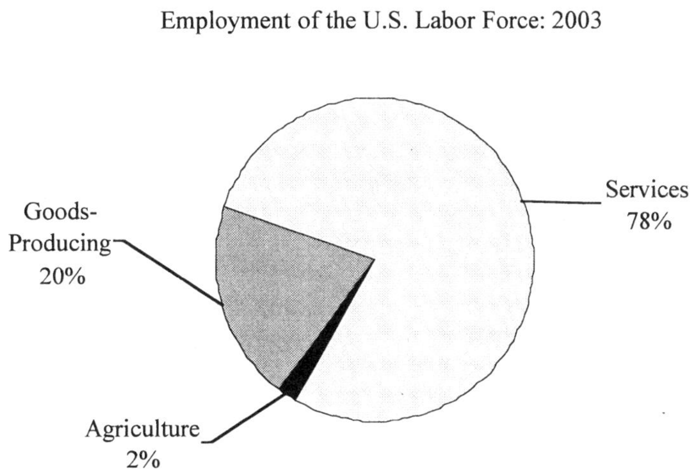

Source: Bureau of Labor Statistics, "Table A-21," October 2003.

had earned high school diplomas, while nearly one-third of this same group had earned bachelor's degrees or higher. Economists view education as a key factor in developing a society's human capital, particularly in a modern, dynamic, and information-driven economy. Economists use the term *human capital* to emphasize the positive impact of education and training in expanding workers' skills and abilities. Table 7.2 shows the educational attainment of American workers in 2003.[6] Note that there is a direct relationship between the labor force participation rate and workers' educational attainment. Also note that workers with higher levels of education are less likely to be unemployed. The direct relationship between

Table 7.1
Labor Force Participation Rate: 1900–2003*

Year	Women		Men	
	Number (thousands)	Participation Rate (%)	Number (thousands)	Participation Rate (%)
1900	5,319	18.8%	30,092	80.0%
1950	18,389	33.9%	43,819	83.7%
2003	68,055	60.4%	77,738	74.6%

*Data for 1900 are based on total labor force; data for 1950 and 2003 are based on the civilian labor force.
Source: U.S. Department of Labor/Bureau of Labor Statistics, *News,* April 4, 2003, 9; and U.S. Bureau of the Census, *The Statistical History of the United States,* 127–28.

Table 7.2
Education and Employment: March 2003 (civilian population 25 years and over)

Educational Attainment	Number in Civilian Labor Force (thousands)	Labor Force Participation Rate	Unemployment Rate
Less than high school diploma	12,874	45.0%	9.8%
High school graduate, no college	37,911	64.0%	6.0%
Some college or associate degree	34,103	73.5%	5.0%
Bachelor's degree and higher	39,603	78.7%	2.9%

Source: U.S. Department of Labor/Bureau of Labor Statistics, *News,* April 4, 2003, 11.

the educational attainment of workers and their earning power is shown in Figure 7.5 later in this chapter.

A fourth feature of the American labor force is its growing flexibility. Today, workers exercise greater choice in determining the time and location of their employment. For example, the number of full-time workers on flexible schedules more than doubled from 1985 to 2001, climbing from 12.4 million workers to nearly 29 million. Flexible schedules typically allow workers to start and end their workdays at nonstandard times. By the early 2000s, the highest concentrations of workers benefiting from flexible work schedules were employed in managerial and professional occupations. In addition, in 2001 about 20 million workers opted to perform at least some of their regular work at their homes rather than the factory, office, or other workplace. New technology supported this trend toward work in the home. By the early 2000s, about 80 percent of those who did some work at home used computers, and most also used e-mail or the Internet while working at home.[7]

Worker Behavior in the American Economy

Workers respond to market incentives in much the same way that consumers, savers, and other groups do. That is, workers exercise their freedom of choice in the labor markets. In the American economy, workers are free to choose an occupation, free to train for alternative employment, and free to set a career path that best satisfies their financial and psychological needs. Workers are also free to make choices about how much time they devote to work and to leisure. From an economic perspective, time spent in paid productive activity is classified as work. Leisure time represents all other uses of time, including recreational activities, household chores, shopping, and even sleep. All workers make trade-offs between work time and leisure time. A **trade-off** occurs when people choose to use a resource, in this case time, in one way rather than another. A worker's final decision about how much time should be spent on the job, or spent in leisure activities, is influenced by a number of factors. Two of the most important factors are the substitution effect and the income effect of a change in wages.

The **substitution effect of a wage increase** states that as the wage rate for a worker increases, the worker will work more hours. In other words, there is a positive relationship between the wage rate and hours worked, as shown in Figure 7.2. For example, when the wage rate climbs from $4 per hour to $6 per hour, the worker will trade off five hours of leisure in order to work five additional hours. As the wage rate continues to increase, additional hours of leisure are foregone so that the worker can work still more hours. If the positive relationship between wage increases and the corresponding increases in the quantity of labor is graphed, the result is the labor supply curve. Where the substitution effect of a wage increase dominates, the supply curve for labor is upward sloping to the northeast.

The **income effect of a wage increase** states that as the wage rate or other monetary compensation for a worker increases, the worker will work fewer hours. In other words, there is an inverse relationship between the higher wage rate and the number of hours a person is willing to work. The income effect seems to contradict the substitution effect. But consider the financial position of a popular entertainer, a skilled brain surgeon, or a top rock star. In each of these occupations, the worker is able to command a high wage for each performance, and, over time, each comes to enjoy a high standard of living and financial security. Under these conditions, the entertainer, surgeon, or rock star may choose to reduce the number of performances, in effect trading off work in order to have more leisure time. Hence, there is an inverse relationship between higher wages and the quantity of labor supplied, as shown in Figure 7.3. Note that the supply curve of labor tends to travel backwards. This shows that as the compensation per performance increases from $2 million to $4 million, and so on, this popular entertainer schedules fewer and fewer performances. Where the income effect of a wage increase dominates, the supply curve is upward sloping to the northwest.

Entrepreneurs: A Special Category of Labor

An **entrepreneur** is a person who starts a new business, develops a new product, or devises a better way to produce a product. Entrepreneurs are an important part of the American labor force. They tend to be innovative thinkers and risk-takers. They also expect to be compensated handsomely if their business activities are profitable. There are two main types of entrepreneurship: venture initiation and intrapreneurship. **Venture initiation** occurs when entrepreneurial activity results in the creation of a new business. From 1990 to 2000, venture initiation accounted for the birth of 575,000 new firms, on average, each year.[8] **Intrapreneurship** is entrepreneurial activity that occurs within an existing business, typically a large corporation. Intrapreneurs develop new products and in-

Figure 7.2
The Substitution Effect of a Wage Increase

Labor Supply Schedule: The Substitution Effect

Wage Rate (per hour)	Number of Hours Worked (per week)
$4.00	5
$6.00	10
$8.00	15
$10.00	20
$12.00	25

Labor Supply Curve: The Substitution Effect

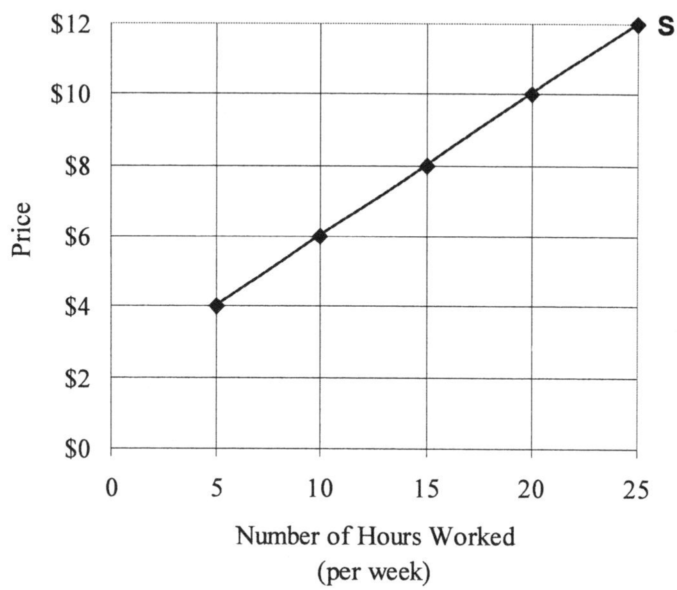

Figure 7.3
The Income Effect of a Wage Increase

Labor Supply Schedule: The Income Effect

Wage Rate (per performance)	Number of Performances (per month)
$2,000,000	5
$4,000,000	4
$6,000,000	3
$8,000,000	2
$10,000,000	1

Labor Supply Curve for a Popular Entertainer
(wage rate per performance in $ millions)

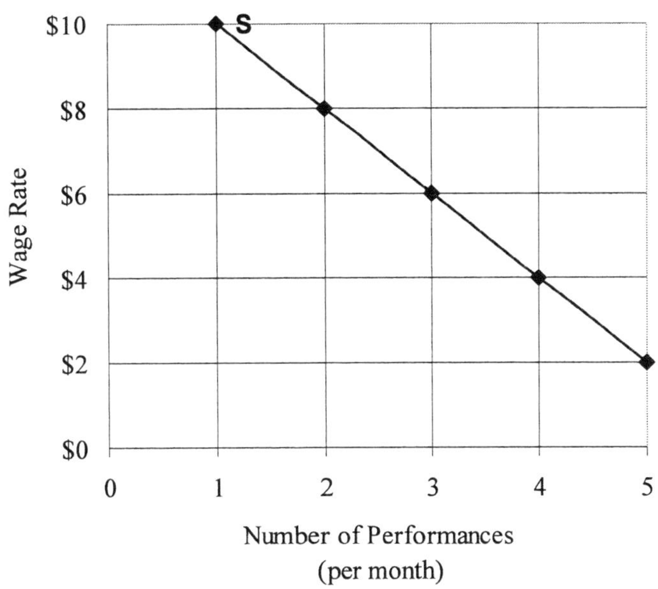

stigate changes in the production, marketing, or distribution of the good. Hence, corporate intrapreneurs might be scientists, engineers, researchers, managers, or other change agents within the firm. Entrepreneurs own and operate millions of small and large businesses in the U.S. economy.

At one end of the spectrum, entrepreneurs initiate business activity through the creation of small nonemployer businesses. These are firms that produce a good or service but do not hire employees. According to the U.S. Census Bureau, more than 70 percent of all businesses, some 17 million firms in all, were classified as nonemployer businesses in 2001. The great majority of nonemployer businesses were organized as sole proprietorships (14.8 million), while the remaining 2.2 million were organized as partnerships or corporations. Entrepreneurial activity takes place in a variety of venues ranging from mom and pop shops, to professional offices, to home-based businesses. Examples of occupations in nonemployer businesses include authors, barbers, builders, childcare providers, real estate agents, and tax preparers. While nonemployer businesses comprised more than 70 percent of all business firms in the U.S. economy, their $730 billion in business receipts represented just 3 percent of the nation's business activity.[9] (See chapter 5 for more on the types of business organization.)

At the other end of the spectrum, entrepreneurs create businesses that grow into corporate giants. In the early twentieth century, entrepreneurs such as King C. Gillette (safety razor), Frederick L. Maytag (washing machine), and William H. Hoover (vacuum cleaner) founded businesses to mass produce consumer goods. Other entrepreneurs during the early century, such as Henry Ford, revolutionized a production process. Ford's application of the moving assembly line to the production of automobiles not only increased technical efficiency, but also significantly reduced auto prices for consumers. The spirit of entrepreneurship continues to spark new technologies and new business ventures in modern America. The American economic landscape is dotted with the results of entrepreneurial vision in industries as diverse as fast-food (Ray Kroc, McDonald's), retail trade (Sam Walton, Wal-Mart), and computer software (Bill Gates, Microsoft). The entrepreneur, past and present, has been an engine of growth in the dynamic U.S. economy.

WAGE DETERMINATION IN LABOR MARKETS

A **labor market** consists of any situation in which individuals voluntarily supply their labor in exchange for a wage or salary. Because labor is a factor of production, labor markets represent one of the three main types of exchanges that occur in a nation's factor market, joining land markets and capital markets (see chapter 3 for more on factor markets).

Labor markets are often defined by different characteristics, such as geographic region or occupation. For instance, economists might analyze the labor market in a certain metropolitan area, a study that would deal with a broad range of labor exchanges within a central city and its suburbs. Labor markets might also be more narrowly defined by a specific occupation or job specialty. In the early 2000s, for example, many towns and cities across the United States were confronted with labor shortages in certain labor markets, such as teachers, nurses, and other professionals. There are many other ways to designate a labor market, such as skilled and unskilled labor markets, unionized and nonunionized labor markets, and so on. One common feature of virtually all labor markets, however, is that the dynamic forces of supply and demand affect the wages that workers will receive.

Determining an Equilibrium Wage

The demand for labor resources, like the demand for natural resources and capital goods, is a **derived demand.** That is, the demand for a certain type of worker is derived from the demand for the output produced by that worker. For example, the U.S. Department of Labor predicts a significant increase in the demand for business services, health services, and social services between 2000 and 2010. Hence, experts anticipate significant growth in the number of jobs that produce these services, such as computer software engineers and support specialists, registered nurses, home health care and medical aides, physical therapists, and so on. Conversely, some jobs in manufacturing, mining, and agriculture are expected to grow more slowly or even decline from 2000 to 2010. Thus, the Labor Department predicts job losses in occupations such as sewing machine operators, typists, switchboard operators, farmers and ranchers, and others.[10]

The forces of supply and demand are responsible for determining an equilibrium wage in most labor markets. An **equilibrium wage** occurs at the point of intersection between the labor supply curve and the labor demand curve. In the nation's factor market, households supply labor resources, while employers in the private and public sectors demand labor. On the supply side of the market, an increase in the wage rate typically results in an increase in the quantity of labor supplied, while a decrease in the wage rate causes a reduction in the quantity of labor supplied. The direct relationship between wages and the quantity of labor supplied is illustrated on the upward-sloping labor supply curve shown in Figure 7.4. On the demand side of the market, an increase in the wage rate decreases the quantity of labor demanded, while a decrease in the wage rate causes an increase in the quantity of labor demanded. The inverse relationship between wages and the quantity of labor demanded is illustrated on the downward sloping labor demand curve shown in Figure 7.4. The equilibrium wage for workers in this labor market is $10 per hour. The equilibrium quantity of labor is 6,000 workers. The equilibrium wage and quantity represents the best compromise between the interests of workers and producers.

The interplay between the supply of and demand for workers in U.S. labor markets is dynamic, as changes in economic conditions alter both sides of the market. Recall that the demand for labor is a derived demand. That is, the demand for certain types of labor exists only when there is a demand for the goods or services produced by that labor. There are also factors that influence the supply of labor in the overall economy and in specific labor markets. On the national level, the overall supply of labor increased dramatically over the past century due mainly to population growth and a higher labor force participation rate. From 1900 to 2003, the U.S. population climbed from 76 million to 292 million. During the same period of time, the labor force participation rate also rose steadily, fueled mainly by the influx of women entrants into the labor force. Table 7.3 shows the remarkable growth of the U.S. civilian labor force from 1950 to 2010.[11] Note that the U.S. population more than doubled during this 60-year period, while the labor force increased by nearly 100 million workers.

Other factors affect the labor supply in thousands of specialized labor markets in the U.S. economy. These factors include required education and skills, workplace conditions, and job location. Many specialized occupations re-

Figure 7.4
The Equilibrium Wage

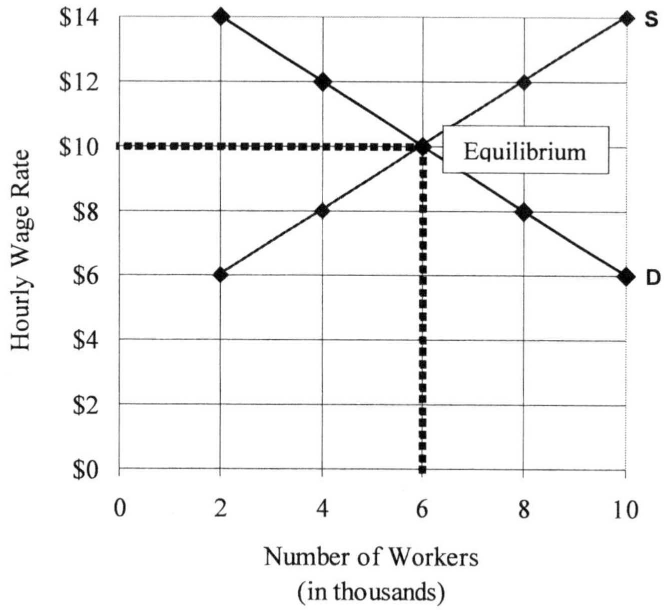

Table 7.3
U.S. Population and the Labor Force: 1950–2010

Year	Resident Population (millions)	Noninstitutional Adult Population (millions)	Civilian Labor Force (millions)	Labor Force Participation Rate (%)
1950	151.3	106.6	62.2	58.3%
1960	179.3	117.2	69.6	59.4%
1970	203.3	137.1	82.8	60.4%
1980	226.5	167.7	106.9	63.8%
1990	248.7	189.1	125.8	66.5%
2000	281.4	209.7	140.9	67.2%
2010*	299.9	233.6	157.7	67.5%

* Estimate
Source: Statistical Abstract of the United States: 2002, 560, 561; *The Statistical History of the United States.*

quire extensive education and advanced academic degrees, professional internships, and other credentials as a condition of employment. For example, professional or doctoral degrees are required of physicians, pharmacists, lawyers, physicists, and biological scientists. The limited supply of these highly skilled workers contributes to higher wage rates. Jobs that require less education or training, such as cashiers, retail salespersons, and personal care and home health aides, command lower wage rates. The direct relationship between level of education and income is illustrated in Figure 7.5.[12]

Figure 7.5
Education and Income: 2000

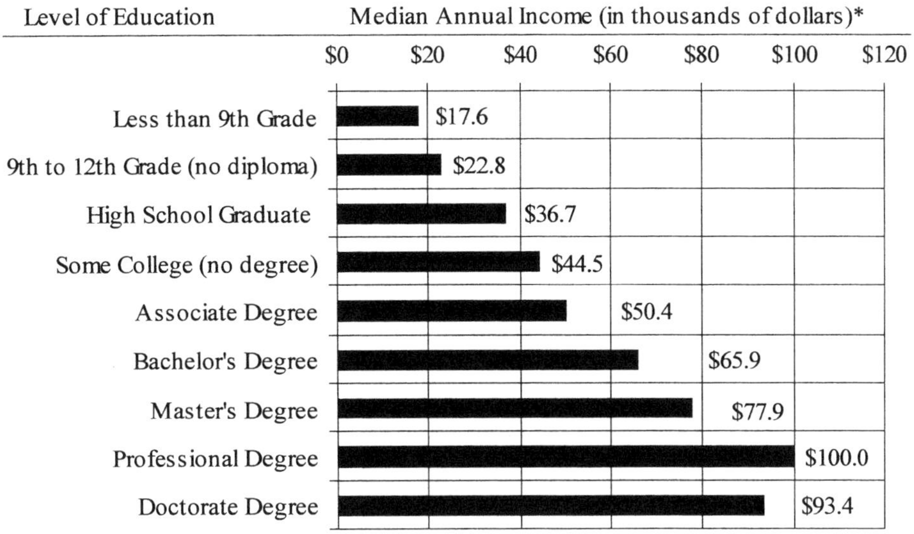

* Data for persons 25 years and older; includes wages and other forms of income.
Source: U.S. Census Bureau, *Statistical Abstract of the United States: 2002.*

A second factor affecting the supply of labor in certain labor markets is working conditions. Workplaces that are uncomfortable, dangerous, or otherwise unattractive tend to discourage entry into these fields and thus limit the labor supply in these labor markets. To attract a sufficient number of workers to less desirable workplaces, higher wage rates are offered, a practice often referred to as *compensating differentials.* That is, workers often receive higher compensation for jobs that involve risks to their health or well-being, and tend to receive lower compensation for comparable jobs in safer, friendlier environments. For example, relatively high wage rates are offered to some firefighters, police officers, construction workers, and miners as compensation for the personal risks inherent in their jobs.

A third factor affecting the labor supply in some labor markets is job location. Generally, the supply of labor is more limited in remote or inhospitable locations. As a result, a higher wage rate is necessary to attract workers to these locations. For example, high wages were paid to workers to build the Alaska pipeline in the 1970s, to cap burning oil wells in Kuwait in 1991, and to rebuild the war-torn Iraqi infrastructure in 2003.

Government and Wage Determination

The government influences wage rates for some workers in the U.S. economy through federal legislation and economic policies. Most federal laws related to wage rates and the conditions of employment promote equal opportunity and equity in the American workplace. For example, the Equal Pay Act of 1963 requires employers to pay the same wage rate to workers performing identical jobs, regardless of the worker's gender. This act allows differences in pay if the differential is based on seniority, worker productivity, or merit incentives, however. The Equal Pay Act was reinforced by the passage of the Civil Rights Act of 1964. Under Title VII of the Civil Rights Act, it became unlawful for employers "to fail or refuse to hire or to discharge any individual, or otherwise discriminate against any individual with respect to his compensation, terms, conditions, or privileges of employment, because of such individual's race, color, religion, sex, or national origin."[13] The Civil Rights Act of 1964 also created the Equal Employment Opportunity Commission (EEOC), a federal agency designed to ensure compliance with antidiscrimination laws. Since the mid-1960s, other landmark legislation has been enacted by Congress to promote equality of opportunity in the workplace, including the Age Discrimination in Employment Act of 1967 and the Americans with Disabilities Act of 1990.

Government, mainly at the state level, has also grappled with the issue of comparable worth in the workplace. **Comparable worth** refers to the equalization of pay rates between different jobs in a workplace, jobs that require essentially the same types of skills and that have about the same value to the employer. Supporters of comparable worth legislation argue that laws are needed to reduce wage rate discrepancies between jobs traditionally held by women and those held by men. The fact that median salaries of women were just 76 percent of those earned by men in the early 2000s fueled demands by some advocacy groups and legislators to support comparable worth laws. Opponents counter that such government intervention disrupts the efficiency of labor markets, which rely on the forces of supply and demand to establish an equilibrium wage. Further, opponents argue that there are legitimate reasons for wage discrepancies between jobs, including differences in education or training, productivity, seniority, and personal choices related to job selection and family responsibilities. By the early 2000s, dozens of state legislatures were considering bills compatible with the goals of comparable worth. On the national level, two bills—the Paycheck Fairness Act and the Fair Pay Act—were introduced to Congress in 2001.

The most direct way for the government to affect the wages of certain workers is to establish a **minimum wage,** a price floor that sets a minimum hourly wage rate for employees. Under the provisions of the Fair Labor Standards Act (FLSA), the first national minimum wage was established in 1938 at an hourly wage rate of $0.25. Since 1938, the minimum wage has been raised 20 times. The most recent increase occurred in 1997, when the hourly rate increased from $4.75 to $5.15.[14] Originally, the federal minimum wage applied to workers whose jobs were related to interstate commerce. During the 1960s and 1970s, coverage under the FLSA was expanded to include most other employees in both the private and public sectors of the economy. The FLSA also included provisions that defined the maximum workweek, originally 44 hours and today 40 hours of work per week. The FLSA mandated a wage rate of at least time and a half for the hours employees work beyond the maximum workweek.

In addition, by the early 2000s, 11 state governments had established their own minimum wages above the federal rate of $5.15. All of these states were located in the Northeast or the West. In 2003 the highest state minimum wages were found in Alaska ($7.15 per hour), Washington ($7.01 per hour), Connecticut ($6.90 per hour; scheduled to increase to $7.10 per hour in 2004), and Oregon ($6.90 per hour). Several states, including Alaska, Washington, and Oregon, also adjust the state minimum wage upward each year to account for inflation.[15]

The minimum wage affects different labor markets in different ways. For example, employees in most skilled trades and the professions are largely unaffected by the minimum wage because compensation in these occupations is already significantly above the federal or state minimum wage standards. The minimum wage is felt more keenly in lower-wage occupations that require less training and fewer specialized skills, such as cashiers, retail salespersons, office clerks, and home health aides.

There has been an ongoing debate about the timing and size of minimum wage increases since the late 1930s. Today's $5.15 minimum wage, which has been the national standard since 1997, spawned similar controversy. Supporters of a higher minimum wage argue that an hourly wage rate of $5.15 cannot provide for a minimum standard of living in the United States. For example, a full-time minimum wage employee who worked all 52 weeks in 2002 would earn an annual income of just $10,712. If this employee headed a family of four, the household's income would fall $7,680 below the poverty line of $18,392.[16] In addition, the federal minimum wage, which is not adjusted annually for inflation, automatically declines in value as inflation erodes the purchasing power of the wage. Opponents of a higher minimum wage counter that higher wages increase business costs and may cause employers to cut jobs in some unskilled labor markets. They also note that a only small percentage of the U.S. labor force earns the minimum wage, and that the wage rate for many of these workers quickly rises above the minimum standard. In 2001 only 2.2 million workers, about 3 percent of employed wage and salary workers in the U.S. economy, earned an hourly wage of $5.15 or less, and most of these workers held part-time jobs.[17]

The impact of a higher minimum wage on some low-wage labor markets might resemble that shown in Figure 7.6 Note that the equilibrium wage in this labor market occurs where the supply curve and demand curve for labor intersect, in this case an hourly wage rate of $4 and a quantity of 5,000 employed workers. Suppose that a minimum wage of $7 is applied to this labor market, as shown in Figure 7.6. The result is a drop in the number of workers demanded, from 5,000 to just 2,000, as shown on the demand curve. At the same time, the number of workers willing to work at this higher wage rises from 5,000 to 8,000, as shown on the supply curve. Hence, a labor surplus of 6,000 workers is created because the quantity supplied (8,000) far exceeds the quantity demanded (2,000) at the new government-imposed wage rate. This theoretical model perhaps overstates the job loss that would occur due to an increase in the minimum wage, but it illustrates the potential for unemployment in certain labor markets.

Figure 7.6
The Minimum Wage and Labor Markets

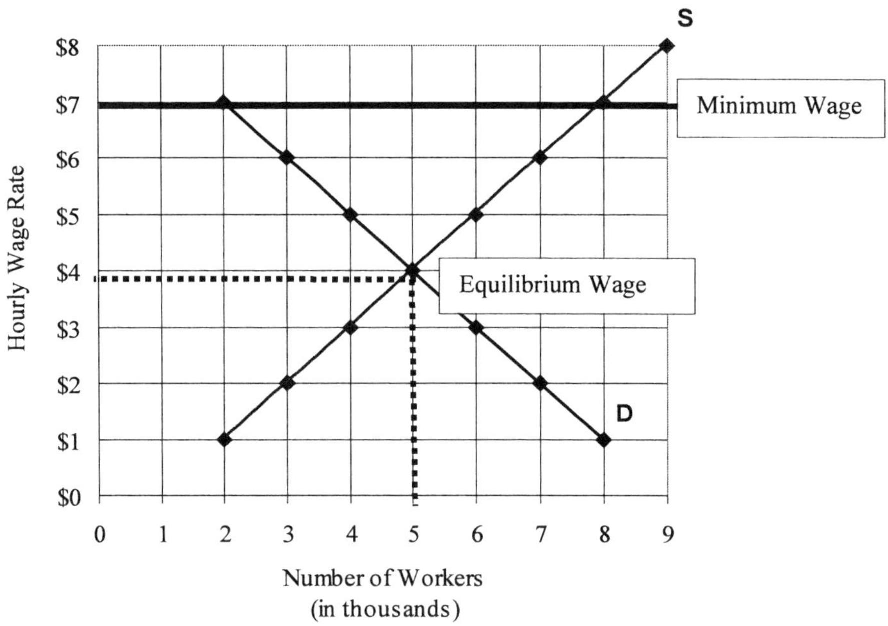

THE LABOR MOVEMENT AND LABOR POWER

The **labor movement** represents the collective actions of laborers, mainly workers who belong to labor unions, to improve wages, the conditions of employment, and the overall quality of life for workers. A **labor union** is a formal association of workers empowered by members to negotiate labor contracts with employers, a process called **collective bargaining.** Labor unions also influence labor reforms and labor legislation at the state and national levels. The labor movement grew alongside the Industrial Revolution as the power of large manufacturers in Europe and the United States dwarfed the power of individual laborers in the industrial workplace. In the United States, the pace of industrialization accelerated during the post–Civil War era, spawning more powerful national labor unions. Like most economic and social movements, the American labor movement progressed in fits and starts. During the late nineteenth and early twentieth centuries, for example, labor unions struggled not only with big business, but also with a suspicious public and an unsympathetic government. By the 1930s, however, unionism had gained significant acceptance and power within the American economy.

The American Labor Movement: The Early Years

The origins of the American labor movement can be traced to the first glimmers of worker consciousness, which occurred more than 200 years ago. In the late 1700s, long before the Industrial Revolution took root in the United States, conflicts between employers and their workers, including the use of strikes, had already taken place in certain trades. Not until the mid-1800s, however, were the first national unions formed. The short-lived National Trades Union (1834–1837), founded in New York City, was the first national union in the United States. The National Trades Union recruited members from local crafts unions, mainly from eastern cities located between Boston, Massachusetts, and Baltimore, Maryland. The union proposed the 10-hour workday, equal pay for equal work, and other economic benefits. It opposed direct union involvement in the political process. The Panic of 1837, a severe recession, stifled union activity and led to the demise of the National Trades Union.

Another early attempt to organize workers on the national level was undertaken by the National Labor Union (1866–1872). The National Labor Union (NLU) was founded in Baltimore by William H. Sylvis and was organized as a loose confederation of unions. Sylvis believed that union power was best achieved through mass membership; thus he courted both skilled and unskilled workers. The NLU lobbied aggressively for the eight-hour workday. It also supported immigration restrictions, the creation of a federal department of labor, and improved working conditions for women. The untimely death of Sylvis in 1869 and an economic slump in the early 1870s contributed to the NLU's collapse in 1872.

The Knights of Labor: Unionism for All

The American labor movement was bolstered by the creation of the Noble and Holy Order of the Knights of Labor by Uriah H. Stephens in 1869. At first, the Philadelphia-based Knights was organized as a secret society of wage earners. Secrecy was necessary to avoid reprisals by employers. Workers who organized or joined labor unions were often branded as agitators or radicals, and were punished accordingly. One severe penalty for so-called labor agitators was blacklisting, a practice whereby employers fired union workers and then circulated their names on a blacklist to discourage their rehiring. The fear of being blacklisted was compounded by the undercover detective work of the Pinkertons, agents of the Allen Pinkerton Detective Agency of Chicago. Pinkertons were contracted by businesses to infiltrate budding labor unions and expose labor leaders. They were also hired by employers as personal body guards and as security guards for factories and mines. Under these conditions, membership in the Knights grew slowly during the 1870s. In these early years, most members hailed from the skilled crafts. Heavily represented were blacksmiths, carpenters, machinists, stonecutters, and others in the manual trades. The Knights' vision was to create a mass union for nearly all workers, however, excluding only the small professional class.

In 1879, when Terence V. Powderly assumed leadership of the Knights, membership stood at nearly 10,000. The flamboyant Powderly capitalized on the discontent of many common workers who had suffered arbitrary wage cuts and other abuses at the hands of employers. He soon removed the veil of secrecy from the organization and shortened the union's name to the Knights of Labor, a move that not only made the union more accessible to workers but also more acceptable to the Catholic Church. Powderly made strategic alliances, gaining favor with aggressive women labor activists such as Mary (Mother) Jones, who rallied thousands of women under the Knights' banner (see the biography of Mary Jones).

While generally opposed to strikes, Powderly and the Knights gained additional credibility by supporting a successful railroad strike in 1885, an act that paralyzed the Wabash line headed by Jay Gould, one of the most powerful financiers and railroad magnates in the country. At issue was the firing of workers due to their affiliation with the Knights. Surprisingly, Jay Gould rescinded the firings, and, in doing so, increased the prestige of the union. By 1886 membership in the Knights swelled to over 700,000 workers. As the chief voice of the labor movement in the United States, the Knights took center stage in pressing for labor rights and reforms. Included in their demands were the eight-hour day, equal wages for women, and prohibitions against child labor, convict labor, and contract labor—particularly contract labor imported from China. On a broader scale, the Knights sought reforms to promote a more equitable distribution of wealth in the United States, including the creation of consumer cooperatives and producer cooperatives and the introduction of a progressive federal income tax.

The peak in union membership coincided with a series of unfortunate events, however, which precipitated the Knights' decline. By the mid-1880s, a growing militancy among local units of the union created internal turmoil. This militancy boiled over into a series of unauthorized and unsuccessful strikes in 1886, crippling the reputation of the Knights. The Knights were also blamed for the rise in labor violence. Most sensational was the Haymarket Square riot, which occurred on May 4, 1886, in Chicago. While this riot was the handiwork of bomb-throwing anarchists, the union was held responsible. Public opinion turned decidedly against the Knights, and, virtually overnight, membership plummeted. In fact, just a few weeks later, a number of the skilled crafts unions previously associated with the Knights of Labor joined the newly formed American Federation of Labor (AFL). During the 1890s, the Knights of Labor faded into obscurity in the United States, but maintained some clout in Canada. The torch of the American labor movement was thus passed from the Knights to the AFL.

The American Federation of Labor: Pure and Simple Unionism

The American Federation of Labor (AFL) was a federation of skilled craft unions. A **craft union** is a labor organization of skilled workers in a single trade, such as carpenters, masons, and printers. While the AFL was officially established in 1886, its foundation was laid with the creation of the Federation of Organized Trades and Labor Unions in 1881. Samuel Gompers, who led the AFL for all but one year from 1886 to 1924, designed the AFL as a federation of craft unions in order to guarantee autonomy for each local craft union (see the biography of Samuel Gompers). During his tenure as president of the AFL, Gompers supported "pure and simple" unionism. To Gompers, this meant that union activity focused on bread-and-butter issues such as higher wages, shorter working hours, and better working conditions. Even before the AFL was formed, a close ally of Gompers, Adolph Strasser, summarized the sentiments of pure and simple unionism in testimony before Congress: "We have no ultimate ends. We are going from day to day. We are fighting only for immediate objects—objects that can be realized in a few years. . . . [W]e want to dress better and to live better, and become better off. . . . [W]e are opposed to theorists. . . . We are all practical men."[18] Throughout his career at the helm of the AFL, Gompers consistently opposed membership for unskilled workers, African Americans, and women, groups that he believed would swell certain labor markets and depress wages.

AFL membership increased during the late nineteenth and early twentieth centuries, and topped 4 million members in 1920, about 80 percent of all unionized workers. From the mid-1880s to the mid-1930s, the AFL represented the most important voice of the American labor movement. During this period of time, there were significant gains for workers in the U.S. labor force. For example, between 1890 and 1925, the average workweek for unionized workers in manufacturing industries fell from over 54 hours to 46 hours. Wages for unionized workers during the same period of time climbed by more than 200 percent, from 32 cents per hour to 99 cents per hour. Nonunionized workers in manufacturing also benefited from a shorter workweek and higher wages during the period but, in 1925, still worked about 4.5 hours longer per week for about two-thirds the hourly wage rate of unionized workers.[19]

Serious problems confronted the AFL during the 1920s and 1930s, however. A post–World War I recession sparked thousands of strikes, mainly the result of disputes over wages and union security. The Republican administrations of Presidents Harding, Coolidge, and Hoover, all adherents of laissez-faire capitalism, were generally unsympathetic to the demands of organized labor. The onset of the Great Depression in 1929 further eroded support for unionism as workers struggled to hold onto their jobs at any wage. Also divisive were the internal squabbles among the union's leadership over the inclusion of industrial unions into the American Federation of Labor. The AFL, rooted in craft unionism since the 1880s, viewed industrial unionism as a direct threat to skilled crafts unions that already operated in certain factories, mills, and other workplaces. Thus, the AFL rejected dual unionism, the coexistence of craft unions and industrial unions operating side-by-side. Differences on this issue were irreconcilable by the mid-1930s, causing the birth of a rival union, the Congress of Industrial Organizations.

The Congress of Industrial Organizations: The Industrial Union

The Congress of Industrial Organizations (CIO) was born out of the turbulence and discord of the 1935 AFL convention. At the heart of this conflict was a proposal to allow industrial unions to join the AFL, a proposal that was defeated at the convention. An **industrial union** is a labor organization that includes all workers within an industry, regardless of their skill level or job description. Some union leaders saw great potential for industrial unions as a means to expand worker power in the United States, particularly in the growing mass-production industries such as automobiles, textiles, rubber, and steel. This faction of the AFL formed an ad hoc Committee for Industrial Organization (CIO), which began to organize workers along industrial lines in the mass-production industries. All workers—regardless of skill level, race, or gender—were recruited to join these industrial unions. In 1936 the AFL leadership retaliated by expelling several CIO unions, thus splintering the federation into two rival camps. In 1938 the Committee for Industrial Organization christened a new labor union, the Congress of Industrial Organizations (CIO), and selected John L. Lewis as its first president.

Even before the Congress of Industrial Organizations was formed in 1938, a number of associated industrial unions were demanding higher pay, better working conditions, and union recognition in key industries. At times, agreements were made through negotiations. In 1937, for example, the steelworker's union successfully negotiated a favorable contract, including union recognition, with the U.S. Steel Corporation. At other times, industrial unions became embroiled in bitter labor strikes against major corporations. In 1936–1937 the United Auto Workers (UAW) staged a bitter sit-down strike against General Motors (GM). In a sit-down strike, workers declare a work stoppage and then occupy the plant, refusing to allow strikebreakers, called scabs, to replace the strikers. The sit-down strike against GM gained certain contract concessions from the auto giant, including recognition of the UAW as the bargaining unit for auto workers at GM plants. Sit-down strikes were used with varying degrees of success until 1939, when the Supreme Court banned further use of this labor practice.

Despite the growing militancy of some industrial unions and the rift between the AFL and CIO, union membership grew rapidly from the mid-1930s to the 1960s, as shown in Table 7.4.[20] The election of the more pro-labor President Franklin D. Roosevelt in 1932, and the enactment of pro-labor legislation during the 1930s, rejuvenated the spirit of unionism even as the country reeled from the effects of the Great Depression. The Norris-La Guardia Act (1932) outlawed the yellow dog contract, which prohibited workers from joining a union. The National Labor Relations Act (1935), more commonly called the Wagner Act, secured workers' right to form unions and bargain collectively with employers. It also created the National Labor Relations Board (NLRB) to prevent unfair labor practices by employers or labor unions. The Fair Labor Standards Act (1938) established a minimum wage of $0.25 per hour for some workers and a maximum workweek of 44 hours. In 1955 a merger between the AFL and CIO created the AFL-CIO, an action that restored some unity to the American labor movement.

The Radical Fringe of the Labor Movement: The Mollies and the Wobblies

Labor radicalism was also a feature of the American labor movement. The tactics of the Molly Maguires during the late 1800s, and of the Industrial Workers of the World (IWW) in the early 1900s, illustrated the militancy of some labor groups. The Molly Maguires, often called the Mollies, was a secret

Table 7.4
U.S. Union Membership: 1900–2000

Year	Total Union Membership (thousands)	Union Membership as a Percentage of Nonagricultural Labor Force	Membership in the AFL (thousands)	Membership in the CIO (thousands)	Membership in Independent Unions (thousands)
1900	791	4.2%	548	–	243
1910	2,116	8.2%	1,562	–	554
1920	5,034	16.2%	4,079	–	955
1930	3,632	11.6%	2,961	–	671
1940	8,944	26.9%	4,247	3,625	1,072
1950	14,823	31.5%	8,494	3,713	2,616
1960	18,117	31.4%	AFL-CIO	15,072	3,045
1970	20,752	27.4%	AFL-CIO	15,978	4,773
1980	19,843	21.9%	AFL-CIO	13,602	6,241
1990	16,740	16.1%	AFL-CIO	13,933	2,807
2000	16,258	13.5%	AFL-CIO	12,952	3,306

Table Notes: Data for 1900–1930 include Canadian union members; data for 1950 cite NBER rather than BLS source.
Source: U.S. Bureau of the Census, *The Statistical History of the United States: From Colonial Times to the Present*, 127, 176–77; U.S. Census Bureau, *Statistical Abstract of the United States: 2002*, 411; *Directory of Labor Organizations 2001*.

society comprised of Irish immigrants. The Mollies had a long and stormy history marked by violence against the British and the propertied classes in Ireland. The first Mollies arrived in the United States in the mid-1840s, and many congregated in the coal-mining regions of Pennsylvania. Here they worked in company towns—towns owned and operated by the mine owners. Low wages, dangerous working conditions, and abusive bosses mobilized the Mollies, who resorted to sabotage and physical violence against mine owners. During the 1870s, a Pinkerton detective infiltrated the Mollies and provided law enforcement officials with evidence to convict many members for their criminal activities. The execution of 19 Mollies and the imprisonment of many others marked an end to the reign of terror that gripped the anthracite coal mines of Pennsylvania. The fall of the Mollies did not end the horrific working conditions that inspired these acts of terror, however.

The Industrial Workers of the World (IWW), or Wobblies, was a revolutionary labor organization founded in Chicago in 1905. Among its founders were a disparate collection of labor activists, socialists, and revolutionaries. The Wobblies grew in strength during the early 1900s under the leadership of William (Big Bill) Haywood. Unlike the AFL and most other unions, the Wobblies directly challenged the capitalist economic system, including private property rights and the practice of wage labor. The organization's Preamble supported ongoing struggle between the working class and the employing class "until the workers of the world organize as a class, take possession of the earth and the machinery of production, and abolish the wage system."[21] Under the slogan "One Big Union," the Wobblies supported an extreme version of industrial unionism and scored some labor victories in the mining and lumbering regions of the Pacific Northwest. The union lacked the organizational skills to maintain its presence in the textile mills of New England and other workplaces, however. Many other factors contributed to the Wobblies' rapid decline during the late 1910s and early 1920s, including its opposition to U.S. entry into World War I, the imprisonment and harassment of union officials by the government, internal disputes, and the antiunion climate of the 1920s.

The AFL-CIO: The Labor Movement's Modern Era

The merger of the AFL and CIO in 1955 created a new union, the AFL-CIO. With a membership of 16 million workers from 139 local affiliates, 9 out of every 10 unionized workers in the United States now belonged to the organization. The 1950s and early 1960s also represented the heyday of organized labor in the United States, when over 30 percent of the civilian labor force was unionized. Since that time, union membership, as a percent of the civilian labor force, has declined steadily. In 2003 15.8 million workers, just 12.9 percent of the civilian labor force, claimed union membership.[22]

The decline in union membership is rooted in some fundamental economic changes in the American economy over the past half-century. First, the standard of living for most Americans improved over time. Higher wages, better fringe benefits, and an expanded safety net of social programs made most households more financially secure and prosperous. Prosperity, in turn, made workers more complacent and less inclined to form or join unions. Second, federal legislation addressed important workplace issues. The Wagner Act (1935) promoted union security, while the Occupational Safety and Health Administration (1970) ensured compliance with safety regulations in the workplace. Third, a fundamental shift in economic activity sapped traditional union strongholds. Goods-producing industries, which historically provided the bedrock of union support, continued to shrink, while less unionized services-producing industries grew in importance. By the early 2000s, services-producing industries employed four out of every five workers in the economy. Fourth, global economic pressures hurt unionism. New global competitors, nonunion domestic competitors, and threats of plant relocation to low-wage countries conspired to reduce union affiliation. Fifth, unions suffered from negative public opinion. The rampant corruption within the International Brotherhood of Teamsters and its expulsion from the AFL-CIO in the late 1950s tarnished the image of unions.

The general decline in unionism also resulted from antiunion government policies at the federal and state levels. At the federal level, the Taft-Hartley Act (1947) banned the **closed shop,** an arrangement that required employers to hire only labor union members. This act also broadened the authority of government to block certain strikes through injunctions. The Landrum-Griffin Act

(1959), which was enacted after Teamsters' corruption was exposed in the 1950s, set rules for the selection of union leaders and the conduct of union business. President Ronald Reagan's decision to break the air traffic controllers strike in 1981 also fueled antiunion sentiments. By 2003, 22 state legislatures, mainly in the South and Midwest, had also enacted right-to-work laws to create an open shop arrangement. In an **open shop,** workers are free to choose whether to join an existing union at a workplace. Unions prefer the **union shop,** however, an arrangement that requires workers to join an existing union after they are hired.

Despite the decline in union membership since the 1960s, today's labor movement shows signs of vitality. The AFL-CIO, the flagship organization in the movement, pledges "to improve the lives of working families—to bring economic justice to the workplace and social justice to our nation."[23] Today the AFL-CIO represents 13 million workers from 65 associated national and international labor unions. Its membership includes workers from all economic sectors—services-producing, goods-producing, and agricultural—and from all socioeconomic groups. Its mission reflects the need to mobilize the power of workers and give voice to their concerns at the local, national, and international levels.

Amid the general decline of unionism in the United States, there have also been some encouraging signs for organized labor. For example, the number of public-sector employees enrolled under a union banner has increased significantly in recent decades. In 2003, 37.2 percent of all government employees in the civilian labor force belonged to unions. In addition, while only 8.2 percent of all private-sector workers were union members, many of the nation's leading industries are heavily unionized including utilities (26.2%), construction (16%), information (13.6%), and manufacturing (13.5%).[24] Union leaders can also look with some satisfaction at union wage rates. In 2003 the median weekly earnings for union workers was $760, compared to $599 for nonunionized workers. During the early 2000s, the average hourly wage rate for unionized workers was nearly $4 per hour higher than the hourly wage of nonunion workers.[25] The labor movement's agenda for the twenty-first century will surely evolve with changes in the composition of the labor force, technology and production techniques, and the effects of globalization.

Defining the Rights of Labor: Setting a Global Standard

The labor movement, at home and abroad, struggled for more than a century to define the rights of labor. Over time, national labor movements secured concessions from employers and from governments. Since its founding in 1919, the International Labor Organization (ILO) has advocated for the rights of labor and has coordinated the efforts of national labor unions in this pursuit. In 1946 the ILO became a specialized agency within the United Nations system. The ILO is not a labor union, however. Instead, it is an international organization of 175 nations designed to promote cooperation among labor groups, business interests, and governments.

In 1998 the ILO adopted the Declaration on Fundamental Principles and Rights at Work.[26] Today it is the most widely recognized statement of labor's rights in the global economy. It identifies four universal rights for workers:

- Freedom of association and the right to bargain collectively with employers
- Protection from all forms of forced labor
- Elimination of child labor
- Equal opportunities and treatment in the workplace

In 1999 other major documents were also introduced to protect workers' rights, including the UN's "Global Compact" and the Reverend Leon H. Sullivan's "Global Sullivan Principles of Corporate Social Responsibility."

BIOGRAPHIES: SHAPERS OF ECONOMIC THOUGHT

Samuel Gompers: Pure and Simple Unionism

Samuel Gompers (1850–1924) was among the most important leaders of the American labor movement and father of the American Federation of Labor (AFL). Gompers was born in London, England. He received a basic primary education at the Jewish free school in London, but out of financial necessity left school to become an apprentice cigarmaker at the age of 10. While working as a cigarmaker in London, the young Gompers not only became skilled at his craft but also observed the operation of the cigarmakers' union. He immigrated to the United States in 1863, settled in New York City, and plied his cigarmaking trade. During the 1860s and 1870s, he flirted with socialism, which he later opposed, and gradually became more active in the Cigarmakers' International Union. His dream of a federation of craft unions took form in 1881, when Gompers helped give birth to the Federation of Organized Trades and Labor Unions of the United States and Canada. Five years later, Gompers became the driving force behind the founding of the American Federation of Labor (AFL), an organization of skilled craft unions.

Gompers led the AFL for all but one year between 1886 and his death in 1924. His unwavering support for pure and simple unionism caused him to be pragmatic, to strive for limited and attainable goals, and to avoid divisive alliances with political parties and special interest groups. His distrust of government also steered Gompers away from any dependence on legislation to correct imbalances between employer power and employee power. Instead, Gompers was committed to the creation of worker power through skilled craft unions. To create a strong, unified AFL, Gompers insisted on dues payments from local affiliates. In exchange, he promised financial support to members who lost their jobs or were on strike. Gompers supported the judicious use of strikes to pressure employers to meet worker demands. While still in the Cigarmakers' Union, he defended the use of strikes before a congressional committee by arguing that "Strikes ought to be, and in well-organized trades unions they are, the last means which workingmen resort to to protect themselves against the almost never satisfied greed of employers."[27] Gompers approached his union-building tasks with zeal throughout his career. As a result, AFL membership swelled to over 1 million by 1901 and 4 million by 1920.

At his death in 1924, Gompers was widely recognized as the single most important labor activist and organizer in the United States. He made compromises on some issues, notably the de facto exclusion of African Americans, women, and others from membership in the AFL. He also drew sharp criticism from local AFL affiliates over the national organization's determination to remain nonpartisan in political elections. Yet, Gompers's universe was built around the vision of a stronger labor movement, one that acknowledged the unique needs of a working class and that worked toward its improvement.

Mary (Mother) Jones: The Most Dangerous Woman in America

Mary Harris Jones (1830?–1930), more commonly called Mother Jones, was a leading socialist labor organizer in the United States. Mother Jones was born Mary Harris in Cork, Ireland. Her family immigrated to Toronto, Canada, in the late 1830s in part to escape British retribution for political activities. After graduating from the Toronto Normal School in 1859, Mary Harris worked briefly as a teacher. Soon thereafter, she came to the United States, where she married George Jones, an ironworker and union activist, in Memphis, Tennessee. The marriage was short-lived; George and her four children died during a yellow fever epidemic in 1867. By the early 1870s, Mary Harris Jones was absorbed in her work on behalf of workers, labor unions, and the American labor movement.

Mother Jones championed many labor causes from the 1870s until her death in 1930. Much of her time and energy was devoted to the plight of miners. She was involved in strikes, demonstrations, and other forms of labor activism from Pennsylvania to Colorado. Her fiery words derided mine owners for their harsh treatment of men, women, and children laborers. Her socialist beliefs put her at odds with American capitalism, which she believed was responsible for the inequalities that permeated society. Her activism often put her in harm's way, and on occasion she landed in a prison cell. Undaunted, Jones recruited thousands of women to join the Knights of Labor in the 1870s, helped found the United Mine Workers of America (UMW) in 1890 and the Industrial Workers of the World (IWW) in 1905, and crusaded on behalf of the Socialist Party in the early 1900s. To some, Mother Jones was the "Miner's Angel." To others she was "the most dangerous woman in America."

Mother Jones was also concerned with the plight of workers in the clothing, steel, railway, and textile industries. During the 1880s and 1890s, for example, she was exposed to the horrific working conditions and low pay of women and children textile workers in the southeastern region of the United States. By 1903 she was prepared to focus the nation's attention the abuse of labor, particularly child labor, in the textile mills. She organized and led "the march of the

Child laborers, called doffers, work in a North Carolina textile Mill, 1908. Photograph by Lewis Wickes Hine. © Library of Congress.

mill children" from the mills of Kensington, Pennsylvania, to the home of President Theodore Roosevelt in Long Island, New York. In her autobiography, Jones explained: "We want President Roosevelt to hear the wail of the children who never have a chance to go to school but work eleven and twelve hours a day in the textile mills of Pennsylvania. . . . Fifty years ago there was a cry against slavery and men gave up their lives to stop the selling of black children on the block. Today the white child is sold for two dollars a week to the manufacturers."[28] While President Roosevelt refused to meet with Mother Jones and the marchers, the publicity generated by the march instigated new child labor laws in several northeastern states. Mother Jones was loved and feared for her radicalism. With sometimes biting criticisms of capitalism and its trappings, she labored to improve the lives of working people.

Frances Perkins: New Deal Labor Reformer

Frances Perkins (1882–1965) was an economist, social activist, and reformer. As secretary of labor during the administration of Franklin D. Roosevelt, she was also the first woman cabinet member in U.S. history. Perkins was born to an upper-middle-class family in Boston, Massachusetts. She earned a bachelor's degree from Mount Holyoke College in 1903 and a master's degree in social work from Columbia University in 1910. In the early years of the twentieth century, her compassion for the working poor, the homeless, women and children, and the unemployed was deepened by her work in philanthropic organizations in Philadelphia, the Consumers League in New York City, and a number of settlement houses—including Chicago Commons in Chicago. Over the years, her reputation as an advocate for social justice grew. Perkins was appointed to influential state government positions in New York under two governors, Al Smith and Franklin D. Roosevelt (FDR). As state industrial commissioner of New York, Perkins researched and supported social insurance programs for the unemployed and the aged. Soon after FDR was elected president in 1932, he appointed Perkins to the position of secretary of labor, a position she occupied throughout the Great Depression and World War II (1933–1945).

During the Great Depression, many of Perkins's ideas were channeled into New Deal legislation. She supported the creation of public works jobs to reduce the suffering of displaced workers and to build confidence in the U.S. economy. Millions of public works jobs resulted from government programs such as the Works Progress Administration (WPA), the Civil Works Administration (CWA), and the Civilian Conservation Corps (CCC). Perkins supported the National Labor Relations Act (1935), which affirmed workers' right to organize and join labor unions and to bargain collectively with employers. This act also outlawed worker blacklisting, a dreaded union-busting tactic. As the chairperson of the Committee on Economic Security, Perkins was the chief architect of the Social Security Act of 1935. Under this act, a system of social insurance was created for the elderly, the unemployed, mothers with children, and people with disabilities. Perkins was relentless in her support of the Fair Labor Standards Act (1938), which established the first national minimum wage of $0.25 per hour, the maximum workweek of 44 hours, and mandatory overtime pay for hours worked beyond 44. This act also prohibited child labor in many industries.

As a public official within the federal government, Frances Perkins was not considered part of the American labor movement. Yet the enormity of her contributions to workers and to the general welfare cannot be overstated. Even after Perkins resigned as secretary of labor in 1945, she continued to work on behalf of the American people in the public and private sectors. During her career, Perkins also penned two books, *People at Work* (1934) and *The Roosevelt I Knew* (1946). In recognition of her long and energetic service to the public welfare, the U.S. Department of Labor headquarters in Washington, D.C., was named the Frances Perkins Building in 1980.

Cesar Chavez: The United Farm Workers

Cesar E. Chavez (1927–1993) was an American labor organizer and founder of the United Farm Workers (UFW), the nation's first successful agricultural workers' labor union . Chavez was born near Yuma, Arizona. For much of his youth, he lived in poverty. The Chavez family lost its modest business and property during the Great Depression and, in 1937, traveled to California in search of new opportunities. The family soon joined thousands of migrant farmers who harvested seasonal crops, lived in migrant labor camps, and endured substandard wages and working conditions. As a migrant worker, Chavez's formal education was fragmented. He quit school in 1942 after completing the eighth grade. Chavez's informal education continued for the remainder of his life, however, as he studied economics, labor history, philosophy, and other subjects.

Chavez's career as a labor activist spanned four decades, beginning in the early 1950s and ending upon his death in 1993. From 1952 to 1962, Chavez was employed by the Community Service Organization (CSO), rising through the ranks to become the organization's national director in 1958. While working within the CSO, Chavez advanced the political and economic rights of agricultural workers, mainly Mexican-American migrant workers. In 1962 Chavez resigned from the CSO to form a labor union, the National Farm Workers Association (NFWA). The NFWA focused its attention on improving the standard of living of migrants and other farmworkers. Many farmworkers suffered from low pay, inadequate housing, abusive bosses, harsh working conditions, and health hazards such as pesticide poisoning. In 1966 the NFWA merged with a smaller AFL-CIO-sponsored labor organization, the Agricultural Workers Organizing Committee (AWOC), to form the United Farm Workers (UFW). The UFW immediately affiliated with the AFL-CIO.

Chavez committed the UFW to nonviolent action as a means to promote agricultural reforms in wage rates and conditions of employment, and union security for the UFW. His patient but persistent nonviolent labor activism took many forms, including labor marches, demonstrations, fasts, strikes, picketing, and consumer boycotts. Often, different labor tactics were combined into a coordinated campaign to pressure employers to make concessions to workers. The most famous coordinated campaign originated in Delano, California, in 1965 and ended five years later. Strikes and picketing of vineyards in the region were complemented by a national consumer boycott of table grapes. Chavez defended unionism and the use of strikes, arguing that strikes represent "all the farm workers standing up together and saying from this day we demand to be treated like the men we are! We are not slaves and we are not animals. And we are not alone."[29] In 1970 most leading vineyards reluctantly recognized the UFW as the legitimate bargaining agent for agricultural workers, and UFW contracts protecting tens of thousands of workers were negotiated with growers. Despite this victory, the unfinished struggle for better pay, better working conditions, and union security occupied the remainder of Chavez's life. In 1994, one year after his death, President Bill Clinton awarded Cesar Chavez the Medal of Freedom—the nation's highest civilian honor—to recognize his steadfast pursuit of economic security and social justice for America's migrant workers.

NOTES

1. U.S. Department of Labor (DOL), Bureau of Labor Statistics (BLS), "The Employment Situation, Table A. Major Indicators of Labor Market Activity, Seasonally Adjusted," *News,* April 4, 2003, 2.

2. DOL/BLS, "The Employment Situation, Table A"; U.S. Bureau of the Census, "Series D 1–10. Labor Force and Its Components: 1900 to 1947," *The Statistical History of the United States: From Colonial Times to the Present* (New York: Basic Books, Inc., 1976), 126; and DOL, *Occupational Outlook Handbook: 2002–2003 Edition,* www.bls.gov/oco/oco2003.htm.

3. BLS, "Table A-21. Employed Persons by Industry and Occupation," www.bls.gov/pub/suppl/empsit.cpseea21.txt; U.S. Bureau of the Census, *The Statistical History of the United States,* 139; and DOL, *Occupational Outlook Handbook: 2002–2003 Edition.*

4. DOL/BLS, "The Employment Situation, Table A-1. Employment Status of the Civilian Population by Sex and Age," *News,* April 4, 2003, 9; and U.S. Bureau of the Census, "Series D 11–25. Labor Force Status of the Population: 1870 to 1970," *The Statistical History of the United States,* 126–27.

5. U.S. Bureau of the Census, "Series H 598–601. High School Graduates, by Sex: 1870 to 1970," *The Statistical History of the United States,* 379; and U.S. Census Bureau, "No. 212. Educational Attainment by State: 1990 and 2000," *Statistical Abstract of the United States: 2002,* 122nd ed. (Washington, DC: Hoover's Business Press, 2003), 141.

6. DOL/BLS, "The Employment Situation, Table A-4. Employment Status of the Civilian Population 25 Years and Over by Educational Attainment," *News,* April 4, 2003, 11.

7. DOL/BLS, "Workers on Flexible and Shift Schedules in 2001 Summary," *BLS News,* April 18, 2002, www.bls.gov/news.release/flex.nr0.htm; and DOL/BLS, "Work at Home in 2001," *BLS News,* March 1, 2002, www.bls.gov/news.release/homey.nr.0.htm.

8. U.S. Small Business Administration, Office of Advocacy, "Employer Firm Births and Deaths by Employment Size and Firm, 1989–2000," *Firm Size Data: Statistics of U.S. Businesses and Nonemployer Statistics,* www.sba.gov/advo/stats/data.html#us.

9. U.S. Census Bureau, "Table 1. Nonemployer Statistics for the United States: 2001," *Nonemployer Statistics: 2001* (Washington, DC: Author, September 2003), 1; and U.S. Census Bureau, "'Mom-and-Pop' Shops Increase," *United States Department of Commerce News,* October 22, 2002, www.census.gov/Press-Release/www/2002/cb02-138.html.

10. DOL, "Chart 9. Job Increases in Occupations with the Largest Numerical Increases in Employment, Projected 2000–10," and "Chart 10. Occupations with the Largest Numerical Decrease in Employment, Projected 2000–10," *Occupational Outlook Handbook: 2002–2003 Edition,* www.bls.gov/oco/images/ocotjc09.gif and www.bls.gov/oco/images/ocotjc10.gif.

11. U.S. Census Bureau, "No. 1. Population and Area: 1790 to 2000," "No. 560. Employment Status of the Civilian Population: 1960 to 2001," "No. 561. Civilian Labor Force Participation Rates, with Projections: 1980 to 2010," *Statistical Abstract of the United States: 2002,* 122nd ed., 8, 367; U.S. Bureau of the Census, "Series D 11–25. Labor Force Status of the Population," 127–28; and Population Reference Bureau (PRB), "World's Largest Countries in 2003," *2003 World Population Data Sheet of the Population Reference Bureau* (Washington, DC: Author, 2003), 1.

12. U.S. Census Bureau, "No. 654. Money Income of Households—Distribution by Income Level and Selected Characteristics," *Statistical Abstract of the United States: 2002,* 122nd ed., 434.

13. "Title VII of the Civil Rights Act of 1964" (Pub. L. 88–352, Sec. 2000e-2), *United States Code* 42, www.eeoc.gov/laws/vii.html.

14. DOL, Employment Standards Administration, "History of Federal Minimum Wage Rates under the Fair Labor Standards Act, 1938–1996," www.dol.gov/esa/minwage/chart.htm.

15. DOL, Employment Standards Administration, "Minimum Wage Laws in the States," June 30, 2003, www.dol.gov/esa/minwage/america.htm#1.

16. Bernadette D. Procter and Joseph Dalaker, "The Official Measure of Poverty," in *Poverty in the United States: 2002* (Washington, DC: U.S. Department of Commerce/Census Bureau, 2003), 4.

17. U.S. Census Bureau, "No. 616. Federal Minimum Wages Rates: 1950 to 2000," and "No. 617. Workers Paid Hourly Rates by Selected Characteristics: 2001," *Statistical Abstract of the United States: 2002,* 122nd ed., 405.

18. Adolph Strasser, "Testimony of Cigar Makers' International Union President Adolph Strasser before the U.S. Senate Committee on Education and Labor (1883), www.uwm.edu/Course/448-440/pure.htm.

19. U.S. Bureau of the Census, "Series D 765–778. Average Hours and Average Earnings in Manufacturing, in Selected Nonmanufacturing Industries and for 'Lower-Skilled' Labor 1890 to 1926," *The Statistical History of the United States,* 168.

20. U.S. Bureau of the Census, "Series D 11–25. Labor Force Status of the Population: 1870 to 1970," "Series D 927–939. Labor Union Membership, by Affiliation: 1935 to 1970," "Series D 940–945. Labor Union Membership, by Affiliation: 1897 to 1934," "Series D 946–951. Labor Union Membership and Membership as Percent of Total Labor Force and of Nonagricultural Employment: 1930 to 1970," *The Statistical History of the United States,* 127, 176–78; and U.S. Census Bureau, "No. 628. Labor Union Membership by Sector: 1983 to 2001," *Statistical Abstract of the United States: 2002,* 411.

21. Industrial Workers of the World, "IWW Preamble as amended in 1908," in *The American Labor Movement,* ed. Leon Litwack (Englewood Cliffs, NJ: Prentice-Hall, Inc., 1962), 42.

22. U.S. Bureau of the Census, "Series D 927–939. Labor Union Membership, by Affiliation: 1935 to 1970," *The Statistical History of the United States,* 176; and BLS, "Union Members Summary (2003)," January 21, 2004, www.bls.gov/news.release/union2.nr0.htm.

23. American Federation of Labor-Congress of Industrial Organizations (AFL-CIO), "What We Stand For: Mission and Goals of the AFL-CIO," www.aflcio.org/about aflcio/about/mission/index.cfm.

24. DOL/BLS, "Union Members in 2003," and "Table 3. Union Affiliation of Employed Wage and Salary Workers by Occupation and Industry," *BLS News,* January 21, 2004, www.bls.gov/news.release/union2.nr0.htm.

25. BLS, "Table 2. Median Weekly Earnings for Full-Time Wage and Salary Workers by Union Affiliation and Selected Characteristics (2003)," January 21, 2004, www.bls.gov/news.release/union2.t02.htm; and U.S. Bureau of the Census, "No. 610. Mean Hourly Earnings and Weekly Hours for Metro and Nonmetro Areas by Selected Characteristics: 2000," *Statistical Abstract of the United States: 2002,* 122nd ed., 400–401.

26. International Labor Organization (ILO), "Declaration on Fundamental Principles and Rights at Work," www.ilo.org/public/english/standards/decl/declaration/faq/index.htm.

27. Samuel Gompers, "Testimony of Samuel Gompers (August 16, 1883)," in *The People Shall Judge: Readings in the Formation of American Policy,* Vol. II, ed. The Staff

of the Social Sciences at The College of the University of Chicago (Chicago: The University of Chicago Press, 1949), 16.

28. Mary Harris Jones, *The Autobiography of Mother Jones* (*Mother Jones* magazine online special edition, 2001), 31, www.motherjones.com/about_us/Mjbio.pdf.

29. Cesar Chavez, "The Union and the Strike," www.sfsu.edu/~cecipp/cesar_chavez/strike.htm.

SELECTED READINGS

Brexel, Bernadette. *The Knights of Labor and the Haymarket Riot: The Fight for an Eight-Hour Workday.* New York: Rosen Publishing Group, 2004.

Chavez, Cesar, Richard J. Jensen, and John C. Hammerback, eds. *The Words of Cesar Chavez.* College Station, TX: Texas A&M University Press, 2002.

Dubofsky, Melvyn, and Joseph A. McCartin, eds. *We Shall Be All: A History of the Industrial Workers of the World.* Champaign, IL: University of Illinois Press, 2000.

Erem, Suzan. *Labor Pains: Inside America's New Union Movement.* New York: Monthly Review Press, 2001.

Featherstone, Liza, and United Students against Sweatshops. *Students against Sweatshops: The Making of a Movement.* New York: Verso Books, 2002.

Ferriss, Susan, and Ricardo Sandoval. *The Fight in the Fields: Cesar Chavez and the Farmworkers Movement.* Orlando, FL: Harvest Books, 1998.

Gifford, Court D. *Directory of U.S. Labor Organizations 2002.* Washington, D.C.: Bureau of National Affairs, 2002.

Gompers, Samuel. *Labor and the Common Welfare.* reprint ed. Manchester, NH: Ayer Company Publishing, 1974.

Hinshaw, John H., Paul Le Blanc, and Paul Leblanc, eds. *U.S. Labor in the 20th Century: Studies in Working-Class Struggles and Insurgency.* Amherst, NY: Humanity Books, 2000.

Jenkins, Rhys O., Ruth Pearson, Gill Seyfang, and Caroline E. Koube, eds. *Corporate Responsibility and Labour Rights: Codes of Conduct in the Global Economy.* Washington, DC: Earthscan Publications, Ltd., 2002.

Joel, Lewin G. III. *Every Employee's Guide to the Law: What You Need to Know about Your Rights in the Workplace—And What to Do If They Are Violated.* New York: Pantheon Books, 2001.

Jones, Mary H. *Mother Jones Speaks,* ed. Philip S. Foner. Atlanta, GA: Pathfinder Press, 1983.

Josephson, Judith P. *Mother Jones: Fierce Fighter for Workers' Rights.* Minneapolis: Lerner Publications Company, 1997.

Kenny, Kevin. *Making Sense of the Molly Maguires.* New York: Oxford University Press, 1998.

Le Blanc, Paul, and Paul Leblanc. *A Short History of the U.S. Working Class: From Colonial Times to the Twenty-First Century.* Amherst, NY: Humanity Books, 1999.

Lichtenstein, Nelson. *State of the Union: A Century of American Labor.* Princeton, NJ: Princeton University Press, 2002.

Nelson, Patricia M., ed. *Affirmative Action Revisited.* Huntington, NY: Nova Science Publishers, Inc., 2001.

Pasachoff, Naomi E. *Frances Perkins: Champion of the New Deal.* New York: Oxford University Press Children's Books, 2000.

Smith, Robert M., and Scott Malloy. *From Blackjacks to Briefcases: A History of Commercialized Strikebreaking and Unionbusting in the United States.* Athens, OH: Ohio University Press, 2003.

Spencer, Barbara, et al. *Big Book of Jobs 2003–2004.* Lincolnwood, IL: McGraw-Hill/Contemporary Books, 2002.

Theriault, Reg. *The Unmaking of the American Working Class.* New York: New Press, 2003.

U.S. Department of Labor. *Occupational Outlook Handbook: 2002–2003.* Indianapolis, IN: Jist Works, 2002.

Wheeler, Hoyt N. *The Future of the American Labor Movement.* New York: Cambridge University Press, 2002.

CHAPTER 8

Financial Markets: The Arteries of Economic Activity

Chapter 8 deals with the role of financial markets in the American economy. Modern economies rely on money, credit, and a variety of financial institutions to support business activity. Some financial institutions such as banks and thrift institutions—savings and loan associations, savings banks, and credit unions—accept deposits and pool savings for productive investments and consumer loans. Depository institutions are supervised and regulated by a number of federal agencies, including the Federal Reserve System (Fed), the nation's central bank. In addition to its regulatory role, the uniquely structured Fed determines the nation's monetary policy and provides key financial services to the government and banking system. Other financial institutions, such as stock and bond markets, are also instrumental in raising money for business start-ups and other productive investments. Stock and bond markets, mutual funds, and futures markets are regulated internally and by government agencies. By saving and investing money, people forego some present consumption in order to reap future financial rewards including interest payments, dividends, and capital gains.

MONEY AND CREDIT IN THE U.S. ECONOMY

Money is any item that is commonly accepted in payment for goods, services, or debts. Money has been used by societies for thousands of years to facilitate business and financial transactions. The use of money is a far more efficient mechanism of exchange than **barter,** the direct exchange of one good for another. Barter requires a double coincidence of wants and tedious negotiations about the relative value of goods in the marketplace (see chapter 2 for more on the origins of money). The use of credit also facilitates marketplace exchanges, but credit cards, charge cards, and other types of credit accounts are not considered money.

Money: Its Functions, Characteristics, and Types

Money has three primary functions in an economy. First, it serves as a medium of exchange. That is, the item that used as money must be commonly accepted in payment for products. Second, money serves as a unit of accounting. Monetary units in the United States are stated in dollars and cents. Hence, a product's price allows people to assess the value of one product compared to the value of a second product. Third, as a store of value, money holds its worth over time. The ability of money to retain its purchasing power increases people's confidence in saving and investing money. In the words of Alan Greenspan, chairman of the Federal Reserve System: "[A]t root, money—serving as a store of value and medium of exchange—is the lubricant that enables a society to organize itself to achieve economic progress. The ability to store the fruits of one's labor for future consumption is necessary for the accumulation of capital, the spread of technological advances and, as a consequence, rising standards of living."[1]

Throughout history, societies have struggled to create and maintain a monetary system that could satisfy these three interrelated functions. Four characteristics help distinguish good money from bad money. Good money must be commonly accepted in payment for goods, stable in value, divisible, and portable. The acceptability of money is derived mainly from its scarcity and the confidence people have in the issuing body, usually a national government. Acceptability is also enhanced by traditional perceptions of value, which helps explain why gold and silver coins have been accepted as money over the centuries. The second characteristic of money, stability, is measured by the ability to hold value over time. The relative scarcity of money is vital to its stability. If too much money is released for public use, its value generally decreases. Economists agree that too much money chasing too few goods is a cause of inflation, a type of monetary instability in which the general price level in an economy rises. The stability of money is also enhanced by its durability, the ability to be used without breaking, rotting, or otherwise deteriorating over time. The third characteristic, divisibility, creates precise monetary units and thus facilitates business and financial transactions. U.S. money is highly divisible, with several denominations of coin and paper currency. Coins are measured in units of cents, with 1, 5, 10, 25, 50, and 100 cent pieces. U.S. paper currency is subdivided into units called dollars, with $1, $2, $5, $10, $20, $50, and $100 notes. Larger denominations of $500, $1,000, $5,000, and $10,000 were issued until 1969, but have since been removed from circulation. Finally, the portability of money enables it to be transported easily from place to place. Historically, the use of paper currency and checks expanded the portability of money. Today, electronic funds transfer (EFT) technology has eased many types of transactions through the use of debit cards, automated teller machines, computer banking, and so on.

Economists generally identify three types of money: commodity money, representative money, and fiat money. **Commodity money** is an item that is commonly accepted as a medium of exchange and also has value it itself. Bales of tobacco were often used as a type of commodity money in colonial Virginia and

The Bureau of Engraving and Printing in Washington, D.C. produces U.S. paper currency. © Bureau and Engraving and Printing/U.S. Department of the Treasury.

Maryland during the 1600s and early 1700s. Commodity money often lacks portability and divisibility. Maintaining the stability of commodity money is also difficult because its value fluctuates with the supply of the crop, animal skin, mineral, or other item that is used as money. **Representative money** is a type of money that has no inherent value, but represents something of value. During the early twentieth century, the U.S. government issued gold certificates, a type of representative money that could be redeemed for gold. Gold redemption ended in 1934, however, and most gold certificates were removed from circulation. U.S. silver certificates, another type of representative money, were issued until 1957 and were redeemable for silver until 1968.[2] In each case, the redemption of paper notes for gold and silver depleted U.S. supplies of these precious metals and forced the government to discontinue the use of these forms of representative money. **Fiat money** is a type of money that derives its value by government decree, or fiat. That is, the government declares its currency to be valuable without backing it with gold, silver, or other precious items. Federal Reserve Notes, which today comprise about 99 percent of the paper currency in the United States, represent legal tender for all debts and thus must be accepted in all types of transactions. The stability of the U.S. government and the confidence people have in the government are vital to maintaining the purchasing power of the nation's fiat money.

The Money Supply: M1, M2, and M3

The **money supply,** or money stock, consists of the total amount of money in circulation in an economy, the money that is available for use in a variety of transactions and investments. The money supply does not include money that is stored away by the Federal Reserve System, the Treasury Department, or other federal agencies. Economists use three measures to determine the size of the money supply, the M1, the M2, and the M3. **M1,** often called transactions money because it can readily be spent, is the narrowest measurement of the nation's money supply. The four main components of M1 are coin and paper currency, demand deposits, other checkable deposits, and traveler's checks, as shown in Figure 8.1.[3] Coin and paper currency account for about half of the M1. Demand deposits, which represents the money held in individual checking accounts in banks, account for another quarter of M1. Other checkable deposits (OCDs), such as negotiable order of withdrawal (NOW) accounts and share draft accounts at credit unions, account for most of the remainder. Less than 1 percent of M1 consists of traveler's checks, which are used to protect travelers' money from loss or theft. In May 2003 the M1 in the United States stood at nearly $1.3 trillion.

The other measurements of the money supply, M2 and M3, are broader indicators of the nation's total stock of money. The **M2** consists of the M1 plus near monies such as savings deposits, small-denomination time deposits of less than $100,000, and retail money market mutual funds. Near monies are highly liquid assets than are easily converted into money. In 2003 nearly $3 trillion was deposited in savings deposits at commercial banks and thrift institutions, which

Figure 8.1
The U.S. Money Supply (M1): 2003

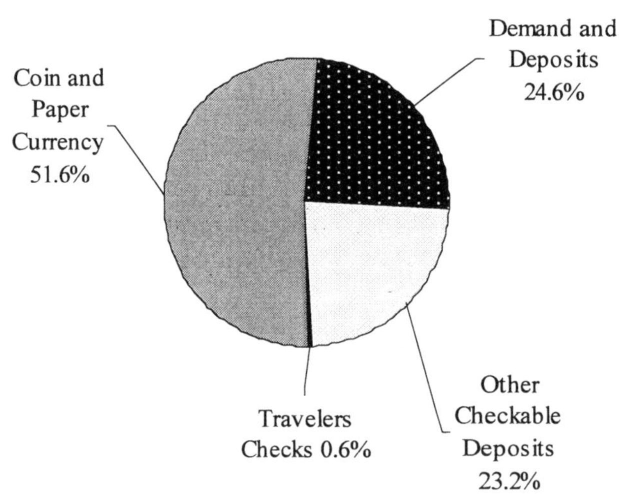

Source: Federal Reserve System, *Federal Reserve Statistical Release,* June 19, 2003.

made savings the largest single component of M2. Combined, the near monies of M2 added $4.7 trillion to the M1, meaning that the M2 totaled about $6 trillion in 2003. The **M3** consists of the M2 plus institutional money market funds, large-scale time deposits, repurchase agreements (RPS) of government securities, and certain eurodollars. Combined, these factors added $2.7 trillion to the M2, elevating the M3 to nearly $8.7 trillion, as shown in Table 8.1.[4]

The Use of Credit: Credit Cards and Charge Cards

People often refer to a credit card or a charge card as *plastic money* because credit instruments add convenience to financial transactions. Yet, economists do not consider credit and charge cards to be money, mainly because these cards do not serve as a unit of accounting or as a store of value. Instead, credit and charge cards represent a type of loan made by the institution that issued the card to the cardholder. The use of credit and charge cards allows consumers to buy now, but the cardholder is expected to finalize the transaction each month by paying the issuing company the amount shown on the credit statement. These payments are made with money, usually by check. Credit cards and charge cards share some common features, but there are some notable differences.

Table 8.1
The U.S. Money Supply: 2003 (dollars in billions)

Money Supply	Components	Amount	Measurement (M1, M2, M3)
M1	Currency	$646.4	
	Demand deposits	$308.4	
	OCDs	$289.6	
	Traveler's checks	$7.5	
		$1251.9	M1 = ($1,251.9)
M2	Savings deposits	$2966.0	
	Small time deposits	$862.6	
	Retail money funds	$884.1	
		$4712.7 + M1 = M2 ($5,964.6)	
M3	Institutional money funds	$1118.9	
	Large time deposits	$826.2	
	RPs	$513.6	
	Some Eurodollars	$235.2	
		$2693.9 + M2 = M3 ($8,658.5)	

Source: Federal Reserve System, "Money Stock Measures," *Federal Reserve Statistical Release,* June 19, 2003.

A **credit card** is a payment card that allows the cardholder to purchase goods at a variety of venues. In addition, credit cards permit the rollover of unpaid balances from one billing cycle to the next. Credit cards are issued by banks, thrift institutions, credit card companies, or other businesses and are used to buy goods and services at department stores, restaurants, grocery stores, gas stations, and so on. The three dominant credit cards in the United States are Visa, MasterCard, and American Express. Credit card companies charge relatively high interest on unpaid balances. In spring 2003 the average annual percentage rate (APR) was 13 percent to 14 percent. Some issuing companies also charge annual fees and fees for cash advances.

A **charge card** is a payment card that allows the cardholder to purchase goods at a specific business. Charge cards often require full payment for transactions at the end of each billing cycle. Charge cards are issued by a variety of retailers such as Sears, Macy's, Abercrombie & Fitch, and the Gap. Some charge cards carry annual fees and interest is charged on unpaid balances for cards that have rollover privileges. Some businesses also provide installment credit for major purchases. Installment credit requires buyers to repay the principal plus interest in monthly installments over a period of months or years. This practice is common in businesses that produce and sell furniture, consumer durables, home entertainment systems, and automobiles.

The use of credit fuels consumer spending on goods and services in the U.S. economy. Providing credit is also a big business. In 2002 there was nearly $1.8 trillion in outstanding consumer credit in the U.S. economy, most of which was held by commercial banks, finance companies, or credit unions as shown in Figure 8.2. Consumer credit includes credit purchases by people, but excludes money borrowed for home mortgages. Mortgage credit is the largest type of consumer borrowing, however. In 2002 U.S. financial institutions held over $8 trillion in mortgage debt.[5] Since the 1960s, a flurry of consumer legislation has been enacted to regulate business practices and protect consumer rights in the consumer credit industry (see chapter 6 for more on credit abuse and personal bankruptcy). Major legislation includes:

- *Truth in Lending Act (1968).* This act requires a clear disclosure of the costs of using credit, bans unsolicited issuance of credit cards, and limits cardholders' liability for unauthorized use of credit cards to $50.
- *Fair Housing Act (1968).* This act prohibits discrimination in the sale, rental, or financing of dwellings based on race, color, national origin, gender, religion, disability, or familial status. The act is found in Title VII of the Civil Rights Act of 1968.
- *Fair Credit Reporting Act (1970).* This act requires credit bureaus to keep accurate and timely credit information, to reinvestigate disputed information, and to correct errors.
- *Equal Credit Opportunity Act (1974).* This act requires equal access to credit regardless of an applicant's race, color, national origin, gender, religion, marital status, age, or whether the applicant receives public assistance.
- *Fair Debt Collection Practices Act (1977).* This act prohibits the harassment of debtors by issuers of credit or by debt collection agencies.

Figure 8.2
Holders of Consumer Credit: 2002

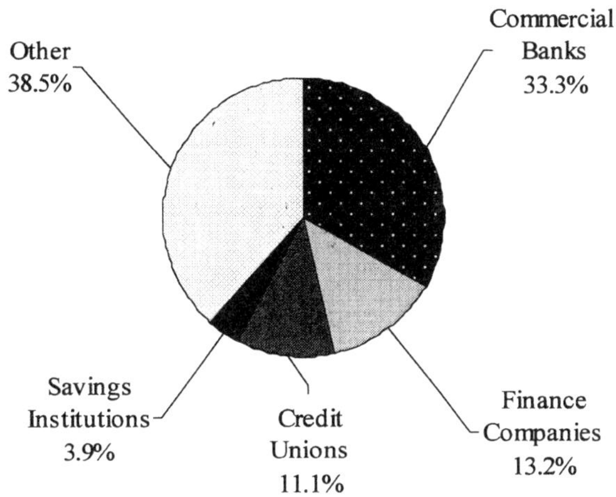

Source: Federal Reserve System, *Federal Reserve Statistical Release,* April 2003.

- *Fair Credit and Charge Card Disclosure Act (1988):* This act requires that all solicitations by credit card issuers, by mail and other means, clearly explain the terms of credit.

THE UNITED STATES BANKING SYSTEM

The **banking system** of the United States consists of a central bank, commercial banks, and thrift institutions such as savings and loan associations, savings banks, and credit unions. The banking system provides a variety of financial services to individuals, businesses, and the government, thus stimulating both the supply side and the demand side of markets. In recent years, new information technology, such as electronic banking, has increased the efficiency and sophistication of the U.S. banking system. You will read more about the role of America's central bank, the Federal Reserve System, later in the chapter.

Commercial Banks and Other Depository Institutions

Depository institutions accept deposits from savers and extend loans to borrowers. There are two main categories of depository institutions: commercial banks and thrift institutions—savings and loan associations (S&Ls), savings banks, and credit unions. In 2002 about 19,000 depository institutions operated in the United States, with combined assets of $9 trillion. An overview of U.S. depository institutions is shown in Table 8.2.[6]

Commercial banks are private financial corporations owned by stockholders and operated by professional management for profit. Commercial banks are the largest type of depository institution, controlling 79 percent of all indus-

Table 8.2
U.S. Depository Institutions: 2002

Type of Depository Institution	Number of Institutions	Total Assets ($ billions)
Commercial banks	7,887	$7,075
S&Ls, savings banks	1,467	$1,359
Credit unions	9,814	$539
All depository institutions	19,168	$8,973

Source: FDIC, "FDIC Statistics on Banking;" OTS, *2002 Fact Book*; and *NCUA, 2002 Midyear Statistics for Federally Insured Credit Unions*.

try assets. Originally founded to attend to the financial needs of businesses, commercial banks evolved to provide a variety of services to businesses and consumers, such as savings accounts, checking accounts, credit cards, and other financial services. Commercial banks pool money by accepting savers' deposits, collecting interest payments on loans, or earning profits from other investments such as the purchase of U.S. government securities. The Federal Deposit Insurance Corporation (FDIC), an agency of the U.S. federal government, insures deposits in savings accounts up to $100,000. Consumer loans, also called personal loans, enable bank customers to purchase consumer durables, renovate their homes, buy cars, or pay off debts. The largest personal loan for many households is the home mortgage loan. Business loans enable firms to upgrade or expand plant and equipment, finance mergers or acquisitions, or satisfy other business needs. By the close of 2002, outstanding commercial bank loans totaled $4.2 trillion. Of all new loans granted by commercial banks in the early 2000s, roughly 60 percent were channeled to business clients. Ranked by assets, the largest American commercial banks in 2002 were the Chase Manhattan Bank ($622 billion), Bank of America, NA ($565 billion), Citibank, NA ($499 billion), First Union National Bank ($319 billion), and Bank One, NA ($218 billion).[7]

Savings and loan associations and savings banks are often classified as savings institutions. In 2002 they accounted for 15 percent of all industry assets and granted $900 billion in loans. **Savings and loan associations** (S&Ls) are savings institutions designed to meet the financial needs of households rather than businesses. S&Ls were originally formed in the early 1830s to pool investors' money for home mortgage loans. Today, S&Ls continue to supply mortgages, other real estate loans, and a variety of personal loans to members. Since the passage of the Depository Institutions Deregulation and Monetary Control Act of 1980, S&Ls have also provided checking accounts, retirement accounts, and other financial services. S&Ls can be organized as stock institutions or as mutual institutions. Stock institutions are owned and operated by stockholders, while mutual institutions are owned by depositors. In 2002 most federally insured S&Ls remained mutual institutions. The Savings Association Insurance Fund (SAIF) and the Bank Insurance Fund (BIF) insure deposits in S&Ls up to $100,000. The Office of Thrift Supervision (OTS) and the FDIC oversee and regulate S&Ls. In 2003 the largest U.S. savings and loan association was Astoria Federal Savings, an institution with $22 billion in assets.[8]

Savings banks are savings institutions that focus on providing home mortgages and personal loans. Savings banks have existed in the United States for about a century and a half and are concentrated in the northeastern states. Originally, almost all savings banks were organized as mutual institutions. Mutual savings banks are owned by depositors, who are called members, and are operated as nonprofit institutions. Profits that accrue are distributed to members. Since the 1980s, many savings banks have been organized as, or have converted to, stock savings banks. Stock savings banks are owned by stockholders and operated for profit. In 2002 most federally insured savings banks operated as stock institutions. Savings deposits in most savings banks are insured by the SAIF or BIF up to $100,000, and are regulated by the OTS or FDIC. Ranked by assets, the largest U.S. savings bank in 2003 was Washington Mutual, Inc. ($268 billion).[9]

Credit unions are nonprofit financial cooperatives that are owned and operated by their members. Like S&Ls and savings banks, credit unions are considered thrift institutions. Originally, membership in a credit union was restricted to people directly associated with the founding organization, such as a corporation, labor union, or other group. Today, eligibility for membership in some credit unions has been expanded to serve people who reside in certain geographic regions or who are employed in certain occupations or industries. Originally, credit unions accepted deposits from members, paid interest on these deposits, and extended relatively small personal loans to members. More recently, deregulated financial markets have enabled credit unions to offer a wider array of financial services, including share drafts, a type of checking account. Today, credit unions also provide loans for home mortgages. In 2002, $96 billion was devoted to first-time home mortgages, about 29 percent of all lending by credit unions. Other major categories of loans included used cars (21%), new cars (18%), and other real estate (14%). By the early 2000s, about 80 million Americans were members of credit unions. The National Credit Union Share Insurance Fund (NCUSIF) insures members' savings up to $100,000. The National Credit Union Administration (NCUA) supervises the nearly 10,000 credit unions that operate nationwide. Ranked by total assets, the largest credit unions in the early 2000s included the U.S. Navy ($15.1 billion), State Employees' ($8.2 billion), the Pentagon ($4.3 billion), and Boeing Employees' ($4.0 billion).[10]

Savings and Types of Deposit Accounts

People save money in depository institutions to earn interest income, to ensure the security of saved money, and to prepare for future financial needs such as college tuition payments or retirement. The personal savings rate is the percentage of people's total disposable income that is saved in a depository institution. In 2003, for example, the personal savings rate in the United States was 2.1 percent. The calculation of the personal savings rate is straightforward. People's disposable income is determined by subtracting taxes and other mandatory payments to government ($990.6 billion) from people's personal income ($9,203.7 billion), as shown in Figure 8.3. Thus, in 2003 Americans' disposable personal income, sometimes called after-tax income, was $8,213.1 billion. There are essentially two things people can then do with their disposable income, save it or spend it. In 2003 Americans chose to spend about $8 trillion, or 97.9 percent of all disposable income, and save $170.1 billion, or 2.1 percent.[11] The nation's gross savings rate includes personal savings by individuals and savings by businesses and the government. In 2001 gross savings was nearly $1.7 trillion, and the gross savings rate, which is expressed as a percentage of the nation's gross domestic product, was 16.5 percent.[12] (See chapter 9 for more on gross savings.)

Depository institutions offer a wide variety of deposit accounts, but most fall into one of four categories: savings accounts, money market deposit accounts, certificates of deposit, or checking accounts. Many people have more than one type of deposit account to meet their different financial needs. All deposit accounts offer security, as depositors' money is protected from theft or other loss and is insured by the FDIC, SAIF, BIF, or NCUSIF. Still, there are differences among deposit accounts in terms of yield, liquidity, check-writing privileges, associated fees, and minimum deposits.

A regular saving account is one common deposit account. The two types of regular savings accounts are the passbook account and the statement account. The passbook savings account requires the depositor to present a passbook when transactions are made. In a statement savings account, a record of monthly transactions is mailed to the depositor. The interest payment on regular accounts is usually the lowest of any deposit account. Liquidity is high because withdrawals from the account can be made quickly. Savings accounts do not offer check-writing privileges, however. Some banks and thrifts assess a monthly fee if the minimum monthly balance falls beneath a certain dollar amount. Credit unions call their savings accounts *share accounts*.

Figure 8.3
Personal Income, Spending, and Saving: 2003

Personal Income	$9,203.7
Minus: Taxes and Nontax Payments	–$990.6
Equals: Disposable Personal Income	$8,213.1
Minus: Personal Outlays (spending)	–$8,043.0
Equals: Personal Savings	$ 170.1

Source: U.S. Department of Commerce/Bureau of Economic Analysis, "Personal Income and Its Disposition," March 26, 2004.

A money market deposit account (MMDA) typically pays a higher rate of interest than does a regular savings account. Interest rates on MMDAs are variable, fluctuating with the interest the depository institution receives on its own investments. Liquidity is relatively high because six transfers, including three checks, are allowed each month. Monthly fees are often imposed on MMDAs by depository institutions. Many institutions also require a minimum balance of at least $1,000 to maintain an MMDA.

A certificate of deposit (CD), also called a time deposit, requires money to remain in an account for a specified period of time. CDs offer a relatively high fixed rate of interest to depositors. This high rate of interest is designed to compensate depositors for the use of their money over an extended period of time. Thus, liquidity is relatively low compared with other deposit accounts. The CD's term, or length of time between the purchase and the maturity date, may be stated in days or years. Financial institutions assess financial penalties for early withdrawals from CD accounts. Further, checks cannot be written against CD accounts. The minimum deposit for CDs ranges from a few hundred dollars to $100,000. Credit unions call CDs *share certificates.*

A checking account is a fourth type of deposit account. Regular checking accounts typically offer no interest and often require that a small minimum balance be maintained. Special checking accounts, called negotiable order of withdrawal accounts (NOW accounts), pay interest to depositors but also require a larger minimum balance. Because checking accounts offer instant access to money, they are highly liquid. Liquidity is further enhanced by electronic funds transfer technology, which permits depositors to gain access to their funds through ATM machines, the use of debit cards, and home computer banking. Depository institutions often levy fees on checking accounts, the use of ATMs, and other checking transactions. Credit unions call checking accounts *share draft accounts.*

Retirement Accounts: Saving for the Future

Social Security was established in 1935 to assist the elderly, the handicapped, and mothers with dependent children to meet their financial obligations. In the mid-1960s, the Social Security system was expanded to include Medicare, the health insurance program for the elderly. Today, the Federal Insurance Contributions Act (FICA) tax requires most employees and employers to each contribute 7.65 percent of each worker's gross wage to maintain the Social Security and Medicare programs. Yet, financial experts agree that the Social Security payments are insufficient to maintain an average retiree's normal lifestyle. To help people prepare for a more financially secure future, a number of retirement plans have been created. Three important retirement plans are individual retirement accounts (IRAs), Keogh plans, and 401(k) plans. All offer tax deferment, but the federal government does not insure savings in any of these accounts.

- *Individual retirement accounts (IRAs).* A traditional IRA is a tax-deferred retirement account for employees. Taxes are not paid on the amount contributed or on the interest that accrues until the money is withdrawn during retirement. There are limits on the annual contribution to an IRA and penalties for early withdrawal. In 2003 the maximum contribution for most people was $3,000 per year, a sum that was scheduled to increase to $5,000 by 2008. The Employee Retirement Income Security Act (1974) created the first IRAs. A Roth IRA is a retirement account in which a worker contributes after-tax money to the account. The main benefit of a Roth IRA is that the principal, plus all interest earned during the life of the account, is tax-free when withdrawn during retirement. The Taxpayer Relief Act (1997) created the Roth IRA.

- *Keogh plan.* A Keogh plan is a retirement plan for the self-employed. Income contributed to a Keogh plan is tax-deferred until it is withdrawn from the account during retirement. By the early 2000s, self-employed workers could contribute up to 25 percent of their self-employment income to a Keogh plan as long as the sum did not exceed $30,000. The Self-Employed Individuals Tax Retirement Act (1962) established the Keogh plan.
- *401(k) plans.* A 401(k) plan is a retirement plan set up by an employer. Under 401(k) plans, the employer may match the employee's contribution to the plan. The employee's contribution is tax deferred; neither the contribution nor accrued interest payments are taxed until withdrawals are made during retirement. The risks involved in 401(k) plans were demonstrated when the collapse of Enron and other large corporations during the early 2000s wiped out several large 401(k) plans. The Internal Revenue Code of 1978, Section 401(k), created these plans.

THE FEDERAL RESERVE SYSTEM: THE NATION'S CENTRAL BANK

The **Federal Reserve System** (the Fed) is America's central bank and, thus, is an important component in the U.S. banking system. The Fed serves two categories of clients, banks and the U.S. government. It neither accepts deposits from nor extends loans to individuals or business firms. The Fed was established by the Federal Reserve Act in 1913, and within a year the Fed was up and running. Congressional debates over the need for a central bank, as well as its structure, were conducted in the shadow of two devastating economic downturns, the Panic of 1893 and the Panic of 1907. Not surprisingly, the Fed's mission stressed the importance of promoting economic stability. The Fed's current mission statement pledges "to foster the stability, integrity, and efficiency of the nation's monetary, financial, and payment systems so as to promote optimal macroeconomic performance."[13]

Brief History of Central Banks in the United States

Shortly after the Constitution of the United States was ratified in 1788, disagreements erupted over the proper role of government in the new nation's economic affairs. One divisive issue was whether the United States should create a central bank. The chief proponent of a central bank was Alexander Hamilton, the first secretary of the treasury. Hamilton insisted that Congress had the power to create a central bank under the "necessary and proper" clause of the

Constitution (Article I, Section 8, Clause 18). Hamilton was convinced that a central bank would strengthen the nation's monetary system and credit (see the biography of Alexander Hamilton). The most outspoken critic of a central bank was Thomas Jefferson, the nation's first secretary of state. Jefferson challenged the constitutionality of a central bank. He argued that the Constitution made no mention of a national bank. Jefferson, a champion of rural and agricultural interests, also feared that a powerful central bank would trample the rights of states and impede the natural development of local economies.

Congress narrowly supported Hamilton's view and created the First Bank of the United States in 1791. With its 20-year charter, the First Bank (1791–1811) served as a commercial bank by accepting deposits, making consumer and business loans, and providing other financial services. It also served as the fiscal authority for the federal government by collecting taxes, paying the government's bills, issuing banknotes, and handling the purchase and sale of government securities. The First Bank did not have the power to supervise or regulate state banks, however. From its headquarters in Philadelphia and branch banks in Baltimore, Boston, Charleston, and New York City, the First Bank brought order and stability to America's financial system during the early republic.

The creation of the Second Bank of the United States (1816–1836) followed a period of financial disorder, from 1811 to 1816. This economic chaos was due in part to the nonrenewal of the First Bank's charter in 1811. During this five-year period, the number of small state-chartered banks mushroomed, many new banknotes appeared, and inflation soared. In addition, the federal government was left without a stable bank from which to conduct its business of raising, storing, and spending money. The economic turmoil caused Congress to reconsider its position on a central bank, and in 1816 the Second Bank of the United States was created. The Second Bank's (1816–1836) 20-year charter gave it many of the same functions as the First Bank. It also inherited the distrust of many common people and the animosity of powerful political leaders, including the nation's seventh president, Andrew Jackson, who served from 1829 to 1837. In 1832, four years before the Second Bank's charter was to expire, Congress approved a bill to recharter the Second Bank for another 20 years. President Jackson vetoed this bill, however. The Second Bank's charter quietly expired in 1836. The United States waited nearly 80 years for the creation of its next central bank, the Federal Reserve System.

The Structure of the Federal Reserve System

A central bank is a nation's single most important monetary authority. Today, virtually all countries have a national financial institution that serves as a central bank. Examples include the Deutsche Bundesbank (Germany), Banco Central do Brazil, the Bank of England, and the Federal Reserve System (United States). While no two central banks are identical, most share common features. For instance, central banks hold cash reserves of member banks. These reserves enable central banks to respond to economic crises in a timely manner. Central banks typically issue currency, regulate and supervise the banking system, and devise a national monetary policy. Most central banks are nonprofit institutions that are owned and operated by the federal government to promote economic stability and growth.

The structure of the Federal Reserve System, or Fed, in the United States rests mainly on two institutions: the Board of Governors, located in Washington, D.C., and the regional Federal Reserve Banks. The Fed's structure is unique. First, the Fed operates through 12 regional Federal Reserve Banks located in cities across the nation, rather than a single national bank. Second, the Fed is largely autonomous. Self-described as an "independent entity within the government,"[14] the Fed's policies do not need the approval of the president or Congress. Congressional oversight of the Fed is an important check on Fed policies, however. Third, only nationally chartered banks, those chartered through the Office of the Comptroller of the Currency in the Treasury Department, are required to join the Fed. State-chartered banks may apply for membership or remain state nonmember banks. Fourth, the federal government does not own the Federal Reserve System. Instead, the law requires member banks in each of the 12 Fed districts to buy stock in their regional Reserve Bank. Hence, member banks own the 12 Federal Reserve Banks. Finally, the Fed is a self-supporting, nonprofit institution, Yet, the Fed often earns profits, which are called net earnings. Most net earnings are derived from the purchase or sale of government securities, interest from loans, or fees for financial services. Net earnings are not distributed to stockholders, but instead are handed over to the Treasury Department. In 2002 the Fed's net earnings totaled $24.5 billion.[15]

The Board of Governors sits at the top of the Fed's organizational structure. This board is organized as a federal agency and consists of seven members, each appointed to a 14-year term by the president and subject to confirmation by the Senate. The president also appoints the chairman of the board, selecting from among the seven board members, for a four-year term of office. Alan Greenspan, current chairman, completed the previous Fed chair's term of office from 1987 to 1988, and was reappointed to the Board's top spot for a historic five terms, most recently in May 2004 by President George W. Bush (see the biography of Alan Greenspan). The board has broad responsibilities in the realm of promoting a sound banking system and economic stability—stable prices, full employment, and economic growth. It supervises and regulates banks, collects and shares economic information with policymakers and ordinary citizens, participates in multilateral organizations, and is a powerful voice in the formulation of the nation's monetary policy (see chapter 10 for more on the board's role in forming monetary policy). The board also meets regularly with three advisory committees: the Federal Advisory Council, which deals with general economic and banking issues; the Consumer Advisory Council, which deals with consumer credit and related issues; and the Thrift Institutions Advisory Council, which deals with financial concerns of S&Ls, savings banks, and credit unions. The Board of Governors and its 1,700 staff workers operate from its headquarters in Washington, D.C.

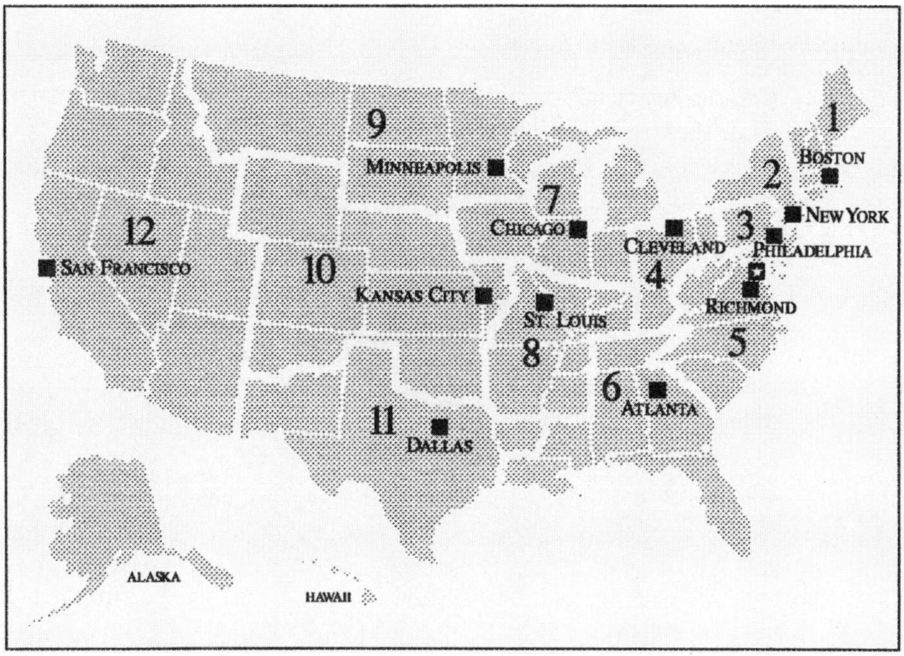

The Federal Reserve System.

The 12 regional Federal Reserve Banks and the 25 Branch Reserve Banks represent a second tier in the Fed. Each of the 12 Reserve Banks serves a specific district in the United States: (1) Boston, (2) New York, (3) Philadelphia, (4) Cleveland, (5) Richmond, (6) Atlanta, (7) Chicago, (8) St. Louis, (9) Minneapolis, (10) Kansas City, (11) Dallas, and (12) San Francisco. A nine-member Board of Directors administers each Reserve Bank. Three directors represent the interests of commercial banks in the region, while the six remaining directors represent the interests of the public—consumers, labor, industry, agriculture, and so on. The nine directors, in turn, select the Reserve Bank's president, a selection that requires the approval of the Board of Governors in Washington, D.C. Similarly, a Board of Directors governs each of the 25 Branch Reserve Banks. The Federal Reserve Banks are often referred to as "the operating arms of the central banking system" because of their role in bank supervision, currency distribution, and the implementation of monetary policy.[16]

The member banks are the principle instruments through which Fed policies are administered. All commercial banks and bank trust companies that hold national charters are required by law to belong to the Fed. Membership is optional for state-chartered banks. Member banks are required to purchase stock in the regional Federal Reserve Bank and receive an annual dividend for this investment. In 2002 there were 7,944 commercial banks operating in the U.S. economy. Of this total, 3,049 were member banks, including all 2,101 nationally chartered commercial banks and 948 state-chartered commercial banks. The remaining 4,895 state-chartered commercial banks did not belong to the Fed. Figure 8.4 summa-

Figure 8.4
Commercial Banks and the Fed: 2002

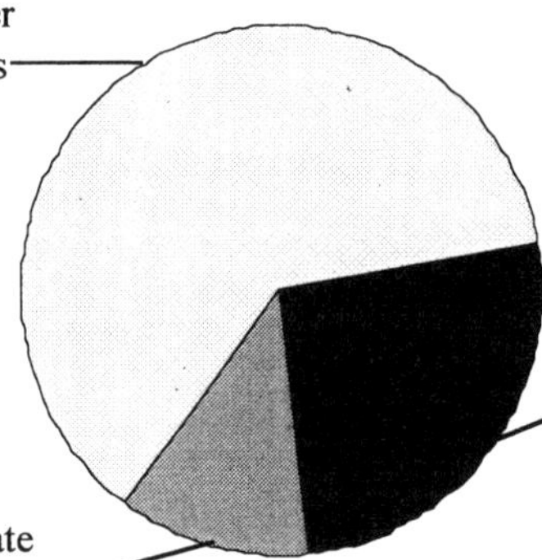

Source: Board of Governors, *89th Annual Report: 2002,* 295.

rizes the membership status of U.S. commercial banks. While member banks represented just 38 percent of all commercial banks in the United States, these banks and their 50,000 branches and offices accounted for 74 percent of all commercial banking services.[17] Thrift institutions, including S&Ls, savings banks, and credit unions, are not eligible to become member banks. In reality, most of the distinctions between member and nonmember state banks have disappeared over time. The Depository Institutions Deregulation and Monetary Control Act of 1980 also extended most of the requirements and benefits of membership to the thrifts.

Functions of the Federal Reserve System

The Fed has several major functions in the U.S. economy, all of which are related to its mission of creating a stronger and more stable monetary and financial system. First, the Fed formulates and implements the nation's monetary policy. **Monetary policy** is the actions of a nation's central bank to alter the money supply and the cost of credit in pursuit of national economic goals, mainly economic growth and stability. The primary tools of monetary policy are open market operations, the discount rate, and the reserve requirement. During economic downturns, or recessions, these monetary tools are used to increase the money supply and lower interest rates. These actions stimulate business activity to help the sluggish economy rebound. Conversely, to slow inflation the Fed's monetary tools are used to decrease the money supply and increase interest rates. By withdrawing money from the economy and making credit more expensive, the Fed reduces inflationary pressures that result from too much money chasing too few goods (see chapter 10 for more about monetary policy).

A second function of the Fed is the supervision and regulation of depository institutions. This function is designed to ensure the stability of financial institutions and the security of depositors' savings. Supervision deals with the Fed's oversight of business practices employed by member and nonmember financial institutions and their compliance with existing banking laws. The Fed's supervisory role is sometimes performed in conjunction with other federal agencies such as the FDIC, OTS, or NCUA. The Fed's regulatory role focuses on the creation of rules and guidelines by which financial institutions are organized and run. Fed regulations also deal with bank mergers and acquisitions, margin requirements in securities markets, and the business conduct of foreign banks operating in the United States. Since 1978, the Federal Financial Institutions Examinations Council (FFIEC) has brought representatives from federal and state regulatory agencies together to coordinate regulations in the banking industry.

A third function of the Fed is to supply important financial services to banks, the U.S. government, and the American people. The Fed's electronic payments systems, which include the automated clearinghouse (ACH) and the Federal Reserve Communications System (Fedwire), speed transactions among financial institutions, government agencies, and citizens. ACH processes payments electronically. It was designed to reduce the use of cumbersome paper checks for recurring payments, such as the direct deposit of payroll, direct payment of mortgages and other bills, interest and dividend payments, tax refunds, and Social Security and other government transfer payments. In 2002 the Fed's ACH system processed 5 billion payments worth more than $10 trillion. Fedwire links the Federal Reserve Banks and 7,800 depository institutions, enabling larger transfers of money and securities between banks. In 2002 Fedwire transferred $406 trillion in funds and $229 trillion in securities through its system.[18] A second important Fed service is check clearing. The Fed operates dozens of check-clearing centers across the country to sort and process checks. In 2002 these centers processed about 16.6 billion checks, about 40 percent of all checks written in the United States. A third Fed service is regulating the nation's money stock. The Fed is alert to shifts in business activity and changes in the demand for money at different times of the year, such as holiday seasons and planting seasons. In response to seasonal fluctuations, the Fed infuses currency and coin into the economy or withdraws them from the economy. It also replaces damaged, or unfit, money when necessary. The Fed receives its supply of paper currency from the Treasury Department's Bureau of Engraving and Printing, and its supply of coins from the Bureau of the Mint. Fourth, the Fed serves as the fiscal agent of the U.S. government. In this role, the Fed provides a number of services to the federal government. It collects and deposits federal tax receipts, issues and redeems government securities, manages government agencies' accounts, and processes government checks to business vendors and citizens.[19]

STOCK EXCHANGES AND OTHER FINANCIAL MARKETS

Trillions of dollars flow through the U.S. banking system each year, providing security and interest income for savers and a pool of funds that can be loaned to borrowers. Thus, the banking system is an important feature within the larger financial system of the country. There are other important components of the U.S. financial system, however. Some of the key institutions include stock markets, bond markets, mutual funds, and futures exchanges.

Stock Markets

A **stock market,** or stock exchange, is a mechanism by which stocks are traded. That is, a stock market provides a way to link buyers and sellers of stocks, and a means to negotiate a price that is agreeable to both parties. Only stocks of publicly traded companies are eligible to be listed on a stock exchange. Some stock markets are situated in a single building or complex. For example, the **New York Stock Exchange** (NYSE), the largest floor-based exchange in the United States, is located on Wall Street in New York City. The **NASDAQ Stock Market** (NASDAQ), however, is a decentralized network of investors and stock dealers that communicate and trade stocks through electronic trading systems. NASDAQ is an abbreviation of North American Stock Dealers Automated Quotations. Ranked by the volume of shares traded, NASDAQ is the largest stock market in the United States. In 2002 stock trading on NASDAQ resulted in 442 billion shares changing hands. The NYSE recorded the second largest volume, with 366 billion shares traded. Over 90 percent of the stocks traded in U.S. stock markets were traded on NASDAQ and the NYSE.[20] In 2003 other U.S. stock markets included the American Stock Exchange, Archipelago Exchange, Arizona Stock Exchange, Boston Stock Exchange, Chicago Stock Exchange, Cincinnati Stock Exchange, and Philadelphia Stock Exchange.

Stock markets are an important component in U.S. financial markets for a variety of reasons. First, they are a vehicle for raising investment capital for corporations in primary markets. Stock trading in a primary market occurs when a business issues new stocks for sale to investors. Established companies and newly formed corporations can benefit from a new issue of stock to the public. The proceeds from the sale of new issues in primary markets generate funds for corporations to build plants, purchase real capital, and attend to other business expenses. A corporation's first issue of stock to investors is called an initial public offering (IPO). For example, in 2004 Google, the world's largest Internet search engine, announced an IPO to raise $2.7 billion. Second, stock markets provide a way for investors to earn profits, called capital gains, in the secondary markets. Stock trading in a secondary market involves the purchase and sale of previously issued stocks. Capital gains occur when the investor is able to sell a stock for more than the purchase price. Of course, all investments involve some risk, and an investor can also incur capital losses, which occur when a stock sells for less than its original purchase price. Third, stock markets send market signals throughout the economy. These market signals indicate investors' confidence in specific firms, in specific industries, in different economic sectors, and in the direction of the overall U.S. economy. The signals influence the buying decisions of individuals as well as the investment decisions of business firms.

The NASDAQ stock trading network, like the floor-based stock exchanges, connects investors who wish to buy and sell stocks. This network is divided into two markets: the NASDAQ National Market for larger firms, and the NASDAQ SmallCap Market for smaller firms. By the early 2000s, there were about 4,100 companies listed in the NASDAQ markets. There are a number of ways a NASDAQ transaction might be completed. One way is for the investor's broker to contact one of the hundreds of dealers who buy and sell stocks for resale at a later date. Since a number of dealers actively seek out each stock listed on the NASDAQ market, the transactions are fluid. Second, brokers access the electronic stock trading systems used in the NASDAQ network, including the alternative trading system (ATS) and the electronic communications network (ECN). These computerized systems can also make a direct link between buyers and sellers of stock without the use of a broker. Third, the Primex Auction System provides a type of electronic auction for stocks. Market participants include dealers and other investors from the ATS and ECN. The performance of NASDAQ stocks is measured by the ups and downs of the NASDAQ Composite Index, which includes all common stocks listed on the exchange. In 1971 the first index was set at 100, and by the spring of 2004 it hovered in the 1,900 to 2,100 range. The Securities and Exchange Commission (SEC) monitors NASDAQ. U.S. brokerage firms must also belong to a self-regulatory organization (SRO), which guard against fraud and unethical behaviors in the securities industry. NASDAQ, the NYSE, and the other stock markets are SROs and are authorized to discipline or expel market participants for breaches in their professional conduct.[21]

The New York Stock Exchange is the largest floor-based stock market in the United States. In 2002 the NYSE listed 2,783 companies that had issued 350 billion shares worth $9.6 trillion. The NYSE is often referred to as an auction market because it brings brokers together under a single roof to negotiate the best deal for their clients. Stock trading takes place on the floor of the exchange, at one of the 20 trading posts. Trading posts are manned by specialists who, as their title suggests, specialize in the trade of a certain group of stocks. Specialists receive buy and sell orders electronically and facilitate the negotiations among brokers gathered at the trading post. Today, most of the buy and sell orders are sent electronically from brokerage firms to the specialists through the NYSE's SuperDot system. Orders are also sped up through the Broker Booth Support System (BBSS), which electronically transmits buy or sell orders from brokerage firms to their brokers on the exchange floor. The NYSE e-Broker system, which relies on wireless handheld communications devices, further streamlines the transaction process. Within seconds of a completed transaction, the specialist sends notice of the deal to the brokerage firms and, through the consolidated tape system, to investors around the world. In 2002 an average of 1.4 billion shares changed hands every business day on the NYSE.[22]

The performance of stocks on the NYSE is often measured by changes in the Dow Jones Industrial Average (the Dow), a stock index of 30 blue-chip stocks. A blue-chip stock is the stock of a prominent well-known company. The

Stock trading on the floor of the New York Stock Exchange. © New York Stock Exchange.

Figure 8.5
The Dow Jones Industrial Average: 1896 and 2004

Dow in 1896 (12 stocks)

American Cotton Oil, American Sugar, American Tobacco, Chicago Gas, Distilling & Cattle Feeding, General Electric, Laclede Gas, National Lead, North American, Tennessee Coal & Iron, U.S. Leather preferred, U.S. Rubber.

Dow in 2004 (30 stocks)

3M Company, Alcoa, Altria Group (formerly Philip Morris Companies), American Express, American International Group (AIG), AT&T, Boeing, Caterpillar, Citigroup, Coca-Cola, DuPont, General Electric, General Motors, Hewlett-Packard, Home Depot, Honeywell International, Intel, IBM, J.P. Morgan Chase, Johnson & Johnson, McDonald's, Merck, Microsoft, Pfizer, Procter & Gamble, SBC Communications, United Technologies, Verizon Communications, Wal-Mart Stores, Walt Disney

composition of the Dow in 1896 and in 2004 is shown in Figure 8.5. In the early 1980s, the Dow was under 1,000 points. The Dow experienced growth during much of the 1990s and eventually peaked at 11,723 on January 14, 2000. A sustained increase in the Dow is called a **bull market.** Soon thereafter, the Dow experienced a prolonged decline, or bear market. Experts generally define a **bear market** as a drop in the value of stocks by 20 percent or more. The trough of the bear market occurred on October 9, 2002, when the Dow dipped to 7,286, a drop of 4,437 points from its earlier peak. The bear market of the early 2000s resulted in a 30 percent fall in the Dow and the evaporation of trillions of dollars in equity on the NYSE and other U.S. stock markets.[23] Federal watchdogs representing the SEC and the in-house SRO at the exchange scrutinize the business conduct of market participants (see the biography of Charles Dow).

Bond Markets

A **bond market** is a mechanism by which corporate bonds and securities issued by the U.S. Treasury, federal agencies, state and municipal governments, and others are bought and sold. Hence the bond market is made up of many types of buyers and sellers of bonds. A **bond** is a type of loan, or IOU. By issuing bonds, corporations and governments borrow money and pledge to repay the borrowed money plus interest in the future. The money generated by the sale of bonds is used in many productive ways. Corporations issue bonds to build or expand productive facilities, purchase new equipment, expand research, or finance other business expenses. In June 2003 General Motors issued a variety of bonds valued at $17.6 billion, the largest corporate bond issuance in history, mainly to finance its pension plans. The federal government issues bonds to finance the public debt and to help finance home mortgages, student loans, and other socially desirable programs. State and local governments issue bonds for local infrastructure construction and repair, and to build schools, hospitals, and other public facilities.

The bond market in the United States is largely run electronically and over-the-counter (OTC), rather than on the floor of formal bond exchanges. Even bond trading on the New York Stock Exchange, which operates the largest bond market of any stock exchange in America, has declined dramatically in recent years. Between 1992 and 2002, total bond trades at the NYSE declined by 70 percent.[24] Today, bond dealers, who are usually employed by securities firms or banks, buy bonds in large quantities directly from bond issuers in primary markets. Later, these dealers resell portions of their inventory of bonds to other dealers or to willing investors in secondary markets. Traditionally, institutional investors such as insurance companies, mutual funds, pension funds, financial institutions, and foreign and domestic governments dominate the purchase of bonds in U.S. bond markets. Individual investors account for just a small fraction of the total bond volume each year. By 2003, the total outstanding bond market debt in the United States was $20.6 trillion, as shown in Table 8.3.[25]

Investing in bonds is attractive for many reasons. First, bonds offer security. For example, U.S. Treasury bonds and notes carry the full-faith-and-credit backing of the federal government. For this reason, Treasury securities are often viewed as among the world's safest investments. Similarly, other government-issued securities, both federal and municipal, are viewed as secure investments. Today, many municipal bonds are also insured, which guarantees the bondholder

Table 8.3
Outstanding Bond Market Debt: 2003

Type of Bond	Amount ($ trillions)	Percent of Bond Debt
Corporate bonds	$4.1	20.2%
U.S. Treasury securities	$3.3	16.1%
Municipal securities	$1.8	8.7%
Federal agencies securities	$2.4	11.6%
Mortgage-related securities	$4.9	23.5%
Money market securities	$2.5	12.2%
Asset-backed securities	$1.6	7.7%
Total outstanding bond debt	$20.6	100.0%

Source: The Bond Market Association, *Research Quarterly,* May 2003.

payment of both principal and interest should the issuer default. Even corporate bonds, because they represent debt rather than ownership, give bondholders a solid claim on the issuing company's assets if the company declares bankruptcy.

Second, bonds offer a steady, predictable rate of return. Most government and corporate bonds offer a fixed rate of interest and a specific maturity date. Treasury notes and bonds, for example, pay a fixed rate of interest semiannually until maturity. Corporate bonds typically pay bondholders a fixed rate of interest on a semiannual or annual basis. Further, since 1997, the Treasury has offered new bonds and notes called Treasury Inflation-Indexed Securities (TIIS) to protect investors from the adverse effects of inflation.

Third, some government bonds have tax advantages. For example, the interest that investors earn from many municipal bonds is exempt from federal taxation and, depending on the issuer, may be exempt from state and local taxes as well. In the early 2000s, over 80,000 state and local governments had issued municipal bonds to finance local projects. In addition, the interest earned on Treasury securities is exempt from state and local taxes.

Fourth, there is high liquidity in most bond markets. While all bonds carry a stated maturity date, most are easily resold on sophisticated electronic secondary markets. There is no guarantee that the bond will sell for full face value, however, and there is often a transaction fee connected with the sale.

Shown below is a summary of major types of bonds in the U.S. economy.

- *Corporate bonds*. Corporate bonds, also called corporates, are debt obligations of issuing companies. They are typically issued in multiples of $1,000 or $5,000, and they pay a fixed rate of interest, often semiannually. The principal is returned to the bondholder with the final interest payment at maturity. Interest rates are usually higher than most government securities, but interest payments are taxed as income. Investment-grade corporates offer less risk than high-yield bonds, which are often called junk bonds.
- *Treasury securities*. Treasury securities are the debt obligation of the U.S. Treasury. Treasury bills (T-bills) mature in 1 year or less, and interest is paid at maturity. Treasury notes mature in 1 to 10 years and offer slightly higher interest than T-bills, paid semiannually. Treasury bonds have traditionally matured in 10 to 30 years and offer higher interest than Treasury notes. The government discontinued the 30-year bonds in 2001. Interest payments on Treasury securities are exempt from state and local taxes.
- *Municipal bonds*. Municipal bonds are debt obligations of cities, counties, states, or other public entities. Maturity varies. The disadvantage of relatively low interest rates is partially offset by the federal tax exemption for many municipal bonds and by the fact that many of these bonds are insured, which guarantees the security of principal and interest.
- *Federal agency securities*. Federal agency securities are debt obligations of federal agencies and government-sponsored enterprises (GSEs). These federal securities support mortgages (Fannie Mae, Freddie Mac, Farmer Mac), student loans (Sallie Mae), the Small Business Administration, and other programs. Maturity varies. Interest is relatively low, but is higher than most Treasury securities. Interest payments are exempt from state and local taxes.

- *Mortgage-related securities*. Mortgage securities are created by institutions that buy loans from mortgage lenders and then issue securities that represent this pool of mortgages. As people make payments on their home mortgages, capital is raised to make interest and principal payments to investors. Securities range from $1,000 to $25,000. The interest rate is often higher than Treasury securities, but interest payments are taxed as income.
- *Money market securities*. Money market securities are types of short-term loans in the form of CDs and commercial paper. Governments and corporations often use money market securities to satisfy financial obligations until longer-term bonds, notes, or bills can be issued. Maturity varies, but virtually all money market securities mature in less than one year. The interest paid to investors is usually higher than prevailing interest rates on bank savings accounts.
- *Asset-backed securities*. Asset-backed securities are created by institutions that buy loans from lenders and then issue securities that represent the pool of loans—such as home mortgage loans, credit card debt, automobile loans, and student loans. As people repay their loans, capital is raised to make interest and principal payments to investors.

Mutual Funds

A **mutual fund** is a pool of assets managed by professional investment managers, called fund managers. Mutual fund companies use investors' money to buy a diversified pool of securities, mainly stocks and bonds, to create an investment portfolio. The amount of risk and the potential for financial gain vary from fund to fund. Investors purchase stock in a mutual fund, which is much like purchasing stock in a corporation. Hence, each investor is a part owner of the mutual fund. The main asset of a mutual fund is its diversified portfolio of securities, rather than plant and equipment. When the securities within the fund's portfolio rise, investors are typically awarded dividends. The value of a successful mutual fund may also rise over time, contributing to capital gains for investors. In many cases, the dividends and capital gains earned by shareholders are ploughed directly back into the fund, which increases the number of shares owned by each investor. In 2002 the largest mutual fund company in the United States was Fidelity Investments, parent to more than 150 mutual funds with combined assets of $723 billion. Total assets for the entire mutual fund industry hit $6.4 trillion, spread across 8,256 different mutual funds—equity funds (4,756 funds), hybrid funds (475), bond funds (2,036), taxable money market funds (679), and tax-exempt money market funds (310), as shown in Figure 8.6. By the early 2000s, 93 million Americans had money invested in mutual funds, distributed in about 250 million shareholder accounts.[26]

Mutual funds offer a number of advantages to investors. First, mutual funds are more secure than investments in individual stocks. This security is derived from the fund's diversified portfolio, which spreads the risk over a broad range of securities. Second, a mutual fund is professionally managed. This feature enables the investor to benefit from the fund manager's experience, expertise, and financial resources. Third, mutual funds expand the investor's choices in terms of risk, capital growth, and income. Investment choices range from

Figure 8.6
Types of Mutual Funds: 2002

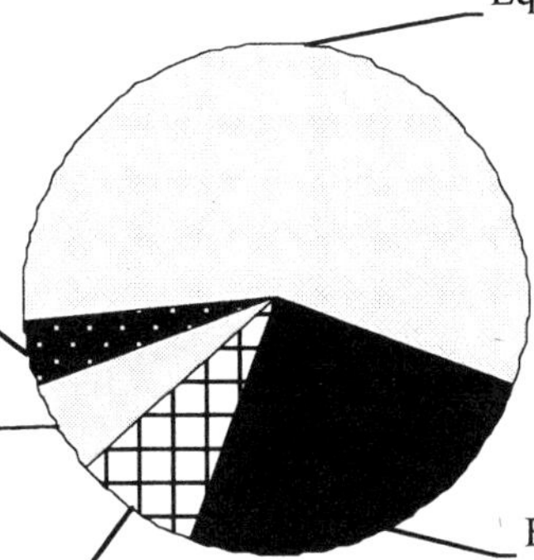

Source: Investment Company Institute/Insurance Information Institute, *Mutual Funds.*

aggressive-growth funds, which are composed mainly of start-up companies and high-risk firms in promising industries, to the more conservative money market funds, which are built around portfolios consisting of U.S. securities, certificates of deposit, and the like. Fourth, mutual funds are simple to buy and sell. The purchase of shares in a mutual fund can be made through stockbrokers and registered financial planners, for a fee. Some funds encourage the direct purchase of shares by mail or phone, with no fees attached. In addition, investors can sell all or a portion of their shares in a mutual fund to the fund itself, which adds to the convenience of mutual fund ownership.

Investors' rights are protected by a number of state and federal laws that regulate the mutual fund industry. The Securities Act of 1933 and the Securities Exchange Act of 1934 mandate accurate investor information and ethical conduct in mutual fund transactions. The Investment Company Act of 1940 requires that fund managers disseminate the investment guidelines for each fund. It also requires the fund to register with the Securities and Exchange Commission. Even with these investor protections, scandal rocked the mutual fund industry in 2003–2004. Some fund managers illegally profited from after-hours trading of mutual fund shares, a practice called late trading. The SEC pledged to pursue fraudulent dealings in the mutual fund industry and prosecute wrongdoers.

Futures Markets

A **futures market,** or futures exchange, is a mechanism by which contracts for items are bought and sold. Thus, the operation of a futures market is similar to the operation of a stock market or bond market. In a futures market, investors buy and sell futures contracts, formal agreements to take a delivery of an item (buy the item) or make a delivery of an item (sell the item) at a specific date in the future. Also listed on the contract is the agreed-upon price for the item, the quantity, and the location for the delivery. As early as the 1860s, futures contracts were used at the Chicago Board of Trade (CBOT) for agricultural products. Under a contract, investors agreed to buy quantities of grain from producers for a set price, and to take delivery later in the year. This system provided some price stability in agricultural markets, as market participants knew in advance the terms of the transaction. A locked-in price enabled the grain producer to calculate with precision the firm's revenues, and enabled the buyer to anticipate the costs of grain in the production of bread or another finished good. Over time, this system also sparked a lively trade in futures contracts. For example, if investors were confident that grain would fetch a higher price than was stated in the futures contract, the contract became more valuable—and a good investment for an investor who wanted to buy low and sell high.

Today's futures markets operate under many of the same basic principles that guided futures markets more than a century ago. Naturally, technological advances and the types of items traded have brought the process into the twenty-first century. Today a wide variety of futures contracts are negotiated for industrial commodities, agricultural commodities, foreign currencies, securities indexes, and interest rates. The negotiations to determine the price for these futures contracts combines sophisticated electronic communications with the shouting and hand signaling of traders in the pit. Contracts are bought and sold rapidly, and much of the action is highly speculative.

Different futures markets in the United States tend to specialize in different types of futures contracts. For example, the Chicago Mercantile Exchange (CME), the largest U.S. futures market, specializes in selected commodities and financial products such as stock indexes, foreign exchange, and interest rates. In 2002, 558 million contracts valued at $329 trillion changed hands on the floor of the CME, through privately negotiated transactions and on CME's GLOBEX electronic trading system. The Chicago Board of Trade (CBOT), the second largest U.S. futures market, deals more with contracts related to U.S. Treasury securities. In 2002, 344 million futures contracts were negotiated on the CBOT.[27] Other futures markets operating in the United States include the Coffee, Sugar and Cocoa Exchange (New York), Kansas City Board of Trade, Mid-America Exchange (Chicago), Minneapolis Grain Exchange, New York Cotton Exchange, and New York Mercantile Exchange.

BIOGRAPHIES: SHAPERS OF ECONOMIC THOUGHT

Alexander Hamilton: Father of the American Banking System

Alexander Hamilton (1757–1804) was the first U.S. secretary of the treasury and father of the American banking system. Hamilton was born on Nevis, a British possession in the Caribbean, and raised by his mother, a single parent. Armed with little more than a keen intellect, the young Hamilton journeyed to New York City in 1772. In 1773 he resumed his formal education at King's College, now Columbia University. The brewing revolution in the American colonies soon interrupted Hamilton's studies, however, and he served the cause of independence with distinction in the early years of the war. His abilities caught the eye of General George Washington. Soon, Hamilton was a member of General Washington's staff, and a lasting friendship developed. President Washington would not forget this friendship when, in 1789, he selected Hamilton as the first secretary of the treasury.

As secretary of the treasury, Hamilton penned a series of reports that outlined an economic agenda for America's growth and prosperity. He believed that America's financial future would rest on its ability to create a sound monetary and banking system and a more diversified economy. In *The Reports on Credit I* (1790), Hamilton proposed that the United States honor all public debts incurred by the federal and state governments during the Revolutionary War. To pay for these past obligations, he proposed that the government issue interest-bearing bonds and enact import tariffs and excise taxes. In *The Reports on Credit II* (1790), Hamilton proposed the creation of a national bank similar to the Bank of England. The national bank would provide security for the federal government's funds, issue a national currency, pool capital for private-sector loans, and help the federal government respond to national emergencies such as war. Hamilton's opponents, including Thomas Jefferson, argued that the creation of a national bank was unconstitutional because the Constitution made no mention of a national bank. Hamilton countered that Congress had certain implied powers under Article 1, Section 8, Clause 18. He argued that a national bank was "an instrument or mean[s] of carrying into execution any of the specified powers,"[28] including the power to tax and to defend the nation from external aggression. In the end, Congress and President Washington sided with Hamilton's view and created the First Bank of the United States. In *The Report on Manufactures* (1791), Hamilton proposed specific policies, such as import tariffs and subsidies to American firms, to support the growth of manufacturing in the United States. Hamilton believed that there was a symbiotic relationship between agriculture, commerce, and manufacturing, and that progress in each of these sectors was necessary for America's economic development.

Underpinning each pillar of Hamilton's economic plan was the principle of federal supremacy over state authority. Hamilton's support for a strong federal government constantly put him at odds with Jefferson, the powerful secretary of state, who favored decentralized decision making. Hamilton's life was cut short in 1804, when he was killed in a duel with political rival Aaron Burr. But Hamilton's contributions to the nation's financial stability, including the First Bank, lived on.

Charles H. Dow: Founder of the Dow Jones Industrial Average

Charles Henry Dow (1851–1902) was a prominent American financial journalist, editor, and founder of the Dow Jones Industrial Average, the most recognized stock index in the world. Dow was born in Sterling, Connecticut, the son of a farmer. His interest soon turned to journalism, and during the 1870s he worked as a reporter for several New England newspapers, including the *Springfield Journal* in Massachusetts and the *Providence Journal* in Rhode Island. Dow's reporting on the silver mining boom in Leadville, Colorado (1879), sparked his interest in financial journalism. Within a year, Dow moved to the financial capital of the United States, New York City, where he joined the staff of a financial news service. In 1882 Dow and fellow reporter Edward D. Jones formed Dow Jones & Company, which was located in a cramped office on Wall Street. Dow and Jones researched financial news and wrote daily financial bulletins, called flimsies, for financial institutions in the city. The firm's size and reputation grew during the 1880s. In 1889 its respected bulletins, originally published as the *Customer's Afternoon Letter,* were transformed into a financial newspaper, the *Wall Street Journal.*

As editor of the *Wall Street Journal,* Dow's articles reached a wider audience. In 1896 Dow developed the Dow Jones Industrial Average (Dow), an index composed of 12 prominent manufacturing companies, to track the performance of stocks on the New York Stock Exchange (NYSE). The Dow followed on the heels of Dow's first stock index, which tracked mainly railroad companies from 1884 to 1896. The composition and number of companies included in the Dow has changed significantly since 1896. By 1929 the Dow had grown to 30 companies, the same number used today. The method of calculating the index has also changed over time. Dow's first index during the 1880s and early 1890s simply added the closing prices of the 11 original companies and divided the sum by 11. Thus, the index measured the average performance of these stocks in dollars. Today's Dow adds the prices of the 30 companies and divides the sum by a divisor. Hence, today's Dow is measured in *points* rather than *dollars.* Despite the changes, the Dow has consistently selected successful blue-chip companies with wide investor interest for inclusion in the index. Over time, additional Dow Jones indexes, including the Dow Jones Transportation Average and the Dow Jones Utility Average, were created to measure the ups and downs of stocks in other industries. The most inclusive of the indexes is the Dow Jones Composite Average, which tracks price changes of all common stocks listed on the NYSE.

Charles Dow is also credited with laying the groundwork for the Dow theory, which is based on his observations and writings. One element of the Dow theory explains fluctuations in the performance of stocks over time. The most important fluctuations were the long-term trends over the course of years, which could be either bullish or bearish. Dow also observed that informed, farsighted investors were in a far more favorable position to make money in the stock market than the general population, mainly because they could better anticipate market swings. Dow died a century ago, but his legacy includes two icons in the nation's financial markets, the Dow and the country's premier financial newspaper, the *Wall Street Journal.*

Carter Glass: Father of the Federal Reserve System

Carter Glass (1858–1946) was an influential American political figure during the early twentieth century. He is also considered the father of the Federal

Reserve System. Glass was born in Lynchburg, Virginia, shortly before the outbreak of the Civil War. The societal chaos that overwhelmed the South during the war and its aftermath cut short Glass's formal education. As a voracious reader, he acquainted himself with history, literature, and philosophy, however. He also gained valuable business skills during the 1870s and 1880s, rising from an apprentice printer in Lynchburg to the owner of several area newspapers. By the late 1890s, Glass entered politics at the state level. In 1902 he represented Virginia in the House of Representatives, where he served until 1918. After a brief stint as secretary of the treasury, Glass returned to Congress as a senator, a position he held until his death in 1946.

Carter Glass had a profound influence on the American banking system during the twentieth century. As a member of the House Committee on Banking and Currency during the early century, Glass understood the weaknesses of the banking system. These weaknesses became more apparent during the Panic of 1907, which threw the entire financial system into chaos. The Panic also motivated Glass to redouble his efforts to create a central bank. In 1912 fellow Democrat Woodrow Wilson was elected president, which not only buoyed Glass's career but also brought a sympathetic ear into the Oval Office. After significant congressional debate, the Federal Reserve Act was passed by both houses of Congress and signed into law by President Wilson on December 23, 1913. Within a year, a uniquely American Federal Reserve System (Fed) began operations, and Carter Glass was hailed as its chief architect. In his book, *An Adventure in Constructive Finance* (1927), Glass chronicled the creation of the Fed. As a senator, Glass also helped craft the Banking Act of 1935, which significantly restructured the Fed. The Banking Act of 1935 replaced the five-member Federal Reserve Board with a seven-member Board of Governors, whose members would serve staggered terms of 14 years. The act increased the Fed's power to devise and implement monetary policy by creating the powerful Federal Open Market Committee (FOMC). It also increased the Fed's independence by removing the secretary of the treasury and the comptroller of the currency from the Board of Governors, effectively making the Fed an independent agency within the federal government.

In the 1930s, Senator Glass and Senator Henry Steagall took the lead in reforming the ailing U.S. banking system, which had witnessed the collapse of 11,000 banks during the first few years of the Great Depression. The Glass-Steagall Banking Act of 1933, also known as the Banking Act of 1933, changed banking practices in two main ways. First, it separated commercial banking from investment banking. This provision took commercial banks out of the risky business of investing in stocks, a practice that had destabilized the banking system and deepened the Great Depression. It wasn't until 1999 that the Gramm-Leach-Bliley Act largely dismantled the wall between commercial and investment banking, leaving government regulators with the unenviable task of implementing the new law. Second, the Glass-Steagall Banking Act created the Federal Deposit Insurance Corporation (FDIC), which guaranteed the safety of depositors' savings up to $2,500. This provision, which Glass only grudgingly supported because he believed it intruded on private enterprise, ended panic runs by depositors on their banks. Today, the FDIC provides federal insurance on deposits up to $100,000 per account.

Alan Greenspan: Chairman of the Board of Governors of the Federal Reserve System

Alan Greenspan (1926–) is a prominent American economist and has served as chairman of the Board of Governors of the Federal Reserve System (Fed) since 1987. Greenspan was born in New York City. After graduating from high school, he briefly studied music at the prestigious Juilliard School. He earned a series of academic degrees in economics from New York University: a bachelor's degree in 1948, a master's degree in 1950, and a doctorate in 1977. In addition, he cofounded an economic consulting firm, Townsend-Greenspan & Co., Inc., where he worked for 30 years, from 1954 to 1974 and 1977 to 1987. Greenspan is best known for appointive positions in public service, however. President Gerald Ford appointed him chairman of the President's Council of Economic Advisors in 1974, a position he held until 1977. In 1987 President Ronald Reagan lured Alan Greenspan back into public service to complete Paul Volcker's term as chairman of the Board of Governors. Greenspan was reappointed to the Fed's top spot five times, in 1988, 1992, 1996, 2000, and 2004.

Throughout his tenure as Fed chairman, Alan Greenspan viewed economic stability as the primary goal of the nation's central bank. One dominant economic concern was the debilitating effects of inflation on the security of individual households and on the overall economy. Hence, Greenspan viewed the Federal Reserve as "the ultimate guardian of the purchasing power of money."[29] To reduce inflationary pressures, Greenspan kept a watchful eye on the growth of the money supply. Another economic concern was periodic brushes with rising unemployment and sluggish economic growth rates. In the recession of 2001–2002, for example, he supported a lower discount rate to encourage borrowing and bolster consumer confidence (see chapter 10 for more on monetary policy).

Greenspan has enjoyed a productive working relationship with Republican and Democratic presidents, Congress, and the larger U.S. banking community since 1987. He has worked to achieve the national economic goals listed in the Employment Act of 1946, including price stability, full employment, and economic growth. He has also voiced support for free trade, deregulation, free markets, and the rule of law. He challenged the business community to end corporate malfeasance and to restore investor confidence in the wake of the crushing financial debacles of Enron, WorldCom, Global Crossings, Tyco, and other corporate giants during the early 2000s. Greenspan received numerous honors and awards over the years, including the Thomas Jefferson Award (1976) for outstanding public service.

NOTES

1. Alan Greenspan, "The Challenge of Central Banking in a Democratic Society," speech delivered to The American Enterprise Institute for Public Policy Research, Wash-

ington, DC, December 5, 1996, www.federalreserve.gov/BOARDDOCS/SPEECHES/19961205.htm.

2. Federal Reserve Bank of Boston, *Currency Points: Understanding Our Money* (Boston: Author), 6.

3. Federal Reserve System, "Table 1. Money Stock Measures," "Table 7. Not Seasonally Adjusted Components of M1," *Federal Reserve Statistical Release*, June 19, 2003, 1, 7, www.federalreserve.gov/releases/h6/Current/h6.pdf.

4. Federal Reserve System, "Table 7. Not Seasonally Adjusted Components of M1," "Table 8. Not Seasonally Adjusted Components of Non-M1 M2," "Table 9. Not Seasonally Adjusted Components of Non-M2 M3," *Federal Reserve Statistical Release*, June 19, 2003, 7–9, www.federalreserve.gov/releases/h6/Current/h6.pdf.

5. Federal Reserve System, "Table G.19. Consumer Credit," *Federal Reserve Statistical Release*, April 2003, www.federalreserve.gov/releases'g19/Current; and "Table b-76. Mortgage Debt Outstanding by Holder, 1949–2002," *Economic Report of the President: 2003* (Washington, DC: U.S. Government Printing Office, 2003), 367.

6. Federal Deposit Insurance Corporation (FDIC), "FDIC Statistics on Banking," December 31, 2002, www.fdic.gov/bank/statistical/statistics/index.html; Office of Thrift Supervision (OTS), "Table 1. Number of Federally Insured Thrift Institutions by Charter Types, 1951–2002," *2002 Fact Book: A Statistical Profile of the Thrift Industry* (Washington, DC: OTS, 2003), 1; National Credit Union Administration (NCUA), *2002 Midyear Statistics for Federally Insured Credit Unions* (Alexandria, VA: NCUA Publications, 2002), 3, 8, 33.

7. FDIC, "FDIC Statistics on Banking"; Board of Governors of the Federal Reserve, "Top Ten U.S. Commercial Banks, by Assets, 2002," compiled by Insurance Information Institute, www.financialservicesfacts.org/financial2/usworld/banks/content.print/.

8. OTS, "Table 1.8. Number of Federally Insured Thrift Institutions by Insurance Fund, 1980–2002," "Table 1.2. Number of OTS-Regulated Thrift Institutions by Charter Type, 1987–2002," *2002 Fact Book*, 2, 8; FDIC, "FDIC Statistics on Banking"; SNL Financial LC, "Top Ten U.S. Thrift Companies, Ranked by Assets, 2003," compiled by Insurance Information Institute, www.financialservicesfacts.org/financial2/usworld/banks/content.print; and OTS, "Total Assets," *Thrift Financial Report System: Line Item Report,* September 2003, 1.

9. Ibid.

10. NCUA, *2002 Midyear Statistics for Federally Insured Credit Unions,* 3, 8; and FDIC, "Top Ten U.S. Credit Unions, 2001," compiled by Insurance Information Institute, www.financialservicesfacts.org/financial2/usworld/banks/content.print.

11. U.S. Department of Commerce/Bureau of Economic Analysis (BEA), "Personal Income and Its Disposition, March 26, 2004, www.bea.doc.gov/brieffrom/tables/ebrd.htm.

12. "Table B-32. Gross Savings and Investment," *Economic Report of the President: 2003* (Washington, DC: U.S. Government Printing Office, 2003), 314–15.

13. Board of Governors of the Federal Reserve System. *89th Annual Report: 2002* (Washington, DC: Board of Governors, 2002), 143.

14. Board of Governors of the Federal Reserve System, *The Federal Reserve System: Purposes and Functions* (Washington, DC: Board of Governors, 1994), 3.

15. Board of Governors of the Federal Reserve System, "Income, Expenses, and Distribution of Net Earnings of the Federal Reserve Banks, 2002 and 2001," *89th Annual Report,* 136.

16. Board of Governors, *The Federal Reserve System: Purposes and Functions,* 11.
17. Board of Governors, *89th Annual Report,* 123, 295, 302.
18. "Fedwire Funds Service" and "Fedwire Securities Service," *Fedwire and National Settlement Services: Annual Volume and Value*, 1–2, www.federalreserve.gov/paymentsystems/fedwire/annual.pdf; Michael Herd, "Federal Reserve Check Volume Decreases for Third Consecutive Year, ACH Volume Continues to Rise," NACHA, The Electronic Payment Association, June 9, 2002, www.nacha.org/news/default.htm; and Federal Reserve Bank of New York, "Automated Clearing Houses (ACHs)," www.ny-frb.org/pihome/fedpoint/fed31.htm.
19. Federal Reserve Board, "Federal Reserve Banks," *The Structure of the Federal Reserve System*, www.federalreserve.gov/pubs/frseries/freri3.htm; Federal Reserve Bank of St. Louis, "Providing Financial Services," *In Plain English,* http://stlouisfed.org/publications/pleng/payment_services.htm; Board of Governors, *The Federal Reserve System: Purposes and Functions,* 71–85, 87–90, 93–111.
20. NASDAQ Educational Foundation, *Market Mechanics: A Guide to U.S. Stock Markets* (New York: The NASDAQ Stock Market, Inc., 2002), 7.
21. Ibid., 8–11, 14.
22. New York Stock Exchange (NYSE), "All NYSE Listed Stocks," and "NYSE Reported Stock Trades, 2002," *NYSE Data Fact Book*, www.nysedata.com/factbook/viewer_edition.asp.
23. Dow Jones Indexes (DJI), "Dow Jones Averages Statistics," www.djindexes.com/jsp/avgStatistics/jsp; DJI, "Dow Jones Industrial Average History," www.djindexes.com/downloads/DJIA_Hist_Comp.pdf; DJI, "Highpoints/Lowpoints," www.djindexes.com/downloads/xlpages/DJIA_Hist_Perf.xls.
24. NYSE, "NYSE Data: NYSE Broker Volume," *NYSE Fact Book.*
25. Michael Decker et. al. "U.S. Bond Issuance Continues to Increase in the First Quarter of 2003," *Research Quarterly* (May 2003): 1.
26. Investment Company Institute (ICI), "U.S. Household Ownership of Mutual Funds in 2001," *Fundamentals: Investment Company Institute Research in Brief* 10, (September 2001): 1; and Insurance Information Institute, "Mutual Funds," www.financialservicesfacts.org/financial2/securities/mutualfunds/content.print.
27. Chicago Mercantile Exchange (CME), "CME at a Glance," www.cme.com/about_cme/cme_at_a_glance/index; Chicago Board of Trade (CBOT), "Greenspan's Support of Derivatives Applauded by CME, CBOT," March 12, 2003, www.cbt.com/cbot/www/cont_detail/0,1493,10+24+109+11426,00.html.
28. Alexander Hamilton, "For the Constitutionality of the Bank of the United States," in *The People Shall Judge: Readings in the Formation of American Policy,* Vol. 1, ed. The Staff, Social Sciences (Chicago: The University of Chicago Press, 1949), 422.
29. Greenspan, "The Challenge of Central Banking in a Democratic Society."

SELECTED READINGS

Benz, Christine, Peter Di Teresa, and Russel Kinnel. *Morningstar's Guide to Mutual Funds: 5-Star Strategies for Success.* New York: John Wiley & Sons, 2002.

Bernstein, Jake. *How the Futures Markets Work.* 2nd ed. Paramus, NJ: Prentice Hall Press, 2000.

Board of Governors of the Federal Reserve System. *The Federal Reserve System: Purposes and Functions.* Washington, D.C.: Board of Governors, 1994.

Boyle, David, and Katrina Brown, eds. *The Money Changers: Currency Reform from Aristotle to E-Cash.* Washington, DC: Earthscan Publications, 2003.
Brumbaugh, R. Dan. *Thrifts under Siege: Restoring Order to American Banking.* Chevy Chase, MD: Beard Group, 1999.
Center for Financial Training. *Banking and Financial Systems.* Cincinnati: South-Western College/West, 2002.
Cohen, Benjamin J. *The Future of Money.* Princeton, NJ: Princeton University Press, 2004.
Cohen, Marilyn. *The Bond Bible.* Paramus, NJ: Prentice Hall Press, 2000.
Engler, Henry, and James Essinger. *The Future of Banking.* Paramus, NJ: Financial Times Prentice Hall, 2000.
Evans, David, and Richard Schmalensee. *Paying with Plastic: The Digital Revolution in Buying and Borrowing.* Cambridge, MA: MIT Press, 2000.
Fitch, Thomas P. *Dictionary of Banking Terms.* 4th ed. Hauppauge, NY: Barrons Educational Series, 2000.
Geisst, Charles R., and Richard A. Grasso. *100 Years of Wall Street.* New York: McGraw-Hill Trade, 1999.
Greenspan, Alan, and Larry Kahaner. *The Quotations of Chairman Greenspan: Words from the Man Who Can Shake the World.* Holbrook, MA: Adams Media Corporation, 2000.
Hamilton, Alexander. *Hamilton: Writings,* ed. Joanne B. Freeman. New York: Library of America, 2001.
Ingebretsen, Mark. *NASDAQ: A History of the Market That Changed the World.* Roseville, CA: Prima Publishing, 2002.
Meltzer, Allen H., and Alan Greenspan. *A History of the Federal Reserve, Vol. 1: 1913–1951.* Chicago: University of Chicago Press, 2003.
Morgenson, Gretchen, and Campbell Harvey. *The New York Times Dictionary of Money and Investing: The Essential A-to-Z Guide to the Language of the New Market.* New York: Times Books, 2002.
Schwager, Jack D. *Stock Market Wizards: Interviews with America's Top Stock Traders.* New York: HarperBusiness, 2003.
Tuccille, Jerome. *Alan Shrugged: Alan Greenspan, the World's Most Powerful Banker.* New York: John Wiley & Sons, 2002.

CHAPTER 9

Perspectives on Economic Growth

Chapter 9 deals with the concept of economic growth. Perspectives on what constitutes economic growth have shifted over time. In the United States, the most widely recognized measurements of economic growth are the real gross domestic product (GDP) and GDP per capita. In recent years, the World Bank and other multilateral organizations have adjusted international economic data using purchasing power parity (PPP). Economic, political, and social factors contribute to sustained economic growth, giving rise to competing growth theories. Economists generally agree that economic growth requires investment in the factors of production, technology, entrepreneurship, and knowledge. They also note the importance of a sophisticated infrastructure, macroeconomic stability, good governance, and economic incentives. Economic growth promotes a higher living standard and quality of life for many people in the United States and in the global economy. Yet economic growth may have negative side effects, including pollution, resource depletion, and gross disparities in income and wealth.

DEFINING ECONOMIC GROWTH

Economic growth occurs when the total output of newly produced goods and services in an economy increases over time. Economists' perspectives on economic growth have shifted in recent years, however. Some economists believe that economic growth occurs only when national output increases per person, as measured by GDP per capita. Others view economic growth qualitatively as well as quantitatively. Hence, these economists are concerned not only with the rising dollar value of output per person, but also with measurable improvements in people's quality of life. This broader view of economic growth blurs the distinction between economic growth and economic development, however. **Economic development** occurs when a nation's output increases, the quality of life of its people improves, and the conditions for future prosperity are sustainable. In reality, there is significant overlap between the terms *economic growth* and *economic development*, and factors that contribute to growth often spill over into the realm of development. Economic growth is illustrated by an outward shift in a nation's production possibilities curve, as illustrated by the curve CD in Figure 9.1. Note that along the outer curve, CD, more consumption goods and investment goods are produced than along the original inner curve AB (see chapter 1 for more on production possibilities curves).

Measuring Economic Growth: The Gross Domestic Product

Measurements of gross domestic product (GDP) are the most cited indicators of economic growth in an economy. The **gross domestic product** is the total market value of final goods and services produced in a nation in a given year. Note that this definition sets conditions about the types of goods and services that are counted in the GDP. First, GDP includes only final goods and services. Final goods are products produced and sold for direct consumption by consumers, producers, or the government. Excluded from the GDP are intermediate goods, or goods that will be further processed for use in the production of another good. For example, an automobile is a final good, while a windshield is an intermediate good. The exclusion of intermediate goods avoids the problem of double counting, counting the same item twice in the GDP. Second, GDP includes only those products produced within the borders of a nation. This includes the final output of all firms operating in the United States, whether

Figure 9.1
Economic Growth: An Illustration

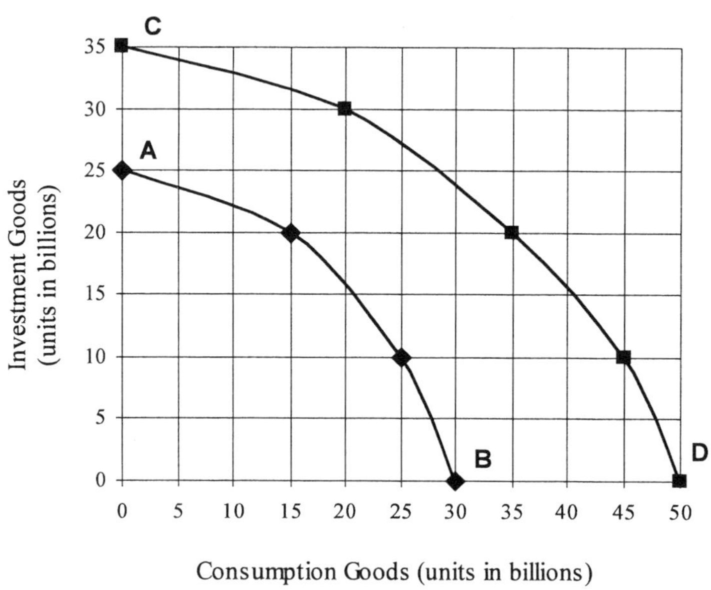

domestic or foreign owned. The output of U.S. firms operating in other countries is counted in the GDPs of foreign host nations. Third, GDP includes only newly produced output in a given year. GDP excludes all transactions of used, or secondhand, items. Fourth, GDP excludes all paper transactions that do not result in new output, including the value of stock or bond transactions, mergers and acquisitions of existing firms, Social Security and other transfer payments, and the resale of existing residential properties.

The GDP and the gross national product are similar measurements of national output. Yet there is one key difference between the two measurements. The **gross national product** (GNP) calculates the total market value of final goods produced by a country's firms, within the country and abroad, each year. Thus, the U.S. GNP includes the market value of output produced by American multinational corporations, independent contractors, and other U.S.-based producers operating anywhere in the world. Simon Kuznets, an American economist and founder of the GNP, introduced this method of national income and product accounting in the 1930s (see the biography of Simon Kuznets). Today there is little difference between the sizes of the GDP and GNP in most countries. In 2003, for example, the U.S. GDP was $10,988 billion and the GNP was $11,032 billion.[1]

The **real GDP** adjusts the current, or nominal, GDP for inflation each year. Real GDP is a more accurate measurement of total national output than nominal GDP because it enables annual growth comparisons based on constant, inflation-adjusted dollars. The GDP price deflator, a price index derived by the government, is used to convert the nominal GDP into the real GDP. The formula for the conversion to real GDP is as follows: nominal GDP divided by the price deflator, times 100, as shown in Figure 9.2. In 2003 the nominal GDP of the United States was $10,998 billion, and the GDP deflator was 105.67. Figure 9.2 shows how an $11 trillion nominal GDP was converted into a $10.4 trillion real GDP.[2]

The GDP per capita states the value of total national output per person in a country. The terms *GDP per capita* and *GNP per capita* are often used interchangeably with *per capita income* (see chapter 12 for more on a newer measurement of economic well-being, gross national income, or GNI). The GDP per capita is calculated by dividing the GDP by the total population of a country. In 2001 the GDP per capita in the United States was $35,277; from 1975 to 2001, the U.S. GDP per capita grew an average of 2 percent per year. In the early

Figure 9.2
Calculating the Real GDP: 2003

$$\frac{\$10{,}998}{105.67} \times 100 = \text{Real GDP}$$

$$103.98 \times 100 = \$10{,}398$$

Source: Bureau of Economic Analysis, *BEA News,* March 25, 2004.

2000s, the U.S. GDP per capita was among the highest in the world. The top five countries, ranked by GDP per capita, were Luxembourg ($42,041), Norway ($36,815), the United States ($35,277), Switzerland ($34,601), and Japan ($32,601).[3] Economists often cite the GDP per capita to compare the relative well-being of people living in different countries. Still, there are limitations to this measure. For instance, GDP per capita states the average income of people, but does not account for the distribution of income. In virtually all economies, the poorest segment of society subsists on a tiny fraction of the national income and wealth. Another limitation is that the GDP per capita deals only with reported business activity and excludes barter and the unreported productive enterprise in the informal sector of economies.

There are a number of ways to compute the GDP. The most commonly used method is the expenditures approach, which tallies the total spending on final goods and services in four areas: consumption (C), investment (I), government (G), and net exports (Xn). The expenditures approach to calculating the GDP can be stated as an equation: C + I + G + Xn = GDP. In this equation, *C* represents the spending by individuals on consumer goods and services. Consumption accounted for the lion's share of the U.S. GDP in 2003. *I* represents the spending by firms and households on new capital, including factories, office buildings, equipment, inventories of products, and houses or apartment buildings. *G* represents spending by government at all levels—federal, state, and local—on final goods and services. Government goods include school buildings, submarines, and libraries, while services are often expressed as salaries of teachers, airport security guards, public officials, and so on. *Xn* represents net exports, the difference between the dollar value of the nation's imports and exports. Note in Table 9.1 that net exports is a negative number in 2003 because the value of U.S. imports was greater than the value of its exports—about $495 billion more. This $495 billion is subtracted from the U.S. GDP because it represents spending on foreign-produced goods rather than American-made goods (see chapter 11 for more on trade deficits). The expenditures approach to the calculation of the nominal GDP is shown in Table 9.1.[4]

Table 9.1
Calculating the Nominal GDP: 2003

Components of GDP	Dollar Value ($ billions)	Percentage of GDP
Consumption spending	$7,757.4	70.6%
Investment spending	$1,670.6	15.2%
Government spending	$2,054.8	18.7%
Net exports	$495.0	-4.5%
Gross domestic product	$10,987.9	100.0%

Source: Bureau of Economic Analysis, *BEA News,* March 25, 2004.

The GDP: A Global Perspective

Economic growth and economic development are crucial to people's quality of life throughout the global economy. Multilateral organizations such as the International Monetary Fund (IMF), the World Bank, and the United Nations collect extensive data on growth and development in the advanced, developing, and transition countries. Traditionally, foreign exchange rates were used to convert the value of currencies, usually into U.S. dollars, to make international comparisons possible. Using the exchange rate conversion process, it was fairly simple to calculate each nation's GDP and other measures of economic progress. In 2001, for example, the U.S. GDP was $10.1 trillion, while Japan's GDP was $4.1 trillion. Using this conversion method, the U.S. economy was more than twice the size of Japan's economy. On an even broader scale, the exchange rate method was used to compile data on the entire global economy. For example, using the exchange rate method, the IMF reported that between 1995 and 2004 the real GDP of the entire world grew from $29 trillion to $36.9 trillion, an annual growth rate of 2.7 percent.[5] During the late 1990s, however, an alternative approach to making cross-border economic comparisons was introduced, purchasing power parity.

The **advanced countries,** also called the advanced economies, are the high-income industrialized countries. The 29 advanced economies include the United States and Canada in North America; Germany, the United Kingdom, and most of the other nations of western Europe; Israel in the Middle East; Australia and New Zealand in Oceania; and Japan and the newly industrialized countries of Asia. The advanced economies have consistently recorded positive economic growth, with annual increases in real GDP and GDP per capita, over the past 20 years, as shown in Table 9.2.[6]

The **developing countries** are the poorer, less industrialized countries of the world. About three-quarters of the 208 economies operating in the global economy are categorized as developing countries. Table 9.2 shows that developing countries, on average, scored significant gains in real output and per capita income over the past 20 years. Yet, more than 30 developing countries experienced negative annual economic growth rates between 1975 and 2001, mainly in the nations

Table 9.2
Economic Growth in the Global Economy: 1985–2004

Classification of Economy	Real Gross Domestic Product		GDP per Capita	
	1985–1994	1995–2004	1985–1994	1995–2004
Advanced	3.0%	2.7%	2.4%	2.1%
Developing	5.2%	5.1%	3.2%	3.5%
Transition	-2.1%	2.8%	-2.6%	3.0%
Global economy	3.3%	3.6%	n/a	n/a

Source: International Monetary Fund, *World Economic Outlook, September 2003,* 173.

of Sub-Saharan Africa. Annual negative growth was especially severe in some of the world's desperately poor nations, including the Democratic Republic of Congo (–5.2% annual negative growth), Sierra Leone (–3.3%), Niger (–2.0%), and Haiti (–2.0%).[7] (See chapter 12 for more on the developing countries.)

The **transition countries** are the nations that are currently transitioning from centrally planned communist economies to more market-oriented capitalist economies. The 28 transition countries, also called the transition economies, are located in eastern and central Europe and western Asia. Some of these countries, such as Poland and Hungary, were part of the Soviet-dominated Eastern bloc during the cold war era. Others, such as Russia and the Ukraine, were republics within the Union of Soviet Socialist Republics (USSR) until 1991, when the USSR dissolved into 15 independent countries. Table 9.2 shows that transition countries, on average, experienced negative annual growth rates and declining income from 1985 to 1994, but rebounded during the next 10-year period. Eleven transition countries experienced negative annual economic growth rates between 1975 and 2001, however. Most of these were the former republics of the USSR, including Russia. Especially severe were the annual declines in the former Soviet republics of Tajikistan (–9.9%), the Ukraine (–7.5%), Turkmenistan (–6.6%), Moldova (–5.6%), and Georgia (–5.5%).[8]

The introduction of purchasing power parity by global institutions has altered the way many people view economic growth, poverty, and other indicators of economic well-being in the global economy. **Purchasing power parity** (PPP) converts nations' currencies into a common currency by assessing the actual buying power of each currency within its own economy. For instance, $1 in U.S. currency would likely buy more goods or services in a developing country, where costs are relatively low, than it would in the United States, where costs are relatively high. When the GDPs of developing countries are adjusted for purchasing power parity, their GDPs tend to rise. Conversely, the GDPs of some of the wealthiest advanced nations tend to fall with the application of PPP rates because the cost of living is relatively high in these countries. Using the PPP rates, global output increased from $34 trillion in 1995 to $54.6 trillion in 2004. Table 9.3 compares the world's largest economies using the traditional exchange rate approach and the PPP approach to figuring GDP.[9] Note that two developing countries, China and India, join the top five nations when PPP rates are employed. Using the PPP valuation of country GDPs, the IMF reported that the 29 advanced economies accounted for 55.7 percent of the world GDP, followed by 125 surveyed developing countries (38.1%) and the 28 transition countries (6.3%).[10] In the early 2000s, the World Bank and other international organizations were still refining standards for data collection and adjusting the intricate formula for determining the PPP rates for over 200 economies worldwide (see chapter 12 for more on PPP).

THE DETERMINANTS OF ECONOMIC GROWTH

The process of economic growth relies on a number of interrelated economic, political, and social factors that work in concert to increase national out-

Table 9.3
The World's Largest Economies: 2001

Rank	Country	GDP: Exchange Rate Approach ($ billions)	Rank	Country	GDP: PPP Approach ($ billions)
1	United States	$10,065	1	United States	$9,793*
2	Japan	$4,141	2	China	$5,111
3	Germany	$1,846	3	Japan	$3,193
4	United Kingdom	$1,424	4	India	$2,930
5	France	$1,310	5	Germany	$2,087

*Theoretically, the exchange rate approach and PPP approach to calculating the U.S. GDP should result in the same dollar amount because the purchasing power of the U.S. dollar in U.S. markets provides the base for all international comparisons. The current conversion formula to PPP rates does not permit this, however.
Source: UNDP, *Human Development Report 2003*, 278–81.

put. At the core of economic growth is the need for productivity gains over time. **Productivity** measures the amount of output that is produced per unit of input. On the national level, the amount of output refers to the real GDP, and the inputs are the factors of production—natural resources, human resources, and capital goods. When the mix of resources used in production results in greater output per unit of input, productivity rises. When the mix of resources produces lesser output per unit of input, productivity falls. The most common measurement of productivity is the productivity of labor, which is calculated by dividing the value of national output by the number of workers in the labor force. For instance, from 1992 to 2003 the productivity of U.S. labor increased by nearly 30 percent.[11] Higher productivity supports higher wages, business formation, and jobs creation in economies. The productivity of labor is inextricably intertwined with other workplace conditions, including the sophistication of physical capital and technology used in production, the education and training of workers, and the organizational skills of management. The Industrial Revolution accelerated the productivity of labor by employing specialized physical capital and a division of labor in the industrial workplace. Over time, economic growth in the industrialized nations created a virtuous cycle of saving, investment, production, and prosperity. Today, economists still debate the underlying causes of economic growth, a topic that has occupied the professional careers of economic giants, including Robert M. Solow (see the biography of Robert M. Solow).

Gross Saving and Investment

Gross saving and investment are pillars upon which economic growth is built. **Gross saving** is the sum of savings by individuals, businesses, and government in an economy. In 2002 the gross savings in the United States was about

$1.6 trillion, a drop from the record $1.8 trillion recorded in 2000. Business saving accounted for over 80 percent of U.S. gross saving in 2002, while personal saving of individuals accounted for the remainder. Gross government saving was negative $22 billion in 2002, a drop of about $450 billion from two years earlier. This dip in government savings reflected deepening budget woes, mainly at the federal level. In 2002 the U.S. gross saving rate, or gross savings as a percentage of GNP, dipped to 15.1 percent, among the lowest in the industrialized world.[12]

Gross savings finance **gross investment,** which consists of private- and public-sector investments in an economy. In 2002 U.S. gross investment hit $1.5 trillion. Most U.S. gross investment emanates from business firms. Businesses invested more than $1 trillion in 2002, mainly on computers and other information-processing equipment ($400 billion), industrial and transportation equipment ($301 billion), and nonresidential production facilities such as factories, retail outlets, and mines ($269 billion). Hundreds of billions of dollars were also invested by individuals and firms in residential structures, mainly single-family houses.[13]

Gross saving and investment in the global economy varies by world region, level of economic development, and changes in global business activity. Sub-Saharan Africa and south Asia, two of the poorest regions in the world, consistently record the lowest national savings, averaging 17 percent and 19 percent respectively from 1996 to 2000. The highest national savings rates consistently appeared in East Asia and the Pacific region, which averaged 37 percent during the same time period. Meanwhile, the high-income countries averaged gross savings of 22 percent of GDP. While the savings rate for high-income countries was lower than in some other parts of the world, it represented over $5 trillion that could be used for investment purposes.[14] (See chapter 8 for more on how financial markets channel savings into productive investments.)

Utilizing the Factors of Production

Production occurs when people use the factors of production, or productive resources, to produce goods and services. The three main factors of production—natural resources, human resources, and capital goods—are unevenly distributed in the world. To achieve economic growth, societies must acquire and seek innovative ways to employ resources in the production process.

Natural resources, or gifts of nature, are things present in the natural environment that are used in production. Natural resources include minerals, oil, natural gas, rivers, oceans, fish, animals, soil, forests, plants, and sunlight. Natural resources provide many of the raw materials needed to produce goods and services. At times, natural resources are plentiful within a region or a country. The United States, for example, is well endowed with abundant land and a suitable climate for agriculture, navigable rivers and deepwater harbors for commerce, substantial quantities of petroleum and minerals for industry, and more. Nations in the Persian Gulf region, including Saudi Arabia, Kuwait, and Iraq, sit on top of large petroleum reserves. Other nations lack essential natural resources, but acquire them through conquest, trade, or foreign investment. European conquest and colonization of the Americas, Africa, and Asia during the sixteenth through twentieth centuries was, in part, motivated by the demand for resources. For centuries, resources from colonial possessions fueled Great Britain's factory system and promoted economic growth. Nations also gain access to natural resources through international trade and foreign investment. Japan's meteoric economic growth during the post–World War II era relied on the import of petroleum, minerals, timber, and other natural resources not readily available in the island nation. In recent years, the accelerated pace of globalization also stimulated foreign investment in resource-rich Nigeria, Indonesia, China, and other countries.

Human resources are the people who are engaged in production. Human resources include assembly-line workers, miners, and contractors in the goods-producing sector; teachers, doctors, and engineers in the services-producing sector; and farmers, loggers, and ranchers in the agricultural sector. By investing in human resources, society creates human capital. **Human capital** refers to workers whose abilities and skills have been enhanced by education, specialized occupational training, and apprenticeships, as well as by adequate health care and nutrition. Skilled, healthy workers are generally more productive and contribute more to a nation's economic growth than do poorly trained workers. Skilled workers are also better able to take advantage of new opportunities and thereby improve the quality of life for themselves and their families. The advanced economies have made significant investments in human capital. For example, 85 percent of the $1.5 trillion spent on public education in 2000 was spent in the 29 advanced countries. On average, per capita spending on education in the advanced economies was 28 times that of developing countries. Not surprisingly, the labor force in advanced economies approaches universal literacy. In low-income developing countries, however, more than one-third of the adult population can neither read nor write. Further, in 2000 the per capita health expenditures in the high-income countries was $2,736, compared to just $21 in south Asia and $29 in Sub-Saharan Africa. Access to quality health care in the advanced economies creates a stable labor force and a population that can expect to live nearly 20 years longer than people residing in low-income countries.[15]

Capital goods are items produced by people that, in turn, are used to produce other products. Capital goods include construction equipment, mine shafts, and factory buildings in the goods-producing sector; television cameras, surgical instruments, and taxicabs in the services-producing sector; and tractors, irrigation systems, and chainsaws in the agricultural sector. Investment in new capital goods increases a nation's **capital stock,** the total amount of capital available to produce goods and services. Capital deepening occurs when a nation's capital stock per worker increases over time.

Investment in new capital goods has sharpened the competitive edge of the advanced countries. For instance, U.S. private investment in information-

Advanced capital goods increase the productivity of American farmers. © U.S. Department of Agriculture. Photograph by David F. Warren.

processing equipment, such as computers and software, averaged nearly a half trillion dollars per year during the early 2000s. This type of investment reinforced the supremacy of U.S. information technology (IT) firms, such as Microsoft, in the global economy and improved productivity in other businesses, ranging from retail sales to engineering and medicine. Similarly, capital deepening in the newly industrialized economies (NIEs) over the past few decades resulted in rapid and sustained economic growth. Recently, these NIEs—Hong Kong, Singapore, South Korea, and Taiwan—have joined the ranks of developed economies. It is important that a nation's capital stock is engaged in production, rather than sitting unused. In the U.S. economy, the **capacity utilization rate** measures the percentage of factory capacity currently being used in productive enterprise. During periods of economic growth, the capacity utilization rate typically tops 80 percent, which means that over 80 percent of the nation's capital in the goods-producing sector is employed. During the recessions of the mid-1970s, early 1980s, and early 2000s, however, the capacity utilization rate dipped into the 74 percent to 75 percent range, contributing to negative growth.[16]

Entrepreneurship and Knowledge

Economic growth is a dynamic process. That is, it thrives on advances in technology, the creation of new products, the expansion of markets, and so on.

Central to the process of change in a dynamic economy are entrepreneurship and knowledge. **Entrepreneurship** refers to the actions of entrepreneurs who develop new products, production methods, or business firms. Entrepreneurship is often considered a factor of production, joining natural resources, human resources, and capital goods. Entrepreneurs are innovators and risk-takers who transform ideas into commercial enterprises. The founding of Apple Computer by Steven Jobs, Microsoft by Bill Gates, and Wal-Mart by Sam Walton testify to the importance of entrepreneurial activity in the U.S. economy. The widely respected *Global Entrepreneurship Monitor 2002* (*GEM 2002*) makes a compelling link between entrepreneurship and economic growth. *GEM 2002* investigated entrepreneurial activity in 37 economies with a combined labor force of 2.4 billion workers. The report found that total entrepreneurial activity (TEA) varied significantly from nation to nation, but concluded "that entrepreneurship is a major mechanism leading to economic growth and adaptation in all economies whether developed, in transition, or developing."[17] The report also estimated that 460 million people in the global economy were directly engaged in entrepreneurial activity in 2002. A ranking of representative countries by the TEA Index, which states the percentage of the labor force that formed or managed a newly formed business, is shown in Table 9.4.[18] (See chapter 7 for more on entrepreneurs.)

Knowledge, as a source of economic growth, promotes **innovation,** the process of converting scientific discoveries and technological advances into profitable products or improved methods of production. Knowledge and innovation often ripple through an economy, sparking business formation and job creation. In recent years, the new growth theory has credited knowledge and innovation for much of the economic growth experienced by the advanced economies (see the biography of Paul M. Romer for more on the new growth theory).

Knowledge and innovation expand through the efforts of individuals, business firms, and the government. One individual who pioneered commercially viable technologies was American inventor Thomas Edison. In 1876 Edi-

Table 9.4
Total Entrepreneurial Activity: 2002

High TEA Countries	TEA Index*	Workers (number in millions)	Low TEA Countries	TEA Index	Workers (number in millions)
Thailand	18.9%	7.6	Japan	1.8%	1.5
India	17.9%	105.9	Russia	2.5%	2.4
Chile	15.7%	1.5	Belgium	3.0%	0.2
South Korea	14.5%	4.7	France	3.2%	1.2
Argentina	14.2%	3.1	Hong Kong	3.4%	0.2

*TEA Index is based on firms that have existed for less than 42 months.
Source: Kauffman Foundation, *Global Entrepreneurship Monitor: 2002 Executive Report*, 8.

son established an "invention factory," the world's first privately owned research laboratory designed to discover, patent, and eventually market new technologies for commercial uses. At his research facility at Menlo Park, New Jersey, and later West Orange, New Jersey, Edison patented hundreds of inventions, such as an improved telephone transmitter, the phonograph, and the incandescent lamp. His incandescent lamp, which required a lighting system, helped give birth to the mass production of electricity.

During the twentieth century, the benefits of research and development (R&D) became more apparent to businesses and to the government. Businesses, especially large corporations, created R&D departments to remain competitive in domestic and global markets. In 2000 total spending on R&D in the United States was $265 billion, or 2.66 percent of the nation's GDP. Private industries supplied $181 billion, more than two-thirds of all money spent on R&D, as shown in Figure 9.3. In the early 2000s, the top private-sector spenders on R&D were the motor vehicle industry, communications, semiconductors and electrical components, software, scientific R&D services, pharmaceuticals, and computer

Thomas Alva Edison at his New Jersey research laboratory, 1901. Underwood & Underwood, publishers. © Library of Congress.

Figure 9.3
Funding Research and Development: 2000

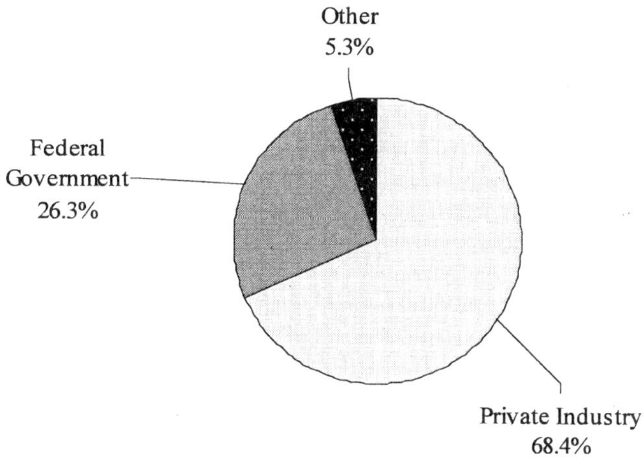

Source: National Science Foundation, *Indicators 2002.*

systems. Other major funding came from the federal government ($70 billion) and from state governments, colleges and universities, and nonprofit organizations ($14 billion).[19]

Government support for R&D took many forms, including grants to colleges and universities, financial aid to private firms, and funding for general purpose technologies. A general purpose technology (GPT) is a technology that eventually might have many possible uses, depending on the creativity of entrepreneurs and other innovators in the economy. Government funding of GPTs is often necessary to defray prohibitive research costs. The Internet, for example, was originally a GPT financed through the U.S. Department of Defense. Since its invention in 1969, the Internet's commercial value has increased due to the introduction of complementary technologies such as e-mail in 1972 and the World Wide Web (WWW) in 1989. By the end of 2002, over 600 million people worldwide were Internet users according to the International Telecommunications Union (ITU). E-commerce over the Internet accounted for $2.3 trillion in 2002, mainly business-to-business (B2B) rather than business-to consumer (B2C) transactions. Some experts have predicted the value of e-commerce transactions to rise to $13 trillion by 2006.[20]

Recently, hubs of innovation have also accelerated the pace of knowledge and innovation in the global economy. Hubs of innovation are geographic regions in which scientists, entrepreneurs, venture capitalists, research labs, start-up companies, corporations, and colleges and universities converge to develop new products and processes. By the early 2000s, 46 hubs existed worldwide, in Europe (16), the United States (13), Asia (9), South America (2), Africa (2), Australia (2), Canada (1), and Israel (1).[21] Other promising hubs were emerging in India, China, and other locations.

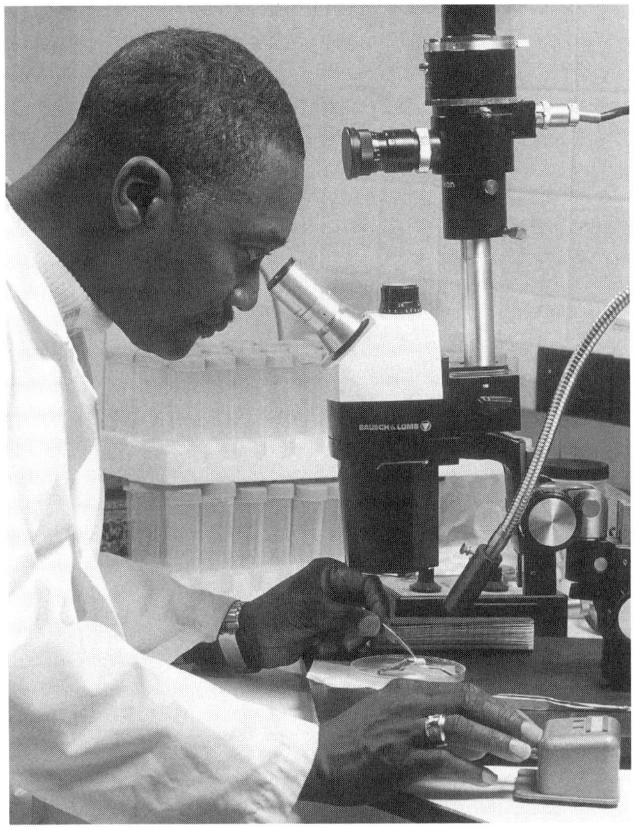

Federal research conducted by the U.S. Department of Agriculture, 2001. U.S. Department of Agriculture. Photograph by Scott Bauer.

Favorable Economic Environment

The process of economic growth is enhanced by a favorable economic environment, which includes a sophisticated infrastructure, supportive economic institutions, and macroeconomic stability. A nation's infrastructure is one of the pillars of sustainable economic growth. Sometimes called **social capital,** the infrastructure includes roads and bridges, airports and seaports, sanitation facilities, hospitals, schools, courts and prisons, and other public goods that support business activity. The construction of social capital is financed by tax dollars. Through taxation, people take collective responsibility for financing public goods necessary for collective well-being. By providing social capital, the government also overcomes the **free rider dilemma**—private firms' hesitancy to build expensive projects, such as roads, because others, the free riders, would benefit without paying the costs. Infrastructure construction and maintenance is a high-priority item in the advanced countries, but often is underfunded in the poorer regions of the world.

Supportive economic institutions, formal and informal, are crucial to economic growth. A significant body of evidence suggests that market-oriented institutions provide the most workable blueprint for sustained growth. Some market institutions are abstract, such as the institutions of private property, voluntary exchange, economic freedom, and profit incentives. Yet these institutions motivate people to work, save, invest, and take financial and business risks in domestic markets and abroad. Other institutions are more tangible. Banks and other depository institutions channel savings into productive investments. Stock and bond markets provide a mechanism to raise funds for business start-ups, expansions, mergers and acquisitions, and other purposes. Public institutions, such as the Social Security system, provide a safety net for people who may need temporary or long-term assistance. Other public institutions, such as the Federal Reserve System and the Securities and Exchange Commission, provide oversight of certain market activities. In 2002, the Department of Justice established a special task force to investigate and prosecute corporate fraud; cases included top executives of Adelphia, Enron, Tyco, WorldCom, and others. Strong economic institutions create the necessary guidelines, practices, procedures, and mechanisms under which production occurs.

Macroeconomic stability, a third component of a supportive economic environment, centers on the maintenance of price stability and full employment. The federal government promotes macroeconomic stability through responsible monetary and fiscal policies. In the U.S. economy, the Federal Reserve System (Fed), the nation's central bank, implements monetary policy. If inflation increases the overall price level, the Fed uses its monetary tools to withdraw money from the economy and thereby reduce the primary cause of inflation—too much money chasing too few goods. If the economy slumps into a recession, Fed tools are used to stimulate economic activity. Similarly, fiscal policies related to government taxation and spending are used to slow an overheated economy or stimulate a sluggish economy (see chapter 10 for more on monetary and fiscal policies).

Favorable Political Environment

A favorable political environment rests on good governance and democratic political institutions. **Good governance** is a broad term that encompasses honesty and competence in the discharge of public service. At the core of good governance is the rule of law, an understanding that all participants in the nation's economic and political life abide by the same rules. Good governance promotes economic growth by encouraging participation in economic activity and creating equal opportunities for success. The advanced economies of the world have a long tradition of good governance. Specific indicators of good governance include a fair system of taxation, enforceable patent and copyright laws, legal protections for private property and private profits, effective antitrust laws, transparency in public- and private-sector business transactions, the absence of corruption and political cronyism, and a host of rules and regulations to protect the rights of marketplace participants, including workers, investors, savers, and consumers. On a broader level, good governance supports human rights, gender equity, tolerance, and democracy.

Democracy and freedom support market-oriented economic institutions and economic growth. **Democracy** is a type of political system that relies on broad-based citizen participation, free elections, and the rule of law. The political freedoms inherent in democracies are compatible with the economic freedoms of capitalism. That is, democracy and capitalism embrace freedom of choice and informed decision making by the people. Studies by the Freedom House, the world's most recognized authority on global political trends and the status of freedom, concluded that a direct relationship exists between freedom and economic growth. The data showed that, over a 10-year period, the economic growth rate for free countries was roughly double that of countries categorized as partly free and not free. This conclusion applied to countries at all levels of economic development. In addition, in 2002 free countries produced 89 percent of the world GDP, compared to 5 percent for partly free countries and 6 percent for not free countries. Freedom House credited political and economic freedoms, an involved citizenry, a free press, and an independent judiciary for the high correlation between freedom and growth.[22] Freedom House research also traced positive trends in the rise of democracies and the rise in freedom in the world during the twentieth century. In 2002, 121 countries had functioning democra-

Table 9.5
Freedom in the World: 1972–2002 (number of countries, number of people in billions)

Year	Free		Partly Free		Not Free	
	Countries	People	Countries	People	Countries	People
1972	43	1.325	38	0.667	69	1.788
1982	54	1.665	47	0.919	64	2.000
1992	75	1.352	73	2.403*	38	1.690
2002	89	2.659*	56	1.282	47	2.153

*The large increase in the number of people living in partly free countries for 1992 reflects a change in India's status from free to partly free in 1992. The large increase in the number of people living in free countries for 2002 reflects, in part, India's status change from partly free to free in 1999.
Source: Freedom House, *Freedom in the World 2002,* 1–4.

cies, 89 of which were classified as free due to their exemplary record in protecting human rights and the civil liberties of citizens. Table 9.5 shows the status of freedom in the world from 1972 to 2002.[23]

THE COSTS AND BENEFITS OF ECONOMIC GROWTH

Economic growth occurs when the total value of goods and services produced in a nation rises over time. Most people simply assume that higher national output and pro-growth policies are good for the economy. Yet, there are costs and benefits attached to economic activities, including the process of economic growth. Economic growth involves a variety of production and consumption decisions, all of which involve trade-offs. **Trade-offs** occur when individuals, businesses, government, or other groups choose to produce or consume more of one thing at the expense of a second. Trade-offs also occur when a production or consumption decision benefits some people at the expense of others. To evaluate current economic activities and policies, people weigh the costs and benefits of their decisions.

The Costs of Economic Growth

For decades economists, sociologists, and scientists have warned that unbridled economic growth is unsustainable. For example in *Small Is Beautiful: Economics as if People Mattered* (1973), E. F. Schumacher warned that the planet was on a "collusion course" with economic collapse and that humanity must "begin to see the possibility of evolving a new life-style, with new methods of production and new patterns of consumption: a life-style designed for permanence"[24] (see the biography of E. F. Schumacher). Schumacher, Rachel Carson (*Silent Spring,* 1962), Paul R. Ehrlich (*The Population Bomb,* 1968), Barry Commoner (*The Closing Circle,* 1971), and others have challenged people to consider the costs and benefits of their economic choices. The costs of economic growth generally fall into one of three main categories: environmental degradation, resource depletion, and a decline in people's quality of life.

Some environmental degradation is an inevitable result of production, a fact that illustrates the classic trade-off between economic growth and environmental decay. On the one hand, increased output produces many of the comforts of life. On the other hand, production fouls the air, water, and land with pollutants; creates wastelands with strip-mining, aggressive timbering, overgrazing, and overplanting; and destroys natural habitats with urban sprawl. Critics of growth note that these negative consequences of production are readily visible. Less visible, however, are impending global nightmares wrought by economic growth. For example, fossil fuels, which power production facilities and motor vehicles, release greenhouse gases such as carbon dioxide, methane, and nitrous oxide into the atmosphere. Evidence suggests that trapped greenhouse gases create a greenhouse effect and global warming, effects that may radically alter global climate and destroy many natural habitats. Emissions of chlorofluorocarbons (CFCs) into the atmosphere result in ozone depletion, which allows the sun's dangerous UV rays to penetrate to Earth's surface. Other industrial emissions cause acid rain, airborne pollutants that are carried with the wind and returned to Earth with precipitation. Acid rain destroys forests, sterilizes lakes, and corrodes structures. *World Resources: 2000–2001,* a cooperative effort of the World Resources Institute, the World Bank, and the United Nations, warned that "we have the ability to change the vital systems of this planet, for better or worse. To change them for the better, we must recognize that the well-being of people and ecosystems is interwoven and that the fabric is fraying. We need to repair it."[25]

A second cost of economic growth is resource depletion. Resource depletion occurs when resources are used in production and are not replaced. **Nonrenewable resources,** including petroleum and natural gas, are consumed in the production process and cannot be reclaimed for further use. Further, nonrenewable resources are in finite supply. **Renewable resources,** such as forests, fish, and animals, can be replenished. Critics of economic growth have traditionally focused on the inevitable depletion of the world's finite supply of nonrenewable resources. In *The Closing Circle* (1971), Barry Commoner presented the problem of resource depletion as "a fundamental paradox of man's life on earth: that human civilization involves a series of cyclically interdependent processes, most of which have a built-in tendency to grow, except one—the natural, irreplaceable, absolutely essential resources represented in the earth's minerals and the ecosphere."[26] More recently, the authoritative *World Resources 2000–2001* quantified resource depletion of some basic resources. For example, 40 percent of the world's population deals with a serious shortage of fresh water, 70 percent of which is used to irrigate croplands. Likewise, 40 percent of the soil used in agriculture is deemed strongly or very strongly degraded due to erosion, nutrient depletion, or another cause. Since the dawn of the agricultural age, between 20 percent and 50 percent of the world's forests have disappeared due to farming, logging, settlement, or other uses.[27]

A third cost of economic growth is a decline in some people's quality of life. Quality of life reflects people's income and the overall conditions under which they live, including access to education, health care, social programs, and so on. A generation ago, the Club of Rome issued an influential report, *The Limits to Growth* (1972). The report warned that economic growth and the population explosion would accelerate resource depletion and cause misery for many marginalized peoples in poorer world regions. Thirty years later, the gap in income and living conditions had widened between the advanced countries and the least developed countries. The Club of Rome could not have foreseen the revolutionary changes in information and communications technologies (ICTs) that reshaped the global economy during the 1990s and early 2000s. Yet, today the digital divide, or ICT gap between the rich and poor countries, is among the most important economic chasms in the global economy. The richer countries, which invested heavily in ICTs such as computers, software, fiber optics, satellite communications, and so on, embraced the digital revolution. They also profited handsomely from its commercial uses in the production, marketing, and distribution of output. Conversely, the lack investment dollars in the poorer nations limited their ICT use and their access to global opportunities.

The Benefits of Economic Growth

The benefits of economic growth are intertwined with the conditions that make growth possible, such as high rates of saving; significant investment in human capital, physical capital, infrastructure, and technology; economic freedom and entrepreneurship; high incomes and high consumption levels; and good governance and the rule of law. Economic growth provides opportunities for an improved standard of living, a higher quality of life, and greater production efficiency.

Economic growth increases total national output and national income, each of which contributes to the material well-being of people. Economic growth in the United States and many European countries gained momentum during the Industrial Revolution, largely the result of technological advances, specialization in production methods, and a division of labor. Over time, rising national output and real wages elevated the standard of living for the working class in these countries. For example, between 1900 and 1950, the real income of U.S. workers rose by about 170 percent, while the real output per worker tripled.[28] As a result, a member of the blossoming middle class was able to purchase a residence, an automobile, consumer durables, and other consumer goods. More recently, the U.S. Census Bureau reported that the real per capita money income of Americans doubled between 1967 and 2001.[29] Economic growth has consistently increased the standard of living in the advanced economies and in many developing countries. By 2000, one in four people living in the developing world owned a radio, and nearly one in five owned a television.[30]

A second benefit of economic growth is an improved quality of life for people. A higher quality of life implies a higher standard of living plus other improvements in the human condition. Economic growth helps create the wealth necessary for public investments in education, health care, infrastructure, social programs, and so on. The size of public investments in these programs is dependent on the amount of tax revenues collected from society's private sector, however. Advanced economies make significant public investments that increase people's economic opportunities, expand their choices, and attend to their needs. Investments in higher education encourage people to explore personal interests, prepare for careers, or both. Investments in health care and sanitation systems reduce the infant mortality rate and debilitating diseases, and increase life expectancy. Investments in highways, airports, and mass transit systems increase the convenience of travel and reduce personal costs in terms of travel time. Investments in the law enforcement and judicial systems improve personal security and people's confidence in the rule of law. Investments in social programs improve living conditions for the needy, including the elderly, the poor, and the handicapped.

A third benefit of economic growth is its ability to maintain the virtuous cycle of development. Growing, prosperous societies are able to save money, a prerequisite for investments in new technology, private and social capital, human capital, and entrepreneurship. Motivated by self-interest and private profits, business investment results in new and better products, more business start-ups and jobs, and technological advances. Growing, dynamic economies are the wellspring of product innovation, as evidenced by improvements in computers, software, electronic calculators, digital cameras, and a variety of other goods. In the meantime, competitive markets weed out less efficient producers and those that cannot adapt to changing tastes in the marketplace—a process colorfully described by economic Joseph Schumpeter as "creative destruction" (see the biography of Joseph A. Schumpeter). In addition, economic growth stimulates aggressive exploration and research to develop key resources. For instance, improvements in geological exploration and extraction technologies have improved the sophistication of mining and drilling techniques for primary energy sources. Total known reserves of natural gas more than doubled since 1975, topping 5,500 trillion cubic feet in 2003. Similarly, the Energy Information Administration (EIA) predicted that known oil reserves in the world will increase by 730 billion barrels between 2000 and 2025.[31]

BIOGRAPHIES: SHAPERS OF ECONOMIC THOUGHT

Simon Kuznets: Father of the Gross National Product

Simon Kuznets (1901–1985), a twentieth-century American economist, is widely hailed as the father of the gross national product (GNP). Kuznets was born in Kharkiv, Russia, where he began his postsecondary studies. He immigrated to the United States in 1922 and entered Columbia University in 1923. After earning his doctorate at Columbia in 1926, Kuznets jumped into a professional career that involved teaching, writing, and public service. He joined the staff of the National Bureau of Economic Research (NBER) in 1927, a position he held for more than three decades. As a member of NBER, Kuznets was involved in the collection and analysis of economic data related to national income and product accounting. Kuznets also held prestigious teaching positions at the University of Pennsylvania (1931–1954), Johns Hopkins University (1954–1960), and Harvard University (1960–1971). During his career, Kuznets authored numerous books, including his classic two-volume *National Income and Its Composition, 1919–1938.*

Kuznets is best known for the meticulous collection of macroeconomic data related to national output and national income, and for the application of these data to economic growth, business cycles, and economic development. In *National Income and Its Composition, 1919–1938*, Kuznets identified key features of national income and product accounts. He stressed the need to determine national income with "consistency and explicitness," yet recognized that limitations existed in estimating aggregate output—the gross national product (GNP). For example, excluded from GNP were goods and services provided "outside of the market system,"[32] such as the services of housewives and business activity in the unreported informal sector of the economy. GNP calculation also failed to account for the value of leisure, which increased steadily during the twentieth century. Still, the pioneering work of Kuznets provided the foundation of GNP calculations, the primary framework for measuring U.S. economic performance in the post–World War II era.

Kuznets's interest in business cycles and economic development broadened his contribution to economic science. He helped shape a strand of economic theory called development economics, which deals with the process of economic development in the poorer world regions. He concluded that economic development is not a uniform process in the global economy. Instead, each nation's unique economic circumstance colors its path toward development. Many insights on economic development appear in his book, *Economic Growth of Nations* (1971). (See chapter 12 for more on development theory.). For his many contributions to the field of economics, Kuznets won numerous awards, including the Nobel Prize in Economic Science in 1971.

Joseph A. Schumpeter: Entrepreneurship and Creative Destruction

Joseph A. Schumpeter (1883–1950) was a prominent economic historian, author, and teacher. Schumpeter was born in Triesch in the former Austria-Hungary (now the Czech Republic) and received a first-rate education in Graz and Vienna. In 1901 he entered the School of Law at Vienna University, where he became well versed in economics, political science, law, history, and other disciplines. Armed with a doctor of law degree (1906), Schumpeter vacillated between practicing law, teaching economics, authorship, and government service. By the mid-1920s, Schumpeter's niche in teaching and writing was firmly established. His appointment as an economics professor at the University of Bonn (1925–1932), Germany, and at Harvard University (1932–1950) in the United States cemented his credentials as one of the world leading economists. During his lifetime, Schumpeter authored 10 books in the fields of economic growth theory, business cycles, economic systems, and economic history. His most famous work, *Capitalism, Socialism, and Democracy* (1942), was written during his Harvard years.

Schumpeter made significant contributions to growth theory during his career. While teaching at the University of Graz, Schumpeter penned *Theory of Economic Development* (1911). In this book he stressed the central role that entrepreneurs play in economic growth and development. Entrepreneurs champion innovation in dynamic economies and reap entrepreneurial profits. Schumpeter is most noted for his classic *Capitalism, Socialism, and Democracy* (1942). In this book he coined the now-famous term *creative destruction* to explain the role of innovation in an economy. According to Schumpeter, capitalism was built on innovation, a process that improved products and production methods, but also rendered some older industries and jobs obsolete. Schumpeter argued: "The essential point to grasp is that in dealing with capitalism we are dealing with an evolutionary process. . . . The fundamental impulse that sets and keeps the capitalist engine in motion comes from the new consumers' goods, the new methods of production or transportation, the new markets, the new forms of industrial organization that capitalist enterprise creates."[33] Schumpeter concluded that capitalism breeds a type of "industrial mutation," which constantly changes "the economic structure *from within,* incessantly destroying the old one, incessantly creating a new one. This process of Creative Destruction is the essential fact about capitalism."[34]

Schumpeter was a prolific writer and dedicated teacher. He marveled at the dynamism of capitalism and, while rejecting Marx's views on the inevitability of communism, believed that capitalism would eventually evolve into a form of socialism. He also received a number of honors. In 1933 he founded and served as president of the Econometric Society and, just one year prior to his death, served as president of the American Economic Association.

E. F. Schumacher: *Small Is Beautiful*

Ernst Friedrich (E. F.) Schumacher (1911–1977) was a British economist, philosopher, author, and advocate of appropriate technology in nations' economic growth and development. Schumacher was born in Bonn, Germany. In 1930 he was selected to represent his homeland as a Rhodes Scholar at Oxford in England. Horrified by the rise of Nazism in Germany, Schumacher and his young family immigrated to Great Britain in 1936. The outbreak of World War II in 1939 cast suspicion on the German-born Schumacher. In England he was branded an enemy alien and was even held for a short time at a detention center. Soon after the war ended, however, Schumacher became a British citizen and served in a number of important government posts, including chief economic adviser to the National Coal Board of Britain. As a United Nations economic consultant in Burma during the mid-1950s, Schumacher was much influenced by the simplicity of the Burmese lifestyle. Other trips to Asia cemented his belief that the Western model for economic growth and development was not applicable to the developing world.

In his most famous book, *Small Is Beautiful: Economics as if People Mattered* (1973), Schumacher supported appropriate technology as the basis for production and economic development. For the economies of the developing world, appropriate technology lay somewhere between the modern capital-intensive methods employed by the West and the traditional indigenous techniques, a middle path that Schumacher called "intermediate technology." To fit the local environment, intermediate technology had to utilize equipment that "would be fairly simple and therefore understandable, [and] suitable for maintenance and repair on the spot."[35] In addition, Schumacher proposed using intermediate technology to create millions of small-scale businesses and employ millions of workers. Even before *Small Is Beautiful* was published, Schumacher was one of the world's chief proponents of appropriate technology. In the mid-1960s, he founded the Intermediate Technology Development Group (ITDG) to research and disseminate information about appropriate technologies for small-scale enterprises.

Schumacher was highly critical of unbridled economic growth, abusive business practices of large multinational corporations, and unwise decisions by governments, which too often sacrificed natural and human resources on the alter of economic growth. During the 1960s and 1970s, his writings ran contrary to mainstream opinion about economic growth and development, which glorified technological advance, specialization and a division of labor, economies of scale, and economics of bigness. Schumacher's work caused people to be more mindful of the costs of economic growth, especially those that affected people's quality of life and created stresses on the natural environment. Today, Schumacher's humanism lives on through his books, the work of the ITDG, and the instructional methodology at Schumacher College in India.

Robert M. Solow: Technology, the Engine of Growth

Robert M. Solow (1924–) is a prominent American economist, teacher, and author whose work in economic growth theory shaped mainstream thinking in the field for decades. Solow was born and raised in New York City. He entered Harvard University on an academic scholarship in 1940. Upon America's entry into World War II, however, Solow interrupted his studies to join the U.S. army. He participated in the U.S. war effort in North Africa, Sicily, and Italy from 1942 to 1945. Solow returned to his studies at Harvard in 1945 and earned his doctorate in 1949. In 1950 he accepted an assistant professorship at nearby Massachusetts Institute of Technology (MIT), an institution that he would call home for his entire professional career. MIT proved fertile ground for Solow's keen intellect. He was elevated to associate professor in 1954, full professor in 1957, and institute professor in 1973. As a prolific writer, Solow penned numerous articles and books. Among the best known is *Growth Theory: An Exposition* (1970), which examined the key requirements for economic growth.

In *Growth Theory: An Exposition,* Solow examined the complexities of production, a process that relied on the skillful use of productive resources and technology. He concluded that technological development, more than any other factor, was the true engine of long-term economic growth. In addition, he noted that technological advances and innovation progressed at uneven intervals over time. Yet, in the long run, these random bursts of technology and innovation bolstered the productivity of labor and, thus, stimulated growth. Solow's earlier articles paved the way for these conclusions, including "A Contribution to the Theory of Economic Growth" (1956), "Technical Change and the Aggregate Production Function" (1957), and "Investment and Technical Progress" (1960). Solow's emphasis on technological advance as the primary determinant of economic growth departed from mainstream economic thought. Traditional growth theory rested on the so-called knife-edge path to growth, an inflexible set of growth conditions related to national savings, the labor supply, and real capital. Solow created a more flexible growth model, which permitted adjustments for new technologies and other variables. Solow's theories created a new economic mainstream in the field of growth and development.

Over time Solow's work branched out in a number of directions. For instance, Solow explored the long-neglected economics of natural resources. These studies considered the impact of economic growth on the natural environment and on the supply of finite resources. He supported the opening of international trade and foreign direct investment to promote economic growth in the developing world, but was highly critical of the uneven distribution of wealth wrought by globalization. Some of Solow's recent books illustrate his intellectual breadth, including *Work and Welfare* (1998), *Inflation, Unemployment, and Monetary Policy* (1998), and *Learning for "Learning by Doing": Lessons for Economic Growth* (1997). In recognition of Solow's groundbreaking contributions to growth theory, he was awarded the prestigious Nobel Prize in Economic Science in 1987.

Paul M. Romer: The New Growth Theory

Paul M. Romer (1956–) is a leading American economist and chief architect of the new growth theory. Romer was born in Colorado, the son of Roy Romer, who later became governor of Colorado. He earned a doctorate in economics from the University of Chicago in 1983. His doctoral dissertation, which dealt with the new growth theory, revolutionized the way people viewed the sources of economic growth. He held teaching positions at the University of Rochester (1982–1988), the University of Chicago (1988–1990), and the University of California at Berkeley (1990–1996) before accepting his current position in the Graduate School of Business at Stanford University. Romer has published dozens of scholarly articles dealing with the new growth theory, reinvigorating discussions about the role of knowledge and innovation in the growth process.

The new growth theory states that economic growth is mainly the result of new knowledge, ideas that stimulate new technologies and innovation. New knowledge is created through investments in education, R&D, and other means. According to Romer, heavy investment in knowledge by the United States and by Japan during the post–World War II period was the driving force behind growth and development in these nations. Further, Romer argued that knowledge is not subject to the law of diminishing returns. The law of diminishing returns states that as additional inputs are used in production, progressively smaller amounts of additional output are created. Instead, Romer contended, knowledge spawns increasing returns, as the boundless applications and adaptations of new ideas create limitless commercial possibilities. Key to Romer's theory is that people are the change agents in an economy. People direct the flows of technological advance according to market incentives, and reap the profits derived from their brainpower.

The new growth theory created a firestorm among economists by challenging traditional explanations of economic growth, which emphasized labor and capital as the chief determinants of productivity, while minimizing the impact of ideas and innovation in the growth equation. Romer rejected the traditional notion that technological advances and innovation were random phenomena. Instead he theorized that the growth of knowledge occurred in proportion to society's investment in it. Romer's new growth theory also stoked public policy debates. In the United States, Romer favored government subsidies to universities that agree to train scientists and engineers for private-sector R&D jobs. The modest cost of this type of government investment, he argued, would be more than offset by future benefits. Likewise, for the developing world he supported changes in public policy to encourage quality educational systems and technology transfers from the richer countries to foster growth. Aside from his teaching responsibilities at Stanford, the controversial Romer is a senior fellow at the Hoover Institution and at the Center for Economic Policy Research.

NOTES

1. Bureau of Economic Analysis (BEA), "Table 3. Gross Domestic Product and Related Measures and Change from Preceding Period," *BEA News*, March 25, 2004, www.bea.gov/bea/newsarchive/2004/gdp403f.pdf.

2. BEA, "Table 3. Gross Domestic Product and Related Measures and Change from Preceding Period," and "Table 6. Price Indexes for Gross Domestic Product," *BEA News*, March 25, 2004, www.bea.gov/bea/newsarchive/2004/gdp403f.pdf.

3. United Nations Development Program (UNDP), "Table 12. Economic Performance," *Human Development Report 2003* (New York: Oxford University Press, 2003), 278–81.

4. BEA, "Table 3. Gross Domestic Product and Related Measures and Change from Preceding Period," *BEA News*, March 25, 2004, www.bea.gov/bea/newsarchive/2004/gdp403f.pdf.

5. International Monetary Fund (IMF), "Table 1. Summary of World Output," *World Economic Outlook, April 2002* (Washington, DC: IMF Publications, 2002), 171.

6. Ibid.

7. UNDP, "Table 12. Economic Performance," *Human Development Report 2003,* 278–81; IMF, "Table 1. Summary of World Output," *World Economic Outlook, April 2003* (Washington, DC: IMF Publications, 2003), 171.

8. IMF, "Table 1. Summary of World Output," *World Economic Outlook, September 2003* (Washington, DC: IMF Publications, 2003), 173.

9. UNDP, "Table 12. Economic Performance" and "Box 5. The Why's and Wherefore's of purchasing power parities," *Human Development Report 2003,* 278–81, 147.

10. IMF, "Table A. Classification of World Economic Outlook Groups and Their Shares in Aggregate GDP, Exports of Goods and Services, and Population, 2002," *World Economic Outlook, September 2003,* 164.

11. "Table B-49. Productivity and Related Data, Business Sector, 1959–2002," *Economic Report of the President: 2003,* 334; Bureau of Labor Statistics (BLS), "Table 1. Business Sector: Productivity, Hourly Compensation, Unit Labor Costs, and Prices, Seasonally Adjusted 2001–2003," *BLS News,* March 4, 2004, 10, www.bls.gov/news.release/pdf/prod2.pdf.

12. BEA, "Table 5.1. Gross Saving and Investment," April 25, 2003, www.bea.gov/bea/dn/nipaweb/TableViewFixed.asp; "Table B-32. Gross Saving and Investment, 1959–2002," *Economic Report of the President: 2003,* 314.

13. BEA, "Table 5.4. Private Fixed Investment by Type," April 25, 2003, www.bea.gov/bea/dn/nipaweb/TableViewFixed.asp.

14. World Bank, *World Development Indicators: 2002* (New York: Oxford University Press, 2002), 196–97.

15. UNDP, "Table 1. Human Development Index" and "Table 10. Literacy and Enrolment," *Human Development Report 2003,* 237–40, 270–73; World Bank Group, "Global Poverty Goals within Reach but Only with Strong Action on Trade, Aid and Investing in People," April 13, 2003, www.worldbank.org/WBSITE/EXTERNAL/NEWS/0,,contentMDK:20104957~menu.

16. "Table B-54. Capacity Utilization Rates, 1955–2002," *Economic Report of the President: 2003,* 339.

17. Paul D. Reynolds, William D. Bygrave, Erkko Autio, Larry W. Cox, and Michael Hay, *Global Entrepreneurship Monitor: 2002 Executive Report* (Babson Park, MA: Babson College; London: London Business School; Kansas City, MO: Ewing Marion Kauffman Foundation, 2002), 39.

18. Ibid., 3, 33.

19. Raymond M. Wolfe, "U.S. Industry Sustains R&D Expenditures during 2001 Despite Decline in Performers' Aggregate Sales," *InfoBrief* (October 2003), 1–3; and National Science Foundation (NSF), "U.S. and International Research and Development: Funds and Alliances: R&D Support in the United States," *Indicators 2002,* www.nsf.gov/sbe/srs/seind02/c4/c4s1.htm.

20. United Nations Conference on Trade and Development (UNCTAD), *E-Commerce and Development Report 2002* (New York: United Nations, 2002), 1, 7–8.

21. UNDP, *Human Development Report 2001* (New York: Oxford University Press, 2001), 38.

22. Freedom House, "Freedom and Economic Growth," *Freedom in the World: 2000–2001* (New York: Freedom House, Inc., 2000), www.freedomhouse.org/research/freeworld/2001/essay1g.htm; Freedom House Survey Team, *Freedom in the World 2002: Liberty's Expansion in a Turbulent World* (New York: Freedom House, Inc., 2003), 15.

23. Freedom House Survey Team, *Freedom in the World 2002,* 1–4.

24. E. F. Schumacher, *Small Is Beautiful: Economics as if People Mattered* (New York: Harper & Row, 1973), 21.

25. World Resources Institute (WRI), UN Development Program, UN Environment Program, and World Bank, *World Resources 2000–2001: People and Ecosystems, The Fraying Web of Life* (Washington, DC: WRI, 2000), 239.

26. Barry Commoner, *The Closing Circle: Nature, Man and Technology* (New York: Alfred A. Knopf, 1971), 119.

27. WRI et. al., *World Resources 2000–2001,* 54, 88, 104, 110.

28. U.S. Bureau of the Census, "Series D 722–727. Average Annual Earnings of Employees: 1900 to 1970" and "Series 683–688. Indexes of Employee Output (NBER): 1869 to 1969," *The Statistical History of the United States: From Colonial Times to the Present* (New York: Basic Books, Inc., 1976), 162, 164.

29. U.S. Census Bureau, "Table P-1. Total CPS Population and Per Capita Money Income: 1967 to 2001," www.census.gov/hhes/income/histinc/p01.html.

30. World Bank, *World Development Indicators: 2002,* 318.

31. Energy Information Administration (EIA), U.S. Department of Energy, "Table 11. Estimated World Oil Resources, 2000–2025" and "Figure 43. World Natural Gas Reserves by Region, 1975–2003," *International Energy Outlook: 2003* (Washington, DC: Author, 2003), 37, 49.

32. Simon Kuznets, *National Income and Its Composition, 1919–1938,* vol. I (New York: National Bureau of Economic Research, Inc., 1941), 9.

33. Joseph A. Schumpeter, *Capitalism, Socialism, and Democracy,* 2nd ed. (New York: Harper & Brothers Publishers, 1947), 82–83.

34. Ibid., 83.

35. E. F. Schumacher, *Small Is Beautiful: Economics as if People Mattered,* 181.

SELECTED READINGS

Alcaly, Roger. *The New Economy: What It Is, How It Happened, and Why It Is Likely to Last.* New York: Farrar Straus & Giroux, 2003.

Bluestone, Barry, Bennett Harrison, and Richard C. Leone. *Growing Prosperity: The Battle for Growth with Equity in the Twenty-first Century.* Berkeley, CA: University of California Press, 2003.

Cetindamer, Dilek. *The Growth of Venture Capital: A Cross Cultural Comparison.* Stamford, CT: Ablex Publishing, 2003.

Commoner, Barry. *The Closing Circle: Nature, Man and Technology.* New York: Alfred A. Knopf, 1971.

Davidson, Eric A. *You Can't Eat GNP: Economics as if Ecology Mattered.* Cambridge, MA: Perseus Publishing, 2000.

Easterly, William. *The Elusive Quest for Growth: Economists' Adventures and Misadventures in the Tropics.* Cambridge, MA: MIT Press, 2002.

Economic Report of the President: 2003. Washington, DC: U.S. Government Printing Office, 2003.

Hart, David M. *The Emergence of Entrepreneurship Policy: Governance, Start-Ups, and Growth in the U.S. Knowledge Economy.* New York: Cambridge University Press, 2003.

Haverman, Robert H., Andrew Bershadker, Jonathon A. Schwabish, and Alexander A. Schmemann. *Human Capital in the United States from 1975 to 2000: Patterns of Growth and Utilization.* Kalamazoo, MI: W.E. Upjohn Institute for Employment Research, 2003.

Jones, Charles I. *Introduction to Economic Growth.* 2nd ed. New York: W.W. Norton & Co., 2002.

Karatnycky, Adrian, Aili Piano, and Arch Puddington. *Freedom in the World 2003: The Annual Survey of Political Rights and Civil Liberties.* Landham, MD: Rowman & Littlefield, 2003.

Kudyba, Stephan, and Romesh Diwan. *Information Technology, Corporate Productivity, and the New Economy.* Westport, CT: Quorum Books, 2002.

Kuznets, Simon. *National Income and Its Composition, 1919–1938.* 2 vols. New York: National Bureau of Economic Research, 1941.

Madrick, Jeff. *Why Economies Grow: The Forces That Shape Prosperity and How We Can Get Them Working Again.* New York: Basic Books, 2002.

Meadows, Donella H., Dennis L. Meadows, Jorgen Randers, and William W. Behrens III. *The Limits to Growth: A Report for the Club of Rome's Project on the Predicament of Mankind.* New York: Universe Books, 1972.

Reynolds, Paul D., William D. Bygrave, Erkko Autio, Larry W. Cox, and Michael Hay. *Global Entrepreneurship Monitor: 2002 Executive Report.* Babson Park, MA: Babson College; London: London Business School; Kansas City, MO: Ewing Marion Kauffman Foundation, 2002.

Schumacher, E. F. *Small Is Beautiful: Economics as if People Mattered.* New York: Harper & Row, 1973.

Schumpeter, Joseph A. *Capitalism, Socialism, and Democracy.* New York: Harper & Brothers Publishers, 1942.

Solow, Robert M. *Growth Theory: An Exposition.* New York: Oxford University Press, 1970.

Tucker, Robert. *Driving Growth through Innovation.* San Francisco: Berrett-Koehler, 2002.

Wolff, Edward N. *Theories of Economic Growth.* New York: Cambridge University Press, 2004.

World Bank. *World Development Report 2003: Sustainable Development in a Dynamic World: Transforming Institutions, Growth, and Quality of Life.* New York: Oxford University Press, 2003.

World Resources Institute (WRI), UN Development Program, UN Environment Program, and World Bank. *World Resources: 2000–2001: People and Ecosystems, The Fraying Web of Life.* Washington, DC: World Resources Institute, 2000.

CHAPTER 10

In Search of Economic Stability

Chapter 10 deals with macroeconomic instability and related economic issues. The three main types of macroeconomic instability are inflation, unemployment, and recession. The government promotes economic stability through monetary and fiscal policies. Over time, different schools of economic thought have offered different approaches to stabilization. The leading twentieth-century schools include the Keynesian school, monetarism, supply-side economics, and the new classical economics. Related economic topics include taxation, the national debt, and poverty.

ECONOMIC INSTABILITY

Prior to the Great Depression of the 1930s, the American economy rested on laissez-faire capitalism, a form of capitalism that shunned most types of government intervention in economic activity. The severity of the Great Depression and the sacrifices necessary to mobilize America's war effort during World War II irrevocably altered people's perceptions about the legitimate role of government in promoting economic stability. The initial guidelines for government's expanded economic role were stated in the Employment Act of 1946, which declared it to be "the continuing policy of the Federal Government to use all practicable means . . . to promote maximum employment, production, and purchasing power."[1] Later, the Full Employment and Balanced Growth Act of 1978, also called the Humphrey-Hawkins Act, reinforced the government's commitment to economic stability. This act authorized the Federal Reserve System to promote maximum sustainable economic growth, price stability, full employment, and moderate interest rates.

The Business Cycle: Tracking Economic Activity

The **business cycle** illustrates the short-term ups and downs in the real gross domestic product (GDP). The business cycle is comprised of two phases, expansion and contraction, as shown in Figure 10.1. The real GDP climbs during an expansion. An expansion is typically accompanied by increased employment opportunities and greater business investment. Job security during expansions also fuels consumer confidence and spending. The real GDP declines during a contraction. A contraction of at least two consecutive quarters, or six months, is considered a **recession.** Recessions are marked by a decline in national output, higher unemployment, and lower business investment. A **depression** is a severe, prolonged recession. The business cycle also has two points, a peak and a trough. The peak represents the highest point on a business cycle, while the trough is the lowest point. Business cycles illustrate short-term changes in national output. Yet some economists are more concerned with long-term growth trends over 20, 50, or even 100 years as the best measure of national economic performance (see chapter 9 for more on economic growth).

Economists use three types of **economic indicators** to predict and assess the duration of business cycles in the U.S. economy. The leading economic indicators predict the direction of a business cycle for the upcoming few quarters. Leading economic indicators can signal an expansion or a contraction. Leading indicators that point to an expansion include increases in business start-ups, building permits, the average manufacturing workweek, new orders for producer and consumer goods, and the Dow Jones Industrial Average (Dow). Declines in the leading indicators suggest that the economy is headed for a contraction.

Figure 10.1
The Business Cycle Model

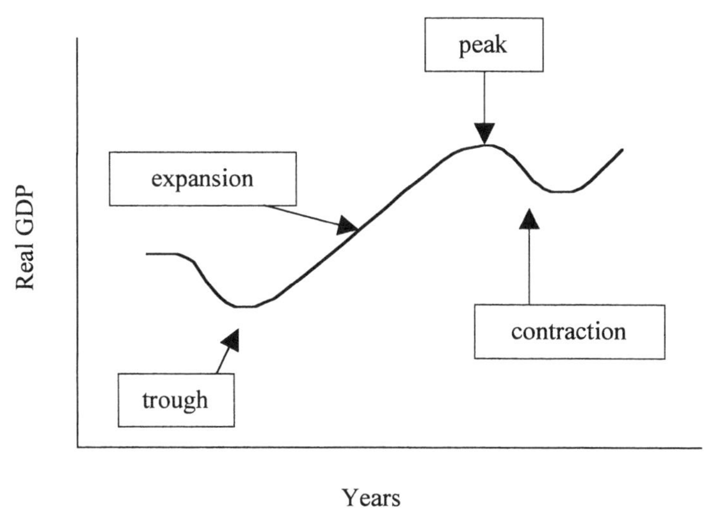

The coincident economic indicators occur in conjunction with a change in the business cycle. As an economy enters an expansion, for example, personal income, sales volume, and production levels rise. Conversely, when an economy enters a contraction, personal income, sales, and production tend to decline.

The lagging economic indicators occur months after a change in the business cycle. These indicators are important consequences of the business cycle change. During expansions, for example, lagging indicators include a drop in the unemployment rate and more robust consumer borrowing. During contractions, however, the unemployment rate rises and consumer borrowing falls.

Price Instability: Inflation and Deflation

Inflation and deflation, the two types of price instability, have mainly negative impacts on the national economy. **Inflation** is an increase in the overall price level in an economy. Demand-pull inflation results from excess demand. That is, aggregate demand is greater than the aggregate supply. As a result, too much money is chasing too few goods, and people bid up prices of products. Cost-push inflation, a second type of inflation, is caused by an increase in the costs of production, such as higher wages or resource prices. Higher costs, in turn, require producers to cut back on production and charge higher prices for their output. The oil price shocks of the mid-1970s and late 1970s demonstrated the negative impact of higher resource costs on price levels in the United States.

Inflation reduces the purchasing power of money and imposes costs on different groups. Inflation erodes the real value of workers' wages, savers' deposits, and consumers' disposable income. Unanticipated inflation harms many groups in the private sector of the economy. It is especially severe for people on fixed incomes, including those who rely on public assistance programs such as Temporary Assistance for Needy Families, a federal transfer program not indexed to the inflation rate. Uncertainty caused by unanticipated inflation also sours business investment in new capital, retards job creation, and dims prospects for economic growth.

The **inflation rate** measures the percentage increase in the overall price level over time. Economists view creeping inflation, an inflation rate of 1 percent to 3 percent per year, as normal in a growing economy. In most years since the early 1990s, the United States has experienced creeping inflation. The nation's most severe post–World War II bouts with inflation occurred in 1979 (11.3%), 1980 (13.5%), and 1981 (10.3%).[2]

While double-digit inflation in the United States is considered a major economic problem, it pales when compared to the galloping inflation and hyperinflation that has plagued some economies. *Galloping inflation* refers to a wide range of inflation rates, perhaps 20 percent, 100 percent, or even higher. In 2002 a number of countries around the world faced galloping inflation, including Angola (109% inflation), Turkey (45%), Argentina (25.9%), the Democratic Republic of Congo (25.7%), and Venezuela (22.4%). *Hyperinflation* refers to inflation rates that climb uncontrollably into thousands of percent or higher. In the early 1990s, several countries were ravaged by hyperinflation, including the Democratic Republic of Congo (23,760% inflation in 1994), Brazil (2076% in 1994), and Russia (1735% in 1992).[3] Average inflation rates for advanced, developing, and transition countries are shown, by decade, in Table 10.1.[4]

In the United States, the consumer price index is used to calculate the inflation rate. The **consumer price index** (CPI) measures the percentage increase in the price of a uniform market basket of goods and services every month. The starting point for the CPI is the base year, a point at which the government says $1 equals 100 percent of its value. At this point, the CPI is set at 100. When the price of the market basket of goods increases, the CPI rises. Likewise, when the price of the market basket falls, the CPI declines. One commonly used base year is 1982–1984, a spread of three years. Government CPI data collected every month since 1982–1984 showed an increase in the CPI from 100 to 179.9 by 2002. This meant that it would take about $1.80 in 2002 to purchase the same amount of goods that $1.00 would have purchased 20 years earlier. The annual inflation rate is calculated by dividing the net change in CPI from year 1 to year 2 by the CPI in year 1. Note in Figure 10.2 that the net change in the CPI from 2001 to 2002 was 2.8 index points. Thus, the inflation rate for 2002 was 1.6 percent (2.8 divided by 177.1). A similar index, called the **producer price index** (PPI), measures price changes for raw materials, intermediate goods, and other items used in the production of goods and services.

Deflation, sometimes called negative inflation, occurs when the general price level in an economy decreases. Deflation is most often the result of insufficient aggregate demand in an economy, and it is most likely to occur when large numbers of people are unemployed during a recession or depression. The United States suffered from severe deflation during the post–World War I economic downturn in 1921 (–10.5%) and 1922 (–6.1%) and during the early years of the Great Depression in 1931 (–9.0%), 1932 (–9.9%), and 1933 (–5.1%).[5] Deflation sends signals to producers and consumers that hinder economic growth. For instance, many businesses respond to deflation by reducing production, a predictable response to the expectation of lower prices for their output. Production cutbacks ripple through the economy, causing worker layoffs and lower

Table 10.1
Global Inflation Rates: 1985–2004

Classification of Country	1985–1994 Average	1995–2004 Average
Advanced	3.8%	2.0%
Developing	49.2%	9.2%
Transition	97.1%	29.9%

Source: International Monetary Fund, *World Economic Outlook, April 2003,* 182.

Figure 10.2
Calculating the Inflation Rate: 2002

$$\frac{2002\ \text{CPI} - 2001\ \text{CPI}}{2001\ \text{CPI}} = \text{Inflation Rate for 2002}$$

$$\frac{179.9 - 177.1}{177.1} = \frac{2.8}{177.1} = 1.6\%$$

business investment. Deflation also discourages consumer spending on automobiles, consumer durables, and other discretionary items. These delays in spending are the result of job insecurity as well as expectations of still lower prices for goods in the future. Persistent deflation in the Japanese economy during the 1990s and early 2000s stunted that nation's economic growth.[6]

Unemployment

Unemployment refers to the number of people in the labor force who do not have jobs. The **unemployment rate** is the percentage of the labor force that is without work. Unemployment is another type of macroeconomic instability. The unemployment rate is typically high when an economy sinks into a recession or depression. At the height of the Great Depression in 1933, for example, the U.S. unemployment rate hit 25 percent of the labor force. More recently, severe U.S. recessions resulted in high unemployment rates in 1975 (8.5%) and 1976 (7.7%), 1982 (9.7%) and 1983 (9.6%), and 1992 (7.5%).[7] In the United States, full employment is a national economic goal, as stated in the Employment Act of 1946 and the Full Employment and Balanced Growth Act of 1978. Economists sometimes disagree about the definition of full employment, however (see chapter 7 for more on the labor force).

A closer look at the three main types of unemployment helps clarify the full-employment debate. Frictional unemployment is temporary joblessness that occurs naturally in a dynamic economy. It includes workers who are between jobs, are reentering the job market, or are new entrants. Economists view frictional unemployment as normal, even healthy, in a fast-changing economy. The frictionally unemployed simply need time to find the best match between their job skills and available jobs.

Structural unemployment is a longer-term type of unemployment that results from a mismatch between workers' skills and job opportunities. Structural unemployment often occurs when workers' skills become obsolete. The recent loss of certain manufacturing jobs in America's "sunset" industries illustrates this process.

Cyclical unemployment is job loss that stems from downturns in the business cycle, including recessions and depressions. Economic downturns require businesses to cut production levels and jobs, as occurred during U.S. recessions in the mid-1970s, early 1980s, and early 1990s.

Most economists agree that full employment is achieved when the economy hits its natural rate of unemployment. The **natural rate of unemployment** is often equated with the percentage of the labor force that is frictionally and structurally unemployed. That is, the natural functioning of dynamic economies is bound to displace some workers while creating opportunities for others. Cyclical employment, on the other hand, results from a change in the business cycle rather than the structure of the economy itself. Today, many economists say that the natural rate of unemployment in the U.S. economy is between 5 percent and 6 percent. Government stabilization policies are most concerned with cyclical unemployment.

GOVERNMENT STABILIZATION POLICIES

The role of the federal government in promoting price stability, full employment, and economic growth has grown dramatically since the Great Depression. The most influential Depression-era theorist was British economist John Maynard Keynes. Keynes rejected the premise that depressions were self-correcting. Instead, he advocated government intervention to increase aggregate demand during recessions or depressions (see the biography of John M. Keynes). **Aggregate demand** is the total demand for goods and services in an economy. The application of Keynes's theories, sometimes called the Keynesian revolution, shaped U.S. monetary policy and fiscal policy over the next several decades. Later, other schools of thought challenged the Keynesians, including the monetarists, supply-siders, and new classical economists.

Monetary Policy: Stabilization by the Federal Reserve System

Monetary policy represents the actions of the Federal Reserve System, America's central bank, to regulate the nation's money supply and the cost of credit. Since the Great Depression, most mainstream economists have favored the use of monetary policy to regulate aggregate demand in the economy. The goals of monetary policy are to moderate sharp economic upswings and downswings and to regulate fluctuations in unemployment and price levels. The two types of monetary policy are easy and tight monetary policies. An easy monetary policy expands the nation's money supply, which increases aggregate demand and stimulates business activity and employment opportunities. A tight monetary policy contracts the nation's money supply, which decreases aggregate demand and reduces inflationary pressures caused by too much money chasing too few goods. The Fed's three main monetary policy tools are open market operations, the discount rate, and the reserve requirement (see chapter 8 for more on the Fed's structure).

Open market operations are the government's purchase or sale of government securities, such as Treasury bills and notes. The Federal Open Market Committee (FOMC), the Fed's top decision-making body, decides when to buy or sell government securities on the open market. The FOMC is composed of all seven governors who serve on the Fed's Board of Governors, plus five Reserve Bank presidents. Purchases and sales of government securities are conducted through the trading desk at the Federal Reserve Bank of New York.

To increase aggregate demand, the FOMC buys securities from dealers in the banking system. The purchase of securities increases banks' cash reserves, which enables the banking system to make additional loans and other investments. A larger pool of loanable funds also tends to reduce interest rates, which encourages individuals and businesses to borrow money. The purchase of securities is designed to stimulate business activity during times of recession.

To decrease aggregate demand, the FOMC sells securities to dealers in the banking system. The sale of government securities withdraws money from the banking system, which reduces banks' ability to make loans and investments. The sale of securities also tends to increase interest rates charged by banks, thus discouraging borrowing by individuals and businesses. The sale of securities is designed to slow an overheated economy, reduce inflation, or both, mainly during the expansion phase of the business cycle. Open market operations are conducted daily at the Federal Reserve Bank of New York and are considered the Fed's most important monetary policy tool.

The **discount rate** is the interest rate charged by the Fed for short-term loans made to member and nonmember banks. The discount rate is set by the Board of Directors at each of the 12 district Reserve Banks, subject to the approval of the Board of Governors in Washington, D.C. To increase aggregate demand, Reserve Banks lower the discount rate, which encourages borrowing from the Fed. To decrease aggregate demand, Reserve Banks increase the discount rate, which discourages borrowing from the Fed. In recent years, changes in the discount rate have sent strong signals to the banking system about the direction of the Fed's overall monetary policy. Banks typically use changes in the Fed's discount rate to adjust the **federal funds rate,** the interest rate banks charge for short-term loans to other banks. To counter the recession in 2001, for example, the Fed reduced the discount rate numerous times from January 2001, when the rate stood at 5.75 percent, to November 2002, when it had dropped to just 0.75 percent. Following the Fed's lead, banks lowered the federal funds rate from 6 percent to 1.25 percent during the same period.[8]

The **reserve requirement** is the percentage of transactions deposits that depository institutions must hold as reserves, either in their own vaults or at their district Reserve Bank. The Board of Governors establishes the reserve requirement, which, under the provisions of the Monetary Control Act of 1980, is limited to 8 percent to 14 percent of transactions deposits. In 2002, for instance, the reserve requirement was set at 10 percent on personal transactions deposits such as checking accounts and negotiable order of withdrawal (NOW) accounts; 9 percent on nonpersonal time deposits; and 0 percent on nontransactions accounts such as savings accounts and certificates of deposit (CDs). To increase aggregate demand, the Fed lowers the reserve requirement, which increases the amount of loanable funds. To decrease aggregate demand, the Fed raises the reserve requirement, which reduces the supply of loanable funds. The reserve re-

Picture of the Federal Reserve Bank of New York. Federal Reserve Bank of New York.

quirement is the least used monetary tool mainly because changes in required reserves disrupt banks' long-term loan and investment strategies. In addition, changes in the reserve requirement have a relatively small impact on economic activity, since reserves are restricted to transactions deposits in the nation's M1 (see chapter 8 for more on M1, M2, and M3).

Fiscal Policy: Stabilization by Congress and the President

Fiscal policy represents the actions of Congress and the president to promote macroeconomic goals of economic growth and stability. Most administrations since the Great Depression have used fiscal policy to regulate aggregate demand to stabilize business activity, employment, and prices. Fiscal policy is often divided into two strands, discretionary fiscal policy and nondiscretionary fiscal policy. The tools of fiscal policy include taxation, government spending, and certain automatic stabilizers.

Discretionary fiscal policy refers to the conscious actions by Congress and the president to stabilize the economy, mainly through tax policies and government spending. Often, these actions consist of new legislation. There are two types of discretionary fiscal policy, expansionary and restrictive. An expansionary fiscal policy uses tax cuts and additional government spending to increase aggregate demand, policies that the Keynesians referred to as "priming the pump." Expansionary policies inject money into the economy, which encourages higher consumption and production. Expansionary fiscal policy is used to fight recessions and depressions. A restrictive fiscal policy requires higher taxes and lower government spending to decrease aggregate demand. Restrictive policies withdraw money from the economy to slow inflation or curb the exuberant growth that may accompany an expansion in the business cycle. Over the past 75 years, many economists, Keynesians and non-Keynesians alike, have supported tax breaks and government spending programs to promote the goals of growth, full employment, and price stability.

Nondiscretionary fiscal policy refers to the built-in, or automatic, stabilizers that exist within the tax system and federal spending programs. Automatic stabilizers tend to inject money into the economy when the economy dips into recessions, and withdraw money when the economy recovers. The two main automatic stabilizers in the U.S. economy are the progressive income tax and public transfer payments. For instance, the progressive income tax is based on the size of people's income, mainly income derived from wages. During recessions, some workers lose their jobs or work fewer hours. As wages decline, people automatically pay lower taxes to the government. During expansions, however, people's wages tend to rise, as do their tax obligations. By automatically increasing tax obligations during an expansion, the tax structure helps prevent the economy from overheating. Similarly, public transfer payments inject additional money into the economy during downturns and withdraw money during expansions. For instance, unemployment insurance, a major public transfer payment offered to the temporarily unemployed, increases during recessions when the unemployment rate is high, and decreases during expansions when unemployment subsides. In 2000, the final year of a prolonged U.S. expansion, just 2.1 million unemployed workers claimed $21 billion in unemployment insurance. In 2001, a year marred by recession, over 3 million workers made unemployment insurance claims of $32 billion.[9]

Different Schools of Thought Shape U.S. Stabilization Policy

The Keynesian school of thought championed demand-management economics from the 1930s to the 1960s. Demand-management economists believed that economic stabilization was best achieved by changing aggregate demand to counter changes in the business cycle and price instability. The heyday of the Keynesians occurred in the 1960s, when the demand-management approach was used to bring the U.S. economy out of the recession of 1960–1961. To reverse this economic slump, the Fed employed an easy monetary policy by purchasing government securities on the open market, lowering the discount rate from 4 percent to 3 percent, and reducing the reserve requirement. Simultaneously, the administration of John F. Kennedy and Congress supported an expansionary fiscal policy by reducing taxes on individuals and businesses and initiating new government spending programs. These policies resulted in a stunning economic turnabout, marked by healthy GDP growth, lower unemployment, and price stability. Prevailing thought was that economists had finally learned how to fine-tune the economy and keep it on an even keel. The Keynesians' celebration was premature, however. Rising inflation by the late 1960s, a severe recession in the mid-1970s, and the introduction of stagflation during the 1970s rained on their parade. **Stagflation** is the simultaneous occurrence of recession, rising unemployment, and high inflation. The Keynesian approach to stabilization was poorly equipped to fight both recession and inflation at the same time. New economic problems sent policymakers scrambling for new stabilization approaches (see the biography of John M. Keynes).

Monetarism, a competing school of economic thought, gained momentum during the 1970s. **Monetarism** supported a Fed policy that established a fixed, predictable rate of growth in the nation's money supply. Hence, the money supply was the key to long-term macroeconomic stability—real economic growth, full employment, and stable prices. Monetarists also believed that free markets and a resilient private sector should guide economic activity. Milton Friedman, the chief spokesman for the monetarists, condemned the Keynesians for their ill-advised attempts to fine-tune the macroeconomy. In fact, Friedman and other monetarists argued that aggressive monetary and fiscal policies were inherently destabilizing. By the late 1970s, spiraling inflation caused Fed Chairman Paul Volcker to institute strict guidelines on growth in the nation's money supply, a policy supported by the monetarists. Eventually, this policy reigned in inflation, but it also contributed to a severe recession in the early 1980s. The debate between the Keynesians and the monetarists dominated the 1970s, but the economic costs associated with each approach caused many people to seek a different solution (see the biography of Milton Friedman).

Supply-side economics stressed the role of incentives to instigate higher productivity and economic growth. The supply-side school of thought relied on the expansion of **aggregate supply,** the total output of goods and services in an economy. The origins of supply-side theory can be traced to French economist Jean Baptiste Say, who in the early 1800s postulated that "supply creates its own demand." Modern supply-siders argued that, to increase aggregate supply, government should provide market incentives to promote work, saving, investment, entrepreneurial risk-taking, and productivity. President Ronald Reagan, who served two terms in the White House from 1981 to 1989, staunchly supported the supply-side approach. Reagan believed that proper supply-side incentives must include tax cuts and reductions in business regulations and wasteful government spending. The centerpiece of Reagan's supply-side agenda was the Economic Recovery Act of 1981, which cut personal and corporate income taxes by 25 percent between 1982 and 1984. Economist Arthur Laffer, through his Laffer curve, explained that lower tax rates would generate greater tax revenues by expanding the tax base. Economists still debate whether the massive tax cuts of the early 1980s had a greater impact on aggregate supply or aggregate demand. They also debated the impact of supply-side policies on the prolonged expansion that stretched into the early 1990s, and on the national debt, which quadrupled from $1 trillion in 1981 to $4 trillion 12 years later.[10] (See the biography of Jean B. Say.)

In recent years, new classical economics has become an influential school of thought in the realm of macroeconomics. New classical economics assumes that both wages and prices are flexible and that people have sufficient economic information to anticipate government economic policies. Much of what is new in the new classical economics centers on the rational expectations hypothesis, a theory developed by Nobel laureate Robert E. Lucas, Jr., and other economists at the University of Chicago. According to the rational expectations hypothesis, people are privy to an immense body of economic information, and by using all available information they will, on average, accurately predict future economic events, including monetary policy and fiscal policy. People's economic forecasts color their present economic behaviors, such as saving, investing, and spending, which limit the effectiveness of future stabilization policies. Supporters of the rational expectations hypothesis point out that microeconomic theory rests on rational behaviors by individuals and firms. Critics of the rational expectations hypothesis argue that people have neither the time nor the inclination to collect sufficient economic information to form rational expectations on the larger macroeconomic stage. Measuring the impact of people's expectations on the macroeconomy will provide research opportunities for economists well into the twenty-first century.

ISSUES IN THE NATIONAL ECONOMY

Much of the work economists do in the macroeconomy deals with economic growth and stability. Yet other economic goals are interrelated with these macroeconomic concerns. For example, economic equity is often discussed when examining the fairness of tax policies and income distribution in the U.S. economy. Similarly, people's economic security is intertwined with macroeconomic problems, such as unemployment and sluggish national production.

Taxes: Raising Revenue and Influencing Behavior

A **tax** is a mandatory payment by individuals or businesses to the federal, state, or local government. The three types of taxes assign different tax burdens to different income groups. A **progressive tax** takes a larger percentage of income in taxes from high-income households than from low-income households. The federal personal income tax is a progressive tax. The Jobs and Growth

Tax Relief Reconciliation Act of 2003, which lowered taxes for many Americans, established six income tax brackets of 10 percent, 15 percent, 25 percent, 28 percent, 33 percent, and 35 percent. Low-income households paid a lower percentage of their income in taxes, while higher income households paid incrementally higher percentages on different portions of their taxable income. A **proportional tax** takes the same percentage of income in taxes from all households. A few state income taxes are proportional. A **regressive tax** takes a larger percentage of income in taxes from low-income than from high-income households. A state sales tax is regressive mainly because low-income groups spend most of their limited income to make ends meet, and much of this spending is on goods subject to sales tax. Many states soften the regressive nature of sales taxes by exempting certain necessities such as food, medicine, and some clothing.

The subject of tax fairness strays into the realm of normative economics. Economists point to two principles of taxation to evaluate tax equity, however. First, the ability-to-pay principle states that people with more income or wealth should pay more in taxes, since these wealthier people are more financially able to contribute. The federal personal income tax is based on the ability-to-pay principle. Second, the benefit-received principle states that people should be taxed in proportion to the benefits they receive from government goods, such as schools, roads, or libraries. Highway tolls are based on the benefit-received principle because toll revenues are often used for highway construction and repair.

Taxes are designed to raise money to finance government programs and to influence the behavior of people. Taxes are the most important source of government receipts. In 2003, federal, state, and local governments across America collected nearly $3 trillion per year from taxpayers, $1.78 trillion at the federal level, and $1.16 trillion at the state and local levels.[11] In 2003 the most impor-

Table 10.2
Federal Tax Receipts by Category: FY 2004

Federal Tax	Tax Receipts (in billions)	Percentage of Receipts
Personal income tax	$765	42.6%
Social insurance tax	$732	40.7%
Corporate income tax	$169	9.4%
Other	$132	7.3%
Total tax receipts	$1,798	100.0%

Source: Office of Management and Budget, *Budget of the United States Government, Fiscal Year 2005,* 30.

tant sources of tax receipts at the federal level were the personal income tax, social insurance tax, and corporate income tax, as shown in Table 10.2. In that same year, major categories of federal spending, called outlays, included Social Security payments (21.4% of federal outlays), national defense (19.6%), Medicare and other health (22.2%), net interest on the national debt (6.7%), and other (30.1%).[12] In the early 2000s, the largest categories of state and local receipts were the sales tax (20.1% of all receipts), revenues from the federal government (18.9%), property taxes (16.2%), and state income taxes (13.7%). State and local spending was dominated by expenditures on education (34.6%), public welfare (15.8%), and highways (6.7%).[13]

In addition to raising revenues for government, taxes also influence people's economic behaviors. That is, some taxes have incentive or disincentive functions. For example, tax incentives are evident in America's enterprise zones. Enterprise zones are economically distressed regions, usually located within core cities, in which tax breaks encourage business investment and job creation. Tax breaks include tax credits for wages paid to new employees and relief from local property taxes. Taxes can also discourage certain behaviors. For example, an excise tax, which is levied on a specific product, increases the product's price and thereby discourages its purchase. The so-called sin taxes on gasoline, tobacco products, and alcoholic beverages are excise taxes designed in part to discourage the consumption of these goods.

The Federal Budget: Budget Deficits and the National Debt

Each year the federal government formulates and approves a **federal budget,** a document that outlines how the government plans to raise and spend money during the upcoming fiscal year (FY). The FY for the federal government begins on October 1 and ends on September 30 of the following year. The original budget proposal is drafted by the Office of Management of Budget (OMB) and is often called the president's budget because it reflects the president's views on tax policy and spending priorities. The president's budget is transmitted to Congress in February, where it is studied, debated, and amended on a timeline that permits implementation by October 1. For instance, the president's budget proposal for FY 2004 was transmitted to Congress in February 2003 and, after the usual political wrangling in Congress, was approved by September 30, 2003. The budget is actually 13 separate appropriations bills, each of which must be passed by Congress and signed by the president. A continuing resolution (CR) is approved by Congress and signed by the president if one or more of the appropriations bills has not been approved by September 30. Under a CR, temporary funding keeps programs and agencies functioning until agreement on the appropriations bill is reached.

A federal budget might be balanced, in surplus, or in deficit. In a balanced budget, planned receipts are equal to planned expenditures. A budget surplus occurs when planned receipts are greater than planned expenditures. A budget deficit occurs when planned receipts are less than planned expenditures.

From the start of the Great Depression in 1929 to 2008, the federal budget has been in deficit 68 times, and in surplus 12 times. Over time, many factors contributed to America's budget deficits. First, national emergencies such as World War II (1941–1945), the Gulf War (1991), and the U.S.-led invasion of Iraq (2003) increased budget deficits by requiring massive government spending for military campaigns. Second, economic crises such as the Great Depression (1930s) slowed tax receipts and increased government spending on relief efforts. Third, the rapid growth of some social programs, including Social Security and Medicare, resulted in large increases in federal spending. In 1966, for example, the $21 billion spent on Social Security and Medicare represented about 15 percent of the federal budget. In FY 2004 spending on these two programs had jumped to $767 billion, about one-third of all federal expenditures.[14] Budget deficits over the past few decades have grown progressively steeper. During the 1970s, the average annual budget deficit was about $37 billion, in the 1980s about $157 billion, and in the 1990s about $192 billion. The most recent budget surpluses appeared in the late 1990s and early 2000s. Significant budget deficits are forecast for the foreseeable future, as shown in Table 10.3.[15]

The **national debt,** also called the federal debt, is the accumulated debt of the federal government over time. By the end of 2003 the national debt stood at about $6.8 trillion. The national debt is divided into two categories: debt held by the public ($3.9 trillion) and intragovernmental holdings ($2.9 trillion) The

Table 10.3
Budget Surpluses and Deficits: 1980–2009

Year	Surplus or Deficit ($ billions)	Year	Surplus or Deficit ($ billions)
1980	-$74	1995	-$164
1981	-$79	1996	-$108
1982	-$128	1997	-$22
1983	-$208	1998	+$69
1984	-$185	1999	+$126
1985	-$212	2000	+$236
1986	-$221	2001	+$127
1987	-$150	2002	-$158
1988	-$155	2003	-$375
1989	-$152	2004*	-$521
1990	-$221	2005*	-$364
1991	-$269	2006*	-$268
1992	-$290	2007*	-$241
1993	-$255	2008*	-$238
1994	-$203	2009*	-$237

Source: Office of Management and Budget, *Budget of the United States Government, Fiscal Year 2005 (Historical Tables).*
*OMB estimates.

debt held by the public is the sum total of the money the federal government has borrowed from individuals, companies, state and local governments, and foreign investors. The government borrows from the public through the sale of government securities such as Treasury bills, notes, bonds, and savings bonds. Government borrowing is necessary to cover annual budget shortfalls in revenues, or budget deficits. Intragovernmental holdings represent debts that the government owes to itself. For example, government money in the Social Security Trust Fund that is invested in federal securities puts the U.S. Treasury in debt to the Trust Fund. In 1982 the national debt topped the $1 trillion mark for the first time, a sum that represented 35 percent of the nation's gross domestic product. The 2003 national debt totaled $6.8 trillion, or 63 percent of GDP.[16] Two main concerns about the growing national debt include debt servicing and crowding out. *Debt servicing* refers to the government's obligation to pay interest on past loans, a sum that amounted to $161 billion in 2003. Crowding out occurs when increased government borrowing soaks up more of society's savings and raises interest rates. Higher interest rates discourage borrowing by firms, which reduces business investment. Higher interest rates also reduce consumer borrowing and spending, which erodes aggregate demand.

Income Distribution and Poverty

The distribution of income and wealth in the United States and other nations is uneven. There are many reasons for the disparities between the different economic classes in the U.S. economy. Income distribution is influenced by the compensation workers receive in labor markets, as well as income derived from interest payments, dividends, rents, entrepreneurial profits, and a variety of public transfer payments. Over the past quarter century, a widening income gap between America's richest and poorest citizens has emerged, as shown in Table 10.4. Note that between 1975 and 2000 the percent of money income received by the richest 20 percent of the population climbed from 40.7 percent to 47.4 percent, while the percent of money income received by all four of the lower quintiles declined.[17] By the early 2000s, nearly half of all income went to people in the top quintile. Stricter regulations on public assistance for the poor and higher

Table 10.4
Distribution of U.S. Money Income: 1975–2000

Income Quintiles	1975	1980	1985	1990	1995	2000
Lowest quintile	5.6	5.3	4.8	4.6	4.4	4.3
Second quintile	11.9	11.6	11.0	10.8	10.1	9.8
Third quintile	17.7	17.6	16.9	16.6	15.8	15.5
Fourth quintile	24.2	24.4	24.3	23.8	23.2	22.8
Highest quintile	40.7	41.1	43.1	44.3	46.5	47.4

Source: U.S. Bureau of the Census, *Statistical Abstract of the United States: 1999, 2002.*

salaries for the highly educated and well-connected professional classes helped account for the growing income gap. Even greater disparities existed in the distribution of society's wealth, as families with incomes of at least $100,000 had an average net worth of $1.7 million, compared to an average net worth of just $40,000 for families with annual incomes of less than $10,000.[18]

The distribution of income has a major impact on the national poverty rate. Even with detailed income data, poverty is difficult to measure, however. In the United States, the Census Bureau uses a family's money income, size, and composition to distinguish the poor from the nonpoor. In 2002, for example, a family of two was poor if its money income dipped below $11,756; a family of four was poor if its income fell below $18,392; and a family of nine or more was poor if its income fell below $37,062.[19] The income level that separates the poor from the nonpoor is called the poverty line or poverty threshold. In the United States, the poverty line is calculated by multiplying a typical family's annual food budget times three. Thus, the poverty line inches upward each year as price levels rise. Over the past three decades, the number of American falling below the poverty line has ranged from a low of 23 million in 1973 to a high of 39 million in 1993. In 2002 about 34.6 million people were considered poor, and the poverty rate, which measures the percentage of Americans living in poverty, was 12.1 percent.[20]

Since the 1960s, a comprehensive welfare system has created some economic security for America's poor. A major expansion of the nation's welfare system began during the presidency of Lyndon B. Johnson, who served from 1963 to 1969. Like his predecessor, John F. Kennedy, President Johnson was dismayed by the fact that more than one in five Americans lived in poverty by the early 1960s. Author Michael Harrington, who wrote *The Other America* in 1962, awakened the nation to the plight of the poor (see the biography of Michael Harrington). The Johnson administration initiated the Great Society program to address a variety of social ills. Great Society expanded civil rights protections, educational opportunities, and the safety net of social programs for the nation's most needy. Great Society programs enacted during the mid-1960s included the food stamp program, Medicare, and Medicaid. Today's most important public assistance programs—programs that provide cash and noncash transfer payments to people in need—are listed below. In 1996 the Personal Responsibility and Work Opportunity Reconciliation Act (PRWORA) and the Contract with America Advancement Act increased eligibility requirements for some public assistance programs.

- *Temporary Assistance for Needy Families.* An income assistance plan created in 1996 by PRWORA that replaced the previous income assistance program, Aid to Families with Dependent Children (AFDC).
- *Supplemental Security Income (SSI).* An income assistance plan created in 1974 to provide income and other assistance to people in need, mainly the elderly with little income and no assets.
- *Medicaid.* A health insurance plan for the poor created in 1965 as an amendment to the Social Security Act of 1935; it is the nation's most expensive noncash public assistance program.

- *Food stamp program.* A food assistance program created by the Federal Food Stamp Act of 1964; other food assistance programs include the Child and Adult Care Food Program and the Special Supplemental Food Program for Women, Infants, and Children (WIC).

The redistribution of income to the poor is a widely debated issue in the United States. At the heart of the public debate is the concept of economic equity, a controversial national goal related to fairness in the economy. Supporters of income redistribution argue that public assistance programs are necessary to guarantee the poor a minimum standard of living. They note that many people living in poverty are victims of circumstances beyond their control. This is especially true for children born into poverty. In 2002, 12.1 million children lived in poverty, making up more than one-third of all poor people in the United States.[21] Other distressed groups included the sick, the handicapped, and others denied an opportunity to succeed. Opponents counter that income redistribution violates basic market freedoms, including the freedom to acquire and freely exchange private property. Critics liken income redistribution to a government confiscation of earned income, "robbing Peter to pay Paul." Critics also argue that the unintended consequences of income distribution are severe. For instance, high taxes required to fund welfare programs discourage upper-income people from working, saving, and investing. Generous welfare programs might also serve as a disincentive for poorer people to find and hold jobs.

BIOGRAPHIES: SHAPERS OF ECONOMIC THOUGHT

Jean Baptiste Say: The Classical Approach to Stabilization

Jean Baptiste Say (1767–1832) was a successful French industrialist and economist who popularized the theory of laissez-faire capitalism, a basic tenet of the classical school of economics. Say was born in Lyon, France, the son of textile merchants. During the 1780s and 1790s, he learned about business operations through apprenticeships and employment in the private sector. By the early 1800s, the enterprising Say tested his entrepreneurial skills by founding a cotton factory, a business venture that earned him a fortune. During this same period of time, Say also became a disciple of Adam Smith, the famous British economist and author of *The Wealth of Nations* (1776). In 1803 Say published the *Treatise on Political Economy,* his most influential book. In this text, Say identified entrepreneurs as the wellspring of innovation in dynamic market economies. He also introduced one of the classical school's most famous economic laws, Say's law (see chapter 2 for more on the classical school of economics).

Say's law, which Say referred to as "the law of markets," states that supply creates its own demand. Say reasoned that the process of production created income for people in the form of wages, rents, interest, and profits. Income, in turn, provided people with the financial means to buy goods and services. In other words, the process of supplying goods was directly linked to the purchase of goods. Say believed that free markets were self-regulating, efficiently balancing the total supply of and total demand for goods without meddlesome government interventions. Periodic economic downturns, Say claimed, were merely temporary misallocations of resources, the overproduction of goods for which there was little demand. He noted, however, that profit incentives would soon steer businesses toward a more efficient use of society's resources and, thus, restore the nation's economic health.

Say's wealth, and his prestigious teaching positions at the Conservatoire National des Arts et Metiers and the College de France, increased his influence on Europe's intellectual community. His unwavering support for free markets and his opposition to government intervention in business activity were bedrocks of classical theory for more than a century. In many parts of the industrialized world, Say's law and the laissez-faire doctrine were not seriously challenged until the global depression of the 1930s. The severity of the global depression opened the doors for alternative views on economic stabilization, especially the views of John M. Keynes that supported a more active role for government in jump-starting economic activity. By the 1980s, however, Say's law and laissez-faire principles were once again in the limelight, revived by supply-side economists and policymakers in Great Britain and the United States.

John Maynard Keynes: The Keynesian Revolution

John Maynard Keynes (1883–1946) was a British economist, teacher, and author and is widely considered the most influential economist of the twentieth century. Keynes was born to a prominent intellectual family in Cambridge, England. His father was a noted economist, and his mother was mayor of Cambridge for a time. A child of privilege, Keynes attended Eton and later graduated from Cambridge University. While at Cambridge, he was encouraged by Alfred Marshall to pursue his interests in economics. After graduation from Cambridge, Keynes had a number of careers in the British civil service, teaching, finance, and writing. By the time Keynes published his most famous book, *The General Theory of Employment, Interest, and Money* (1936), he was already widely recognized as among the world's leading economists.

The controversial Keynes published *The General Theory* during the depths of a global depression called the Great Depression in the United States. In this book. Keynes rejected orthodox laissez-faire economic doctrine, which maintained that economic slumps were self-correcting. Instead, he argued that economic downturns were the result of insufficient aggregate demand and that market forces alone were not sufficient to end sluggish business investment and consumer spending. To Keynes, the solution to inadequate aggregate demand was government intervention in the economy. He proposed that the government inject money into the economy through greater federal spending and tax cuts. Keynes recognized that federal budget deficits and a rising national debt would occur in the short-term, but believed that these debts could be paid off when the nation's economic health improved. Keynes's views reshaped the economic landscape and created nothing less than a Keynesian revolution in economic thought during the twentieth century.

The Keynesian school of economic thought, which evolved around his thinking, influenced government policy in the United States and elsewhere for decades. President Franklin D. Roosevelt (FDR) embraced the Keynesian approach to stabilization during the Great Depression. FDR increased federal spending on public works jobs, public construction projects, and business subsidies to stimulate aggregate demand and business activity. The reign of the Keynesians continued into the 1960s and early 1970s, when new economic conditions prompted economists to explore different avenues toward economic growth and stability.

Milton Friedman: The Monetarists

Milton Friedman (1912–) is a prominent American economist and the undisputed leader of the monetarist school of thought. Friedman was born in New York City, the son of immigrant parents who hailed from the former Austria-Hungary. The Friedman family soon moved to nearby Rahway, New Jersey. Upon graduation from Rahway High School in 1928, Friedman attended Rutgers University, where he earned his bachelor's degree in 1932. Shuffling between the University of Chicago and Columbia University to complete his graduate studies, with stints at the National Bureau of Economic Research and the U.S. Treasury, Friedman eventually earned his doctoral degree in economics from Columbia in 1946. Soon thereafter, he accepted a position as professor of economics at the prestigious University of Chicago, where he spent the next three decades as a teacher, researcher, and author. At the University of Chicago, Friedman earned his reputation as a scholar. He soon became the chief spokesperson for the Chicago School monetarists.

Friedman had solid credentials to lead the Chicago School. In *A Monetary History of the United States, 1867–1960,* which he co-authored with Anna Schwartz, Friedman documented the dominant role of the money supply on changes in the price level and economic activity in the country. In this book and other works, he articulated the core elements of monetarism. First, the monetarists maintained that the Federal Reserve should allow the money supply to grow at a steady rate to foster long-term economic growth. Second, the monetarists stated that government monetary and fiscal policies designed to fine-tune economic activity in the short term inevitably destabilized the economy. This observation put Friedman and the Chicago School at odds with the dominant Keynesian school of thought during the 1960s and 1970s. Third, the monetarists favored free market capitalism. Friedman developed this theme of laissez-faire capitalism in books such as *Capitalism and Freedom* (1962) and the best-selling *Free to Choose: A Personal Statement* (1979), which he co-authored with his wife Rose. In *Capitalism and Freedom* Friedman identified the "role of competitive capitalism . . . as a system of economic freedom and a necessary condition for political freedom."[22]

Friedman is among the world's best known and respected contemporary economists. He served as president of the American Economic Association in 1967, and, after teaching economics at the University of Chicago for 30 years, became a senior research fellow at the Hoover Institute at Stanford University. In recognition of his authorship and other contributions to the field of economics, Friedman received the Nobel Prize in Economic Science in 1976.

Michael Harrington: *The Other America*

Michael E. Harrington (1928–1989) was a controversial American political activist, author, and reformer who exposed the plight of the poor in the United States and advocated socialism as an workable alternative to U.S. capitalism. Harrington was born to a middle-class Irish-Catholic family in St. Louis, Missouri. In 1947, at the age of 19, the academically talented Harrington earned his bachelor's degree at Holy Cross College in Worcester, Massachusetts. In that same year, he entered Yale to study law, but other interests cut his studies short. In 1948 he entered the University of Chicago, where he pursued his interests in poetry and earned a master's degree in English literature in 1949. During the 1950s, Harrington's worldview expanded, partly as a result of the dire poverty he witnessed in St. Louis, Chicago, and New York City, and partly due to his associations with socialist and civil rights organizations. In 1962 he published his most influential book, *The Other America: Poverty in the United States,* which caused a firestorm of public debate about poverty in the world's most prosperous country.

In *The Other America,* Harrington examined American poverty and critiqued the country's unwillingness to confront the plight of the poor, a subgroup consisting of nearly one-quarter of the entire U.S. population. Harrington observed that the poor were well hidden from public view. He noted: "The millions who are poor in the United States tend to become increasingly invisible. Here is a great mass of people, yet it takes an effort of the intellect and will even to see them."[23] This invisibility was caused by the isolation of rural and urban pockets of poverty, general appearances of affluence across the nation, and the political impotence of the poor. In Harrington's words: "[The poor] are without lobbies of their own; they put forth no legislative program. As a group, they are atomized. They have no face; they have no voice."[24] The power of Harrington's words reached President John F. Kennedy, and later influenced the creation of President Lyndon B. Johnson's Great Society programs.

Harrington's activism on behalf of social justice spanned four decades. During this time, he wrote 15 books, organized labor unions, participated in demonstrations, and led the Democratic Socialists of America. He also served as a professor of political science at Queens College in New York City for most of the 1970s and 1980s. Harrington never came to grips with capitalism, which, in *The Twilight of Capitalism* (1976), he described as "outrageously unjust" and "self-destructive."[25] Yet, working within the democratic framework in the United States, Harrington tweaked the conscience of America in the name of social justice.

NOTES

1. National Archives and Records Administration, "Joint Committee on the Economic Report (1946–56), JC.093," in *Guide to Federal Records in the National Archives of the United States, 1789–1988,* www.archives.gov/records_of_congress/house_guide/chapter_23_joint_economic_report.html.

2. U.S. Department of Labor/Bureau of Labor Statistics (BLS), "Consumer Price Index," ftp://ftp.bls.gov/pub/special.requests/cpi/cpiai.txt.

3. International Monetary Fund, "Table 12. Developing Countries—by Country: Consumer Prices" and "Table 13. Countries in Transition: Consumer Prices," *World Economic Outlook, May 2000* (Washington, DC: IMF, 2000), 212–15.

4. IMF, "Table 8. Summary of Inflation," *World Economic Outlook, April 2003* (Washington, DC: IMF, 2003), 182.

5. Ibid.

6. "Table B-108. Industrial Production and Consumer Prices, Major Industrial Countries, 1979–2002" and "Table B-112. Growth Rates in Real Gross Domestic Product, 1984–2002," *Economic Report of the President: 2003* (Washington, DC: U.S. Government Printing Office, 2003), 400, 404; IMF, *World Economic Outlook, April 2003,* 28–29.

7. "Table B-42. Civilian Unemployment Rate, 1955–2002," *Economic Report of the President: 2003,* 326.

8. Federal Reserve Bank of New York, "Historical Changes of the Fed Fund and Discount Rate (1971–Present)," www.ny.frb.org/pihome/statistics/dlyrates/fedrate.html.

9. "Table B-45. Unemployment Insurance Programs, Selected Data, 1972–2002," *Economic Report of the President: 2003,* 329.

10. U.S. Department of the Treasury, "Historical Debt Outstanding—Annual, 1950–2000," www.publicdebt.treas.gov.

11. Office of Management and Budget (OMB), "Table 15.1—Total Government Receipts in Absolute Amounts and as Percentages of GDP: 1947-2003," *Budget of the United States Government, Fiscal Year 2005, Historical Tables* (Washington, DC: U.S. Government Printing Office, 2004), 288.

12. OMB, "Table 2.1—Receipts by Source: 1934–2009," and "Table 3.1—Outlays by Superfunction and Function: 1940–2009," 30, 52.

13. "Table B-86. State and Local Government Revenues and Expenditures, Selected Fiscal Years, 1927–2000," *Economic Report of the President: 2003,* 377.

14. OMB, "Table 3.1," 52; and "Table B-80. Federal Receipts and Outlays, by Major Category, and Surplus or Deficit, Fiscal Years 1940–2004," *Economic Report of the President: 2003,* 371.

15. OMB, "Table 1.1—Summary of Receipts, Outlays, and Surpluses or Deficits: 1789–2009," 22.

16. OMB, "Table 7.1—Federal Debt at the End of the Year: 1940–2009," 118–19.

17. U.S. Census Bureau, "No. 751. Share of Aggregate Income Received by Each Fifth and Top 5 Percent of Families: 1970 to 1997," *Statistical Abstract of the United States: 1999,* 479; U.S. Census Bureau, "N. 659. Share of Aggregate Income Received by Each Fifth and Top 5 Percent of Families: 1980 to 2000," *Statistical Abstract of the United States: 2002* (Washington, DC, 2002), 437.

18. U.S. Census Bureau, "No. 677. Family Net Worth—Mean and Median Net Worth in Constant (1998) Dollars by Selected Family Characteristics: 1992 to 1998," *Statistical Abstract of the United States: 2002*, 445.

19. Bernadette D. Proctor and Joseph Dalakar/U.S. Census Bureau, *Poverty in the United States: 2002* (Washington, DC: U.S. Government Printing Office, September 2002), "The Official Poverty Measure," 4.

20. Ibid., "Table 1. Number in Poverty and Poverty Rate by Race and Hispanic Origin: 2001 and 2002," 2; and U.S. Census Bureau, "Historical Poverty Tables," www.census.gov/hhes/poverty/histpov/hstpov2.html.

21. Proctor and Dalakar, *Poverty in the United States: 2002,* "Table 5. People with Income below Specified Ratios of Their Poverty Thresholds by Selected Characteristics: 2002," 12.

22. Milton Friedman and Rose D. Friedman, *Capitalism and Freedom* (Chicago: University of Chicago Press, 1962), 4.

23. Michael Harrington, *The Other America: Poverty in the United States* (Baltimore, MD: Penguin Books, 1962), 10.

24. Ibid., 13.

25. Michael Harrington, *The Twilight of Capitalism* (New York: Simon & Schuster, 1976), 320.

SELECTED READINGS

Blinder, Alan S., and Janet L. Yellen. *The Fabulous Decade: Macroeconomic Lessons from the 1990s.* New York: Twentieth Century Fund, 2001.

Card, David E., and Rebecca M. Blank, eds. *Finding Jobs: Work and Welfare Reform.* New York: Russell Sage Foundation, 2000.

Friedman, Milton, and Rose D. Friedman. *Capitalism and Freedom.* Chicago: University of Chicago Press, 1962.

Friedman, Milton, and Anna J. Schwartz. *Monetary History of the United States, 1867–1960.* Princeton: Princeton University Press, 1971.

Harrington, Michael. *The Other America: Poverty in the United States.* Baltimore, MD: Penguin Books, 1962.

Healey, Nigel, and Mark Cook. *Supply Side Policies.* Westport, CT: Heinemann Educational Books—Secondary Division, 2001.

Keith, Robert, and Allen Schick. *The Federal Budget Process.* Huntington, NY: Nova Science Publishers, Inc., 2003.

Keleher, Robert E. *Monetary Policy.* New York: Cambridge University Press, 2004.

Keynes, John M. *The General Theory of Employment, Interest, and Money.* rep. ed. Amherst, NY: Prometheus Books, 1997.

Lutz, Arnold G. *Business Cycle Theory.* New York: Oxford University Press, 2002.

Page, Benjamin I., and James R. Simmons. *What Government Can Do: Dealing with Poverty and Inequality.* Chicago: University of Chicago Press, 2000.

Posen, Adam, ed. *The Future of Monetary Policy.* Malden, MA: Blackwell Publishers, 2004.

Seidman, Laurence S. *Automatic Fiscal Policies to Combat Recessions.* Armonk, NY: M.E. Sharpe, 2003.

Solow, Robert M., and John B. Taylor. *Inflation, Unemployment, and Monetary Policy.* Cambridge, MA: MIT Press, 1999.

CHAPTER 11

Globalization: Creating a Global Marketplace

Chapter 11 deals with globalization and its role in creating a more interdependent global economy. Globalization has progressed in fits and starts over the past 150 years. Its pace accelerated after World War II, however. The core elements of globalization are international trade, foreign direct investment, and cross-border financial flows. Over time, globalization has been fueled by new technologies, transnational corporations, receptive national governments, and multilateral organizations such as the World Bank, International Monetary Fund, and World Trade Organization. The costs and benefits of globalization are hotly debated. Major issues include financial contagion, corporate social responsibility, protectionism, and grassroots challenges to globalization.

THE PILLARS OF GLOBALIZATION

The **global economy** is the international network of individuals, businesses, multilateral organizations, and governments that make production, distribution, and consumption decisions. Ancient civilizations in Egypt, China, Greece, Rome, and elsewhere conducted cross-border business activity by land and sea, and thus participated in a global economy. Modern globalization has stitched the fabric of today's global economy more tightly than ever before. **Globalization** refers to freer cross-border movements of goods and services, labor, technology, real capital, and financial capital to create an integrated and interdependent global economy (see the biography of Jagdish Bhagwati for more on the benefits of globalization).

In modern history, globalization's two spurts are often labeled the first and second great ages of globalization. The first great age of globalization was dominated by Great Britain, which aggressively supported global trade and investment throughout its sprawling empire during the nineteenth and early twentieth centuries. Technological advances supported global economic connections. For instance, during this period steamships joined steam-powered locomotives to speed the transport of goods and people, while the telegraph and telephone made communications more convenient than ever before. The second great age of globalization was led by the United States, the dominant economic and military superpower during the post–World War II era. New technologies in transportation and communications strengthened global connections. Technological advances in high-speed railways, transport ships, jet airplanes, and motorized vehicles opened new avenues for long-distance business enterprise. Similarly, the rapid growth of information and communications technologies (ICTs) such as fiber optics, microelectronics, computers, software, the Internet, and the World Wide Web accelerated connectivity in the global economy. These technologies supported the three pillars of globalization—international trade, foreign direct investment, and cross-border financial flows.

International Trade

International trade is the cross-border exchange of goods or services. Such exchanges occur when individuals, businesses, governments, or other entities import or export goods or services. An import is a product that is purchased from another country, while an export is a product that is sold to another country. The benefits of international trade are built on the principle of mutual benefit and the theory of comparative advantage. The principle of mutual benefit emphasizes that both parties can be better off as a result of an exchange. The theory of comparative advantage, first presented by David Ricardo, stresses the need for nations to specialize in the production of goods that they can produce most efficiently relative to other countries (see the biography of David Ricardo). Since World War II many of the world's leading economies have embraced free trade to stimulate production efficiency, product innovation, consumer choice, and higher living standards. Under the watchful eyes of the General Agreement on Tariffs and Trade from 1947 to 1994 and the World Trade Organization from 1995 to the present, countries dismantled many traditional barriers to trade. A **barrier to trade** is a government restriction on the import or export of goods or services. Barriers to trade include:

- *Tariffs.* A federal tax on an imported good, a tariff discourages consumption of the imported product by making it more expensive in domestic markets.
- *Import quotas.* A federal limit on the quantity of a product allowed into a country, an import quota restricts the availability of the imported product in domestic markets.
- *Voluntary quotas.* A voluntary quota is a negotiated limit on the quantity of an import (voluntary restraint agreement) or a negotiated means to expand the quantity of an export (voluntary import expansion) and is often negotiated to reduce a trade imbalance.
- *Embargoes.* An embargo is the federal stoppage of all or some imports from or exports to a second country; it is often politically motivated to pressure the second country to change a domestic or international policy.

The global trading system represents the sum total of international trade, plus the institutions and practices that influence cross-border exchanges of goods and services. Exchanges in the global trading system increased dramatically in recent years, recording an annual growth rate of 6.5 percent from 1990 to 2000. In 2002 international trade in merchandise ($6.4 trillion in exports) and commercial services ($1.5 trillion in exports) topped $7.9 trillion. These figures represented an increase of 4 percent in traded merchandise and a 5 percent increase in traded services from 2001. World exports were expected to climb to $9.4 trillion in 2004.[1] Ranked by value of exports, the top three world regions in the global trading system during the early 2000s were western Europe, Asia, and North America, respectively. The top five exporting and importing nations in the global economy are shown in Table 11.1.[2] (See the biography of Jeffrey D. Sachs for more on trade liberalization.)

The **balance of trade** measures the difference between the value of a country's imports and exports. A country's balance of trade rarely settles at a breakeven point, a position in which the value of its imports and exports is equal. Instead, most countries experience a trade deficit or a trade surplus. A trade deficit occurs when the value of a country's imports is greater than the value of its exports. A trade surplus occurs when the value of a country's exports is greater than the value of its imports.

The U.S. balance of trade has deteriorated since 1975, the last year in which the economy recorded a trade surplus. Since then, average annual trade deficits have climbed from $85 billion during the 1980s, to $105 billion during the 1990s, and $410 billion during the early 2000s. In 2003 the U.S. trade deficit hit $489 billion as the value of U.S. imports ($1,508 billion) exceeded the U.S. exports ($1,019 billion). The balance of trade is divided into its two parts, merchandise and commercial services. Over time, the huge U.S. merchandise trade deficits have been partially offset by modest trade surpluses in services. In 2003, for example, the U.S. merchandise trade deficit stood at a record $549 billion, which, when combined with a trade surplus in services of $60 billion, resulted in an overall trade deficit of $489 billion.[3] According to U.S. Census data, half

Table 11.1
Top Exporting and Importing Nations: 2002

Rank	Country (Exporters)	Value ($ billions)	Rank	Country (Importers)	Value ($ billions)
1	United States	$961.3	1	United States	$1,420.9
2	Germany	$707.1	2	Germany	$636.1
3	Japan	$480.7	3	Japan	$441.7
4	France	$413.5	4	Britain	$437.8
5	Britain	$396.9	5	France	$390.7

Source: World Trade Organization, *World Trade Report 2003,* 68, 70.

of the entire U.S. trade deficit resulted from trade with just three countries: China (–$124 billion), Japan (–$66 billion), and Canada (–$55 billion). The main categories of U.S. merchandise exports in 2003 included capital goods (41% of merchandise exports), industrial supplies (24%), consumer goods (12%), and automotive and parts (11%). Leading U.S. services exports were private educational, financial, business, and professional services (43% of services exports), travel (22%), royalties and fees (16%), and other transportation (10%). The main categories of U.S. merchandise imports in 2003 were consumer goods (27% of merchandise imports), industrial supplies (25%), capital goods (24%), and automotive and parts (17%). Key U.S. services imports included private services (31%), travel (23%), and transportation (18%).[4] The **balance of payments** (B/P), which records all transactions between people in one country and foreigners, is an even broader measure of inflows and outflows of money than the balance of trade. The balance of payments, for example, measures monetary inflows and outflows of money that result from international trade, foreign direct investments, foreign aid, and other sources.

The global trading system relies on the orderly functioning of the **foreign exchange market,** a highly integrated network of major financial institutions, such as commercial banks and investment banks, which convert and trade currencies. By providing a mechanism to convert one currency into an equivalent amount of a foreign currency, the largely unregulated foreign exchange market promotes trade between nations. In today's flexible exchange rate system, the value of a currency is determined mainly by the forces of supply and demand in the foreign exchange market. When the demand for a currency is high, the currency tends to gain value relative to other currencies. Conversely, when the demand for a currency falls, the currency tends to lose value against other currencies. The exchange rate states the value of one currency against other currencies at a moment in time. Table 11.2 shows the exchange rate between the U.S. dollar and the Mexican peso on February 23, 2004.[5] The column labeled "U.S. Equivalent" shows that the peso was worth about 9 cents compared to the U.S. dollar. Under "Currency per U.S. Dollar," the table shows that it would take 11 pesos to equal 1 U.S. dollar. At times, the government intervenes in the foreign exchange market to stabilize the value of a currency. This intervention has caused some economists to use the term *managed exchange rate system* to describe the government's impact on exchange rates. (The role of foreign exchange markets in currency trading is examined later in this chapter.)

Table 11.2
Exchange Rates: February 23, 2004

Country/currency	U.S. Equivalent	Currency per U.S. Dollar
Mexico/peso	.090400	11.0620

Source: The New York Times, February 24, 2004, C15.

Foreign Direct Investment

A second pillar of globalization is foreign direct investment. **Foreign direct investment** (FDI) is a cross-border investment that results in one company's gaining ownership or control of productive facilities in another country. Implied in this definition of FDI is that the relationship is long term in nature. The two types of FDI are mergers and acquisitions, and greenfield investments. Mergers and acquisitions (M&As) represent a legal joining of two existing companies under a single ownership. The great majority of all FDI occurs through M&As of companies. Greenfield investments occur when transnational corporations construct new production facilities, such as factories or plantations, in a foreign country. A **transnational corporation** (TNC), also called a multinational corporation, is composed of a parent company and its foreign affiliates, businesses in which the TNC has controlling interest. FDI grew rapidly during the 1990s and peaked at $1.3 trillion in 2000. A global slump during the early 2000s interrupted the FDI growth trend, as FDI inflows and outflows dropped by nearly half between 2000 and 2002. Still, in 2002 the foreign affiliates of TNCs accounted for nearly $18 trillion in sales and employed 53 million workers, as shown in Table 11.3. In that same year, the advanced economies received 71 percent of all FDI inflows, compared to 25 percent in the developing countries and just 4 percent in the transition countries.[6]

Foreign direct investment strengthens economic integration and interdependence in the global economy. In the early 2000s, the world's 65,000 TNCs operated about 850,000 foreign affiliates. Cementing the economic relationship between parent company and foreign affiliates were foreign assets worth $26.5 trillion and affiliates' output, which added $3.4 trillion to the global gross domestic product.[7] Ranked by foreign assets, the largest TNC in 2001 was Vodafone, as shown in Table 11.4.[8] In addition, new production strategies, such as production sharing, wove different businesses, peoples, and nations together in

Table 11.3
Selected Indicators of Transnationals: 1982–2002 (billions of dollars)

Indicator	Dollar Values at Current Prices			
	1982	1990	2000	2002
FDI inflows	$59	$203	$1,271	$651
FDI outflows	$28	$233	$1,150	$647
Sales of foreign affiliates	$2,541	$5,479	$15,680	$17,685
Total assets of foreign affiliates	$1,959	$5,759	$21,102	$26,543
Employment of foreign affiliates (in thousands)	17,987	23,858	45,587	53,094

Source: UNCTAD, *World Investment Report 2003*, 3; and *World Investment Report 2001* (Overview), 2.

Table 11.4
Largest Nonfinancial Transnational Corporations: 2001 (ranked by foreign

Rank	TNC	Home Country	Industry	Foreign Assets ($ billions)
1	Vodafone	United Kingdom	Telecommunications	$188
2	General Electric	United States	Electrical	$180
3	BP	United Kingdom	Petroleum	$111
4	Vivendi Universal	France	Diversified	$91
5	Deutsche TelekomAG	Germany	Telecommunications	$91

Source: UNCTAD, *World Investment Report 2003*, 187.

common cause. **Production sharing** occurs when a business produces a good in stages in a number of different locations around the world. Production sharing is motivated by a firm's desire to minimize production costs, and it is supported by the liberalization of trade and investment. Thousands of foreign-owned maquiladoras, duty-free assembly and manufacturing plants that are located in Mexico, illustrate production sharing in today's global economy. Finally, FDI transfers more than capital across national borders. It also stimulates cross-border technology transfers and introduces new management techniques and business practices into host countries.

The rapid expansion of FDI during the 1990s was fueled by new telecommunications technologies, changes in financial regulations, and trade and investment liberalization. Advanced telecommunications allowed TNCs to tap a broader pool of financial resources in global financial markets, funds that were used to fund M&As and greenfield investments. Many countries have relaxed rules and regulations governing banks and other financial institutions. These regulatory changes reduced restrictions on cross-border financial transactions, permitted mergers of banks with insurance and investment companies, and encouraged economies of scale through consolidation in the banking industry. The trend toward liberalization, which allowed the market to drive business activity, also stimulated FDI by increasing cross-border mobility of natural, human, and capital resources and the output produced by these resources. The General Agreement on Tariffs and Trade (1947–1994) and the World Trade Organization (1995–present) fostered trade liberalization. Since the 1980s, the proliferation of bilateral investment treaties has signaled liberalization in many nations' investment regimes. Bilateral investment treaties (BITS) are formal agreements between two countries designed mainly to promote mutually beneficial investment opportunities. Nearly 2,200 BITS were in effect by the close of 2002.[9]

In recent years the liberalization of trade and FDI has intensified public debate over outsourcing, also called offshoring. **Outsourcing** occurs when a firm in one country contracts with workers or other firms in another country, or builds production facilities in another country, to produce or provide a good or service. The practice of outsourcing is not a new phenomenon in the global economy. For decades companies in the United States, Japan, and other industrialized countries lowered their production costs by outsourcing certain manufacturing and assembly tasks to firms in low-wage developing countries. By the early 2000s the pace of outsourcing accelerated, however, dipping into high-tech industries such as information technologies, computer programming, and engineering. The potential loss of millions of U.S. jobs in these professions stoked debates over the long-term effects of outsourcing on the U.S. economy.

Cross-Border Financial Flows

The third pillar of globalization is the flow of financial capital across national borders. Economists have coined the term *financial globalization* to describe the integration of global financial markets. Financial globalization is encouraged by many of the same forces that stimulate foreign direct investment—sophisticated information and communications technologies (ICTs), supportive financial regulatory regimes, and the market-oriented liberalization of trade and investment. Combined, these forces instigated significant changes in the global financial system, changes that increased its size, complexity, and efficiency.

Changes in market participants, financial instruments, the exchange rate system, and investment strategies have influenced business activity in the global financial system. First, the rise of nonbank sources of financial capital created a more competitive financial environment. Leading nonbank financial institutions include securities firms, mutual funds, insurance companies, investment banks, pension funds, and other institutional investors. Second, new types of tradable securities entered the system. Expanded financial instruments, including a $1.4 trillion per day market in derivatives, offer new opportunities for profit in global financial markets. Third, the transition from a fixed exchange rate system to a flexible exchange rate system opened the door to currency trading. Today, a highly integrated foreign exchange market provides a mechanism for foreign exchange trading—the buying and selling of currencies by currency dealers for profit. In 2001 more than half of global turnover in foreign exchange, often called *forex* or *fx*, took place in just three countries—the United Kingdom (31.1% of foreign exchange turnover), the United States (15.7%), and Japan (9.1%). The Bank for International Settlements (BIS) reported that daily foreign exchange trading hit $1.2 trillion in 2001, a dip from peak daily trading of $1.5 trillion in 1998.[10] Fourth, the rise of highly speculative investment strategies threatened the stability of global finance. Sophisticated communications technologies, deregulated financial markets, and the absence of global investment rules enabled speculators to alter inflows and outflows of financial capital from countries at a moment's notice. The panic selling of securities in certain East Asian countries during the late 1990s brought several economies perilously close to financial meltdown.

The Shanghai Stock Exchange, located in the Pudong New Area, is one symbol of China's expanding role in the global economy. Changing China Fulbright-Hays Group Projects Abroad, 2002. Photograph by Ted Hartsoe.

MAJOR INSTITUTIONS OF THE GLOBAL ECONOMY

Over the past half-century, a number of transnational organizations have been founded to oversee global business activity and promote growth and stability in the global economy. These institutions have generally encouraged freer trade, FDI, cross-border financial flows, and other programs and policies to encourage participation in the global economy (see chapter 12 for more on sustainable economic development).

The Big Three Multilateral Organizations

The Big Three are the multilateral organizations mainly responsible for overseeing economic relations among countries: the World Trade Organization, the International Monetary Fund, and the World Bank Group. The **World Trade Organization** (WTO) is a multilateral organization designed to promote free and fair trade in the world economy. It was founded in 1994 by the Treaty of Marrakesh, one of the crowning achievements of the Uruguay Round—the eighth round of trade negotiations conducted under the General Agreement on Tariffs and Trade (GATT). The Treaty of Marrakesh signaled the end of GATT, which had guided global trade relations from 1947 to 1994. The WTO, which began operations in January 1995, inherited many of GATT's basic principles, including the reduction of trade barriers, such as tariffs and import quotas; equal treatment of foreign goods in domestic markets; and most-favored nation (MFN) status, which ensures that trade concessions granted to one WTO member apply to other WTO members. The WTO has more muscle than its GATT predecessor. The WTO, for example, has a number of dispute settlement bodies and the authority to impose retaliatory economic sanctions for noncompliance with its rulings. In 2003, for example, the WTO authorized the European Union (EU) to enact trade sanctions on the United States in retaliation against federal tax breaks supplied to U.S. exporters. EU sanctions, which included tariffs on U.S. agricultural products, textiles, information technologies, and other goods, took effect in March 2004. From 1995 to mid-2003, 299 trade disputes were brought to the WTO by member nations, with a mixed record of success in dispute resolution. WTO membership in 2003 stood at 146 nations.

The **International Monetary Fund** (IMF) is a multilateral organization designed to stabilize the international monetary system. The IMF was founded at the 1944 Bretton Woods (New Hampshire) Conference. In December 1945 delegates from 29 countries signed the IMF's charter, and by spring of the following year the IMF began operations as a specialized agency within the United Nations system. By 2003 IMF membership had grown to 182 countries, each of which was obliged to contribute to IMF coffers through quota subscriptions, or quotas. Since 1946, 5 countries have contributed about 40 percent of all quotas: the United States (17.6%), Japan (6.5%), Germany (6.2%), France (5.1%), and the United Kingdom (5.1%). By 2003 the IMF's total quotas topped $290 billion.[11] The cash reserves generated through quota subscriptions finance the IMF's stabilization functions, which include surveillance, technical assistance, and financial assistance. Surveillance involves active monitoring of and consultation with member countries to encourage sound domestic policies. Technical assistance provides the financial know-how to create and maintain effective economic institutions, such as a central bank and a treasury, and policies related to taxation, accounting practices, and so on. Financial assistance consists of short-term loans, called credits, which are extended for terms of six mouths to four years. Financial assistance helps countries stabilize currencies, honor foreign debt obligations, pay for imports, or increase foreign reserves. The IMF does not extend loans for major development projects, however. The IMF's credits are granted in Special Drawing Right (SDR), which serves as the organization's unit of accounting. Since the 1940s, the largest IMF borrowers have been Mexico, South Korea, Russia, Brazil, and Argentina. In 2002 alone, the IMF's commitments topped SDR 39 billion ($50 billion), much of which was destined for economic restructuring in Argentina, Brazil, and Turkey. Total outstanding credit for all IMF borrowers in 2003 was SDR 76 billion ($104 billion).[12]

The **World Bank Group** is a multilateral development organization. Like the IMF, it was founded at the Bretton Woods Conference in 1944 and began operations in 1946 as a specialized agency within the United Nations system. In its early years, the World Bank consisted of a single organization, the International Bank for Reconstruction and Development (IBRD). IBRD's initial goal was to help rebuild war-torn Europe, a continent ravaged by World War II. Over time, the World Bank's composition and mission expanded. Today, the World Bank Group consists of five mutually supporting development institutions. Its financial resources come from the sale of securities in global financial markets, interest payments on past loans, and contributions from donor countries. Today, the overarching goal of the 184-member World Bank Group is the reduction of global poverty.

IBRD and its closest partner, the International Development Association (IDA), supply most of the World Bank Group's development assistance. IBRD extends 15- to 20-year low-interest development loans to the more creditworthy, higher-income developing countries. Development loans build schools, health facilities, and other infrastructure projects. Loans also target disease prevention and environmental protection. In 2002 IBRD granted $11.5 billion to support 96 projects in 40 countries. The International Development Association (IDA) was founded in 1960 to extend 35- to 40-year interest-free loans to low-income developing countries. In 2002 the IDA supplied $8 billion to finance 133 projects in 62 low-income developing countries. The International Finance Corporation (IFC) was founded in 1956 to encourage private-sector investment. Thus, IFC financial and technical assistance is granted to private firms rather than to governments. The International Center for Settlement of Investment Disputes (ICSID) was created in 1966 to help reconcile disputes between foreign investors and host governments. Since the 1960s, the dispute resolution mechanisms of ICSID have promoted FDI and have influenced numerous investment laws and BITs. Finally, the Multilateral Investment Guarantee Agency (MIGA) was established in 1988 to promote FDI in the developing world. MIGA provides investment insurance to protect investments against nonfinancial losses that might result from government expropriations of property, civil war, or other changes in the business environment. By the early 2000s, MIGA insured more than 500 projects in 78 developing countries.[13]

Regional Economic Integration: The Rise of Regional Trade Agreements

Over the past 50 years, the rise of regional trade agreements (RTAs) has promoted regional economic integration. In many cases, RTAs form a trade bloc—a formal association of countries designed to promote cooperation on trade and other economic issues. Membership in a trade bloc is often limited to countries located in a world region, such as Europe, North America, or Southeast Asia. The World Trade Organization (WTO) identified 159 RTAs in the world economy by the early 2000s and estimated that intraregional trade among bloc members accounted for 43 percent of the world's total merchandise trade.[14] The expansion of RTAs in the global economy has stirred some controversy, since these agreements extend certain trade and investment preferences just to member countries. Yet, the WTO's Article 24 has given the green light to RTAs so long as they do not impose additional trade restrictions on nonmembers. There are several ways to categorize RTAs. One broad distinction divides RTAs into two camps, free trade areas and customs unions.

A **free trade area** is a trade bloc that eliminates trade barriers among members, but permits individual members to devise their own restrictions on imports from nonmembers. Many regional trade blocs are organized as free trade areas, including the North American Free Trade Agreement (NAFTA), the Common Market of the South (MERCOSUR), the Association of Southeast Asian Nations (ASEAN), and the Economic Community of West African States (ECOWAS). Steps toward creating a U.S.-Central American Free Trade Agreement (CAFTA) and an even more expansive Free Trade Area of the Americas (FTAA) among the 34 democracies of the Western Hemisphere were also underway during the early 2000s. Ranked by total national output, NAFTA, which is made up of Canada, Mexico, and the United States, is the world's largest RTA.[15] Article 102 of the NAFTA agreement states its main objectives: to "(a) eliminate barriers to trade in, and facilitate the cross-border movement of, goods and services between the territories of the Parties; (b) promote conditions of fair competition . . . ; (c) increase substantially investment opportunities."[16] The implementation of NAFTA on January 1, 1994, paved the way for the removal of trade barriers between the United States and Canada by 1998 and for the phase-out of trade barriers between the United States and Mexico by 2008. Under NAFTA, trade among the three member nations grew significantly. In 2003 the United States conducted more total trade with Canada ($394 billion) and Mexico ($236 billion) than with any other country.[17] Total trade measures the dollar value of all U.S. imports to and exports from its NAFTA partners. Despite the growth in trade, NAFTA remained controversial, with disputes arising over issues related to job security in the United States and people's quality of life in Mexico.

A **customs union** creates a free trade zone for members and establishes uniform trade policies and barriers on imports from nonmember countries. Over time, the European Union (EU) evolved from a free trade area to a customs union—and more. In 2001 the European Union recorded $1.4 trillion in intra-RTA merchandise exports, the largest of any regional trade agreement in the world.[18] The European Union is defined as "a unique, treaty-based, institutional framework that defines and manages economic and political cooperation among its fifteen European member countries."[19] The EU's roots can be traced back to founding of the European Coal and Steel Community in 1951. The Maastricht Treaty on European Union (1993) established the present EU. This and later treaties created the institutions and practices needed to integrate members' economic, political, and social policies. For instance, economic integration among member nations focused on creating a single market by forming common policies in the realms of foreign trade, agriculture, transportation, labor mobility, research and technology, regional development, foreign aid, energy, and the environment. The crowning achievement of European integration was the adoption of a single currency, the euro. The euro, which was phased in over a three-year period, replaced the national currencies of 12 EU countries in January 2002. These countries, which comprise the European

Monetary Union (EMU) or euro zone, are Austria, Belgium, Finland, France, Germany, Greece, Italy, the Republic of Ireland, Luxembourg, the Netherlands, Portugal, and Spain. The 3 EU countries that retained their own currencies were Denmark, Sweden, and the United Kingdom. In 2002 the EU also approved its fifth enlargement by recommending admission of 10 candidate countries: Cyprus, the Czech Republic, Estonia, Hungary, Latvia, Lithuania, Malta, Poland, the Slovak Republic, and Slovenia. These countries officially joined the EU on May 1, 2004, increasing the number of member nations from 15 to 25 and advancing the EU's goal of European integration.

CHALLENGES TO GLOBALIZATION

The race toward economic globalization has been supported by new technologies, the liberalization of trade and investment, and a variety of profit incentives for businesses to conduct cross-border transactions. Yet an undercurrent of uncertainty about the functioning and direction of the globalization juggernaut, and visible glitches in the global economy, have rallied opposition to globalization.

Globalization: Grassroots Discontent

Much of the opposition to globalization comes from grassroots organizations, including nongovernmental organizations and civil society organi-

Euro denomination notes are 5, 10, 20, 50, 100, 200, and 500 euro; Euro coins are 1, 2, 5, 10, 20, 50 euro cents, and 1 and 2 euro coins/European Commission Delegation, Washington, D.C.

zations. **Nongovernmental organizations** (NGOs) are special interest groups that research issues, share information, and pressure governments, multilateral organizations, and TNCs to reform policies or practices. For example, Amnesty International advocates for human rights, Jubilee 2000 for foreign debt forgiveness, and Greenpeace for environmental protection. The United Nations estimated that 37,000 international NGOs operated in the global economy by 2000. In *Global Civil Society Yearbook 2002,* the Center for Civil Society and Center for the Study of Global Governance put the number of NGOs at 55,000, however.[20]

Civil society organizations (CSOs) include NGOs and other nonprofit groups that seek to improve the human condition. Examples of CSOs include community organizations, foundations, student organizations, trade unions, and other stakeholders that constitute civil society. In recent years, NGOs and CSOs have become powerful voices in global decision making. Multilateral organizations such as the WTO, United Nations, and World Bank have solicited their participation. Civil society organizations have also staged mass events. In 1999 CSOs disrupted the WTO's Ministerial Conference in Seattle, Washington, the unofficial kick-off to the WTO's Millennium Round of trade negotiations. Similar protests interrupted meetings of the World Bank, IMF, World Economic Forum, and other organizations. In 2003 Porto Alegre, Brazil, hosted the third World Social Forum, the largest civil society gathering in history. This forum attracted 100,000 participants from 156 countries to discuss poverty, environmental degradation, human rights, and other issues of global concern. In 2004 the fourth World Social Forum drew a similar following to Mumbai, India.[21]

Other Challenges to the Globalization Juggernaut

Some experts view the march toward globalization as inexorable, while others see a road pitted with potholes. One major challenge to globalization is financial contagion. **Financial contagion** refers to the uncontrollable spread of a financial crisis from one country to other countries or regions. At the heart of financial contagion are highly interdependent financial markets and the ability to transfer financial resources across national borders with lightning speed via ICTs. During the 1990s, financial contagions emanating from Brazil, Russia, and Thailand spread financial chaos in South America, eastern and central Europe, and East Asia, respectively. The East Asian financial crisis of 1997–1998 had the most widespread global consequences, rippling from its epicenter in Thailand to the doorsteps of New York City, Tokyo, and London. Most experts blame the speculative exuberance of foreign investors who, during the early and mid-1990s, bid up prices for Thai assets such as stocks, real estate, and businesses. Speculative booms inevitably peak, however, and as the panic selling of assets commences, the value of securities and other assets collapses. The economic meltdown in Thailand fueled investor panic throughout East Asia. Speculators rushed to sell off assets in other East Asian countries, a process often referred to as herd behavior. This herd behavior caused similar chaos in

Malaysia, Indonesia, and South Korea. Soon the profitable East Asian export markets soured, causing hardships for American, Japanese, and other exporters. The International Monetary Fund, Asian Development Bank, World Bank, and United States finally extended an aid package totaling $125 billion to stabilize the region. While this economic bailout succeeded in stopping the domino-like collapse of economies, it was clear that weaknesses existed in the global financial architecture. Since the late 1990s, governments, international organizations, NGOs, and other participants in the global economy have studied ways to strengthen the global financial system.

A second challenge is the perceived exploitation of human and natural resources by TNCs, often referred to as the race to the bottom. Some CSOs and NGOs argue that irresponsible TNC behaviors result in the mistreatment of overseas workers, the destruction of ecosystems, and disrespect for local cultures. During the 1990s, for example, Nike subcontractors created sweatshops in Asia to produce popular Nike athletic wear. To pressure Nike to reform its business practices, CSOs and NGOs initiated a global consumer boycott of Nike products. In recent years, most TNCs have adopted corporate codes of conduct. These voluntary codes list the rights of workers to safe and fair workplaces and decent pay. Outside organizations have also drafted standards, called codes of conduct for multinationals, to promote corporate social responsibility. The International Labor Organization's Declaration on Fundamental Principles and Rights at Work and the Reverend Leon H. Sullivan's Global Sullivan Principles of Corporate Social Responsibility emphasize workers' rights to free association, equal opportunities, workplace safety, and respect. On an even broader level, the United Nations' Global Compact identifies nine core principles aimed at protecting human rights, workers' rights, and the environment.

A third challenge to globalization is protectionism. **Protectionism** is the government's use of trade barriers, such as tariffs and import quotas, to restrict foreign imports. Protectionists argue that import restrictions are often necessary to protect domestic jobs, infant industries, and defense-sensitive industries. Protectionists also believe that trade barriers are a justifiable response to unfair foreign trade practices such as dumping. Dumping occurs when a good is sold in a foreign market at a price lower than its production costs. In recent years, the United States has retaliated against dumping by slapping tariffs on foreign imports that range from Russian steel to Vietnamese catfish. Over the past two decades, the new trade theory suggested that the judicious use of trade barriers could benefit economies (see the biography of Paul R. Krugman for more on the new trade theory). Free traders criticize the use of trade barriers, however, fearing trade wars and economic paralysis. The U.S. Smoot-Hawley Tariff of 1930 illustrated how protectionist policies could spark a global trade war and retard global economic growth.

A fourth challenge to globalization stems from an attitudinal preference favoring the local over the global. Notable in this regard are two movements, one flying under the banner of the new protectionism and the other under relocalization. The **new protectionism** demands greater government restrictions on and control over foreign trade and FDI. Supporters of the new protectionism argue that globalization favors rich and powerful TNCs over indigenous peoples, whose local cultures and lifestyles are endangered by foreign economic interests. Relocalization seeks to make local economies more self-sufficient, relying on local factors of production to meet local production needs. The new protectionism and relocalization favor economic diversification over specialization and seek to minimize the role of foreign trade, FDI, and other foreign intervention in local business activity.

A final challenge to globalization is anticompetitive behaviors by business firms and national governments. For example, producer cartels restrict competition and disrupt the orderly flow of goods or services in certain markets. A **cartel** is an agreement or organization that coordinates the production decisions of independent producers of similar or identical products to influence the product's supply and price. The world's most powerful producer cartel is the Organization of Petroleum Exporting Countries (OPEC), which sets quotas on the production of oil for each of its 11 member nations: Algeria, Indonesia, Iran, Iraq, Kuwait, Libya, Nigeria, Qatar, Saudi Arabia, the United Arab Emirates, and Venezuela. Cuts in OPEC production quotas in April 2004 contributed to spiraling world oil prices, which topped $41 per barrel by May of that year. Over the past few decades other cartels have imposed production quotas to raise product prices, including the Association of Coffee Producing Countries, De Beers (diamonds), the International Bauxite Organization, the International Copper Council, the International Rubber Agreement, and the International Tin Council. By influencing the supply of essential products, cartels wield above-normal market power—power that can be used to stabilize or disrupt business activity and global economic development.

BIOGRAPHIES: SHAPERS OF ECONOMIC THOUGHT

David Ricardo: The Theory of Comparative Advantage

David Ricardo (1772–1823) was a leading British economist, a staunch supporter of free trade, and a chief architect of the classical school of economics. Ricardo was born to a prominent family, the third of 17 children. His scant formal education was complemented by extensive experience in the world of finance. He worked for his father at the London Stock Exchange and, after a family disagreement, established his own securities firm. Ricardo's financial insights made him fabulously wealthy, allowing him to retire to a country estate at the age of 41. In retirement, Ricardo wrote extensively on controversial economic issues and, as a member of the British Parliament, pressed for free trade policies. These themes were featured in Ricardo's most famous book, *Principles of Political Economy and Taxation* (1817).

In *Principles of Political Economy,* Ricardo introduced the theory of comparative advantage, an economic theory that guided free trade policies for nearly two centuries. The theory of **comparative advantage** stated that nations should specialize in the production of goods that they can produce more efficiently than can other nations, and then exchange their surpluses. Ricardo illustrated the theory of comparative advantage with the wine and bread trade between Portugal and England. Ricardo demonstrated that, even if Portugal had an absolute advantage in the production of both wine and bread, it was in both countries' best interest to specialize in the product in which it enjoyed its greatest advantage, or least disadvantage. **Absolute advantage** occurs when one country produces a product more efficiently than a second country. Specialization, Ricardo argued, would increase efficiency in both countries, expand total output, and improve prospects for prosperity. Ricardo's theory of comparative advantage had major implications for England's trade policy. Through his writings and his influence in Parliament, Ricardo pushed for the abolition of England's protectionist trade policies and the creation of a trade system built on free trade.

Ricardo's influence on British trade policy and on the rise of laissez-faire economics is difficult to overstate. For instance, his steadfast opposition to England's Corn Laws, which severely restricted the import of low-priced grains, helped in their eventual repeal in 1846. The repeal of the Corn Laws not only encouraged Britain to shift resources to more profitable enterprises in manufacturing and commerce, but also stimulated production of raw materials and semi-finished goods in foreign mines, plantations, and other businesses. Over the next hundred years, Great Britain became the hub of global economy. Today, Ricardo's theory of comparative advantage is an honored economic principle and the heart of arguments favoring free trade.

Paul Krugman: The New Trade Theory

Paul R. Krugman (1953–) is an influential American economist, professor of international economics, and prolific writer in the field of trade policy. Krugman was born in Long Island, New York, the only son of a middle-class family. He earned his bachelor's degree in economics from Yale University in 1974 and his doctorate from MIT in 1977. Krugman's first teaching position as a professional economist was at Yale, where the idea of the new trade theory began to crystallize. Krugman also taught at MIT, Stanford, and most recently at Princeton. Of the 20 books he authored or co-authored, none made a bigger splash than *Market Structure and Foreign Trade: Increasing Returns, Imperfect Competition, and the International Economy* (1985) and *Trade Policy and Market Structure* (1989), each co-authored with Elhanan Helpman.

In *Market Structure and Foreign Trade*, Krugman and Helpman developed the new trade theory, which complements rather than replaces Ricardo's time-honored theory of comparative advantage. At the heart of the new trade theory are two insights. First, the theory postulates that economies of scale, in conjunction with nations' endowments of productive resources, stimulate specialization and trade. **Economies of scale** refers to the benefits of larger-scale enterprise. The most important benefit of the economies of scale is the progressively lower average cost of producing additional units of output by large firms. Krugman and Helpman state: "Economies of scale provide an additional incentive and will give rise to trade even if countries are identical in tastes, technologies, and factor endowments."[22] Thus, even when there is no appreciable comparative advantage in the production of a good, there is still a reason for trade to take place. Second, the new trade theory accounts for the reality of different market structures operating in the global economy. Krugman and Helpman recognized the importance of imperfectly competitive industries, including monopolistic competition and oligopoly, in the global arena. Imperfectly competitive industries, by definition, have some degree of market power due to product differentiation and other barriers to entry. This reality distinguishes the new trade theory from traditional theories built around a single market structure, perfect competition.

In *Trade Policy and Market Structure* (1989), Krugman and Helpman identify policy implications for the new trade theory. First, given the realities of the global marketplace there may be instances in which "mild protectionism can—if it is not retaliated against—raise national welfare."[23] Mild protectionism might include temporary subsidies or tariffs to support selected industries. Second, the authors' research generally supports free trade as the basis of international exchanges in the global economy. In fact, Krugman and Helpman warn people to be on guard lest the new trade theory be inappropriately used to "support highly dubious political causes" or "crude protectionism."[24] Since the 1980s, Krugman's interests have extended into other areas of public policy. In his books and in columns for major publications such as *Fortune, Slate,* and *The New York Times,* Krugman plies his trade with vigor, offering viewpoints on a wide variety of topics.

Jeffrey D. Sachs: The Challenge of Economic Integration

Jeffrey D. Sachs (1954–) is a leading American economist, author, and consultant in the field of international economics and trade. Sachs was born in Detroit, Michigan, the son of a prominent lawyer. In his youth, Sachs traveled with his parents to different countries. These trips sparked his interest in alternative economic and political systems. Sachs pursued these interests at Harvard University, where he earned a bachelor's degree (1976), master's degree (1978), and doctorate (1980). Sachs joined the Harvard faculty in 1980, where he remained until the summer of 2002. While at Harvard, Sachs became one of the most recognized and influential economists in the world. As a prolific writer and consultant, he influenced economic policies in countries in Latin America, eastern and central Europe, Asia, and Africa. Sachs was Harvard's first director of the Center for International Development (CID), a position he held from 1998 to 2002. Since July 2002, Sachs has served as an economics professor and as director of the Earth Institute at Columbia University.

Sachs is best known for his shock therapy prescription for growth and stability in Poland, Russia, and other transition economies in eastern and central Europe during the late 1980s and 1990s. Shock therapy relied on aggressive economic policies designed to replace government controls with market incentives as the surest way to promote business activity. Sachs advised transition governments to privatize businesses, end most government controls on wages and prices, protect competitive markets, and expand global connections. Entry into the global economy, Sachs argued, would allow transition countries to rejoin Europe and share in the prosperity derived from foreign trade and foreign direct investment (FDI). In addition, foreign trade and FDI would help create a realistic price structure for goods and services, thus speeding the shift of productive resources into profitable ventures. Sachs's book, *Poland's Leap to the Market Economy* (1993), examines the implementation of shock therapy in eastern Europe (see chapter 4 for more on transition economies).

In recent years much of Sachs's work has focused on sustainable economic development in the poorer world regions. While director of the CID at Harvard, Sachs worked with development issues related to disease prevention, overpopulation, environmental stresses, biodiversity, international poverty, and other topics of global concern. In 2002 UN Secretary General Kofi Annan appointed Sachs as his special adviser on the UN Millennium Development Goals, a series of eight poverty reduction initiatives devised under the auspices of the United Nations and supported by many international organizations, including the World Bank, International Monetary Fund (IMF), and Organization for Economic Cooperation and Development (OECD). Since July 2002, Sachs's work as an economics professor and director of the Columbia University Earth Institute has enabled him to explore global problems related to economic growth, human health, and the environment.

Jagdish Bhagwati: The Benefits of Globalization

Jagdish Bhagwati (1934–), a prominent Indian-born economist, is one of the world's most powerful supporters of globalization. Bhagwati was born and raised in India, but earned his advanced academic degrees at Western universities, including Cambridge, MIT, and Oxford. After teaching economics at the Indian Statistical Institute and the Delhi School of Economics for much of the 1960s, Bhagwati accepted teaching positions in the United States, first at MIT (1968–1980) and then at Columbia (1980–2001). Bhagwati has written hundreds of scholarly articles and about 40 books, the most recent of which are *The Wind of the Hundred Days: How Washington Mismanaged Globalization* (2001) and *Free Trade Today* (2002).

Bhagwati's central message is that the benefits of globalization outweigh its costs. In Bhagwati's view, there are five interrelated components of globalization: the liberalization of international trade, foreign direct investment, cross-border financial flows, technology transfers, and immigration. In *Free Trade Today,* Bhagwati identified five benefits of trade: its positive impact on the economies of scale, consumer choice, productivity, technology sharing, and productive investment.[25] Bhagwati was also attentive to the question of how to promote free trade. He opposed aggressive unilateralism, which bullies other countries into reducing their trade barriers. He also opposed the use of preferential trade agreements (PTAs), such as regional and bilateral trade agreements, which discriminate against nonmembers. Instead, Bhagwati favored conventional unilateralism, whereby countries reduce their own trade barriers. He also favored multilateral trade negotiations (MTN), such as WTO talks, which guarantee equal benefits under the most-favored nation principle. Bhagwati summarized his views more colorfully by arguing "that both conventional unilateralism and MTN reciprocity have a useful role to play in freeing trade, whereas both aggressive unilateralism and PTAs are a pox on the world trading system."[26]

Bhagwati's widely respected views have influenced policies of governments and multilateral organizations and have shaped public opinion. His work has encouraged free trade, competitive markets, and other market-driven reforms in his native India and other countries. The General Agreement on Tariffs and Trade (GATT), United Nations, and World Trade Organization (WTO) have also solicited Bhagwati's advice on matters of global concern. Bhagwati's articles, which appear regularly in leading newspapers such as *The Financial Times, The New York Times,* and the *Wall Street Journal,* have spread the gospel of globalization to millions of readers. He has also sought to expand the voices of traditionally marginalized peoples by supporting NGO participation in global decision making.

NOTES

1. World Trade Organization (WTO), "Appendix Table 1A.1. Leading Exporters and Importers in World Merchandise Trade, 2002" and "Appendix Table 1A.3. Leading Exporters and Importers in World Trade in Commercial Services, 2002," *World Trade Report 2003* (Geneva, Switzerland: WTO, 2003), 68, 70; and International Monetary Fund (IMF), "Table 22. Summary of World Trade Volumes and Prices," *World Economic Outlook, April 2003* (Washington, DC: The Fund, 2003), 199–200.
2. WTO, "Table 1A.1" and "Table 1A.3,"; and "Table 1.8. Share of Goods and Commercial Services in the Total Trade of Selected Regions and Economies, 2001," *International Trade Statistics 2002,* 25, 27–28.
3. U.S. Census Bureau, Foreign Trade Division, "U.S. Total Trade Balance in Goods and Services (exhibit 1)," www.census.gov/foreign-trade/statistics/historical/gandsbal.pdf; and U.S. Census Bureau, "Annual Trade Highlights: 2003 Highlights," www.census.gov/foreign-trade/statistics/highlights/3/annual.html.
4. U.S. Census Bureau and U.S. Department of Commerce, "Exhibit 1. U.S. International Trade in Goods and Services," "Exhibit 3. U.S. Services by Major Category—Exports," "Exhibit 4. U.S. Services by Major Category—Imports," "Exhibit 6. Exports and Imports of Goods by Principle End-Use Category," (FT 900—U.S. International Trade in Goods and Services December 2003), February 13, 2004, 4, 6–7, 9; and U.S. Census Bureau and U.S. Department of Commerce, "Top Ten Countries with Which the U.S. Has a Trade Deficit," *Foreign Trade Statistics,* www.census.gov/foreign-trade/top/dst/2003/12/deficit.html.
5. "Foreign Exchange," *The New York Times,* February 24, 2004, C15.
6. United Nations Conference on Trade and Development (UNCTAD), "Table 1.1. Selected Indicators of FDI and International Production, 1982–2002" and "Table 1.2. FDI Inflows to Major Economies, 2001 and 2002," *World Investment Report 2003: FDI*

Policies for Development: National and International Perspectives (New York: United Nations, 2003), 3, 7; and UNCTAD, "Table 1. Selected Indicators of FDI and International Production, 1982–2000," *World Investment Report 2001,* Overview (New York: United Nations, 2001), 2.

7. UNCTAD, "Table 1.1," 3.

8. UNCTAD, "Annex Table A.1.1. The World's Top 100 Non-financial TNCs, Ranked by Foreign Assets, 2001," *World Investment Report 2003,* 187.

9. UNCTAD, *World Investment Report 2003,* 21.

10. Bank for International Settlements (BIS), *Triennial Central Bank Survey: Foreign Exchange and Derivatives Market Activity in 2001* (Basel, Switzerland: Author, 2002), 1, 5, 12.

11. International Monetary Fund (IMF), "What Is the International Monetary Fund?" August 2002, www.imf.org/external/pubs/ft/exrp/what.htm; IMF, "IMF's Financial Resources and Liquidity Position, 2001—April 2003," www.imf.org/external/np/tre/liquid/2003/0403.htm.

12. IMF, *Annual Report 2002* (Washington, DC, 2002), 57–8; IMF, "What Is the International Monetary Fund?"; and IMF, "Total IMF Credit Outstanding for All Members from 1984–2003," www.imf.org/external/np/tre/tad/extcred1.cfm.

13. World Bank Group, "What Is the World Bank? http://web.worldbank.org/WBSITE/EXTERNAL/EXTAABOUTUS/0,,CONTENTmdk:200405; World Bank Group, "International Development Association," http://web.worldbank.org/WBSITE/EXTERNAL/EXTABOUTUS/IDA/0,,pagePK:118644; International Finance Corporation (IFC), "About the IFC," http://ifcln.ifc.org/ifcext/about.nsf; World Bank Group, "About ICSID," http://www.worldbank.org/icsid/about/main.htm; Multilateral Investment Guarantee Agency (MIGA), "About MIGA," http://www.miga.org/screens/about/about.htm.

14. WTO, *International Trade Statistics 2002,* 8.

15. Delegation of the European Commission to the United States, "Facts and Figures on the European Union and the United States, Basic Statistics 2001," www. eurunion.org/legislat/agd2000/agd2000.htm.

16. Office of NAFTA and Inter-American Affairs/International Trade Administration (ITA), "NAFTA Treaty, Article 102: Objectives," www.mac.doc.gov/nafta/chapter1.htm.

17. U.S. Census Bureau and U.S. Department of Commerce, "Top Ten Countries with Which the U.S. Trades," *Foreign Trade Statistics,* www.census.gov/foreign-trade/top/dst/2003/12/balance.html.

18. WTO, *International Trade Statistics 2002,* 8.

19. Delegation of the European Commission, *The European Union: A Guide for Americans* (Washington, DC: Delegation of the European Commission, 2002), 3.

20. United Nations General Assembly, "Strengthening of the United Nations: An Agenda for Further Change," Document A/57/387, September 9, 2002, 23, www.globalpolicy.org/ngos/int/un/access/2002/1109strengthen.htm; and Marlies Glasius, Mary Kaldor, and Helmut Anheier, eds., *Global Civil Society Yearbook 2002* (Oxford, UK: Oxford University Press, 2002), 336–38.

21. Marlies Glasius, Mary Kaldor, and Helmut Anheier, eds., "Table 1.4: List of World, Regional, and Thematic Social Forums as of May 2003," *Global Civil Society Yearbook 2003,* 22.

22. Elhanan Helpman and Paul R. Krugman, *Market Structure and Foreign Trade: Increasing Returns, Imperfect Competition, and the International Economy* (Cambridge, MA: MIT Press, 1985), 261.

23. Elhanan Helpman and Paul R. Krugman, *Trade Policy and Market Structure* (Cambridge, MA: MIT Press, 1989), 178.

24. Ibid., 8.

25. Jagdish Bhagwati, *Free Trade Today* (Princeton: Princeton University Press, 2002), 35–6.

26. Ibid., 95.

SELECTED READINGS

Bannock, Graham, and William Manser. *International Dictionary of Finance.* 4th ed. London: Economist Books, 2003.

Bhagwati, Jagdish. *Free Trade Today.* Princeton, NJ: Princeton University Press, 2002.

Bird, Graham. *International Financial Institutions and the World Economy.* Northampton, MA: Edward Elgar Pub, 2004.

Cavanaugh, John, et al. *Alternatives to Economic Globalization.* San Francisco: Berrett-Koehler Pubs, 2002.

Center for Civil Society and the Center for the Study of Global Governance. *Global Civil Society Yearbook 2002.* New York: Oxford University Press, 2003.

Desai, Padma. *Financial Crisis, Contagion, and Containment: From Asia to Argentina.* Princeton, NJ: Princeton University Press, 2003.

Dimand, Robert W., ed. *The Origins of International Economics.* New York: Routledge, 2004.

Eckes, Alfred E., Jr., Richard L. Brinkman, and William Anthony Lovett. *US Trade Policy: History, Theory, and the WTO.* 2nd ed. Armonk, NY: M. E. Sharpe, 2004.

Europa Publications. *A Chronology of International Organizations.* London: Europa Publications, 2003.

Friedman, Thomas L. *The Lexus and the Olive Tree: Understanding Globalization.* New York: Anchor Books, 2000.

Gilpin, Robert. *The Challenge of Global Capitalism: The World Economy in the 21st Century.* Princeton, NJ: Princeton University Press, 2002.

Gotthelf, Philip. *Currency Trading: How to Access and Trade the World Biggest Market.* New York: John Wiley & Sons, 2002.

Hakim, Peter, Robert E. Litan, and Strobe Talbott. *The Future of North America Integration: beyond NAFTA.* Washington, DC: Brookings Institution Press, 2002.

Helpman, Elhanan, and Paul R. Krugman. *Market Structure and Foreign Trade: Increasing Returns, Imperfect Competition, and the International Economy.* Cambridge, MA: The MIT Press, 1985.

Hoekman, Bernard M., Aaditya Mattoo, and Philip English, eds. *Development, Trade, and the WTO: A Handbook.* Washington, DC: World Bank, 2002.

Lang, Tim, and Colin Hines. *The New Protectionism: Protecting the Future against Free Trade.* New York: New Press, 1993.

Northrup, Cynthia Clark, ed. *World Trade: From Ancient Times to the Present.* Armonk, NY: M. E. Sharpe, 2004.

Obstfeld, Maurice, and Alan M. Taylor. *Global Capital Markets: Integration, Crisis, and Growth.* New York: Cambridge University Press, 2003.

O'Connor, David E. *Demystifying the Global Economy: A Guide for Students.* Westport, CT: Greenwood Publishing Group, 2002.

Ricardo, David. *Principles of Political Economy and Taxation.* Amherst, NY: Prometheus Books, 1996.

Robertson, Robbie. *The Three Waves of Globalization: A History of a Developing Global Consciousness.* New York: Zed Books, 2003.
Sachs, Jeffrey D., and Felipe B. Larrain. *Macroeconomics in the Global Economy.* Old Tappan, NJ: Prentice Hall, 1993.
Stiglitz, Joseph E. *Globalization and Its Discontents.* New York: W.W. Norton & Company, 2003.
United Nations Conference on Trade and Development (UNCTAD). *World Investment Report 2003: FDI Policies for Development: National and International Perspectives.* New York: United Nations Publications, 2003.
World Economic Forum, Peter Cornelius, and Klaus Schwab, eds. *The Global Competitiveness Report 2002–2003.* New York: Oxford University Press, 2003.

CHAPTER 12

The Challenge of Sustainable Economic Development

Chapter 12 explores the prospects for sustainable economic development in the developing world. There are several ways to classify the development status of the world's economies. One common classification divides the world's 208 economies by per capita income, identifying low-income, middle-income, and high-income countries. A similar classification distinguishes advanced countries from developing and transition countries. The vast majority of the world's population lives in low-income or middle-income developing countries. While developing countries have unique histories and cultures, most share some common characteristics that affect their prospects for sustainable economic development. The most important development goal for poorer countries is to transform the vicious cycle of poverty into a virtuous cycle of development. Key to achieving this goal is the efficient use of society's resources, the creation of a pro-growth business environment, and support from external sources.

DEVELOPING COUNTRIES: COMMON CHARACTERISTICS

Developing countries are mainly the world's poorer nations, whose services-producing, goods-producing, and agricultural sectors are underdeveloped. They are often called the global south, largely to acknowledge concentrations of poorer nations in the Southern Hemisphere.

Classifications of the World's Economies

The World Bank and many other international institutions classify countries by their gross national income per capita. **Gross national income** (GNI) measures the nation's total income by adding the value of household spending on consumption goods, business spending on capital goods, and government spending, in a given year. The GNI per capita states people's average annual income by dividing the GNI by the country's population. The World Bank introduced the GNI per capita in 2000. It replaced the gross national product (GNP) per capita as the preferred method of comparing nations' relative well-being.

The World Bank classification identifies four categories of countries: low-income, lower-middle-income, upper-middle-income, and high-income countries, as shown in Table 12.1.[1] The low-income and middle-income countries are generally called developing countries or developing economies. The World Bank emphasizes that the term *developing economies* is a term of convenience, and "it is not intended to imply that all economies in the group are experiencing similar development or that other economies have reached a preferred or final stage of development. Classification by income does not necessarily reflect development status."[2] In fact, a number of high-income countries, such as Monaco, Kuwait, and Bahrain, are not considered advanced economies due to the inadequate size or sophistication of their services-producing, goods-producing, and agricultural sectors. In 2002 representative low-income countries included the Democratic Republic of Congo (annual GNI per capita of $100), Sierra Leone ($140), Cambodia ($300), Bangladesh ($380), Haiti ($440), and India ($470). Lower-middle-income countries include the Ukraine ($780), China ($960), Egypt ($1,470), Thailand ($2,000), Russia ($2,130), and Brazil ($2,830). Upper-middle-income countries include Botswana ($3,010), Malaysia ($3,540), Argentina ($4,220), Poland ($4,570), Mexico ($5,920), and Saudi Ara-

Table 12.1
Classification of the World's Economies: 2003 (measured in $US)*

Country Classification	GNI per Capita	Average GNI per Capita (Exchange Rate Method)	Percentage of the World's Economies	Average GNI per Capita (PPP Method)
Low income	$735 or less	$430	31%	$2,040
Lower middle income	$736–$2,935	$1,390	26%	$5,130
Upper middle income	$2,936–$9,075	$5,040	16%	$9,220
High income	$9,076 or more	$26,310	27%	$27,590
World	(208 economies)	$5,080	100%	$7,570

*Classifications are based on the exchange rate method; dollar figures are for 2002.
Source: World Bank, *World Development Indicators* database.

bia ($8,530). High-income countries include the Republic of Korea ($9,930), Israel ($16,020), Canada ($22,390), Japan ($34,010), the United States ($35,400), and Switzerland ($36,170).[3] The income gap between the richest and poorest countries is widening. By the early 2000s, the average income of the richest 20 nations was about 37 times the average income of the poorest 20 nations—a ratio that has doubled over the past 40 years.[4] (See chapter 9 for more on more on GDP and GNP.)

Thc GNI per capita offers a basis for national comparisons of economic well-being. Yet, there are limitations to this approach to national income accounting. First, income data are generally confined to reported business activity, thus ignoring barter transactions and income generated in the informal economy. As a result, the government may understate national income. Second, income data, particularly data collected in the developing world, are often unreliable. In recent years, the International Monetary Fund and the World Bank have provided technical assistance to help correct weaknesses in data collection and analysis, an important foundation upon which national economic policies are built. Third, GNI per capita, which measures the average annual income per person, cannot assess the actual distribution of that income. In some developing economies, the income disparity between the richest and poorest citizens is severe, as shown in Table 12.2.[5] Note that the income of the richest 20 percent of the population in Brazil is about 30 times that of the poorest 20 percent of the population. In other countries, such as Lesotho and Namibia, the disparity between the richest and poorest segments of society is even steeper. Fourth, GNI data, which classify economies based on the exchange rate conversion process, fail to account for differences in currencies' purchasing power. When income data are adjusted for purchasing power parity (PPP), they more accurately reflect people's buying power (see chapter 9 for more on the exchange rate and PPP approaches to converting currencies).

Table 12.2
Income Distribution in Selected Developing Countries*

Country	Share of Income or Consumption		Inequality Measures
	Poorest 20%	Richest 20%	Comparing Richest 20% to Poorest 20%
Brazil	2.2%	64.1%	29.7 times
South Africa	2.0%	66.5%	33.6 times
Lesotho	1.4%	70.7%	50.0 times
Namibia	1.4%	78.7%	56.1 times

*Income data are taken from selected years during the 1990s.
Source: United Nations Development Program (UNDP), *Human Development Report 2003,* 282–85.

Characteristics of Developing Countries

Low GNI per capita is one characteristic of developing countries. Yet, the statistical classification of countries by per capita income sometimes clouds the human dimension of poverty in the global south. As the world entered the twenty-first century, about 1.1 billion people, or 21 percent of the total population living in low- and middle-income countries, lived in extreme poverty. Extreme poverty is defined as having an income of less than $1 per day. This figure represents a significant improvement in the global poverty picture over the past 20 years. In 1981, 1.45 billion people from low- and middle-income countries lived in extreme poverty, roughly 40 percent of the total population from these poorer regions. In the early 2000s more than 90 percent of all people living in extreme poverty were found in three world regions: South Asia (42% of the total), Sub-Saharan Africa (27%), and East Asia and the Pacific (24%). Further, close to half of the world's population lived on less than $2 per day.[6] The International Labor Organization (ILO) describes the human face of extreme poverty, stating:

> For individuals, poverty is a nightmare. It is a vicious circle of poor health, reduced working capacity, low productivity and shortened life expectancy. For families, poverty is a trap. It leads to inadequate schooling, low skills, insecure income, early parenthood, ill health and early death. For societies, poverty is a curse. It hinders growth, fuels instability, and keeps poor countries from advancing on the path to sustainable development.[7]

While each country in the developing world has a unique history and culture, a set of common economic characteristics apply to many of the world's poorer countries. One common characteristic is a low GNI per capita. Others include growing populations, limited resources, a low quality of life, and high foreign debts.

Rapid population growth is a second common feature and a common concern for most developing countries. World population grew dramatically during the twentieth century, increasing nearly fourfold from 1900 to 2000 as shown in Figure 12.1. Often referred to as the population explosion, this twentieth century growth trend is expected to continue into the twenty-first century. The Population Reference Bureau (PRB) predicts a 3 billion person increase in the world's population between 2000 and 2050. Almost all of this increase in population is expected to occur in the global south.[8] Rising populations create a number of challenges for developing countries. First, rapid population growth creates surplus labor, which often results in unemployment, underemployment, and low wage rates. Second, larger populations hasten the degradation of local ecosystems, as demands for fresh water, farmland, and other resources increase. Third, growing populations force nations to make difficult trade-offs between the production of consumption goods and the production of investment goods. The production of food, clothing, and other consumption goods for a growing population diverts scarce resources

Figure 12.1
Population Explosion: 1900–2050 (in billions of people)

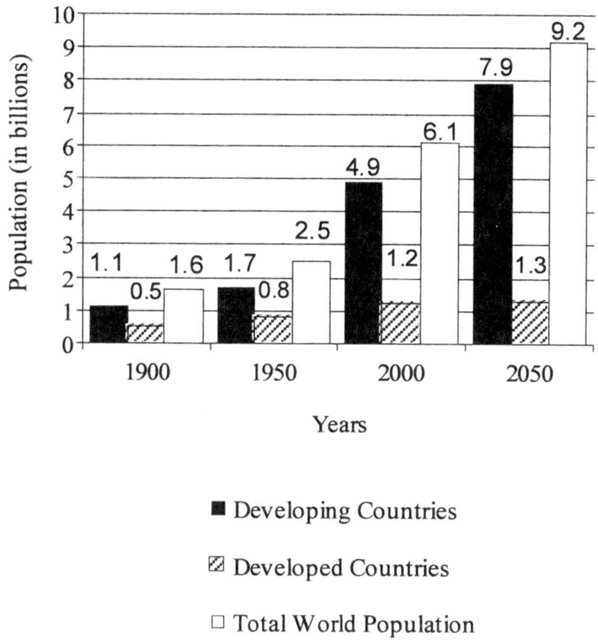

Source: Population Reference Bureau, *2003 World Population Data Sheet* and *Population Bulletin* (vol. 54, no. 1, 1999).

from productive investments in new physical capital and social capital, such as schools, health care facilities, and transportation systems.

A third characteristic of developing countries is limited natural resources. Limited natural resources stem from scant natural endowments and inadequate resource management. The scarcity of natural resources steers some developing countries toward one-crop economies, the reliance on the production of one or a few primary commodities such as foods, beverages, agricultural raw materials, or minerals. Volatile commodity prices in global markets lead to periods of boom and bust, however. In 1995, nonfuel commodity prices boomed by nearly 10 percent in global markets. A bust soon followed when commodity prices dipped by 16 percent in 1998 and by an additional 10 percent in 1999. Overall, nonfuel primary product prices dropped by 1.3 percent per year between 1995 and 2004, which reduced saving and investment in developing countries.[9] Further, about 40 countries that relied on the export of primary products experienced unsustained growth, a decline in GDP per capita over time.[10] Poor resource management aggravates the problem of resource scarcities. Governments, plagued by corruption and inefficiency, have been unable to prevent the waste and destruction of scarce resources. Deforestation, desertification, and other forms of environmental decay also reduce the usefulness of nature's gifts.

Traditional subsistence agriculture in Mozambique, 2002. Eric Miller/The World Bank Group.

A fourth characteristic of developing countries is a low quality of life. **Quality of life** refers to the conditions under which people live. People's quality of life is heavily influenced by economic factors, such as income and growth. Quality of life indicators include people's access to consumer goods and services; to health care, education, personal security, and essential social services; to a sound communications and transportation infrastructure; and to a variety of other factors that support economic opportunities and civil liberties. While it is difficult to make cross-border quality of life comparisons, the fact that 830 million people in the developing world were chronically undernurished in the early 2000s underscored the glaring disparities between the world's rich and poor.[11] Some development economists, such as Amartya Sen, have written extensively on human welfare in the developing world (see the biography of Amartya Sen). Since the early 1990s, the United Nations Development Program (UNDP) has published the Human Development Index (HDI) to rank countries by level of human development. The HDI considers quality of life indicators such as life expectancy, adult literacy, educational achievement, and GDP per capita. In 2001, 55 of the 175 surveyed countries attained high human development status, mostly high-income countries. The HDI also included 85 medium human development and 35 low human development countries. The top 5 spots in the HDI ranking were Norway, Iceland, Sweden, Australia, and the Netherlands. The bottom spots were occupied by Burundi, Mali, Burkina Faso, Niger, and Sierra

Table 12.3
Selected Quality of Life Indicators: 2001

Indicators	Low-income Countries	Middle-income Countries	High-income Countries
Income			
GNI per capita (2002)	$430	$1,840	$26,310
GNI per capita, PPP (2002)	$2,040	$5,630	$27,590
Health			
Life expectancy (years)	59	70	78
Undernourished people (%)	25%	10%	n/a
Infant mortality (per 1,000)	80	31	5
Population			
Total population (millions)	2,515	2,695	936
Urban population (%)	32%	52%	79%
Annual population growth rate, 1975 to 2001	2.2	1.5	0.7
Fertility rate (per woman)	3.7	2.1	1.7
Education			
Adult literacy (%)	63%	87%	99%
Primary school enrollment (%)	74%	93%	97%
Internet users (per 1,000)	6	37	397

Source: United Nations Development Program (UNDP), *Human Development Report 2003;* World Bank, *2003 World Development Indicators* database.

Leone.[12] A comparison of quality of life indicators for high-income, middle-income, and low-income countries is shown in Table 12.3.[13]

A fifth characteristic of developing countries is high foreign debt obligations. **Foreign debt,** also called external debt, is the money owed by a country to foreign governments, commercial banks, multilateral organizations, or other investors. The total foreign debt of low-income and middle-income countries increased by over $400 billion between 1995 and 2004, and topped $2.7 trillion by 2004. Developing countries had accumulated the lion's share of foreign debt ($2.3 trillion), and the transition economies accounted for the remainder ($0.4 trillion).[14] In 2004 developing and transition economies made nearly $400 billion in debt service payments to foreign creditors. Debt servicing, which siphoned scarce financial resources from the public till, crippled poorer countries' ability to finance social welfare programs, public education, infrastructure construction, and other programs vital to sustainable economic development. Some of these countries were saddled with unsustainable debt, foreign debt that could not be repaid without horrific consequences for the domestic population. The financial hardships faced by some severely indebted countries also raised the specter of default, a government repudiation of all foreign debts. By 2003 the

World Bank had identified 50 severely indebted countries, mostly low-income developing countries.[15]

THE DEVELOPMENT PROCESS: THEORY AND PRACTICE

Economic development became a legitimate field of study during the post–World War II era, as decolonization forced government leaders and economists to consider viable development strategies for emerging Third World nations. Early development theories, which defined economic development in terms of economic growth and industrial output, stressed the primacy of national savings and investment in capital goods. Much of the work of economist Sir Arthur Lewis focused on the necessity of saving and investing (see the biography of Sir Arthur Lewis). Some early development economists also constructed linear development models, implying a lockstep development process. W. W. Rostow's book, *The Stages of Economic Growth: A Non-communist Manifesto* (1960), popularized the view that economic development progressed in sequential stages. Rostow's five development stages were the traditional society, the preconditions for take-off, the take-off, the drive to maturity, and the age of mass consumption.[16]

Over time, other theories of economic development evolved. Later development economists expanded the definition of economic development to include not just sustained economic growth, but also measurable improvements in people's quality of life. Important quality of life indicators were a higher adult literacy rate, longer life expectancy, and better diet and nutrition. Predictably, many of these economists concluded that greater investment in human capital, the acquired skills and talents of workers, was the key to sustainable development. Hence, development theories stressed the value of education, health care, nutrition, and access to economic opportunity as prerequisites for long-run prosperity. Later development economists also shunned the linear view of economic development, concentrating instead on how to use existing resources and technology to leapfrog into modernity. Many development economists also advocated an expanded role for government in mobilizing society's resources.

One manifestation of greater government involvement in the development process was economic planning. As the pace of decolonization accelerated during the 1950s, 1960s, and 1970s, leaders of the newly independent nations in Africa, Asia, and the Middle East adopted **development plans,** a type of economic blueprint that outlined the nation's path toward sustainable development. The creation of development plans by Third World nations was a logical step along the road to economic development. Most of the advanced economies of Europe had already embraced some form of economic planning, as did many of the world's leading economists, including Sweden's Karl Gunnar Myrdal (see the biography of Karl Gunnar Myrdal). Even today, economists and government leaders debate the merits of government planning and other government intervention in the economic activities of developing nations.

Development Models

A nation's approach to economic development hinges on its development model. A **development model** establishes the conditions under which economic decisions are made. Development models, like models of economic systems, span a continuum. Some support significant government control over economic activity, and others rely mainly on private-sector decision making.

A command model for economic development relies on centralized decision making by the government. Under the command model, the government directs the use of society's resources to meet national goals. The command model assumes that the government, rather than the private sector, is best able to allocate society's resources. Command economies and totalitarian political systems tend to support the command model for economic development. In the former Soviet Union, for example, a state planning agency dictated the nation's development road map through successive five-year plans. The collapse of communism by the early 1990s highlighted weaknesses in this development strategy. Costly and inefficient federal bureaucracies stifled innovation, incentives, and entrepreneurship. Many dictatorships in the global south also adopted variations of the command model. Dictatorships gave rise to rampant corruption, cronyism, civil strife, and disregard for the rule of law. Self-serving dictators dimmed prospects for sustainable development in much of Africa (Taylor in Liberia), Asia (Pol Pot in Cambodia), the Caribbean (Duvalier in Haiti), Latin America (Somoza in Nicaragua), the Middle East (Hussein in Iraq), and elsewhere. The command model, often couched as socialism or communism, was the dominant development strategy from the 1950s to the 1980s.

A market model for development emphasizes decentralized economic decision making. The market model relies on the private sector—individuals and firms—to allocate society's scarce resources. Countries with capitalist economies and democratic governments embrace the market model. The main institutions of the market model include private property rights, freedom of contract, and other freedoms of the marketplace. The market model has been most successful in the newly industrialized economies of East Asia, including Hong Kong, Singapore, South Korea, and the Chinese Province of Taiwan. The market model is not without its weaknesses, however. Problems include periodic economic downturns, equity issues, and disagreements about the legitimate role of government in the economy. Since the collapse of communism during the early 1990s, the market model has influenced most development strategies in the developing world.

Development Priorities

Developing countries must also define their development priorities. Traditionally, this has meant rechanneling scarce resources from subsistence agriculture to industry and services. In recent decades, the pace of this economic transition has quickened. By 2001 over half of all output produced in the developing world consisted of services, and services represented the fastest growing sector within developing countries.[17] Economists view the transition from subsistence agriculture toward industry and services as a positive step toward modernization and fuller participation of poorer countries in the global economy. Yet, past experience suggests that economic development requires more than capital accumulation, the expansion of a nation's capital stock. Instead, development economists argue that the transition toward modern economies must be accompanied by improvements in human capital, entrepreneurship, incentive systems, and real opportunities to succeed. Despite progress toward modernization in much of the developing world, economic development has proven elusive, especially in the low-income developing countries. In the early 2000s, agricultural output still accounted for over half of GDP in Ethiopia, Laos, the Democratic Republic of Congo, Liberia, and some other low-income countries. Agricultural output in the advanced economies, on the other hand, accounted for a tiny percent of GDP: 1 percent in Germany, 1.4 percent in Japan, and 2 percent in the United States.[18]

Another priority for developing countries is to establish an effective trade policy. As one of the pillars of globalization, trade creates profitable business links between nations. Developing countries often create trade strategies based on either import substitution or export promotion. Under import substitution, nations try to produce goods that replace similar imported goods. Import substitution, however, often requires heavy investment in new physical capital, government subsidies to inefficient domestic producers, and trade barriers to protect inefficient firms from foreign competition. Historically, import substitution policies have been woefully unsuccessful. Under export promotion, nations simply export products that they produce efficiently. Export promotion does not relegate developing nations to the export of commodities and raw materials, however. Instead, the composition of a country's exports can and should evolve as new, efficient industries arise. In recent decades, the export promotion trade strategy fueled economic growth and development in the newly industrialized countries of East Asia.

The push to expand exports from the poorer nations is supported by some advanced economies, the World Trade Organization (WTO), and other multilateral institutions. For example, the United States and the European Union have each devised and implemented a generalized system of preferences (GSP) to encourage selected exports from certain developing countries. GSPs reduce import tariffs, import quotas, and other restrictions on trade. On a broader scale the WTO is committed to free trade as a cornerstone of its strategy to reduce global poverty and promote sustainable economic development. Its 2001 Doha Declaration, a document approved at the WTO's Fourth Ministerial Conference in Doha, Qatar, pledged to redouble efforts to include poorer nations in the global trading system. Hot items for future WTO ministerial conferences will be how to implement the agreements crafted in Doha.

THE VIRTUOUS CYCLE: PROMOTING SUSTAINABLE ECONOMIC DEVELOPMENT

The *virtuous cycle* refers to the upward spiral of investment and production in an economy, which, in turn, leads to sustainable economic development. Broadly defined, **sustainable economic development** includes sustained economic growth and substantive improvements in people's quality of life over time. *Agenda 21,* which was one important outcome of the 1992 United Nations Conference on Environment and Development (the Rio Earth Summit), is one of the world's most authoritative statements on the scope of sustainable development. Under *Agenda 21* guidelines, sustainable economic development embraced policies to expand national output, protect the natural environment, promote worker and human rights, and reduce the glaring income disparities within and between countries. Another respected document giving direction to responsible economic development in the global economy is the UN's *Millennium Declaration* (2000), which established eight Millennium Development Goals (MDGs). Key multilateral organizations rallied around the MDGs, which highlighted the need to end extreme poverty and hunger, promote universal primary education, promote gender equity, improve health, protect the environment, and create partnerships for development.[19] A convergence of many mutually supporting economic, political, and social factors is necessary if the virtuous cycle of development is to replace the vicious cycle of poverty.

Management of Society's Productive Resources

The effective management of productive resources in the developing world is one important step toward creating the virtuous cycle. This means that society's natural resources, human resources, and capital goods must be used efficiently. Key elements in the management of a country's natural resources include policies to reduce environmental degradation, increase the use of renewable resources, and expand the productivity of the land and other gifts of nature. In *World Resources 2000–2001,* the World Resources Institute estimated that two out of every five people on Earth face a serious shortage of fresh water, and that nearly two-thirds of all land used for crops suffers some soil degradation.[20] The magnitude of the challenges to fragile ecosystems in the developing world is staggering. Yet, policies to reduce overgrazing and overfarming of land can reduce desertification, deforestation, and soil erosion. Replanting forests and cultivating new groundcover also protects valuable land resources. In addition, higher productivity is possible through the application of scientific planting techniques and the strategies of the green revolution—the use of high-yield hybrid seeds, fertilizers and pesticides, and capital goods in the production of agricultural products. Uniform and enforceable policies are needed to reduce pollution, prevent strip mining, and curb other destructive practices. Improvements in the storage and transportation of goods, particularly agricultural goods, would also protect valuable output from rot or infestation.

Improving human resources is another essential ingredient in the virtuous cycle. Developing countries lag behind the advanced countries in educational attainment, health care, nutrition, and life expectancy, as was shown in Table 12.3. These deficiencies limit the productivity of labor, national output, and economic opportunities. The virtuous cycle requires advanced human capital in the form of a highly educated and skilled workforce. Three broad policies are supportive of this goal. First, developing countries must increase people's access to primary education and higher education, job training programs, adequate food and fresh water, and health care. These policies improve the overall quality of the labor force. Second, poorer countries must reverse the brain drain. The *brain drain* refers to the exodus of the small, well-educated professional class from developing countries to the advanced countries. To reverse the brain drain, poorer countries must establish suitable financial incentives and a higher quality of life for people. Third, developing countries must nurture domestic entrepreneurship. Programs should expand credit, encourage innovation and risk-taking, and promote inclusion—especially participation by women in business activity. Since the mid-1970s, the Grameen Bank, founded by Muhammad Yunus, has granted microloans of less than $100 to support entrepreneurial activity and self-reliance among the poorest households in Bangladesh. By the early 2000s, thousands of microcredit institutions in the developing world had extended loans to millions of local entrepreneurs. Acknowledging the pivotal role of microcredit in global poverty reduction, the United Nations proclaimed 2005 the International Year of Microcredit.

Capital deepening is a third element in promoting the virtuous cycle. **Capital deepening** occurs when a nation's capital stock per worker increases. Capital goods, also called physical capital, increase the productivity of labor in agriculture, industry, and services. Obstacles to capital deepening in the developing world include low national saving and investment rates, rapid population growth, recurrent civil strife and conflicts, and other disruptions to business activity. Capital deepening is enhanced by three complementary policies. First, developing countries should attract foreign direct investment (FDI) by transnational corporations (TNCs). Responsible FDI infuses new physical capital, technology, and management skills into host economies. TNCs also increase connectivity, linking local businesses with profitable opportunities in the global economy. Through the use of sophisticated information and communications technologies (ICTs), TNCs can also reduce the digital divide, a technological gap that traditionally excluded the global south from globalization's benefits. Second, the poorer countries must work to reduce capital flight. **Capital flight** occurs when the wealthy elite in poorer countries invests its savings in safer, more profitable ventures abroad. Capital flight reduces the already shallow pool of savings in developing countries and thus slows domestic investment. The protection of private property rights and the implementation of responsible stabilization policies to protect the value of domestic currencies are important preconditions to slowing capital flight. Third, poorer countries must end destructive civil wars and domestic violence. The World Bank reported that, during the 1990s, 46 poorer countries were involved in conflicts, mainly civil wars or other civil unrest, "destroying past development gains and leaving a legacy of damaged assets and corrosive mistrust that impedes future progress."[21] The destruction of productive resources often results in negative economic growth and perpetuates the vicious cycle of poverty.

Creating a Pro-Growth Business Climate

The virtuous cycle is enhanced by a pro-growth business climate. A favorable business climate includes stable, transparent, and inclusive economic and political institutions and practices. It relies on a well-developed economic infrastructure, a respect for private property and market institutions, and macroeconomic stability. It is based on good governance. Widespread poverty, budget constraints, lack of business experience, corruption, and so on weaken the business climate in much of the developing world (see chapter 9 for more on pro-growth policies).

Improving the economic environment stimulates business activity and improves people's quality of life. First, a well-developed economic infrastructure includes transportation and communications systems, basic services in sanitation and water supply, health and educational facilities, and a justice system capable of enforcing contracts and administering the rule of law. The infrastructure also includes institutions to attend to the specific needs of the poor and other marginalized segments of society. Second, respect for market institutions provides incentives to work, save, invest, and produce goods. In the developing world, the reform of land tenure laws is an especially important ingredient in nurturing market incentives (see the biography of Hernando de Soto for more on land tenure and incentives). Legal reforms must also open the doors of opportunity to the poor, end discrimination, and protect productive assets from government seizure through nationalization or expropriation. Third, macroeconomic stabilization policies lay the groundwork for price stability, full employment, and growth. Responsible macroeconomic policies attempt to control annual budget deficits, manage external debt, maintain adequate quantities of foreign exchange, implement appropriate monetary policies, and form partnerships with multilateral organizations such as the World Bank, the International Monetary Fund, and regional development banks.

A stable political environment based on good governance also fosters a favorable business climate. *Good governance* refers to honest and competent public service by government officials. Democratic governments in the advanced countries developed principles of good governance over time. These principles were built on the rule of law, the understanding that all participants in the economic or political life of the country must abide by the same rules. Good governance and the rule of law encourage business activity by guaranteeing equal access to business opportunities and equal protections for private property and profits. Good governance has proven elusive for many developing countries, particularly those subjected to extreme poverty, dictatorship, corruption, and civil conflict. In recent years, international development institutions have extended financial and technical assistance to help developing countries create ef-

A traditional Beijing hutong, or residential area, in China. A secondary effect of economic development is the systematic destruction of hutongs in China's cities in favor of infrastructure projects, modern residential and commercial buildings, and other construction. Changing China Fulbright-Hays Group Projects Abroad, 2002. Photograph by Todd Wisdom Jarvis.

fective tax systems, business codes, accounting principles, and public financial institutions. In addition, governments and international institutions have encouraged participation by nongovernmental organizations (NGOs) and civil society organizations (CSOs) to help devise and monitor compliance with the principles of good governance.

Expansion of External Supports

Economic aid to developing countries stimulates the virtuous cycle of development. **Economic aid** refers to cross-border grants, loans, technical assistance, and emergency aid. Foreign governments and multilateral organizations provide most economic assistance. Other sources of assistance include transnational corporations, nongovernmental organizations, civil society organizations, and individual philanthropists. Five of the most important sources of economic aid are the World Bank Group, regional development banks, the International Monetary Fund, the Organization for Economic Cooperation and Development, and the United Nations system.

The **World Bank Group,** which consists of five mutually supporting institutions, provides development assistance to the world's poorer nations. Development assistance includes loans and technical assistance designed to promote sustainable economic development. In recent years, the World Bank Group placed poverty reduction as its top priority. Development assistance is devoted to improving nations' social capital, which, broadly defined, includes not only traditional features of the economic infrastructure but also schools, hospitals, and elements of a social safety net for the needy. Development assistance is also intended to provide support for long-term economic growth within the context of respect for the environment, worker and human rights, and indigenous cultures. During a three-year period in the early 2000s, the World Bank built or upgraded 46,000 clinics and 130,000 classrooms, trained 1.3 million primary health care workers and 1.2 million teachers, and improved access to clean water and sanitation to tens of millions of people.[22] The World Bank is a specialized agency of the United Nations system (see chapter 11 for more on the World Bank Group).

Regional development banks (RDBs) are member-owned, multilateral lending institutions. Some member nations are located within the geographic region served by the bank, while others are located outside the region. RDBs' loanable funds are derived from interest payments on past loans, the sale of securities to foreign investors, and financial contributions by member countries. RDBs extend loans to support poverty-reduction programs and sustainable economic development. The four major RDBs operating in the global economy are the African Development Bank Group (ADB Group), which consists of 77 member nations; the Asian Development Bank (ADB), which consists of 61 members; the Inter-American Development Bank (IDB), which consists of 46 members; and the European Bank for Reconstruction and Development (EBRD), which consists of 60 members. EBRD is concerned not only with promoting sustainable development, but also with facilitating the economic transition of former communist countries in eastern and central Europe and western Asia toward capitalism. Smaller RDBs promote economic development in the Caribbean, Central America, and the Islamic world.

The **International Monetary Fund** (IMF) is a multilateral organization designed to stabilize the international monetary system. Over time, the IMF has redoubled its efforts to promote economic and financial stability in the developing world. Through surveillance, technical assistance, and financial assistance, the IMF supports programs to strengthen nations' financial institutions, policies, and practices. The IMF has also cooperated with the World Bank to support poverty reduction initiatives, including the Heavily Indebted Poor Countries (HIPC) Initiative, which offers foreign debt relief, and the Poverty Reduction and Growth Facility (PRGF), which offers low-interest loans, called *credits*, to low-income countries. By fall 2003, 27 developing countries had received debt-reduction benefits under the HIPC Initiative, saving these countries $52 billion in debt servicing payments over time. By the spring of 2004, 77 poor countries were eligible for low-interest loans under the PRGF.[23] The IMF is a specialized agency of the United Nations system (see chapter 11 for more on the IMF).

The **Organization for Economic Cooperation and Development** (OECD) is an association of 30 countries that collectively discuss global issues and work toward sustainable economic growth and development. Through its 23-member Development Assistance Committee (DAC) foreign aid, called *official development assistance* (ODA), is channeled from the advanced countries to poorer countries. About one-third of all DAC aid is spent on developing countries' social and administrative infrastructure, which includes education, health, water, and government services. Other important categories of spending include economic infrastructure, production, debt relief, and emergency aid. In 2003 ODA totaled $68 billion. The United States was the top donor nation contributingh $15.8 billion to the DAC till, or 23 percent of all ODA. Table 12.4 identifies the top donor countries and the leading recipients of ODA by country, income group, and region.[24]

The **United Nations** (UN) is the world's leading public forum for discussing issues of global concern. The UN's mission centers on preserving peace, promoting economic development, and supporting human rights. Under the umbrella of the United Nations system, a variety of specialized agencies, programs, and funds contribute to improved living standards and a higher quality of life for the peoples of the world. Specialized agencies, programs, and funds are self-governing and self-supporting. Among the key specialized agencies that promote sustainable development are the Food and Agriculture Organization, the International Labor Organization (ILO), IMF, United Nations Educational, Scientific, and Cultural Organization (UNESCO), the World Bank Group, and the World Health Organization (WHO). Important UN programs and funds include the United Nations Conference on Trade and Development (UNCTAD), United Nations Children's Fund (UNICEF), United Nations Development Program (UNDP), United Nations Environmental Program (UNEP), United Nations Population Fund (UNFPA), and World Food Program.

Table 12.4
Official Development Assistance: 2002

		Leading Recipients		
Rank	Donor Countries	Country	Income Group	World Region
1	United States	China	Low income	Sub-Saharan Africa
2	Japan	India	Lower mid-income	Other Asia/Oceania
3	France	Indonesia	Upper mid-income	South and Central Asia
4	Germany	Egypt	High income	Latin America/ Caribbean

Source: Organization for Economic Cooperation and Development/Development Assistance Committee.

BIOGRAPHIES: SHAPERS OF ECONOMIC THOUGHT

Sir Arthur Lewis: Pioneer in Development Economics

Sir William Arthur Lewis (1915–1991) was a prominent British economist and specialist in the field of development economics. Lewis, who used the name Arthur, was born in St. Lucia, a British possession in the West Indies. At age 17, he won a scholarship to attend the London School of Economics, where he earned a bachelor of commerce degree in 1937 and a doctorate in industrial economics in 1940. The London School of Economics appointed Lewis to the position of lecturer in economics from 1938 to 1947, helping to break the color barrier that had long denied blacks the opportunity to advance in academia. In the years to come, Lewis served as an economics professor at other major universities, including the University of Manchester (1947–1958) in England and Princeton University (1963–1968) in the United States. Lewis authored 10 books, including *The Principles of Economic Planning* (1949), *The Theory of Economic Growth* (1955), *Development Planning* (1966).

Lewis was a pioneer in the field of development economics. He drew insights about the plight of the developing world from personal experiences and meticulous study of statistical data and economic history. He concluded that many economies in the developing world operated on two different levels, one pushing toward modernity and growth, and the other clinging to traditional subsistence agriculture. Lewis argued that sustainable development was dependent on raising the domestic savings rate, investment in modern capital goods, aggressive export of agricultural and manufactured goods, and mutually beneficial foreign direct investment (FDI). In addition, Lewis valued the role of education, including the transfer of knowledge from transnational corporations, to expand business and entrepreneurial skills in the developing world. Lewis also noted that the transition from a traditional to a modern economy was pitted with obstacles. For instance, he observed that rising populations and mass migrations of people from rural to urban areas created a nearly unlimited supply of labor. Bloated labor markets depressed workers' wages and living standards, however. Other obstacles to economic development included inefficient government planning, unfavorable trade relationships between the global north and south, and low worker productivity—particularly in the agricultural sector.

While active in academic pursuits for much of his professional career, Lewis was also an agent of change in the developing world. Under the auspices of the United Nations, he served as economic adviser to developing countries in the late 1950s. He also headed the University of the West Indies in the early 1960s and founded the Caribbean Development Bank in the early 1970s. Lewis earned many honors during his career. He was knighted by Queen Elizabeth in 1963, thus earning the title of Sir Arthur Lewis. In 1979 he shared the Nobel Prize in Economic Science in recognition of his groundbreaking work in the field of development economics and economic history.

Hernando de Soto: Harnessing the Informal Sector

Hernando de Soto (1941–) is among the world's most influential development economists. De Soto was born in Arequipa, Peru, the son of a Peruvian diplomat. When he was still a boy, political turmoil in Peru caused the de Soto family to flee to Switzerland, where Hernando de Soto received his early education and business experience. De Soto pursued his university studies in Lima, Peru, and completed his graduate work at the Institut Universitaire de Haute Etudes Internationales in Geneva, Switzerland. After running a successful engineering firm in Europe for a number of years, de Soto returned to his native land in 1980. His attention soon turned to the dysfunctional Peruvian economy, where he discovered the untapped potential of dead capital—productive assets and enterprises that were denied entry into the legal or formal economy by complicated and costly business regulations. In his two best-selling books, *The Other Path: The Invisible Revolution in the Third World* (1989) and *The Mystery of Capital: Why Capitalism Triumphs in the West and Fails Everywhere Else* (2003), de Soto examined Peru's development woes and offered a fresh prescription for sustainable economic development in the global south.

De Soto's development theory stressed the need to transform poorer societies' dual economies, the legal and the extralegal, into a single competitive market. He argued that the informal sector accounted for more than half of all business activity in Peru, and that the same was true in many other poorer countries. Further, he believed that the vitality and entrepreneurial spirit of the informal sector, along with the infusion of its dead capital into the formal economy, was a wellspring for sustainable development. De Soto and his think tank, the Institute for Liberty and Democracy (ILD), recognized that a union between the formal and informal economies would require radical reforms in Peru's economic and political environment. His reform agenda, sometimes called *poor people's capitalism*, included streamlined business regulations and costs, and legal protections for people's property rights. In *The Other Path,* de Soto emphasized the need "to give people access to the system so they can join in economic and social activity and compete on an equal footing, the ultimate goal being a modern market economy."[25] Working with government leaders in Peru, de Soto's ideas became public policy. As a result of ILD initiatives during the late 1980s and early 1990s, over 1 million households were awarded titles to their homes in rural and urban areas, and hundreds of thousands of new businesses were formed in Peru's legal sector.[26] Legal ownership of assets expanded opportunities for the poor, including access to credit and public services. Other ILD initiatives worked toward good governance, tax fairness, financial stability, and improved education.

The success of de Soto's development strategy in Peru soon gained international attention. Under de Soto's leadership, the ILD grew to be one of the world's most influential think tanks. Governments in Africa, Asia, Eastern Europe, Latin America, and the Middle East sought de Soto's advice on development strategies. His prescription for prosperity, which received support from the

World Bank, the U.S. Agency for International Development (USAID), and UN Secretary General Kofi Annan, helped expand the rule of law to protect the property rights of the poor. In recent years, de Soto has also received a number of prestigious awards including the Freedom Prize, the Adam Smith Award, and the CARE Canada Award for Outstanding Development Thinking.

Amartya K. Sen: Welfare Economics and Development

Amartya Kumar Sen (1933–) is a prominent Indian economist specializing in welfare and development economics. As an advocate for the world's poorest citizens, Sen is often referred to the "conscience of economics." Sen was born in Shantiniketan, West Bengal, India, to an intellectual family. He has lived on or near university campuses in India, the United Kingdom, and the United States for most of his life. Sen earned his first bachelor's degree from Calcutta University, India. He continued his studies at the University of Cambridge, United Kingdom, where he earned a second bachelor's degree and then a doctorate in 1959. Over the years, Sen served as a professor of economics at a number of universities, mainly the Delhi School of Economics during the 1960s, the London School of Economics during the 1970s and 1980s, and Harvard University during the late 1980s and the 1990s. In 1998 Sen accepted a position as the Master of Trinity College at Cambridge. Among his best-known books in the field of development economics are *On Economic Inequality* (1973), *Poverty and Famines* (1981), *Development as Freedom* (2000), and *Pathologies of Power: Health, Human Rights, and the New War on the Poor* (2003, co-authored with Paul Farmer).

Most of Sen's work in the field of development economics focused on human welfare. He explored topics such as poverty, famine, the distribution of income and wealth, health care, education, and other factors that affect the quality of life in poor countries. After exhaustive research, Sen concluded that human misery could be reduced if food and other resources were distributed more equitably. As a social activist, Sen's books often featured the normative side of economics, stressing what should be rather than simply describing what is. In *Development as Freedom,* Sen stated that people's freedoms should be expanded as a precondition to sustainable economic development. He argued that expanded freedoms required broader participation by the poor in the economic, social, and political life of developing countries. Free markets and the power of government were necessary to achieve freedom and development. Free markets encouraged business activity and modernization, while government policies promoted social justice and human welfare. To expand people's range of choices, Sen favored public support of education, nutrition, health care, gender equity, and other programs that promoted inclusion. He also supported democratic institutions, including a free and independent press, to help protect personal freedoms.

Sen garnered many awards and honors during his professional career. He held leadership positions in the Econometric Society, the Indian Economic

Association, and the American Economic Association. In 1998 he was awarded the Nobel Prize in Economic Science in recognition of his contribution to development and welfare economics.

Karl Gunnar Myrdal: Economic Planning and Development

Karl Gunnar Myrdal (1898–1987) was a prominent Swedish sociologist, politician, and economist who supported economic planning in the development process. Myrdal was born in Gustafs, a small village in Sweden, the son of working-class parents. He attended Stockholm University, where he earned a law degree in 1923 and a doctorate in economics in 1927. Myrdal's professional career consisted of a colorful blend of scholarship, teaching, and public service to the people of Sweden and the world. He was an economics professor at Stockholm University for much of the 1930s, 1940s, and 1960s. He also was elected to the Swedish Senate during the 1930s, and served as Sweden's Commerce Secretary from 1945 to 1947. Myrdal was appointed secretary general of the UN's Economic Commission for Europe, a post he held from 1947 to 1957. In 1957 he began a 10-year research project on economic conditions in the developing world. His results were published in a three-volume tome, *Asian Drama: An Inquiry into the Poverty of Nations* (1968). Two years later, Myrdal published a summary of *Asian Drama* entitled *The Challenge of World Poverty: A World Anti-Poverty Program in Outline.*

Myrdal's highly acclaimed *Asian Drama* rekindled interest and debate about development strategies for the world's poorer countries. While Myrdal did not offer a blueprint for development in this seminal book, his keen observations and meticulous research identified many obstacles to development that begged for policy reforms. Long an advocate of economic planning, Myrdal argued that the governments in the developing world must control rising populations, expand basic services in education and health care, and reform land tenure laws to enable the poor to own farmland. Further, he challenged developing countries to reform legal codes, which historically had protected the narrow interests of the ruling elite and blocked human progress by the masses. Myrdal also saw a role for the industrialized countries in Third World development through increased foreign aid and trade concessions to poorer nations. In *Asian Drama* and other publications, he made additional prescriptions for prosperity in the developing world. He believed that a workable development strategy must increase labor productivity, halt soil and other environmental degradation, employ new production technologies, and stamp out public-sector corruption. More controversial proposals included recommendations to assign excess labor to cooperative public work projects, such as the construction of roads, wells, and irrigation systems. Myrdal also criticized overconsumption by richer nations, a practice that benefits the rich at the expense of poor.

Myrdal's support for a third way, a development model that blends elements of the command and the market models, represented mainstream thought during much of the post–World War II period. He believed that economic planning, which was a common feature in most Western European countries after the war, was superior to America's reliance on the market mechanism. During his lifetime, Myrdal received many honors and awards in recognition of his groundbreaking work in development economics. He received honorary degrees from leading universities in Europe and the United States, and he was a distinguished member of the Econometric Society, the Royal Swedish Academy of Sciences, and other prominent organizations. In 1974 Gunnar Myrdal shared the Nobel Prize in Economic Science with Friedrich August von Hayek.

NOTES

1. World Bank, "World Bank List of Economies (July 2003)," World Development Indicators Database, www.worldbank.org/data/databytopic/CLASS.XLXS.
2. World Bank Group, "Country Classification," www.worldbank.org/data/countryclass/countryclass.html.
3. World Bank, "Table 1.1. Size of the Economy," *2004 World Development Indicators* (New York: Oxford University Press and the World Bank, 2004), 14–16.
4. World Bank, *World Development Report 2003* (New York: Oxford University Press and the World Bank, 2003), 2.
5. United Nations Development Program (UNDP), "Table 13. Inequality in Income or Consumption," *Human Development Report 2003: Millennium Development Goals: A Compact among Nations to End Human Poverty* (New York: Oxford University Press, 2003), 282–85.
6. World Bank, "Global Poverty Goals within Reach but Only with Strong Action on Trade, Aid and Investing in People," news release, No. 2003/287/S, http://web.worldbank.org/WBSITE/EXTERNAL/NEWS/0,,contentMDK:20104957~menu; and World Bank, *2004 World Development Indicators,* 2–3.
7. International Labor Organization (ILO), "Report of the Director-General," in *Working out of Poverty* (Geneva, Switzerland: Author, 2003), 1.
8. Population Reference Bureau (PRB), *2003 World Population Data Sheet of the Population Reference Bureau* (Washington, DC: Author, 2003), 3; and Alene Gelbard, Carl Haub, and Mary M. Kent, "World Population beyond Six Billion," *Population Bulletin* 54 (March 1999): 4.
9. International Monetary Fund (IMF), "Table 23. Nonfuel Commodity Prices," *World Economic Outlook, April 2003* (Washington, DC: The Fund, 2003), 201.
10. World Bank, "Figure 9. Unsustained Growth, Point-Source Natural Resources, and Conflict," *World Development Report 2003: Overview* (Washington, DC: Author, 2002), 18.
11. World Bank, *2004 World Development Indicators,* 4.
12. UNDP, "Table 1. Human Development Index," *Human Development Report 2003,* 237–240.
13. UNDP, "Table 1. Human Development Index," "Table 5. Demographic Trends," "Table 8. Survival Progress and Setbacks," "Table 11. Technology: Diffusion and Creation," "MDG Goal 1," *Human Development Report 2003,* 237–40, 250–53, 262–65, 274–77, 202; and World Bank, "GNI per Capita 2002."
14. IMF, "Table 38. Summary of External Debt and Debt Service," *World Economic Outlook, April 2003,* 226.
15. World Bank, "World Bank List of Economies (July 2003).".

16. W. W. Rostow, *The Stages of Economic Growth: A Non-communist Manifesto* (London: Cambridge University Press, 1960), 4–11.

17. World Bank, *2003 World Development Indicators* (Washington, DC: World Bank, 2002), 181.

18. Central Intelligence Agency (CIA), *The World Factbook 2003,* www.odci.gov/cia/publications/factbook/geos/cg/html.

19. United Nations, *UN Millennium Development Goals (MDG),* www.un.org/millenniumgoals/index.html.

20. World Resources Institute (WRI), *World Resources 2000–2001, People and Ecosystems: The Fraying Web of Life* (Washington, DC: WRI, United Nations Development Program, United Nations Environment Program, the World Bank, 2000), 54, 88,104, 110.

21. World Bank, *World Development Report 2003*: *Overview*, 3.

22. World Bank, *2004 Partnerships in Development* (Washington, DC: Author, 2004), 22. OECD, "Table: Net Official Development Assistance in 2003, April 16, 2004 (www.oecd.org/dataoecd/42/61/31504039.pdf).

23. World Bank, *2004 Partnership in Development*, 18; and IMF, "The Poverty Reduction and Growth Facility (PRGF), factsheet, April 2004, www.imf.org/external/np/exr/facts/prgf.htm.

24. Organization for Economic Cooperation and Development (OECD), "Net Official Development Assistance from DAC Countries to Developing Countries and Multilateral Organizations," www.oecd.org/dataoecd/43/26/1894401.xls; and OECD, "Total DAC Countries," www.oecd.org/dataoecd/17/39/23664717.gif.

25. Hernando de Soto, *The Other Path: The Invisible Revolution in the Third World* (New York: Harper & Row, Publishers, 1989), 244.

26. Institute for Liberty and Democracy (ILD), "Hernando de Soto," www.ild.org.pe/hernandodesoto.htm.

SELECTED READINGS

Bender, Daniel E. *Sweatshop Work, Weak Bodies: Anti-Sweatshop Campaigns and Languages of Labor.* Piscataway, NJ: Rutgers University Press, 2004.

Birdsall, Nancy. *What Role for Regional Development Banks in Financing for Development?* Washington, DC: Institute for International Economics, 2003.

Buira, Ariel, ed. *Challenges to the World Bank and IMF: Developing Country Perspectives.* London: Anthem Press, 2003.

Fogel, Robert W. *The Escape from Hunger and Premature Death, 1700–2100: Europe, America and the Third World.* New York: Cambridge University Press, 2004.

Kasmauski, Karen. *Impact: On the Frontlines of Global Health.* Washington, DC: National Geographic Society, 2003.

Lewis, W. Arthur. *The Theory of Economic Growth.* London: Unwin Hyman, 1955.

Manning, Richard. *Food's Frontier: The Next Green Revolution.* Berkeley, CA: University of California Press, 2001.

Miller, Margaret J. *Implementing the Millennium Development Goals.* Washington, DC: World Bank, 2003.

Myrdal, Gunnar. *Asian Drama: An Inquiry into the Poverty of Nations.* New York: Pantheon Books, 1968.

Sen, Amartya. *Development as Freedom.* New York: Anchor Books, 2000.

Sogge, David. *Give and Take: What's the Matter with Foreign Aid?* New York: Zed Books, 2002.
Soto, Hernando de. *The Mystery of Capital: Why Capitalism Triumphs in the West and Fails Everywhere Else.* rev. ed. New York: Basic Books, 2003.
Stiglitz, Joseph E., and Ha-Joon Chang, eds. *The Rebel Within: Joseph Stiglitz and the World Bank.* London: Anthem Press, 2002.
Tarp, Finn, ed. *Foreign Aid and Development: Lessons Learned and Directions for the Future.* New York: Routledge, 2000.
United Nations Development Program (UNDP). *Corruption and Good Governance.* New York: United Nations, 2000.
———. *Human Development Report 2003.* New York: Oxford University Press, 2003.
Wilson, Ernest J., III. *The Information Revolution and Developing Countries.* Cambridge, MA: MIT Press, 2004.
World Bank. *World Development Report 2004: Making Services Work for People.* Washington, DC: Author, 2003.
Yunus, Muhammad, Mohammed Yunus, and Alan Jolis. *Banker to the Poor: Micro-Lending and the Battle against World Poverty.* Cambridge, MA: Perseus Books, 1999.

CHAPTER 13

Careers in Economics

Economists are highly trained professionals who study economic activity. They also influence economic decision making in the private and public sectors of the economy. The job market for economists is promising for the immediate future. Most economists in the private sector are employed by businesses. Business economists are mainly concerned with collecting and analyzing economic data to help firms make informed business decisions. Public-sector economists include government economists and academic economists. Government economists are employed at all levels of government—local, state, and national—to aid in public decision making. Academic economists are employed mainly as professors at colleges and universities. In addition to their teaching responsibilities, many academic economists become consultants, advisers, and authors.

ECONOMISTS: A PROFESSIONAL PROFILE

An **economist** is a social scientist concerned mainly with the collection and analysis of economic data. As social scientists, economists study the economic behaviors of people and institutions. They identify patterns of behavior, form generalizations and theories, discern economic trends, and make economic forecasts. Their specialized skills also influence economic decisions made by households, businesses, governments, global institutions, and others. The noted economist Robert L. Heilbroner noted that the ideas of the great economists, whom he called "the worldly philosophers," shaped the fortunes of nations and empires (see the biography of Robert L. Heilbroner).

Today, the U.S. Bureau of Labor Statistics (BLS) classifies economists as social scientists, a type of professional occupation. Other occupational classifications include executive and managerial, marketing and sales, administrative support and clerical, services, mechanical, construction trades, production, and transportation. The BLS estimated that 13,390 economists were employed in the U.S. economy in 2001.[1]

Economists: Earning Potential

Professional economists are highly educated and are well compensated for their acquired skills. Most attend graduate school to earn advanced degrees in specialized fields in economics, such as labor economics, industrial economics, agricultural economics, economic history, or development economics. Most also have strong backgrounds in mathematics and statistics. As a general rule, economists with just a bachelor's degree are relegated to lower-level positions in both public- and private-sector jobs. The path toward professional advancement and higher pay is strongly linked to earning additional academic degrees. In 2001, for example, the federal government paid newly hired economists with bachelor's degrees between $21,900 and $27,200, while new hires with doctorates earned between $40,200 and $48,200.[2] In that same year, the average annual wage for all private- and public-sector economists was $72,350, about double the $34,020 average annual wage for workers in the American labor force.[3] Figure 13.1 shows the average annual wage for economists and other social scientists in the U.S. economy in the early 2000s.[4]

Figure 13.1
Wages of Social Scientists: 2001

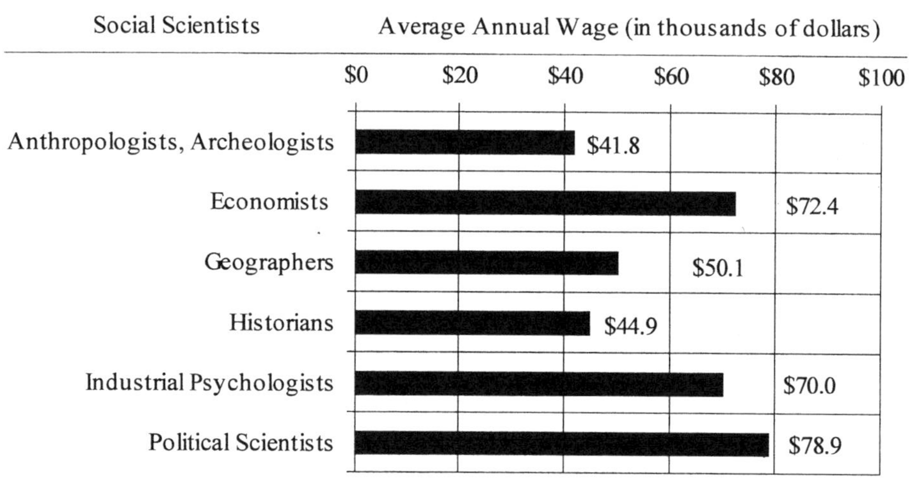

Source: Bureau of Labor Statistics, *2001 National Occupational Employment and Wage Estimates.*

Economists: Growing Diversity in the Profession

The economics profession in the United States has become more diverse over time. The *Statistical Abstract of the United States* reported that in 2001 over half of the 135,000 professionals employed as economists and market and survey researchers were women, about 9.6 percent were African Americans, and 3.6 percent were of Hispanic origin. In 1983 just 37.9 percent of the 98,000 professionals in this group were women, 6.3 percent African American, and 2.7 percent of Hispanic origin.[5]

Recent studies also confirmed a rising percentage of women and minorities earning academic degrees in economics. For example, during the 1990s the percentage of undergraduate economics degrees earned by women climbed several points, to 30 percent at public institutions and 36 percent at private institutions.[6] A growing diversity among recipients of doctoral degrees in economics was also apparent over the past quarter century. For instance, in the 1975–1979 period, women earned about 1 in 10 doctoral degrees in economics, compared to 1 in 4 by 2000. During the same time span, the percentage of doctoral degrees earned by African Americans, Asians and Pacific Islanders, and Hispanics more than doubled. By 2000, more than half the recipients of doctoral degrees in economics were non-U.S. citizens, compared to just 30 percent during the 1975–1979 period.[7]

Employment Opportunities for Economists and Economics Majors

In the *Occupational Outlook Handbook,* the U.S. Department of Labor predicted solid demand for economists in the immediate future. As with other occupations, the demand for economists is a derived demand. That is, the demand for economists is derived from the demand for the services they offer. Enhancing the demand for economists are the skills they acquire during their rigorous academic program. For example, economists typically possess quantitative skills, including statistics, economic modeling, and econometrics; computer skills; research and problem-solving skills; and communications skills, mainly the ability to explain complex ideas clearly in verbal and written form. These skills, in turn, make economists valuable human capital to businesses, government, and academic institutions, especially in today's fast-paced, highly integrated global economy. These skills also make trained economists attractive to employers in related fields such as market research, advertising, finance and banking, insurance, accounting, real estate, and government policymaking.

Other factors contribute to the marketability of an economist in this highly competitive job market. First, to qualify for most positions of leadership or responsibility, an economist must hold an advanced academic degree. This is particularly true for prestigious, high-paying positions at colleges or universities, major corporations, or federal agencies, which often require a Ph.D. Second, job opportunities improve if economists are mobile, willing to live and work in an urban setting. Today, most economists are employed in the cities, where many major businesses and public institutions are located. For example, many economists hired by the federal government live and work in the Washington, D.C., metropolitan region. This is because federal economists fill positions in departments and agencies such as the U.S. Treasury, the Labor Department, and the Commerce Department. Third, economists' job prospects increase when they develop an area of specialization. Specialists in the field of international and development economics are attractive candidates for jobs within multilateral organizations such as the World Bank, International Monetary Fund, United Nations, and regional development banks. Similarly, major labor unions are likely to hire labor economists; banks and securities firms are likely to hire financial economists; and leading newspapers and magazines might hire economic journalists. Entrepreneurial economists often establish their own businesses, including economic consulting firms. Other business, academic, and government economists supplement their income by serving as consultants in the public or private sectors of the economy.

TYPES OF ECONOMISTS

The three main categories of economists are business economists, academic economists, and government economists. The U.S. Department of Labor predicts steady growth in the job market for economists through the first decade of the twenty-first century. The Labor Department expects the strongest demand for economists to come from private industries, "especially in research, testing, and consulting firms, as more companies contract out for economic research services."[8] Some job growth for economists is also expected in the public sector, mainly at the state and local levels, including job opportunities in teaching high school economics. The *Occupational Outlook Handbook* anticipates significant job opportunities in the near future, mainly the result of retirements and career changes by employed economists.

Business Economists

Business economists are employed by private enterprises to analyze economic data and to help management make informed business decisions. Business economists collect and analyze company-specific data to help the firm make reasoned pricing and output decisions, improve productivity, obtain financing for business expansion, make hiring decisions, and so on. Thus, these economists are well versed in the principles of microeconomics, including marginal analyses involved in production and consumption decisions. Business economist also collect and interpret data related to the overall health of the economy, such as economic growth rates and unemployment rates, to predict the strength of consumer demand for the firm's output. Thus, they need to be familiar with macroeconomic topics, including the likely impact of government stabilization policies on business activity. Finally, business economists monitor external forces, such as international crises, to assess possible consequences for the firm's domestic and overseas sales, the cost and availability of key resources, and consumer confidence. Thus, business economists must understand international economics, such as the functioning of foreign exchange markets and the impact of trade policies and agreements on cross-border transactions. Because business economists often have a wide variety of duties and responsibilities, they tend to be generalists rather than specialists.

Jobs for business economists expanded rapidly during the second half of the twentieth century. With the ravages of the Great Depression still fresh in people's minds during the 1940s and 1950s, the management of many firms looked to professional economists to help them anticipate and solve business problems. The acceleration of globalization during the post–World War II years also increased the demand for expert economic analysis of how national and international affairs might affect the business activity of individual firms. Larger corporations sometimes hired a staff of business economists. Smaller firms often employed a single economist with shared responsibilities, or hired outside consultants to attend to their needs. According to the National Association for Business Economics (NABE), the nation's leading professional association in the field of business economics, all business economists share three common qualities, however. That is, business economists are "shrewd observers of what goes on both inside and outside the firm; enlightened analysts who can formulate and test promising ideas in an objective way; and persuasive communicators to management and others on behalf of the firm."[9]

Business economists receive higher pay, on average, than the other categories of economists. The primary determinants of a business economist's wage include educational attainment, years of experience on the job, and the industry in which the economist is employed. In a recent survey, NABE reported that the median base salary of business economists was $85,000 per year, and that more than half received additional compensation from consulting jobs or other employment. The median base salaries of government economists and academic economists were $74,500 and $70,000, respectively. According to the NABE study, the highest paid business economists were employed in the securities and investments sector, as shown in Table 13.1.[10]

Academic Economists

Academic economists are employed mainly by colleges and universities to teach, conduct scholarly research, and publish academic books and arti-

Table 13.1
Annual Salaries of Business Economists: 2000

Type of Industry	Median Base Salary	Additional Compensation	Total Compensation
Securities/investments	$107,500	$50,000	$157,500
Manufacturing	$103,000	$33,750	$136,750
Consulting	$99,999	$19,000	$118,999

Source: National Association for Business Economics, *Careers in Business Economics,* 2002.

cles in the field of economics. Academic economists might also be employed by private foundations, think tanks, and research institutes; serve as consultants to businesses, government, multilateral institutions, nongovernmental organizations, or other elements of civil society; or work under the auspices of competitive grants. Many academic economists, especially professors of economics in colleges and universities, specialize in a defined field of study such as comparative economic systems, econometrics, economic history, economic theory, industrial economics, international economics, labor economics, market structure and regulation, or public finance. Economics professors are expected to conduct research in their area of specialization and regularly publish the results of their research in academic books, journals, newsletters, or other media. Some economists, such as Paul A. Samuelson, have influenced generations of college students by publishing popular economics textbooks. Samuelson's *Economics* has gone through 17 editions since its original publication in 1948 (see the biography of Paul A. Samuelson).

Academic economists have taught economics at colleges and universities around the world for more than two centuries, often under the banner of political economy during the late eighteenth and the nineteenth centuries. Today, some colleges, mainly junior and community colleges, hire economists with master's degrees in economics. A master's degree typically requires one or two additional years of study beyond the bachelor's degree. To teach economics at most four-year colleges, however, a Ph.D. is often required. A doctorate usually takes four additional years of study beyond the bachelor's degree. Included in Ph.D. programs are requirements for original research and authorship of a doctoral dissertation. New hires at four-year colleges or universities are usually offered the rank of instructor or assistant professor. By publishing books and articles, presenting lectures at professional conferences, delivering quality instruction, or making other contributions to the field of economics, an assistant professor can rise to associate professor and eventually to the rank of full professor. Compensation for professors of economics increases with rank and experience. Academic economists earn about $70,000 per year, on average, a lower wage than business or government economists. Many supplement their income as consultants, authors, and public speakers, however. Some have even become television personalities. Milton Friedman's best-selling book, *Free to Choose: A Personal Statement,* which he co-authored with his wife Rose, became a popular movie and television series in the late 1970s and early 1980s. Similarly, *The Commanding Heights: The Battle between Government and the Marketplace That Is Remaking the Modern World,* by Daniel Yergin and Joseph Stanislaw, became a popular PBS series in the early 2000s.

Government Economists

Government economists are employed by federal, state, or local governments to collect and analyze data necessary in the formation of public policy. The federal government hires thousands of government economists to work within its many departments, agencies, and commissions. Many federal economists work in the Departments of Agriculture, Commerce, Health and Human Services, Labor, Transportation, and Treasury. Government economists are also employed at the state and local levels to analyze data related to tax policy, regional economic development, urban planning, infrastructure, environmental protection, consumer advocacy, and so on.

Many federal government economists are specialists. For instance, economists with strong backgrounds in money, finance, and banking are valuable to the Federal Deposit Insurance Corporation (FDIC), which safeguards depositors' savings; the Securities and Exchange Commission (SEC), which protects investors from fraud in securities markets; the Internal Revenue Service (IRS), which helps form and guarantee compliance with tax laws; and the Federal Reserve System (Fed), which ensures the overall integrity of the nation's monetary and banking system. Federal government economists are also employed in agencies associated with the global economy, such as the U.S. Agency for International Development (USAID), which oversees American foreign aid, and the Central Intelligence Agency (CIA), which monitors and reports on international economic conditions. The International Trade Commission (ITC), which investigates unfair trade practices such as dumping, patent and copyright infringement, and tariff structures, is instrumental in supplying the president and Congress with data upon which U.S. trade policy is based. Government econo-

U.S. Department of Agriculture building, Washington, D.C., and other federal departments, employ economists. U.S. Department of Agriculture. Photograph by Ken Hammond.

mists are employed at the state and local levels to analyze data related to tax policy, regional economic development, urban planning, environmental protection, consumer protection, and so on.

The federal government employed the first government economists during the early twentieth century, an era of progressive reform in the United States. Shaken by the Panic of 1907, many reformers supported the hiring of professional economists to assist in the creation of public financial institutions and policies. During the Progressive Era, the Federal Reserve System (1913) was founded to stabilize the nation's financial system; the Sixteenth Amendment (1913) was approved to create a national income tax; and the Clayton Antitrust Act (1914) was enacted to prevent monopolies from forming.

Another spurt in the hiring of federal economists occurred during the Great Depression of the 1930s. Economists helped President Franklin D. Roosevelt and Congress devise New Deal legislation, which reformed the banking system, supported the family farm, created public works jobs, and initiated a Social Security system for the elderly. Frances Perkins, a labor economist from New York, served as secretary of labor during the Depression years, the first woman to achieve cabinet rank.

Employment of government economists snowballed during and after World War II. During World War II, economists were employed to mobilize the nation's resources and coordinate the nation's production and consumption policies to support the war effort. Economists were valued employees of the federal War Production Board, the Office of Price Administration, the War Labor Board, and others. Immediately after the war ended, the historic Employment Act of 1946 pledged government support for economic growth, full employment, and stable prices. It also solidified the central role of economists in public decision making by founding the influential Council of Economic Advisors (CEA), an

Federal Reserve Chairman Alan Greenspan is America's most recognized government economist. U.S. Department of the Treasury/Bureau of Engraving and Printing.

inner circle of economic counselors who help the president develop and implement national economic policy. In 2003 President George W. Bush appointed prominent Harvard economist N. Gregory Mankiw as CEA chair (see the biography of N. Gregory Mankiw).

Today, the job market for government economists is fairly stable. The U.S. Department of Labor predicts a slow decline in the number of economists at the federal level, largely the result of a more generalized downsizing of the federal workforce—a cost-cutting process that will likely reduce the number of federal workers by 8 percent between 2001 and 2010. Thus, competition for government jobs, including economists, will be keen. At the same time, the Labor Department anticipates a slow rise in the number of jobs for economists in state and local governments.[11] Federal government economists were among the highest paid federal employees in the early 2000s, as shown in Table 13.2.[12] The average annual salary of $74,089 for federal economists was nearly 50 percent higher than the average annual salary of $51,565 for all workers in the federal government's.

BIOGRAPHIES: SHAPERS OF ECONOMIC THOUGHT

Paul A. Samuelson: Academic Economist

Paul A. Samuelson (1915–) is the preeminent American academic economist and a self-proclaimed generalist in an era of economic specialization. Samuelson was born in Gary, Indiana, the son of a pharmacist. After graduating from Hyde Park High School in Chicago, Illinois, he enrolled at the University of Chicago, where he earned his bachelor's degree (1935) and master's degree (1936). He continued his graduate program at Harvard University and in 1941 received his doctorate. Having gained an international reputation for scholarship even before his graduation from Harvard, Samuelson

Table 13.2
Top Salaries in the Federal Government: 2001

Rank	Occupation	Salary
1	Patent administrator	$102,392
2	Astronomer	$89,734
3	Attorney	$86,673
4	Financial manager	$79,840
5	Computer scientist	$75,351
6	Economist	$74,089
7	Podiatrist	$73,172
8	Chemist	$70,435
9	Electrical engineer	$69,560
10	Statistician	$68,901

Source: U.S. Department of Labor, Bureau of Labor Statistics, U.S. Office of Personnel Management.

was offered an assistant professorship at the Massachusetts Institute of Technology (MIT) in 1940.

Samuelson's excellence as a researcher, author, and teacher hastened his rise to associate professor in 1944 and a full professor in 1947. In 1947 he also published the highly acclaimed *Foundations of Economic Analysis,* which featured a mathematical approach to analyzing economic topics. During the 1950s and 1960s, Samuelson served as a consultant for federal agencies such as the U.S. Treasury and the Federal Reserve System and as an economic adviser to President Kennedy and President Johnson. Samuelson published many books and hundreds of scholarly articles during his career. His *Economics: An Introductory Analysis* (1948) has run for 17 editions and has ranked as one of the world's most respected economics textbooks for more than a half-century.

Samuelson made many contributions to economic theory throughout his long and productive career as an academic economist. As a generalist, he explored a variety of topics, including consumer behavior, welfare economics, international trade and finance, money and banking, linear programming, the nature of public goods, and monetary and fiscal policies. Samuelson believed that the common language of mathematics, the use of economic models, and precision in the definition of economic vocabulary were essential to the subject of economics and to economic analysis. Samuelson's *Foundations of Economic Analysis* (1947) kicked off the mathematical revolution among professional economists. A year later, his *Economics: An Introductory Analysis* boldly applied mathematical models to contemporary economic issues. Later editions of *Economics* kept pace with new developments in the field and introduced new ideas such as his now-famous neoclassical synthesis. Samuelson's neoclassical synthesis supported aggressive government intervention in the economy to combat recession, high unemployment, and inflation. It also postulated that during times of economic growth and stability, market forces, rather than government interventions, were able to direct economic activity. Even after his 50 years of painstaking work in the field, Samuelson concluded that economics was a discipline that is "still growing and still having a long way to go before approaching the state of a tolerably accurate science."[13]

Samuelson influenced mainstream economic thinking in the United States for more than 50 years. He received numerous awards and honors in recognition of his scholarship, commitment to students, and service to his country. In 1947 the American Economic Association (AEA) honored Samuelson with the John Bates Clark Medal. Later, he served as president of professional associations including the Econometric Association (1951), the AEA (1961), and the International Economic Association (1965). In 1970 Samuelson was the first American economist to win the Nobel Prize in Economic Science, largely to acknowledge his contributions "to raising the level of analysis in economic science."[14]

Alice M. Rivlin: Government Economist, Public Servant

Alice M. Rivlin (1931–) is a distinguished American economist and government official with expertise in public finance, stabilization policy, and social policy. Rivlin was born in Philadelphia and raised in Indiana, the daughter of an academic family. She earned a bachelor's degree in economics from Bryn Mawr College in 1952 and pursued her studies in economics at Radcliffe College (Harvard University), where she earned a master's degree in 1955 and a doctorate in 1958. Rivlin devoted the next 40 years of her life to public service, teaching, and research. She held key federal government posts throughout her career, including founding director of the Congressional Budget Office from 1975 to 1983, director of the Office of Management and Budget from 1994 to 1996, and vice chair of the Federal Reserve Board from 1996 to 1999. She also served as a professor of economics at George Mason University and Harvard University and earned the title of senior fellow while in the employ of the Brookings Institution—an influential think tank in Washington, D.C. She penned several books, most notably *Reviving the American Dream: The Economy, the States, and the Federal Government* (1992). More recently, Rivlin and co-author Robert E. Litan published *Beyond the Dot.coms: The Economic Promise of the Internet* (2001).

Rivlin is recognized as one of the most respected and influential government economists of the twentieth century. She was appointed the first director of the Congressional Budget Office (CBO), a federal agency created by the Congressional Budget and Impoundment Control Act of 1974 to provide Congress with timely information on economic conditions, tax policies, and spending programs. As CBO director, Rivlin was known for her decisiveness and her willingness to work in a nonpartisan manner during the presidencies of Gerald Ford, Jimmy Carter, and Ronald Reagan. As director of the Office of Management and Budget (OMB) during the mid-1990s, Rivlin consistently opposed large budget deficits. The OMB, a federal agency within the executive branch of government, assists the president in forming the federal budget each year. In her role as vice chair of the Federal Reserve Board, Rivlin took a leadership role in administering the Fed's budget and staff. Her views were often controversial and not always popular. In her most famous book, *Reviving the American Dream* (1992), Rivlin proposed a restructuring of American federalism to more clearly divide the functions and responsibilities among the three levels of government—national, state, and local. She argued that the overlapping duties of different levels of government hurt efficiency and accountability. Rivlin also favored devolution, the process of transferring some federal responsibilities to state and local authorities, as a way to increase public accountability and decrease federal budget deficits.

Rivlin earned many honors during her professional career. In 1983 she received the MacArthur Foundation Prize Fellowship. Three years later, while director of economic studies at the Brookings Institution, she became the president of the American Economic Association (AEA), the first of only two women to head the nation's largest organization of professional economists. In recognition of a long and distinguished career in service to America, President George W. Bush presented Alice M. Rivlin with the Elliot L. Richardson Prize for Excellence in Public Service in 2002.

Nicholas Gregory Mankiw: Chairman of the Council of Economic Advisors

Nicholas Gregory Mankiw (1958–) is a prominent American academic economist, turned government economist. Born in Trenton, New Jersey, Gregory Mankiw earned his undergraduate degree in economics at Princeton in 1980 and a Ph.D. four years later at the Massachusetts Institute of Technology. Most of Mankiw's professional life was spent in the classroom. He was an economics instructor at MIT from 1984 to 1985, an assistant professor of economics at Harvard from 1985 to 1987, and a full professor at Harvard from 1987 to 2003. Mankiw, an accomplished researcher, author, and teacher, was one of the youngest academics to earn the title of professor at Harvard. He penned numerous scholarly articles and several books, including multiple editions of two popular textbooks, *Macroeconomics* and *Principles of Economics,* each of which enjoyed healthy sales during the 1990s and early 2000s. In 2003 President George W. Bush appointed Mankiw chairman of the Council of Economic Advisors (CEA).

Mankiw's research dealt mainly with consumer behavior, financial markets, government stabilization policy, and economic growth. Active in macroeconomic policy issues and debates, the young Mankiw stirred some controversy with his biting criticisms of America's flirtation with supply-side economics during the 1980s. He argued that the supply-siders' tax cuts, which were designed to stimulate investment and promote economic growth, had instead saddled the country with crippling federal deficits and a spiraling national debt. Interestingly, as CEA chairman in 2003, Mankiw was in the awkward position of defending President George W. Bush's economic stimulus package, as outlined in the Jobs and Growth Tax Relief Reconciliation Act of 2003. This package included massive tax cuts for millions of Americans through restructured income tax rates and reduced taxes on capital gains and dividend income. These tax cuts were controversial, in part because they were enacted while the nation was amassing the largest federal budget deficit in history.

Mankiw is widely recognized as one of America's most talented macroeconomists. Despite his youth, he has served as an adviser to the Federal Reserve Bank of Boston and to the Congressional Budget Office (CBO). He has also served as director of the Monetary Economics Program at the National Bureau of Economic Research (NBER), a nonprofit think tank located in Cambridge, Massachusetts. As a consultant with the Educational Testing Service (ETS), Mankiw played an important role in the development of the College Board's advanced placement national exam in economics.

Robert L. Heilbroner: Economists as Worldly Philosophers

Robert L. Heilbroner (1919–) is a popular American economic historian and social critic, preferring the titles of philosophical historian or intellectual to economist. Heilbroner was born to a prosperous family in New York City, where he received a private school education at the Horace Mann School for

Boys. He attended Harvard University from 1936 to 1940, earning a bachelor's degree in history, government, and economics. After serving in the U.S. Army during World War II, Heilbroner worked as a business economist for a couple years. A passion for economics and writing inspired Heilbroner to take graduate courses in economics at the New School for Social Research in New York City, where he earned his Ph.D. in 1963. He authored his classic book, *The Worldly Philosophers: The Lives, Times, and Ideas of the Great Economic Thinkers* (1953), while still a student at the New School for Social Research. Since the 1950s, millions of copies of *The Worldly Philosophers* have been sold in the United States and abroad. In 1971 Heilbroner was appointed to the Norman Thomas chair in economics at the New School for Social Research, an institution he called home for the next three decades.

The Worldly Philosophers, the first of many books penned by Heilbroner, explored the lives and times of notable economists such as Adam Smith, David Ricardo, Karl Marx, and John Maynard Keynes. Heilbroner's book dispelled the dismal science image of economics, breathing life into the contributions of the great economists, whom he called "the worldly philosophers." He insisted that "the great economists pursued an inquiry as exciting—and as dangerous—as any the world has ever known. . . . The notions of the great economists were world-shaking, and their mistakes nothing short of calamitous."[15] Heilbroner's passion for economic ideas and economic conditions in a historical context influenced many of his later books. For example, in *The Future as History* (1960), Heilbroner questioned the direction of American capitalism and warned of global instability stemming from the economic chasm between rich and poor countries. He pursued the topic of uneven development in *The Great Ascent: The Struggle for Economic Development in Our Time* (1963), a book that challenged America and the richer nations to support development in the world's poor regions—a great ascent toward global prosperity. He declared: "if the Great Ascent is slow, cruel, even fearsome, it is also irresistible, stirring, grandiose. It is an avenue of history which, however difficult, leads from an eternity of dark suffering toward the possibility of light and life."[16]

Heilbroner is widely recognized as one of the most original thinkers and influential economists of the twentieth century. He bucked the mathematical revolution, which engulfed the economics profession during the second half of the century. Instead, Heilbroner emphasized the study of economics within its historical and social context, as illustrated in major works such as *The Making of Economic Society, An Inquiry into the Human Prospect, The Economic Transformation of America: 1600 to the Present* (with Aaron Singer), and *The Crisis of Vision in Modern Economic Thought* (with William Milberg). In 1994 the New York Council for the Humanities named Heilbroner its scholar of the year.

NOTES

1. Department of Labor (DOL), Bureau of Labor Statistics (BLS), "2001 National Occupational Employment and Wage Estimates, Life, Physical, and Social Sciences Oc-

cupations," www.bls.gov/oes/2001/oes_19Li.htm; and DOL, "Economists and Market and Survey Researchers," *Occupational Outlook Handbook: 2002–2003* (Indianapolis, IN: Just Works, December 23, 2003), 240.

2. DOL, *Occupational Outlook Handbook: 2002–2003,* 241.

3. BLS, "2001 National Occupational Employment and Wage Estimates, 19–3011 Economists," www.bls.gov/oes/2001/oes193011,htm; and BLS, "2001 National Occupational Employment and Wage Estimates, All Occupations," www.bls.gov/oes/2001/oes_00A1.htm.

4. BLS, "2001 National Occupational Employment and Wage Estimates, Life, Physical, and Social Science Occupations."

5. U.S. Census Bureau, "No. 588. Employed Civilians by Occupation, Sex, Race, and Hispanic Origin: 1983 and 2001," *Statistical Abstract of the United States: 2002,* 122nd ed. (Washington, DC: U.S. Government Printing Office, 2002), 381.

6. John L. Siegfried, "Trends in Undergraduate Economics Degrees, 1991–2001," *Journal of Economic Education,* Summer 2002, 294.

7. Charles E. Scott and John J. Siegfried, "Table A-Survey of Earned Doctorates: Demographic Profile of Doctorate Recipients in Economics and Econometrics," in "America Economic Association Universal Academic Questionnaire Summary Statistics," *American Economic Review Papers and Proceedings,* 92 (May 2002): 530.

8. DOL, *Occupational Outlook Handbook: 2002–2003,* 240.

9. National Association for Business Economics (NABE), "The Profession of Business Economics," in *Careers in Business Economics* (Washington, DC: Author, 2002)

10. NABE, "Salaries of Business Economists," in *Careers in Business Economics.*

11. DOL, *Occupational Outlook Handbook: 2002–2003,* 240; and DOL/BLS, *Career Guide to Federal Government, Excluding Postal Service*, 222, www.bls.gov/oco/cg/cgs041.htm.

12. DOL/BLS, "Table 5. Average Annual Salaries in the Federal Government in Selected Occupations, March 2001," *Career Guide to Industries: Federal Government, Excluding Postal Service*, 222.

13. Paul A. Samuelson and William D. Nordhaus, *Economics* 15th ed. (New York: McGraw-Hill, 1995), xxix.

14. The Nobel Foundation, "The Bank of Sweden Prize in Economic Sciences in Memory of Alfred Nobel 1970, Paul A. Samuelson," www.nobel.se/economics/laureates/1970/index.html.

15. Robert L. Heilbroner, *The Worldly Philosophers: The Lives, Times and Ideas of the Great Economic Thinkers,* rev. ed. (New York: Simon and Schuster, 1961), 2.

16. Robert L. Heilbroner, *The Great Ascent: The Struggle for Economic Development in Our Time* (New York: Harper & Row, Publishers, 1963), 158.

SELECTED READINGS

Bannock, Graham, R. E. Baxter, and Evan Davis. *Dictionary of Economics.* 4th ed. Princeton, NJ: Bloomberg Press, 2003.

Buchholz, Todd G., and Martin Feldstein. *News Ideas from Dead Economists: An Introduction to Modern Economic Thought.* rev. ed. New York: Penguin USA, 1999.

Cicarelli, James, and Julianne Cicarelli. *Distinguished Women Economists.* Westport, CT: Greenwood Publishing Group, 2003.

Easterlin, Richard A. *The Reluctant Economist: Perspectives on Economics, Economic History, and Demography.* New York: Cambridge University Press, 2004.

Economist, The. *The Economist Style Guide.* 8th ed. London, UK: Economists Books, 2003.

Freedman, Craig, and Rick Szostak, eds. *Tales of Narcissus: The Looking Glass of Economic Science.* Huntington, NJ: Nova Science Publishers, Inc., 2003.

Gale Research Staff. *Economists and Their Theories for Students.* Farmington Hills, MI: Gale Group, 2004.

Heilbroner, Robert L. *The Worldly Philosophers: The Lives, Times and Ideas of the Great Economic Thinkers.* 7th ed. New York: Touchstone Books, 1999.

Heilbroner, Robert L., and Aaron Singer. *The Economic Transformation of America: 1600 to the Present.* 4th ed. Belmont, CA: Wadsworth Publishing, 1998.

Landsburg, Steven. *Armchair Economist: Economics and Everyday Experience.* New York: Free Press, 1995.

Mankiw, N. Gregory. *Principles of Economics.* 3rd ed. Cincinnati, OH: South-Western College Publisher, 2003.

Samuelson, Paul A., and Michael Szenberg. *Passion and Craft: Economists at Work.* Ann Arbor, MI: University of Michigan Press, 1998.

Skousen, Mark. *The Making of Modern Economics: The Lives and Ideas of Great Thinkers.* Armonk, NY: M.E. Sharpe, 2001.

Swonk, Diane. *The Passionate Economist: Finding the Power and Humanity behind the Numbers.* New York: John Wiley & Sons, 2003.

Szenberg, Michael, ed. *Eminent Economists: Their Life Philosophies.* New York: Cambridge University Press, 1992.

Thompson, William. *A Guide for the Young Economist.* Cambridge, MA: MIT Press, 2001.

Wahid, Abu N. M. *Frontiers of Economics: Nobel Laureates of the Twentieth Century.* Westport, CT: Greenwood Publishing Group, 2002.

Wheelan, Charles. *Naked Economics: Undressing the Dismal Science.* New York: W. W. Norton & Company, 2002.

Zellner, Arnold. *Statistics, Econometrics and Forecasting.* New York: Cambridge University Press, 2003.

Appendix A

Glossary of Selected Terms

Absolute advantage Occurs when one country produces a product more efficiently than another country.

Academic economist An economist employed mainly by colleges and universities to teach, conduct scholarly research, and publish.

Acquisition Occurs when one firm buys some or all of the ownership in a target firm. Pfizer Corporation's acquisition of Pharmacia in 2003 cost Pfizer $63 billion.

Advanced countries The high-income industrialized countries of the global north; also called the developed countries.

Advertising A paid announcement by a business or an industry to inform consumers about a product and to convince people to purchase the good or service.

Aggregate demand The total demand for all goods and services in an economy.

Aggregate supply The total supply of all goods and services produced in an economy.

Agricultural revolution Describes the momentous shift from a nomadic lifestyle during the Paleolithic Age to permanent agriculture during the Neolithic Age.

Agricultural sector An economic sector composed mainly of farms, dairies, poultry and livestock farms, forestry, and fishing and shellfish industries.

Balance of payments Records all transactions between people in one country and foreigners, including international trade, foreign direct investment, and foreign aid.

Balance of trade Measures the difference between the value of a nation's imports and exports. Nations incur a trade deficit when imports are greater than exports, and have a trade surplus when exports are greater than imports.

Banking system A financial system that consists of a central bank, commercial banks, and other depository institutions.

Bankruptcy The legal recognition that a business or an individual is unable to repay its debts; most personal bankruptcies are filed under Chapters 7 or 13 of the bankruptcy code, while most business bankruptcies are filed under Chapter 11.

Barriers to entry Factors that discourage or prevent firms from entering or exiting an industry.

Barter A system of exchange in which one good is exchanged for a second good.

Basic economic questions The universal questions that are answered by economic systems: what to produce and in what quantity? how to produce? for whom to produce?

Bear market A sustained fall in the value of stocks.

Bond A type of loan, or IOU, issued by corporations and governments as a means of borrowing money; investors purchase bonds to earn interest income.

Bond market A mechanism by which corporate and government bonds are traded.

Budget constraint The limits on consumer choice dictated by people's income and the prices of goods.

Bull market A sustained rise in the value of stocks.

Business cycle Illustrates the short-term ups and downs in the real gross domestic product: expansion, peak, contraction, and trough.

Business economist An economist employed by firms to analyze economic data and help management make informed decisions.

Capacity utilization rate Measures the percentage of a nation's factory capacity that is currently being used in productive enterprise.

Capital deepening Occurs when a nation's capital stock per worker increases.

Capital flight Occurs when the wealthy elite in poorer countries invests its savings in safer, more profitable ventures abroad.

Capital goods The items that are designed to produce other products; examples include business computers, delivery trucks, and shopping malls. Capital goods, often called capital, is a factor of production.

Capitalism A type of economic system in which the private sector owns and controls the factors of production.

Capital markets The financial institutions that channel peoples' savings from households to business firms for the purpose of productive investments; examples include commercial banks, insurance companies; and stock exchanges.

Capital stock The total amount of capital goods in a nation.

Cartel An agreement or organization that coordinates the production decisions of independent producers of similar or identical products to influence the product's supply and price. An example is the Organization of Petroleum Exporting Countries (OPEC).

Ceteris paribus An assumption made by economists that all factors within the economy can be held constant for a moment; the *ceteris paribus* assumption permits economists to study a specific cause-and-effect relationship by temporarily excluding other variables.

Charge card A payment card that allows the cardholder to purchase goods at a specific business and repay the money in monthly payments.

Circular flow model An economic model that shows how goods and services are exchanged in a market economy; illustrates the exchanges on the product market and the factor market.

Civil society organizations Formal groups founded to improve the human condition; CSOs include nongovernmental organizations and other nonprofit groups.

Classical school A school of economic thought that favors laissez-faire economic principles, including a reliance on private-sector decision making, competitive markets, and few government interventions in economic activity.

Closed shop An arrangement that required employers to hire only labor union members; the Taft-Hartley Act of 1947 banned the closed shop.

Collective bargaining The power of labor unions to represent the collective interests of workers in formal contract negotiations with management.
Collusion An illegal conspiracy among competing firms designed to fix prices, agree on market share, or otherwise reduce competition.
Command economy A type of economic system in which the government dictates the answers to the basic economic questions; the command economy model and the market economy model represent the extremes along the economic continuum.
Commercial bank A private financial corporation owned by stockholders and operated by professional management for profit.
Commercial revolution An economic transition from localized production to one based on global trade; the commercial revolution (1400s–1700s) stimulated exploration and colonization of peoples by the European powers.
Commodity money An item that is commonly accepted as a medium of exchange and also has value in itself; an example is tobacco money in colonial Virginia.
Communism A type of economic system in which the government owns and controls most of the means of production such as factories and farms; communism is most often associated with the economic system created under Marxist doctrine in the twentieth century.
Comparable worth The process of equalizing pay rates between jobs in the workplace that require similar skills; designed mainly to eliminate gender inequities.
Comparative advantage, theory of States that nations should specialize in the production of goods in which they have the greatest advantage, or the lesser disadvantage; the theory of comparative advantage supports free trade in global markets.
Competition The economic rivalry that exists among producers of similar products.
Complementary good A product that is normally used in conjunction with another good; an example is flashlights and batteries.
Conglomerate merger A merger of firms in unrelated industries.
Consumerism The protection of consumer interests.
Consumer movement The embodiment of the actions, programs, and other forms of activism by individual consumerists and consumerist organizations.
Consumer price index (CPI) Measures the percentage change in the price of a uniform market basket of products over time; the CPI is used to calculate the rate of inflation and deflation.
Consumers People who buy goods and services to satisfy personal wants and needs.
Consumer sovereignty States that informed consumers exercise freedom of choice and, through their buying decisions, signal producers what to produce.
Consumption goods Goods and services designed for immediate use by households, including food, electrical appliances, and legal services.
Corporate state A national economy that places firms, workers, and other aspects of business activity under the control of a dictator; private enterprise and private profits exist, but under the direction of the government. The corporate state existed in twentieth-century fascist governments.
Corporation A type of business that is owned by stockholders, but typically run by professional managers.
Correlation-as-cause fallacy Faulty reasoning, which incorrectly assumes that because two events occur at about the same time the first must have caused the second.
Costs of production The payments made by firms in exchange for the factors of production; costs of production include wages, rents, interest, and profits.

Craft union A labor organization of skilled workers in a single trade, such as carpenters, masons, and printers.

Credit card A payment card that allows the cardholder to purchase goods at a variety of venues and repay the money in monthly payments.

Credit union A nonprofit financial cooperative that is owned and operated by members.

Customs union A trade bloc that eliminates trade barriers among member nations and establishes uniform trade policies, including trade barriers, with nonmember nations.

Deductive approach A method of forming economic theories; the deductive approach begins with a hypothesis or generalization based on observations, followed by data collection and testing.

Deflation The overall decline in the price level in an economy; also called negative inflation.

Demand The amount of a good, service, or resource that people are willing and able to buy at a series of prices at a moment in time.

Democracy A type of political system that relies on broad-based citizen participation, free elections, and the rule of law.

Democratic socialism A type of economic system in which the government owns and controls some of the means of production and provides extensive social programs; examples include Sweden and Norway.

Depository institutions Financial institutions that accept deposits and extend loans to borrowers; the main depository institutions are commercial banks, savings and loan associations, savings banks, and credit unions.

Depression A severe, prolonged recession.

Derived demand The demand for a resource is derived from the demand for the product the resource is used to produce.

Developing countries The poorer, less industrialized countries of the global south.

Development model The conditions under which economic decisions are made in the world's poor nations; some development models lean toward the command model and others toward the market model.

Development plan A type of economic blueprint that outlines a nation's path toward sustainable economic development.

Dialectical materialism A basic Marxist belief that ongoing class conflicts result in the progression of history from one stage to the next; under this interpretation of history, the final stage in human history is perfect communism.

Digital divide The technological chasm between the developing countries and the advanced countries; the *digital divide* usually refers to the gap in availability and use of information and communications technologies (ICTs) between the rich and poor nations.

Diminishing marginal utility, law of States that consumer satisfaction declines as additional units of the same good are consumed in a specified time period.

Discount rate A monetary policy tool used by the Federal Reserve System; the discount rate involves changes in the interest rate charged by the Fed to banks for short-term loans.

Division of labor Specialization applied to labor; the division of labor becomes more sophisticated as economies become more advanced.

Domestic system A system of production that relies on small-scale, labor-intensive cottage industries.

Econometrics The use of highly sophisticated mathematical models to explain or predict economic behaviors.
Economic aid The cross-border grants, loans, technical assistance, and emergency assistance that typically flows from the advanced countries to the poorer nations.
Economic choice Any decision that people make to use resources one way rather than a second way.
Economic development A process that rests on achieving sustainable economic growth, improvements in people's quality of life, and conditions for long-run prosperity.
Economic goals National economic objectives upon which society evaluates the overall performance of the economy; U.S. economic goals include economic freedom, efficiency, equity, security, stability, and growth.
Economic growth An economic goal measured by a sustained increase in a nation's total output; often measured by a sustained increase in the real GDP per capita.
Economic indicators Economic data used to predict and assess the duration of business cycles; types of indicators include leading, coincident, and lagging.
Economic law An economic theory that has survived repeated testing, such the law of demand; also called an economic principle.
Economic model A simplified version of reality designed to focus on a specific relationship between two or more variables; often shows cause-and-effect relationships.
Economics The study of how people choose to use their scarce resources to satisfy their wants and needs; the study deals with production, distribution, and consumption decisions.
Economic sectors The broad categories of production in an economy, including the services-producing sector, goods-producing sector, and agricultural sector.
Economic system The sum total of all economic activity that takes place within a society; economic systems answer the basic economic questions of what, how, and for whom to produce.
Economies of scale The decline in the average cost of producing goods as the rate of output rises; an argument used to support mergers and acquisitions of firms and the existence of natural monopolies.
Economist A professional social scientist who analyzes the production and distribution of goods and services in a society; the three main categories of economists are academic economists, business economists, and government economists.
Employment rate The percentage of the labor force that has a job.
Entrepreneur A person who starts a new business, develops a new product, or devises a new way to produce a product; a risk-taker and innovator.
Entrepreneurship The risk-taking and innovation of entrepreneurs; some economists consider entrepreneurship a factor of production.
Equilibrium wage The point of intersection between the labor demand curve and the labor supply curve in a particular labor market.
European Union The world's most highly integrated custom's union, which includes common economic and political policies and a common currency (the euro).
Expropriation The government seizure of resources, firms, or entire industries without compensating the previous owner.
Factor market Represents all purchases of resources in an economy; also called the resource market. Exchanges in the factor market are illustrated in the circular flow model.

Factors of production The resources needed to produce products, including natural resources, human resources, capital goods; entrepreneurship is often considered a factor of production.

Factory system A system of production that relies on large-scale, capital-intensive production in factories; a system that relies on specialization and a division of labor.

Fallacy of composition Faulty reasoning, which assumes that what is true for a piece is true for the whole.

Fascism A totalitarian system of government headed by a single individual that embraces the superiority of the state over the individual, extreme nationalism, obedience to authority, and the use of force to achieve objectives.

Federal budget A document that outlines how the federal government plans to raise and spend money during the upcoming fiscal year.

Federal funds rate The interest rate that banks charge to other banks for short-term loans.

Federal Reserve System America's central bank, with responsibility for maintaining the stability of the nation's banking system and monetary system.

Fiat money A type of money that derives its value by government decree; an example is the paper currency used in the United States today.

Financial contagion The uncontrollable spread of a financial crisis from one country to other countries or regions; viewed as a threat to global economic stability.

Firm A business entity that produces a good or service.

Fiscal policy The tax and spending policies of Congress and the president that are designed to promote economic growth and stability.

Five-year plan A government economic plan that outlines economic goals, production targets, and resource allocation; commonly associated with communist economies.

Fixed costs Business costs that do not change along with changes in a firm's rate of output; examples include regular rent or lease payments, interest payments.

Foreign debt The money owed by one country to foreign governments, banks, multilateral organizations, or other investors; also called external debt.

Foreign direct investment (FDI) The cross-border investments that result in one company's gaining ownership or control of productive facilities in another country; FDI occurs through mergers and acquisitions, and greenfield investments.

Foreign exchange market A highly integrated global network of financial institutions that converts currencies and trades currencies for profit.

Franchise A business consisting of a parent company called a franchiser, and satellite firms called franchisees; examples include Subway, McDonald's and Holiday Inn.

Freedom of choice A basic economic freedom of consumers in a market-oriented economy; consumers' right to purchase goods that best satisfy their needs.

Freedom of enterprise A basic freedom of business firms in a market-oriented economy; producers' right to produce goods in a manner that generates profits.

Free rider dilemma The problem that results when people are able to benefit from the use of a good or service without having to pay for it; the free rider dilemma is an important justification for government provision of public goods.

Free trade International trade that is not restricted by trade barriers such as import quotas or tariffs.

Free trade area A trade bloc that eliminates trade barriers among members, but permits members to devise their own trade policies with nonmember countries.

Futures market A mechanism by which contracts for items are traded.

Geographic monopoly A single firm that provides a good or service to a certain region.

Glasnost A reform program initiated by Soviet Premier Mikhail Gorbachev to promote a new atmosphere of openness in the political arena during the mid-1980s.

Global economy The international network of individuals, businesses, multilateral organizations, and governments that make production, distribution, and consumption decisions.

Globalization The process of creating a more integrated and interdependent global economy through expanded international trade, foreign direct investment, and cross-border capital flows.

Good governance Honest and competent government that abides by the rule of law.

Goods-producing sector The economic sector that supplies tangible items in an economy, such as final goods, intermediate goods, and resources; the goods-producing sector is composed of all manufacturing, construction, and mining industries.

Government economist An economist employed by any level of government to collect and analyze data necessary in the operation of government or in the formation of public policy.

Government monopoly Exists when any level of government becomes the sole producer of a good or service; examples include local government control of water and sewage services.

Gradualism A cautious approach to economic transition, based on experimentation and gradual infusion of successful market reforms into a command economy.

Great Leap Forward China's flawed economic program to expand its industrial production during the late 1950s and early 1960s.

Gross domestic product The total market value of final goods and services produced in a nation in a given year; includes the output of domestic and foreign firms within the nation's borders.

Gross investment The sum total of private investment and public investment in an economy in a given year.

Gross national income (GNI) Measures a nation's total income by adding the value of household spending on consumption goods, capital goods, and government goods; the GNI per capita is the leading measurement of well-being in the global economy.

Gross national product (GNP) The total market value of all final goods and services produced by a nation's firms operating anywhere in the world; excludes the value of output produced by foreign firms within the nation's borders.

Gross saving The sum total of savings by individuals, businesses, and the government in an economy in a given year.

Horizontal merger A merger of firms that sell similar products in the same market.

Household responsibility system A market-oriented economic reform in China that permits peasants to lease government land and work it for private profit.

Human capital Workers whose abilities and skills have been enhanced, mainly by education or training.

Human resources The people involved in production, such as teachers, factory workers, and farmers; human resources is a factor of production.

Hyperinflation An annual inflation rate that rises into the hundreds or thousands; Russia's hyperinflation soared to nearly 2,000 percent in 1992.

Income effect of a price change States the inverse relationship between the price of a good and a household's economic well-being; as the price of a product falls, people are better off; as the price of a product rises, people are worse off.

Income effect of a wage increase States that as the wage rate for a worker increases the worker will work fewer hours and therefore have more leisure; illustrated on the upper segment of some labor supply curves.

Indicative planning A collaborative, inclusive economic planning process employed by some democratic socialist countries.

Inductive approach A method of forming economic theories; the inductive approach begins with the identification of a problem, followed by data collection, generalizations, and testing.

Industrialization The conversion of an economy from labor-intensive production to large-scale mechanized production; historically, industrialization occurred in conjunction with the Industrial Revolution.

Industrial Revolution The economic transformation of societies from agriculture to mechanized production in the factory system; the origins of the Industrial Revolution are traced to Great Britain in the 1700s.

Industrial union A labor organization composed of all workers within an industry, regardless of skill level or job description.

Industry Represents all the firms that produce a similar product.

Inflation An increase in the overall price level in an economy over time.

Inflation rate Measures the percentage increase in the overall price level over time.

Information and communications technologies The technological advances that radically increased the ability to store, retrieve, and share information; these technologies support the information age and the globalization process.

Innovation The process of converting scientific discoveries and technological advances into profitable products or improved methods of production.

Interlocking directorate Occurs when members of one corporate board of directors also sit on a competitor's board of directors; ruled an anticompetitive behavior.

International Monetary Fund (IMF) A multilateral organization designed to stabilize the international monetary system; the IMF is a specialized agency within the United Nations system.

International trade The cross-border exchange of goods or services; trade is conducted through importing and exporting goods and services.

Intrapreneurship Entrepreneurial activity that occurs within an existing business.

Investment goods Items not designed for present consumption, including capital goods, inventories, and residential housing.

Joint venture A business agreement between two or more companies to produce or sell a good or service; usually a short-term business arrangement.

Keynesian school A school of economic thought centered on the works of John M. Keynes; Keynesians favor government intervention in the economy to promote economic growth and stability.

Labor The human element in production; a factor of production; also called human resources.

Labor force Consists of individuals who are 16 years old or older and who are employed or actively seeking a job.

Labor market Any situation in which individuals voluntarily supply their labor in exchange for a wage or salary.

Labor movement The collective actions of laborers and labor unions over time to improve wages and other conditions of employment.

Labor union A formal association of workers empowered by members to negotiate labor contracts with the management of firms.

Laissez-faire capitalism A doctrine that supports economic freedoms of marketplace participants and opposes most types of government intervention in economic activity.

Law of demand States the inverse relationship between the price of a good and the quantity demanded.

Limited liability company A hybrid business organization that combines features from corporations, partnerships, and sole proprietorships.

Macroeconomics The branch of economics that deals with economic performance of the entire economy, including overall price levels, unemployment, and national output.

Management A process that coordinates the use of resources to achieve an organization's goals; also, the group of people who conduct the four functions of managing an organization: planning, organizing, implementing, and controlling.

Marginalism An economic analysis that considers the additional costs and benefits of a decision; most economic decisions are made at the margin.

Marginalist school A school of economic thought that emphasized rational decision making on both the supply and demand sides of a market; many principles related to decision making at the margin are outgrowths of the marginalist school.

Marginal utility The additional satisfaction that is derived from the consumption of additional units of the same good during a specific time period.

Market Occurs whenever two or more parties freely exchange goods, services, financial instruments, or other transferable items.

Market economy A type of economic system that relies on the private sector to answer the basic economic questions; the market economy and the command economy represent the extremes of the economic continuum.

Market equilibrium The point at which the market demand and the market supply curves for a product intersect.

Market mechanism The interaction of supply and demand in free markets to determine prices and allocate resources without government intervention; the market mechanism supports individual self-interest and competitive markets.

Market structure The competitive environments under which industries are organized; the four types of market structure are perfect competition, monopolistic competition, oligopoly, and monopoly.

Marxism A doctrine, and a school of economic thought, that stemmed from the works of Karl Marx; Marxism is grounded in socialist principles and committed to the overthrow of capitalism and the creation of perfect communism.

Mercantilism The belief that a country's wealth is derived from its ability to accumulate gold and silver.

Merger Occurs when two or more firms combine their assets, or equity, to form a larger firm; the merger of Exxon and Mobil in 1999 formed the Exxon Mobil corporation.

Microeconomics The branch of economics that focuses on specific interactions or behaviors of participants in the economy, such as workers, consumers, and firms.
Minimum wage A price floor that sets a minimum hourly wage rate for employees.
Mixed economy An economy that combines features from the market model and the command model; the term *mixed economy* is often used to describe economies that lean heavily toward the market model, such as the United States.
M1 A measurement of the money supply that includes coin, paper currency, demand deposits, and traveler's checks.
Monetarism A school of thought that supports a fixed, predictable rate of growth in the nation's money supply; the monetarists' goal is macroeconomic stability.
Monetary policy The actions of the Federal Reserve System to alter the money supply and the cost of credit in pursuit of national macroeconomic goals, mainly growth and stability.
Money Any item that is commonly accepted in payment for goods or services or in payment of debts.
Money supply The total amount of money in circulation in an economy; major measurements of the money supply are M1, M2, and M3.
Monopolistic competition A type of market structure in which many firms, perhaps 25, 50, or even 100, produce and sell differentiated products.
M3 A measurement of the money supply that includes M2, plus larger time deposits and money market funds, repurchase agreements, and some eurodollars.
M2 A measurement of the money supply that includes M1, plus near monies such as savings deposits, small time deposits, and money market mutual funds.
Mutual fund A diversified pool of financial assets managed by a professional investment manager; a more secure type of investment than common stocks.
NASDAQ Stock Market The largest stock market in the world, which links investors through sophisticated electronic stock trading systems.
National debt The accumulated debt of the federal government over time; also called the federal debt.
Nationalization A government takeover of a private enterprise with compensation to the previous owner.
Natural monopoly A single producer of a good or service that exists mainly because the economies of scale reduces the average cost of producing additional units of output; natural monopolies, such as local power companies, are regulated by the government.
Natural rate of unemployment The percentage of the labor force that is frictionally and structurally unemployed.
Natural resources The gifts of nature that are used in production, such as sunlight, natural forests, and rivers; natural resources is a factor of production.
New Economic Policy A program of small-scale private enterprise designed to spark production and employment in the Soviet Union during the 1920s; the New Economic Policy was abruptly ended by Joseph Stalin in 1928.
New protectionism Favors additional government restriction on and control over foreign trade and foreign direct investment to help protect peoples' quality of the life.
New York Stock Exchange The largest floor-based stock market in the world; ranked by total trade volume, the NYSE is the second largest stock exchange in the world behind the NASDAQ Stock Market.

Nominal gross domestic product The gross domestic product not adjusted for inflation.

Nonconvertible currency A currency that cannot be exchanged for other currencies due to its uncertain value.

Nongovernmental organization Groups that research issues, share their findings, and advocate for reforms; examples include Amnesty International and Jubilee 2000.

Nonprofit organization An organization designed to provide goods or services to people, but not to earn profits for shareholders, employees, or other stakeholders; examples include the Red Cross, Veterans of Foreign Wars, and the United Way.

Nonrenewable resources Resources that are consumed during production and cannot be replenished, such as natural gas and petroleum.

Normative economics A type of economics concerned with what ought to be or what ought not be; normative economic statements are subjective and cannot be tested objectively.

North American Free Trade Agreement A free trade area comprised of Canada, Mexico, and the United States.

Oligopoly A type of market structure in which several firms, perhaps 3, 6, or 12, dominate the output of an industry; recently, economists say an oligopoly exists when the top 4 firms in an industry produce at least 40 percent of the industry's output.

Open market operations A monetary policy tool used by the Federal Reserve System, which involves the sale or purchase of government securities; open market operations is the most used Fed tool.

Open shop An arrangement that allows workers to join or refuse to join an existing union in a workplace.

Opportunity cost The second best use of limited resources; the good or service that is not produced or consumed.

Organization for Economic Cooperation and Development An association of 30 countries that discusses issues of global concern and coordinates official development assistance to the poorer nations.

Partnership A type of business that is owned by two or more people, called partners.

Perestroika An economic restructuring in the Soviet Union along more market-oriented lines; initiated during the mid-1980s by Premier Mikhail Gorbachev.

Perfect competition A type of market structure in which thousands of independently operating firms produce and sell a homogeneous product; an example is the U.S. wheat industry.

Personal income The sum total of all income households receive after social insurance contributions have been deducted but before personal taxes have been paid.

Physiocratic school An economic school of thought that stressed the primacy of agriculture and the agricultural elite in the nation's economy.

Positive economics A type of economics concerned with what is; positive economics is sometimes called descriptive economics; positive economic statements can be tested objectively.

Price ceiling A government-imposed maximum price that a seller may charge for a good or service; an example is rent control on apartment units.

Price floor A government-guaranteed minimum price for a product or resource; an example is a minimum wage for workers.

Private property Any good, resource, or other asset that is owned and controlled by an individual or a business firm.

Private property rights Legal codes and other protections that guarantee people's right to own, control, buy, sell, and profit from their private property.

Private sector The sector of the economy comprised of households and firms; the nongovernmental sector.

Privatization The process of selling state-owned enterprises to individuals or firms in the private sector of the economy.

Producer cooperative A business that is owned and operated collectively by the firm's employees.

Producer price index Measures the percentage change in the prices of raw materials, intermediate goods, and other items used in the production process.

Producers Firms that make or sell goods and services, mainly to earn profits.

Producer sovereignty Theory that consumer choice is manipulated by big business and advertisers.

Production The process of converting the factors of production into goods and services.

Production possibilities curve Illustrates the range of possible production choices that nations or firms might make at a specific moment in time; the production possibilities curve is used to show the opportunity cost of production decisions.

Production sharing The production of a good in stages, and in a number of different countries, in order to minimize production costs.

Productivity A measurement of output per unit of input; productivity is typically measured in terms of output per unit of labor employed in the production process.

Product market Represents all purchases of finished goods and services in an economy; exchanges in the product market are illustrated in the circular flow model.

Progressive tax A tax that takes a larger percentage of income from high-income households than from lower-income households.

Proportional tax A tax that takes the same percentage of income from all households, regardless of income level.

Protectionism The government's use of trade barriers, such as import quotas and tariffs, to restrict foreign imports.

Public assistance Government transfer programs that provide financial or other assistance to people who have made no financial contribution to the program; examples include Temporary Assistance for Needy Families, Medicaid, and food stamps.

Public goods Goods provided by the government to satisfy a public need; public goods, such as public schools and national defense, are nonexclusionary.

Public sector The sector of the economy composed of government at the local, state, and national levels.

Purchasing power parity A conversion process for nations' currencies that assesses and compares the buying power of money within individual economies.

Real gross domestic product The gross domestic product adjusted for inflation.

Recession A relatively short-term economic downturn in economic activity, marked by a decline in gross domestic product for at least two quarters and a rise in unemployment.

Regional development banks Member-owned, multilateral lending institutions that promote economic development in different world regions, including Africa, Asia, Latin America, and eastern and central Europe.

Regressive tax A tax that takes a larger percentage of income from lower-income households than from upper-income households.

Renewable resources Resources than can be replenished, such as sunlight and forests.

Representative money A type of money that has no inherent value but represents something of value; an example was U.S. silver certificates, which were redeemable for silver until 1968.

Reserve requirement A monetary policy tool used by the Federal Reserve System; the reserve requirement involves changes in the percentage of transactions accounts that banks must hold as reserves.

Savings and loan association A savings institution designed to meet the needs of households rather than businesses.

Savings bank A savings institution designed to provide home mortgages and other personal loans.

Say's law States that supply creates its own demand, also called the law of markets; Say's law is used to support supply-side economic thinking.

School of economic thought A group of economists who share common ideas about how scarce resources should be used to achieve society's goals.

Secondary effects The unintended consequences of an economic decision, policy, or action.

Services-producing sector An economic sector that supplies productive activities; includes companies connected with transportation, communication, retail trade, banking, financial securities, health care, and government services.

Shock therapy An aggressive approach employed by some transition countries to cast off communism and create market-oriented economies.

Single cause fallacy Faulty economic reasoning, which identifies just one cause of a problem when, in fact, there are multiple causes.

Small business A firm that employs fewer than 500 workers.

Social capital The broad infrastructure of a nation, which is financed with tax dollars for the collective welfare of citizens.

Social insurance Government transfer payments that provide financial or other assistance to people who have made a financial contribution to the program; examples include Social Security payments, Medicare, and unemployment compensation.

Socialism A type of economic system based on public ownership and control of key resources and industries; strands include democratic socialism and authoritarian socialism.

Sole proprietorship A type of business that is owned by one person, the proprietor.

Specialization Occurs when individuals or firms produce a specific product or narrow range of products; occurs when regions or nations produce a narrow range of products; specialization promotes interdependence.

Stagflation The simultaneous occurrence of recession, rising unemployment, and inflation.

Statism An economic philosophy that supports active government intervention in the economy, including the nationalization of key industries by government.

Stock A certificate of ownership in a corporation.

Stock market A mechanism by which corporate stocks are traded.

Substitute good A product that can be used in place of a second good; an example is Coca-Cola and Pepsi Cola.

Substitution effect of a price change States that as the price of a good falls, people will buy more of the good and less of a substitute good; and vice versa.

Substitution effect of a wage increase States that as the wage rate increases, the worker will work additional hours and, therefore, will have less leisure; illustrated on the lower potion of most labor supply curves.

Supply The amount of a good, service, or resource that producers are willing and able to sell at a series of prices at a moment in time.

Supply-side economics A school of thought that stresses the role of incentives, such as tax cuts, to stimulate productive investment and increased business activity.

Sustainable consumption Consumption based on the efficient purchase and use of resources and products by consumers, firms, and government.

Sustainable economic development Economic development that includes long-term economic growth and improvements in people's quality of life.

Sweatshop A production facility, such as a factory or a mill, that offers poor working conditions and low pay.

Tax A mandatory payment by individuals or businesses to the federal, state, or local government.

Technological monopoly A single firm that produces a good or service because it alone has the right to employ a patented technology in the good's production.

Total cost The sum total of a firm's fixed costs and variable costs.

Township and village enterprises Profit-making firms in rural China that are owned by local governments or, in special instances, by individuals; a market-oriented reform.

Trade barriers Government policies designed to discourage or prohibit imports; examples include import quotas and tariffs.

Trade deficit Occurs when the value of a nation's exports is less than the value of its imports; also called an unfavorable balance of trade.

Trade-off Occurs when people choose to use a resource in one manner rather than another.

Trade surplus Occurs when the value of a nation's exports is greater than the value of its imports; also called a favorable balance of trade.

Traditional economy A type of economic system that relies on custom or tradition to answer the basic economic questions.

Transfer payments Payments of money, goods, or services that are financed by one group of people and distributed to a second group; government transfer payments are financed by taxpayers and distributed in the form of social insurance or public assistance payments.

Transition economies The 28 eastern and central European countries that endeavored to transform their economies from communism to capitalism, and their political systems from totalitarianism to democracy, during the 1990s and early 2000s; also called transition countries.

Transnational organization A formal group or institution designed to address global issues through collective action; also called a multilateral organization; examples include the World Bank, International Monetary Fund, and World Trade Organization.

Trust An association of corporations whose stock is held by a single board of directors; antitrust laws have been enacted over the past century to protect competitive markets.

Tying agreement An anticompetitive business arrangement that requires buyers of one good to likewise buy related products, mainly complementary goods, from the same supplier.

Unemployment The number of people in the labor force without a job.

Unemployment rate The percentage of the labor force that is without a job.

Utilitarianism Applied to economics, utilitarianism supports economic policies that benefit the greatest number of people.

Utility The amount of satisfaction a person derives from the consumption of a good or service.

Union shop An arrangement that requires workers to join an existing union after they are hired by a firm, agency, or other employer.

United Nations The world's leading public forum for discussing issues of global concern, including world peace, human rights, and sustainable economic development; these goals are supported through a variety of specialized agencies, programs, and funds.

Variable costs Business costs that change along with changes in a firm's rate of output; examples include costs associated with labor and materials used in production.

Vertical merger A merger of firms that produce different goods or resources that are used in the production of a final good; the objective of a vertical merger is to control some output at each phase in the production of a final good.

Venture initiation The creation of a new business through entrepreneurial activity.

War communism The Bolshevik program to mobilize Russia's resources during the civil war that raged between 1918 and 1921; marked by confiscations of agricultural output, expropriations of foreign and domestic firms, and compulsory labor.

Welfare economics A branch of economics that deals with the redistribution of society's income and wealth to promote people's economic well-being.

Welfare state The provision of extensive social programs by the government to provide cradle to grave security for people; most commonly associated with public policies of the democratic socialist countries in Scandinavia.

World Bank Group A multilateral development organization comprised of five mutually supporting institutions; the World Bank is a specialized agency within the United Nations system.

World Trade Organization A multilateral organization designed to support free and fair trade in the world economy; the WTO replaced the General Agreement on Tariffs and Trade in 1995.

World Wide Web Links documents and files on the Internet; relies on the HyperText Transfer Protocol (HTTP) to locate resources stored on other computers on the Internet.

Appendix B

Key Economic Web Sites

This list identifies Web sites that provide timely, authoritative economic information for students, teachers, researchers, and citizens. The Web sites provide convenient access to government departments, agencies, and commissions; nonprofit organizations and advocacy groups; and a variety of multilateral organizations.

AFL-CIO	www.aflcio.org
African Development Bank	www.afdb.org
American Economic Association	www.vanderbilt.edu/AEA
Asian Development Bank	www.adb.org
Association of Southeast Asian Nations	www.asean.or.id
Bank of International Settlements	www.bis.org
Bureau of Economic Analysis	www.bea.gov
Bureau of Labor Statistics	www.bls.gov
Bureau of the Census	www.census.gov
Chicago Board of Trade	www.cbt.com
Chicago Mercantile Exchange	www.cme.com
Conference Board	www.conference-board.org
Congressional Budget Office	www.cbo.gov
Consumer Federation of America	www.consumerfed.org
Consumer Product Safety Commission	www.cpsc.gov
Consumers International	www.consumersinternational.org
Department of Agriculture	www.usda.gov
Department of Commerce	www.doc.gov

Department of Energy	www.doe.gov
Department of Health and Human Services	www.dhhs.gov
Department of Housing and Urban Development	www.hud.gov
Department of Labor	www.dol.gov
Department of the Treasury	www.ustreas.gov
Energy Information Administration	www.eia.doe.gov
Environmental Protection Agency	www.epa.gov
Equal Employment Opportunity Commission	www.eeoc.gov
European Bank for Reconstruction and Development	www.ebrd.com
European Commission to the U.S.	www.eurunion.org
European Free Trade Association	www.efta.int
Federal Communications Commission	www.fcc.gov
Federal Deposit Insurance Corporation	www.fdic.gov
Federal Reserve System	www.federalreserve.gov
Federal Trade Commission	www.ftc.gov
FedStats	www.fedstats.gov
Freedom House	www.freedomhouse.org
Global Policy Forum	www.globalpolicy.org
Inter-American Development Bank	www.iadb.org
Internal Revenue Service	www.irs.gov
International Center for Settlements of Investment Disputes	www.icsid.org
International Co-operative Alliance	www.coop.org
International Development Association	www.ida.org
International Finance Corporation	www.ifc.org
International Labor Organization	www.us.ilo.org
International Monetary Fund	www.imf.org
International Trade Administration	www.ita.doc.gov
International Trade Commission	www.usitc.gov
Multilateral Investment Guarantee Agency	www.miga.org
NASDAQ Stock Market	www.nasdaq.com
National Association for Business Economics	www.nabe.com
National Bureau of Economic Research	www.nber.org
National Cooperative Business Association	www.ncba.org
National Science Foundation	www.nsf.gov
New York Stock Exchange	www.nyse.com
Office of Management and Budget	www.whitehouse.gov/omb
Office of Thrift Supervision	www.ots.treas.gov
Organization for Economic Cooperation and Development	www.oecd.org
Organization of Petroleum Exporting Countries	www.opec.org

Partnership in Statistics for Development	www.paris21.org
Patent and Trademark Office	www.uspto.gov
Population Reference Bureau	www.prb.org
Securities and Exchange Commission	www.sec.gov
Small Business Administration	www.sba.gov
Social Security Administration	www.ssa.gov
United Nations	www.un.org
UN Children's Fund	www.unicef.org
UN Conference on Trade and Development	www.unctad.org
UN Development Program	www.undp.org
UN Educational, Scientific, and Cultural Organization	www.unesco.org
UN Environmental Program	www.unep.org
UN Population Fund	www.unfpa.org
World Bank	www.worldbank.org
World Economic Forum	www.weforum.org
World Health Organization	www.who.org
World Intellectual Property Organization	www.wipo.org
World Resources Institute	www.wri.org
World Trade Organization	www.wto.org
Worldwatch Institute	www.worldwatch.org
World Wide Web Consortium	www.w3.org/consortium

Appendix C

Selected Videotapes

This list includes classroom-tested videos that provide information on basic economic concepts and principles, microeconomy, macroeconomy, and global economy. The list also delves into economic history, movements, issues, and the lives of people who shaped economic thought.

Advertising Tactics. Teacher's Video Company, 2001. 50 minutes (color).

Aligning Supply and Demand: Creating the Right Supply Chain. BBC Production, 1998. 65 minutes (color).

Amazon.com and the World of E-Commerce. Films for the Humanities and Sciences, 1999. 29 minutes (color).

An American Legacy: The Great Depression (Series). Teacher's Video Company, 2002. 60 minutes (color).

America Today: Looking for the Union Label. Films for the Humanities and Sciences, 2001. 29 minutes (color).

Assembly Line. The History Channel, 2001. 50 minutes (color).

Banking on Life and Debt. Maryknoll World Productions, 1995. 30 minutes (color).

Banks: Modern Marvels. The History Channel, 2000. 50 minutes (color).

Bigger Than Enron. PBS, 2002. 60 minutes (color).

Biography: Alan Greenspan, The Man behind the Money. A&E, 1999. 50 minutes (color).

Biography: Dow and Jones, Wizards of Wall Street. A&E, 1996. 50 minutes (color).

Biography: Henry Ford, Tin Lizzy Tycoon. A&E, 1994. 50 minutes (color).

Biography: Ray Kroc, Fast Food McMillionaire, A&E, 1996. 50 minutes (color).

Biography: Sam Walton, Bargain Billionaire. A&E, 1997. 50 minutes (color).

Black Entrepreneurs [The Ebony/Jet Guide to Black Excellence]. Home Video Entertainment, 1991. 35 minutes (color).

Booted Out! Exporting Jobs from the U.S. Films for the Humanities and Sciences. 28 minutes (color).

Bootstrap Capitalism. Films for the Humanities *and* Sciences, 1999. 15 minutes (color).

Branded: The Power of Brand Names (Series). BBC Production. 120 minutes (color).

Brand Marketing: Why We Eat, Drink and Wear Brand Names. Learning Seed, 2000. 18 minutes (color).
Building a Successful Business (Series). Radco Media, Inc., 1997. 450 minutes (color).
Business and Industrial Growth, Part 1: From Boom to Bust. ABC News, 1999. 29 minutes (color).
Business and Industrial Growth, Part 2: Riding the Cycles. ABC News, 1999. 40 minutes (color).
Business Basics (Series). Teacher's Video Company, 2001. 274 minutes (color).
Business Ethics: A 21st Century Perspective. A Meridian Production, 2000. 16 minutes (color).
Capitalism. Teacher's Video Company, 2001. 19 minutes (color).
CEO Exchange: Conversations in Leadership (Series). Films for the Humanities *and* Sciences, 1994–2001. 1,160 minutes (color).
Charge It! Credit Card Secrets. Learning Seed, 2002. 23 minutes (color).
Chinese Capitalism: Moving the Mountain. BBC Production. 50 minutes (color).
Colonialism and Imperialism. Teacher's Video Company, 2001. 25 minutes (color).
Commanding Heights: Battle for the World Economy (Series). WGBH Boston, 2002. 360 minutes (color).
Communism and Socialism. Teacher's Video Company. 25 minutes (color).
Consumers: Know Your Rights! A Meridian Production, 2003. 17 minutes (color).
Copyrights. Teacher's Video Company, 2001. 19 minutes (color).
The Crash. The History Channel, 2001. 100 minutes (color).
Creation of the Computer. The History Channel, 1996. 50 minutes (color).
Credit Card Cautions. A Meridian Production, 2000. 30 minutes (color).
Dotcoms Gone Bust. Films for the Humanities *and* Sciences, 2001. 23 minutes (color).
Dot Con. PBS, 2001. 60 minutes (color).
Economics (Series). New Dimension Media, 1993–1997. 13 minutes per episode (color).
Economics: A Framework for Teaching the Basic Concepts (Series). United Learning, 1997. 84 minutes (color).
Economics at Work (Series). Films for the Humanities *and* Sciences. 330 minutes (color).
Economics USA (Series). The Annenberg/CPB Collection. Revised, 1985, 1992, 2002. 750 minutes (color).
Emerging Powers: Bx4. (Series) Wall Street Journal Video, 1996. 200 minutes (color).
Empowering the World: Technologies for a Sustainable Future. Films for the Humanities *and* Sciences. 30 minutes (color).
Entrepreneurs: An American Adventure. MPI Home Video, 1986. 360 minutes (color).
Ethics in Corporate America: A Crisis of Credibility. NewsHour, 2002. 36 minutes (color).
European Union Educational Videos 2002. European Union, 2002. 99 minutes (color).
Fall of Communism. ABC News Production, 1990. 80 minutes (color).
Fascism. Teacher's Video Company, 2001. 19 minutes (color).
Fast Forward: Life inside Our Ever-Shrinking World. PBS, 1999. 60 minutes (color).
Fate of the Earth. Teacher's Video Company, 1995. 57 minutes (color).
The Fed Today. The Federal Reserve System, 13 minutes (color).
Free to Choose: A Personal Statement (Series). PBS, 1980. 720 minutes (color).
Funding Your Dreams: The Emerging Investor. Merrill Lynch, 1998. 30 minutes (color).
Give Yourself Some Credit. Teacher's Video Company, 2003. 32 minutes (color).
Global Business: New Ways to Improve the Bottom Line (Series). Films for the Humanities *and* Sciences. 300 minutes (color).

The Global Generation: The Human Face behind Globalization (Series). Films for the Humanities *and* Sciences. 156 minutes (color).
Globalization: Winners and Losers. Films for the Humanities and Sciences, 2000. 42 minutes (color).
The Global Marketplace. A&E, 2002. 50 minutes (color).
Great Depression (Series). The History Channel, 1998. 200 minutes (color).
Greatest TV Commercials. A&E, 2000. 50 minutes (color).
Harvest of Shame: Edward R. Murrow Collection. CBS, 1960. 60 minutes (black and white).
The Hidden Army: Women in World War II. Goldhil Home Media International, 1995. 57 minutes (color).
The History of Money. Cambridge, 1997. 55 minutes (color).
Industrial Revolution. Teacher's Video Company, 2000. 46 minutes (color).
Industry and the Environment. Teacher's Video Company, 1999. 60 minutes (color).
Innovations of Silicon Valley. Films for the Humanities and Sciences, 2000. 57 minutes (color).
Inside the Global Economy (Series). The Annenberg/CPB Collection, 1995. 480 minutes (color).
Inside the World's Mightiest Bank: The Federal Reserve. Discovery Channel, 2000. 50 minutes (color).
International Branding in the 21st Century. PBS, 2000. 60 minutes (color).
The International Monetary Fund: Financial Cure or Catastrophe? Films for the Humanities and Sciences, 1998. 35 minutes (color).
The Internet: Doing Business on the Net. Educational Video Network, 1997. 20 minutes (color).
Internet Shopping in the 21st Century. Films for the Humanities and Sciences. 2000. 57 minutes (color).
An Introduction to Online Investing. Investor Videos, 2000. 46 minutes (color).
Introductory Economics (Series). Films for the Humanities and Sciences, 1993. 510 minutes (color).
Inventions That Changed Our Lives. Teacher's Video Company, 1998. 160 minutes (color).
IRS Horror Stories. A&E, 2000. 50 minutes (color).
Japan's Economy: Bursting the Bubble. Films for the Humanities and Sciences, 1999. 13 minutes (color).
Landmark Consumer Rights Trials. World Almanac Video, 1997. 50 minutes (color).
Laws of Money. Lessons of Life. PBS Home Video, 2003. 89 minutes (color).
Market Structure. Teacher's Video Company, 1993. 13 minutes (color).
Merger: Disney and ABC. ABC News, 1995. 30 minutes (color).
Millennium: The IMF in the New Century (Series). Films for the Humanities and Sciences, 2000. 70 minutes (color).
Mobilizing for Growth: Entrepreneurship within Companies. Films for the Humanities and Sciences, 1999. 65 minutes (color).
Modern Marvels: Computers. The History Channel, 2001. 50 minutes (color).
Money and Values: What Is Wealth? Learning Seed, n/d. 22 minutes (color).
Money Never Sleeps: Global Financial Markets. Films for the Humanities and Sciences, n/d. 52 minutes (color).
NAFTA and the New Economic Frontier: Life along the U.S./Mexico Border. Films for the Humanities and Sciences, 2001. 23 minutes (color).

The New Global Economics: A Real World Guide (Series). Films for the Humanities and Sciences, 1999. 300 minutes (color).

Organizing America: The History of Trade Unions. Cambridge Educational Production, 1994. 38 minutes (color).

Patents. Teacher's Video Company, 2001. 25 minutes (color).

A Penny Saved: How to Grow Money. Learning Seed, 2000. 21 minutes (color).

The People Bomb: When Will Overpopulation Explode? CNN Video, 1992. 105 minutes (color).

Peter Drucker. Films for the Humanities and Sciences, 1988. 30 minutes (color).

Pirates of the Silicon Valley. Turner Home Video, 2000. 96 minutes (color).

Population 2000 Series. Library Video Company, 1998. 25 minutes (color).

Preparing Students for Financial Stability (Series). Teacher's Video Company, 1994–2001. 389 minutes (color).

Problem Solving in the Job World. Education Associates, 2000. 18 minutes (color).

The Profits and Pitfalls of Mutual Funds. Teacher's Video Company, 2001. 20 minutes (color).

Quick Tips to Learning Basic Economics Video Series. The Princess Company. 48 minutes (color).

The Road to Riches: The History of Wealth-Building (Series). BBC Production, 2000. 306 minutes (color).

Sell and Spin: A History of Advertising. The History Channel, 2001. 100 minutes (color).

Spend and Prosper: A Portrait of J. M. Keynes. BBC Production, 1981. 51 minutes (color).

The Standard Deviants: Macroeconomics. Cerebellum Corporation, 1995. 120 minutes (color).

The Standard Deviants: Marketing. Cerebellum Corporation, 1998. 105 minutes (color).

The Standard Deviants: Microeconomics. Cerebellum Corporation, 1995. 120 minutes (color).

Stock Exchange. The History Channel, 1997. 50 minutes (color).

Stock Market Basics: Learning without Losing. Learning Seed. 24 minutes (color).

Stopping the Money: An Economic Approach to Counterterrorism. Films for the Humanities and Sciences. 23 minutes (color).

Supply and Demand. Teacher's Video Company, 2001. 19 minutes (color).

Taking Care of Business: CEOs Sound Off (Series). Films for the Humanities and Sciences, 2001. 240 minutes (color).

Thomas A. Edison. Teacher's Video Company, 1994. 50 minutes (color).

Understanding Free Market Economics: Lessons Learned in the Former Soviet Union (Series). Films for the Humanities and Sciences, 1995. 165 minutes (color).

United Nations: It's More Than You Think. Cambridge Research Group, 1991. 30 minutes (color).

The Ups and Downs of Stocks. Teacher's Video Company, 2001. 24 minutes (color).

U.S. Mint. The History Channel, 1998. 50 minutes (color).

The Value of Brand Names. Films for the Humanities and Sciences, 2000. 29 minutes (color).

Why You Buy: 21st Century Advertising. Learning Seed. Revised, 2002. 23 minutes (color).

Winning Our Rights: The History of the Consumer Movement. Learning Zone Express, 1999. 20 minutes (color).

The Women's Bank of Bangladesh. Films for the Humanities and Sciences, 1998. 47 minutes (color).

The World Bank: The Great Experiment. Films for the Humanities and Sciences, n/d. 100 minutes (color).

Your Consumer Rights. Learning Seed, n/d. 19 minutes (color).

Appendix D

Index to Biographies

This index provides a list of the people who are profiled in brief biographies at the ends of the chapters, the chapter and section heading under which the biography appears, and the page number.

Index

Index

About the Author

DAVID E. O'CONNOR is an economics teacher at Edwin O. Smith High School in Storrs, Connecticut. He is the president of the Connecticut Council for the Social Studies, and the author of numerous books and teacher's guides in the fields of economics, ethnic history, and world history.